PERSHING'S LIEUTENANTS

PERSHING'S LIEUTENANTS

AMERICAN MILITARY LEADERSHIP IN WORLD WAR I

EDITED BY

DAVID T. ZĄBECKI

DOUGLAS V. MASTRIANO

OSPREY PUBLISHING
Bloomsbury Publishing Plc
Kemp House, Chawley Park, Cumnor Hill, Oxford OX2 9PH, UK
1385 Broadway, 5th Floor, New York, NY 10018, USA
E-mail: info@ospreypublishing.com
www.ospreypublishing.com

OSPREY is a trademark of Osprey Publishing Ltd

First published in Great Britain in 2020

A catalog record for this book is available from the British Library.

ISBN: HB 978 1 4728 3863 6; eBook 978 1 4728 3864 3; ePDF 978 1 4728 3861 2;
XML 978 1 4728 3862 9

20 21 22 23 24 10 9 8 7 6 5 4 3 2 1

Edited by David T. Ząbecki and Douglas V. Mastriano
Maps by Donald S. Frazier
Index by Zoe Ross

Typeset by Deanta Global Publishing Services, Chennai, India
Printed and bound in Great Britain by CPI (Group) UK Ltd, Croydon CR0 4YY

Front cover (main): General John J. Pershing. (Bettmann/Getty Images). Background flag image from iStock. Cap badge image on front cover, back cover and spine from main cover image.

Osprey Publishing supports the Woodland Trust, the UK's leading woodland conservation charity.

To find out more about our authors and books visit **www.ospreypublishing.com**. Here you will find extracts, author interviews, details of forthcoming events and the option to sign up for our newsletter.

CONTENTS

The editors dedicate this book to the institution we spent our adult lives serving. In doing so, we borrow from the words originally written by Rudyard Kipling.

To the United States Army:

I have eaten your bread and salt.
I have drunk your water and wine.
In deaths ye died I have watched beside,
And the lives ye led were mine.

Rudyard Kipling, from "Prelude"
to *Departmental Ditties and Other Verses*

CONTRIBUTORS

James Corum, PhD, taught military history at Salford University, UK, from 2014 to 2019. He was dean of the Baltic Defence College in Tartu, Estonia, from 2009 to 2014. From 1991 to 2004 he was a professor at the U.S. Air Force School of Advanced Air and Space Studies at Maxwell Air Force Base, Alabama. In 2005 he was a visiting fellow at All Souls College, Oxford, and then served as an associate professor at the U.S. Army Command and General Staff College from 2005 to 2008.

Corum is the author/co-author of 12 books on military and airpower history, including *The Roots of Blitzkrieg: Hans von Seeckt and German Military Reform*; *The Luftwaffe: Creating the Operational Air War, 1918–1940*; *The Luftwaffe's Way of War: German Air Doctrine, 1911–1945*, with Richard Muller; *Airpower in Small Wars: Fighting Insurgents and Terrorists*, with Wray Johnson; and *Wolfram von Richthofen: Master of the German Air War*. His upcoming book is *The Condor Legion* (Osprey, 2020). Currently Corum is researching World War I on the Eastern Front and the 1919 campaigns in the East.

He has also authored more than 60 major book chapters and journal articles on a variety of subjects related to airpower and military history. James Corum is a retired lieutenant colonel in the U.S. Army Reserve with 28 years' service. He holds a master's degree from Brown University, a master of letters from Oxford University, and a PhD from Queen's University, Canada.

G. K. Cunningham, PhD, is professor of strategic landpower at the U.S. Army War College, Carlisle Barracks, Pennsylvania, USA. He directs the

Strategic Landpower of Area of Concentration Program and is a key effectuator for quality assurance and integration of academic and leader development programs dealing with 21st-century theater strategy and campaigning. In addition to organizational leadership roles, he teaches elective courses on military history and campaign planning and analysis.

Carlo D'Este graduated magna cum laude in 1958 from Norwich University, the birthplace of the Reserve Officers' Training Corps (ROTC). Commissioned in the U.S. Army, his five overseas tours included two in Vietnam. He retired as a lieutenant colonel in 1978 to begin a second career as a military historian. His seven books of military history and biography include *Decision in Normandy*, *Patton: A Genius for War*, and *Warlord: A Life of Winston Churchill at War, 1874–1945.* Carlo is the cofounder of the William E. Colby Military Writers' Symposium held annually at Norwich University, where he served for ten years as its executive director. He has lectured widely and written for the *New York Times*, *The Washington Post*, *The Wall Street Journal* and *Armchair General* and *World War II* magazines. D'Este was awarded an honorary PhD from Norwich in 1992 and in 2011 received the Pritzker Museum and Library Literature Award for Lifetime Achievement in Military Writing. He lives in Massachusetts with his wife, Shirley.

Brigadier General (Ret.) Robert Doughty, PhD, retired in July 2005 after 40 years of service in the U.S. Army. He graduated from the U.S. Military Academy in 1965 and received his PhD from Kansas University in 1979. His awards and decorations include the Distinguished Service Medal, Silver Star, and Combat Infantry Badge. He served as the head of the Department of History at the U.S. Military Academy from 1985 until 2005. He is the author of numerous articles and books and currently is working on a paper about Franco–American relations during World War I.

Donald S. Frazier, PhD, (cartographer) is the director of The Texas Center at Schreiner University in Kerrville, Texas. He was formerly professor of history at McMurry University in Abilene, Texas. A graduate of the University of Texas at Arlington and Texas Christian University, Frazier is also the award-winning author of five books on the Civil War, including *Blood and Treasure, Cottonclads, Fire in the Cane Field, Thunder Across the Swamp*, and *Blood on the Bayou*. His other work includes serving as co-author of *Frontier Texas, Historic Abilene*, and *The Texas You Expect*, as well as general editor of *The U.S. and Mexico at War* and a collection of letters published as *Love and War: The Civil War Letters and Medicinal Book of Augustus V. Ball*. In addition to his teaching duties, Frazier has been very involved in work on Civil War and frontier heritage trails in Texas, New Mexico, and Louisiana, and work on historical projects in Europe and Mexico. He is the writer and director for the video *Our Home, Our Rights: Texas and Texans in the Civil War*, a winner of the Mitchell Wilder Award for Excellence in Publications and Media Design from the Texas Association of Museums. Frazier is an elected member of the prestigious Philosophical Society of Texas, the oldest learned organization in the state, and a fellow of the Texas State Historical Association. He has drawn more than 2,000 maps for various publishers and authors during the course of his career.

Patrick Gregory is a journalist and writer based in London. The former managing editor of BBC Political Programmes, Gregory has devoted his time in recent years to the study of the history of the United States' role in World War I. His work, through talks and writing, has been aimed at the wider public understanding of the war. Alongside writing and editing *An American on the Western Front* and contributing to *1914–1918 Online: International Encyclopedia of the First World War*, his articles have appeared in a wide variety of history and news websites in the U.S. and UK. Gregory worked for the BBC for nearly 30 years: as a news editor in politics at Westminster, and before then as a producer in radio news programs covering events such as the fall of the Berlin Wall; the closing years of the Soviet Union; the reshaping of eastern Europe; the First Gulf War; and wars in the Balkans.

He has also produced a number of politics and history documentaries for BBC Radio 4 and the BBC World Service and has lectured on the practice of parliamentary journalism in the Asia–Pacific region.

Lieutenant Colonel (Ret.) Mark E. Grotelueschen, PhD, teaches strategic studies and serves as the Chief of Majors Academics in the

Department of Military and Strategic Studies at the U.S. Air Force Academy. He previously served as professor of history. A 1991 graduate of the U.S. Air Force Academy, he received his MA from the University of Calgary and his PhD from Texas A&M University. He is the author of *Doctrine Under Trial: American Artillery Employment in World War I* and *The AEF Way of War: The American Army and Combat in World War I*, the latter of which has been named repeatedly on the U.S. Army Chief of Staff's Professional Reading List. Most recently he authored *Into the Fight: April–June 1918* for the U.S. Army Center of Military History's Great War Commemoration Series.

J. Mark Jackson was reared in central Ohio. He attended Ohio University on a four-year ROTC scholarship, graduating as a distinguished military graduate with a degree in journalism and a minor in political science. He was commissioned Regular Army. As a cadet he attended Winter Warfare School at Fort Greely, Alaska. Jackson's first tour of duty was with the 2nd Armored Cavalry Regiment in Bamberg, Germany. During his three-year tour, he served as a cavalry platoon leader and support platoon leader. He returned to the United States, completed the Armor Officer's Advanced Course and Airborne, and was subsequently assigned to the 3rd Battalion, 73rd Armor (Airborne) at Fort Bragg, North Carolina. Jackson left the U.S. Army to pursue a career with Goodyear Tire & Rubber Co. After five years with Goodyear, Jackson moved to Cooper Tire Co., where he is employed currently. Jackson took a combat sabbatical and returned to the Army after an 18-year absence when it was announced that the Army was short of 30,000 captains and majors for the Global War on Terror. He was recommissioned captain, promoted to major, and sent to Afghanistan as a mentoring team chief. He earned the Bronze Star and Combat Action Badge. Jackson has written articles for *The Washington Post*, *Reader's Digest*, and appeared on several network television news programs. He is the author of one book, *Touched by Fire*. Additionally, he trained senior government executives on leadership for over a decade, using history as the case study. Jackson holds a master's degree in organizational leadership from Gonzaga University. He is married, has three children, and lives in St. Augustine, Florida.

Robert John Laplander is an independent historian of American participation in World War I; in particular, the activities of I Corps of the American First Army during the Meuse–Argonne offensive. His specific research into the "Lost Battalion" of the 77th Division spans 20 years, while his book on the subject, *Finding the Lost Battalion: Beyond the Rumors, Myths and Legend of America's Famous WW1 Epic*, has become the benchmark work on that event for which he is recognized the world over. Laplander was prominently featured in the third episode of the television event *The Great War*, a six-hour, three-part record of America's contributions in World War I presented as part of the "American Experience" series for PBS, and has appeared on CSPAN, The John Batchelor radio show, Federal News Radio, ABC News Radio, CBS News radio, and a multitude of print outlets. He has also lectured for the U.S. Army to both the old 77th Regional Readiness Command, the 77th Sustainment Brigade, and the 78th (Training) Division, and still lectures to groups of all kinds on the Lost Battalion and the American experience in World War I (with an emphasis on small-unit actions), as well as personal inspiration and leadership. A partner in the U.S. World War I Centennial Commission, he is managing director of *Doughboy MIA*, a site which tracks all 4,423 missing U.S. service personnel from World War I, as well as being a partner with the U.S. Foundation for the Commemoration of the World Wars. Laplander lives with his wife, Trinie, and their three children in the small town of Waterford, Wisconsin.

Sebastian H. Lukasik, PhD, is associate professor in the Department of Airpower at Air Command and Staff College, Maxwell AFB, Alabama. He received a PhD in military history from Duke University. His research and teaching interests include the American military experience of the world wars, combat motivation and soldier morale in modern warfare, and the theory and history of airpower.

Colonel (Ret.) Douglas V. Mastriano, PhD, is the state senator for the 33rd Pennsylvania District. He is an Eagle Scout and the son of a career U.S. Navy man. He served more than 30 years on active duty and began his military service on the Iron Curtain with the 2nd Armored Cavalry

Regiment, West Germany. Serving along the East German/Czechoslovakian borders, he witnessed the end of the Cold War and deployed to Iraq for Operation DESERT STORM. Mastriano's regiment led the attack against Saddam Hussein's elite Republican Guards. Mastriano served in tactical, operational, and strategic assignments in Washington, the 3rd Infantry Division, and U.S. Army Europe. After 9/11, he was lead planner to invade Iraq from Turkey. He served four years with NATO and deployed three times to Afghanistan. Mastriano was the director of the Afghan Joint Intelligence Center, leading 80 soldiers from 18 nations. Mastriano is a historian and earned a PhD from the University of New Brunswick, Canada, and four master's degrees – strategy, strategic intelligence, military operations, and airpower; he also has a bachelor's from Eastern University. He authored the award-winning book *Alvin York: A New Biography of the Hero of the Argonne* and *Thunder in the Argonne: A New History of America's Greatest Battle*. Mastriano has extensive foreign policy experience. He is an expert on Russia and NATO security and senior editor for the Army Chief of Staff study, Project 1704 / Project 1721. He shaped American/NATO strategy, providing strategic guidance for American and European leaders against Russia.

Kevin E. McCall is the former General Walter Bedell Smith Chair for National Intelligence at the United States Army War College, where he taught in the Department of National Security Strategy. He is a retired Army officer with service in a frontline tank battalion in Operation DESERT STORM. His military decorations include the Bronze Star, Armed Forces Expeditionary Medal, Desert Shield/Storm Campaign Medal, Kuwait Liberation Medal, Saudi Arabia Defense Medal, Master Parachutist Badge, and Expert Field Medical Badge. He holds master's degrees from both the U.S. Army War College and U.S. Naval Postgraduate School. McCall and his wife Maureen have three children and four grandchildren.

Colonel (Ret.) Jerry D. Morelock, PhD, is a 1969 West Point graduate who served 36 years in uniform. A decorated Vietnam War combat veteran, his assignments included two Pentagon tours: Leadership

Division, Department of the Army General Staff; and Strategic Plans and Policy Directorate, Joint Chiefs of Staff. His final active duty assignment was director of the Combat Studies Institute, the Command & General Staff College's history department. He has authored several books and published hundreds of journal and magazine articles. His latest book is *Generals of the Bulge: Leadership in the U.S. Army's Greatest Battle*. His writing awards include the Arter-Darby Military History Writing Award for excellence in professional scholarship, the U.S. Field Artillery Association History Writing Award, and Distinguished Essayist in the Chairman of the Joint Chiefs of Staff Essays on Strategy competition. After Army retirement, he was executive director of the Winston Churchill Memorial & Library at Westminster College in Fulton, Missouri – site of Churchill's famed 1946 "Iron Curtain" speech – and is adjunct faculty professor of history and political science at Westminster. From 2004 to 2015 he was editor in chief of *Armchair General* magazine, and currently is senior editor/senior historian for *Historynet's America's Civil War*, *World War II*, and *Vietnam* magazines. His grandfather, Corporal Louie F. Hummel (312th Infantry Regiment, 78th Division) and his great uncle, Private Richard Longren (131st Infantry Regiment, 33rd Division) were World War I combat veterans.

Captain (Ret.) Carl O. Schuster is a retired U.S. Navy officer who served on a variety of U.S. and Allied warships, submarines, and headquarters' staffs during his 26-year naval career. His operational tours included stints in Central America, the Mediterranean, the Western Pacific, South Korea, and the Middle East. Commissioned in 1974, he transferred to intelligence in 1985 and finished his career as the director of operations at U.S. Pacific Command's Joint Intelligence Center. He currently lectures at Hawaii Pacific University in Honolulu, Hawaii, is a military analyst for CNN, and is a widely published author on current events and military history.

Colonel (Ret.) Kenneth Shaw, OD, grew up in South Carolina and has a bachelor's degree in biology from The Citadel, The Military College of South Carolina, a doctorate in optometry from the Pennsylvania College of Optometry (Salus University), and an MA in homeland security and emergency management from American Military University. He served 27 years in the U.S. Army with duty in the 25th Infantry Division (Light), the 3rd Infantry Division (Mechanized), and several U.S. Army hospitals and medical centers. He was a responder during the attack on the Pentagon on 9/11 and is a leading expert in the medical response to chemical, biological, radiological, nuclear, and high-yield explosive (CBRNE) events and running all-hazard medical emergency response teams for special security events. He is married to Janie Shaw, a colonel in the Army Nurse Corps. They have two wonderful children, Ashley and Jacob, and a great Golden Retriever, Louie.

Lieutenant Colonel (Ret.) Dave Theis, EdD, is a retired Army Reservist and a retired educator. He was a teacher and administrator for the Department of Defense Dependent Schools, serving in Europe and Asia for over 40 years. Besides his normal educator duties, he also organized and led many battlefield staff rides for parents and community members, focusing on both World War I and II battles. His Army assignments, in both active and reserve status, included Cavalry, Armor, personnel, nuclear duties, war plans, training, and the NATO Partnership for Peace program. He served for 28 years. His most memorable history mission was being called to active duty to be the lead historian for over 40 members of the U.S. House of Representatives – the Honorable Sonny Montgomery, Speaker of the House, delegation head – for the 50th anniversary of D-Day, held in Normandy.

Master Sergeant (Ret.) William H. Van Husen, U.S. Air Force, received his bachelor's, magna cum laude, from the University of Maryland and his master's in international relations from Troy University. From 1989 to 1994 he taught history and American government for Central Texas College and the University of Maryland European Program. He was assistant editor and contributor to ABC-CLIO's *Encyclopedia of World War II: 1939–1945* and *Germany at War: 400 Years of Military History*, and contributor to the *Encyclopedia of the Korean War*; editor and contributor to Garland Publishing's *World War II in Europe: An*

Encyclopedia; and contributor to Naval Institute Press' *Chief of Staff: The Principal Officers behind History's Great Commanders*. He served in Germany for a total of 38 years both in uniform and as a U.S. Air Force civilian. He is retired and lives in New Hampshire.

Derek Varble, PhD, holds a doctorate in history from Oriel College, University of Oxford, where he researched 20th-century diplomacy. He also completed an undergraduate degree in history at the U.S. Air Force Academy and a graduate degree in history at the George Washington University. He lives in Colorado.

Tim White is a co-founder, owner, and managing director of Johnson & White Wealth Management, LLC. As a Certified Financial Planner practitioner, he is responsible for advising investment clients for Johnson & White. White's education includes a master's in personal financial planning from the College for Financial Planning and a bachelor's in finance from Penn State. White was commissioned into the Regular Army in 1985 after serving as the cadet brigade commander in Army ROTC at Penn State in the academic year 1984–85. He is a recipient of the George C. Marshall Award. His military experience includes a tour with the 2nd Armored Cavalry Regiment in Bamberg, Germany, and commands of a tank company and headquarters company of the 157th Infantry Brigade in Pennsylvania. Today, he serves on the Board for the Second Cavalry Association. White's military experience spawned many years of leadership development for organizations as diverse as the U.S. Mint, Northrop Grumman, L3 Communications, the General Services Administration, and the U.S. Department of Agriculture. His use of Civil War battlefields as leadership laboratories for these and other organizations is built on his knowledge of military history and the use of the staff ride as a teaching tool.

Major General (Ret.) David T. Ząbecki, PhD, is the author, editor, or translator of more than 25 military history books. His ABC-CLIO encyclopedia, *Germany at War: 400 Years of Military History*, won a Society for Military History Distinguished Book Award in 2016. His 2018 book for University of Indiana Press, *The Generals' War: Operational*

Level Command on the Western Front in 1918, won the Tomlinson Book Prize from the World War I Historical Association. He is editor emeritus of *Vietnam* magazine. In 1988 he was the Distinguished Honor Graduate of his year group at the U.S. Army Command and General Staff College, receiving the General John J. Pershing Award. He holds a PhD in military history from Britain's Royal Military College of Science, Cranfield University, where his supervisor was the late Professor Richard Holmes. In 2012 Ząbecki was the Shifrin Distinguished Professor of Military History at the U.S. Naval Academy, Annapolis. He is an honorary senior research fellow in the War Studies Programme at the University of Birmingham (UK). He is a fellow of the American College of National Security Leaders, and a member of both the U.S. and British Commissions for Military History. He enlisted in the U.S. Army in 1966 and served as an infantry rifleman in the 47th Infantry Regiment in Vietnam in 1967 and during the 1968 Tet Offensive. He spent most of his subsequent military career as a field artillery, intelligence, or operations officer. In 2003 he was attached to the U.S. State Department as the senior security advisor on the U.S. Coordinating and Monitoring Mission in Israel, charged with advancing the Roadmap to Peace in the Middle East initiative. In 2004 he commanded the American task forces that supported the 60th anniversary observances of the D-Day Landings, Operation MARKET-GARDEN, and the Battle of the Bulge. In 2005–06 he was the commander of the Southern European Task Force (Rear), and the U.S. Army's senior mission commander in Europe south of the Alps. He is a distinguished member of the 47th Infantry Regiment. He lives in Freiburg, Germany.

FOREWORD

Robert A. Doughty

In April 1917, the United States was woefully unprepared for war, especially a war against a well-armed, well-led foe that had fought for three long years against the major powers of Europe. Prior to the U.S.'s entry into that war, President Woodrow Wilson had pursued a policy of strict neutrality and had prohibited U.S. Army officers from making even limited preparations for such a war. With a reelection slogan in 1916 of "He kept us out of war," Wilson insisted that the United States not be drawn inadvertently into the war by American military leaders preparing for such a contingency. In late February 1917 initial estimates for equipping a million-man army anticipated not having enough rifles on hand until 1 September 1917 and not having enough ammunition, artillery, and machine guns until late 1918. When the war burst on the scene, the U.S. Army lacked modern equipment and arms and soon faced the extraordinary challenge of providing enough weapons and equipment for nearly 4 million men, a much larger number than initially considered. As for war plans, the War Department had incomplete plans that envisaged only defensive actions on the North American continent in the event of a war against Germany. In his memoirs, Major General Robert Alexander, who commanded the 77th Division in the war, wrote: "Any officer, however distinguished, who displayed ordinary foresight by the advocacy of any preparatory measure did so at the jeopardy of his career."[1]

The U.S. made a formal declaration of war against Germany in the early days of April 1917 and immediately began an all-out mobilization that would increase the strength of the Army from 213,557 on 6 April to 3,685,458 on 11 November 1918. With illusions of avoiding war gone, senior military leaders faced a myriad of challenges. Many of these were the enduring challenges of war, especially in the sense of leaders solving problems, motivating subordinates, adapting to unexpected circumstances, and working with allies. Important questions also had to be answered in those early days. What role would the United States play in the war? Would the U.S. transport units/soldiers to Europe? If so, how many? How would soldiers be organized and how would they fight in combat operations? Almost none of the senior American military leaders had foreseen the circumstances they eventually faced or had prepared themselves (or their soldiers) to face such circumstances. They had to build an army from scratch, had to prepare soldiers to fight on an incredibly complex and deadly battlefield, and had to learn not only from their own experiences but also from those of others. Being able to learn and to adapt proved as valuable to these senior officers as courage and charisma.

Nothing was more complex or more difficult in this war than choosing and developing leaders. General John J. Pershing's own experience illustrates this with his rising in a matter of days from the designated commander of a division going to Europe, to commanding general of the American Expeditionary Forces. Officers in World War I who thought they would retire as captains suddenly found themselves commanding battalions or regiments. Others found themselves commanding large units only briefly before being promoted to even higher positions of responsibility. And others found themselves as key staff officers in units or echelons that had not existed in the U.S. Army before the war. These officers' experiences underline the wisdom of educating officers broadly and not focusing exclusively on honing technical skills. The most valuable and successful officers in that war were those such as Colonel George C. Marshall, who could see far beyond the in-box on their desks and adjust to the unexpected situations and demands they faced in the European war.

Officers also had to learn how to conduct successful operations with the units they led. A successful operation in World War I required much more than charging ahead with the infantry and bringing along the artillery and engineers. By April 1917 the French, British, and Germans had sacrificed thousands of their soldiers' lives as they learned how to coordinate complex infantry, artillery, aviation, engineer, intelligence, medical, supply, and transportation assets. Americans soon learned through bitter, bloody experience that fire support, logistics, and communications played as important, if not more important, roles than the military leadership ideals of previous centuries. They also learned that maneuvering units on the ground was far more difficult than moving hands across a map or moving cursors across a computer screen. Staff officers such as Colonel Marshall made contributions that rivaled those of American commanders.

Some of the most challenging issues faced by American officers came from establishing and maintaining relations with allied or coalition units. Those issues serve today as a reminder of the complexities and difficulties of combined operations. Though the allies (Great Britain, France, Italy, and Russia) had fought in the war for almost three years, the Americans sometimes refused to accept their advice or even to listen. While such behavior accorded with their confidence in their own abilities, it resulted from time to time in poorly conducted operations and unnecessary casualties. Nonetheless, the Americans could and did learn a great deal in World War I, sometimes from allies and other times from the enemy. Their learning from allies contrasts sharply with more recent American experiences in places such as Korea, Vietnam, Iraq, and Afghanistan, where the Americans have provided advice and assistance and have trained the indigenous forces.

Much like losing a document on the hard drive of a computer, insights from 1917–18 have been overshadowed in the last century by current events or by competing bureaucratic requirements. In the aftermath of World War II, officers focused on the European or Pacific campaigns in that war, and in subsequent decades on more recent experiences in Korea, Indochina, and the Middle East. They sometimes lost sight of the importance of reading broadly in military history and of understanding how the waging of war has evolved over time. From time to time, they also forgot that no bureaucracy or organization can predict exactly the challenges it will face and that officers have a special responsibility to prepare themselves broadly and gain insights from the experience of others. Since 1917, American soldiers, whether privates or general officers, have had to live and fight among foreign populations and to thrive amidst foreign customs and traditions. Simple tasks, such as obtaining water or communicating with superiors and subordinates, have frequently been overwhelmingly difficult. And much more arduous missions, such as fighting through the Argonne Forest, have been almost impossible.

In war, as Clausewitz has reminded us, the simplest tasks are difficult. Since no one can predict exactly what challenges Americans will face in the future, understanding how senior officers overcame (or did not overcome) challenges in the past will provide valuable insights into how to confront and overcome challenges in the future. And no generation of American officers faced greater challenges than those of World War I.

MAPS

LIST OF ILLUSTRATIONS

Lieutenant Colonel George S. Patton.
Lieutenant Colonel William J. Donovan.
Lieutenant Colonel Theodore Roosevelt, Jr.
Captain Harry S. Truman.
Official U.S. Army Signal Corps photo of General Pershing.

INTRODUCTION

The War to End All War

Douglas V. Mastriano and David T. Ząbecki

Dr. John Lennox of Oxford University perceptively observed that "New things are old things happening to new people."[1] It seems that the past, or human history, is wrought with valuable lessons for the future. For us today, many of these are rooted in World War I. That war was a clash of empires and an epoch of incredible innovations. Four ancient dynasties collapsed in the midst of this war, entire societies were radically altered, a plethora of nations were created or given new life, and the map of the Middle East was redrawn. Many of today's conflicts have their roots in World War I. The existence of Syria and Iraq is due to World War I and the troubles there today are rooted in World War I. Today's tensions with Russia in the Baltics (Estonia, Latvia, and Lithuania) and along the Ukrainian border were likewise borne forth in the aftermath of the Great War.

Beyond these cataclysmic transformations, the very way in which wars were fought was forever changed. Armored warfare was introduced and thousands of tanks were used extensively along the Western Front. The tank became a dominant innovation, in additional to the introduction of chemical warfare, small-unit tactics, flamethrowers, and a plethora of other modernizations that still echo across the ages. The time-proven Napoleonic style of linear fighting was replaced by small-unit infantry tactics, a change forced largely by machine guns that made any audacious frontal assaults unlikely to succeed. Artillery truly became the King of Battle in this war, with infantry units often fighting for high ground to serve as an observation platform for directing lethal artillery fires. Meanwhile, on the open seas, the deployment of a fleet of U-boats by the Germans challenged the age-old ideas of the dominion of a surface fleet.

World War I brought with it not just conflict on the land and sea, but also in the air. The concepts of close air support, interdiction, and thinking of war in a three-dimensional way came out of this period. The building blocks of conducting joint operations with the Army, Navy, and Air Service came out of this clash of arms. The first air campaigns were launched during this fierce struggle, bringing modern warfare to the civilian populations of London and other major European cities. The ideas of strategic bombing and justification of targeting civilian populations took root, setting the conditions for laying waste to entire cities in the next world war. The character of war was forever changed.

America and the Great War

In addition to these cataclysmic changes in nations and how to wage battle, the war had a profound impact on the United States of America. It was America's first truly modern war and its first foray into Europe, something that George Washington advised the nation to avoid during his farewell address in 1796. Yet, it was a different world when President Washington spoke. Speed of transport and expanding world trade made it impractical, if not impossible, for the United States to avoid Europe's entangling alliances. The weight of the decision to break with 121 years of American policy was President Woodrow Wilson's, who won reelection as a peace president in 1916 with the slogan "He kept us out of war." Richard Striner, in his book *Woodrow Wilson and World War I*, captured the dilemma that Wilson faced as a wartime president, writing, "Woodrow Wilson's self-destruction as a wartime leader started early: the mistakes that would make him his own worst enemy began… at the beginning of World War I… Wilson sank into a mental condition that rendered him incapable of strategy. However wise his decisions might have seemed at the time to some, he made his first major blunders right away."[2]

Despite the American "tradition" of steering clear of European conflicts, Woodrow Wilson's feckless strategy of avoiding war at all costs resulted in virtually no national preparation for such an eventuality. When war was declared in April 1917, the United States had just over 200,000 men under arms, a smaller army than prewar Belgium. The Allies would have to wait over a year before enough Americans would arrive in Europe to make an appreciable difference. In the meantime, the French Army would mutiny and find itself on the brink of collapse, the British Army, long relying on its Imperial and Colonial volunteers, was likewise close to its breaking point. Meanwhile, on the Eastern Front, Imperial Russia would quit the war in the aftermath of the Bolshevik Revolution. This freed up more than a million German combat troops, who would be unleashed on the Western Front in early 1918 in the hopes of striking a victorious blow against the British and French before the Americas turned the tide in sheer manpower.

The incredible waste of lives along the Western Front by the American forces was in some part due to the lack of a coherent strategy and preparation of the nation by the American President. It was so incomprehensible that even when the U.S. Army War College commandant, Brigadier General Montgomery M. Macomb, ordered his officers to begin working on assessments of what the United States would need to do if it entered the war, he was rebuked by Wilson for warmongering and ordered to cease such planning. It would take a new generation of leaders to learn the tragic and failed lessons of the Wilson Administration to wrestle victory in a second and bloodier world war.

With considerable help from the French and British, 2.1 million Americans would serve in Europe in 1918. Of these, over 1.2 million served in the Meuse–Argonne campaign, making it one of the nation's largest engagements in its history. Another 2 million men were drafted and in training in the United States preparing for shipment to combat if needed. But the road to building this sizable force was not an easy one.

As the United States hastily created an army in 1917–18, it found that it lacked many of the tools it would need to fight a modern war. As a result, most of the major pieces of equipment that the Army required would come largely from the French. The British too provided equipment, aircraft, and trainers, but it was the French who were the arsenal of democracy in this war, and they provided the fledgling American Army with thousands of pieces of artillery, aircraft, tanks, and, more importantly, experienced officers and non-commissioned officers (NCOs) to help the Americans overcome the training deficit to fight the Germans on the Western Front. Yet, learning while in contact with the enemy is not the best way to prepare for war, and for the American soldiers on the Western Front the price was high. This costly experience during the waning months of the war resulted in large part from the inexperience of the American leaders, the lack of preparation for combat, and clinging to antiquated ideas of how actually to fight a modern war despite the help offered from the Allies.

Commander-in-chief of the AEF

On 10 May 1917 57-year-old Major General John J. Pershing was selected to command the American Expeditionary Forces (AEF). On 6 October that year, Pershing was promoted from major general in the Regular Army to the wartime temporary rank of (full) general in the National Army. That same day, the chief of staff of the U.S. Army, Tasker Bliss, was also promoted to general. Bliss and Pershing were only the fourth and fifth American Army officers to hold four-star rank, following Ulysses S. Grant, William T. Sherman, and Philip Sheridan. Almost a year after the end of the war, Pershing on 3 September 1919 was promoted to the Regular Army rank of General of the Armies. It was a unique rank title, created especially for him. Although he continued to wear only four stars, they were gold, rather than the silver stars worn by all other general officers. When in December 1944 the five-star rank of General of the Army was created, there was widespread agreement that Pershing's General of the Armies would continue to be the superior rank. Pershing remained the senior-ranking U.S. Army officer of all time until America's Bicentennial, when on 11 October 1976 the U.S. Congress passed a special act posthumously conferring the General of the Armies rank on George Washington, with an effective date of 4 July 1776.

Thus, John "Black Jack" Pershing shares a seat with George Washington at the pinnacle of American military history. For more than 50 years after the end of the Great War, Pershing was considered to be one of the greatest, if not *the* greatest, of American generals... but only by Americans. The British have always been extremely critical of Pershing. The French have been condescendingly polite about him, largely in recognition of the key role played by American manpower in tipping the strategic balance against Germany in 1918. Pershing hardly rates a blip on the radar screen of German military historiography. During the course of the last 40 years or so, an increasing number of American military historians have been looking more critically at Pershing's generalship during World War I.

The great German military theorist, Major General Carl von Clausewitz, grouped the entire diverse range of military activities into two primary categories: 1. preparation for war, and 2. the conduct of war proper.[3] Clausewitz further observed that very few generals have ever been equally skilled in both broad categories. History bears him out, and this pattern emerges quite clearly upon close examination of Pershing's record.

Pershing was a brilliant and hard-driving organizer. He was a tireless manager who knew how to make things happen, and he had a talent for overcoming the seemingly insurmountable obstacles faced in establishing the American Expeditionary Forces. He was an efficient trainer – but he was not an effective one. He trained his troops rapidly and well; but he did not train them for the right things. He trained them for a 19th-century war, rather than for the new type of 20th-century war his troops were facing. Pershing came late into the war with an unshakable belief in American national exceptionalism and a steadfast faith in "self-reliant infantry," based on superior American marksmanship and the power of the bayonet. Ignoring the experiences of the previous three years and the advice of the Allies, he believed that the tired and dispirited Europeans hunkering down in their mud-filled and barbed wire-laced trenches could never stand up against his robust and fresh American Doughboys with their M-1903 Springfield rifles. Consequently, Pershing discounted the effects of most of the modern 20th-century weapons, such as machine guns, trench mortars, artillery, and aircraft. He trained his troops to fight the wrong kind of war, and once in action he pushed them forward in relentless frontal attacks.

Despite Pershing's serious shortcomings as a tactical and operational commander, there most likely never would have been an AEF on the European battlefields of 1918 without "Black Jack" Pershing. But his mantra of "Self-Reliant Infantry" and "Open Warfare" as the only solutions for "Trench Warfare" was the foundation of the AEF's official doctrine – a doctrine that became dogma. Although maneuver warfare became the standard approach to warfighting from the mid-20th century on, it was largely impractical through the end of World War I because the necessary military technology was not yet available. Although firepower had become mechanized, increasing its volume and lethality, battlefield mobility through 1918 was still largely based on the limitations of human and animal muscle power.

Pershing's prejudices against modern weapons, his lack of understanding of how firepower and maneuver complemented each other, and his almost blind prejudice against accepting any warfighting advice from his allies, meant that his AEF units were trained and organized inadequately for the war they had to fight. Pershing's misreading of the World War I battlefield was a major factor in the U.S. Army suffering a staggering 117,700 dead and 204,000 wounded in just a little more than six months of major combat operations.

Pershing's background

Born on 13 September 1860, Pershing was the son of a Missouri businessman with no particular family ties to the military. His primary motivation for attending West Point was the free education. Graduating from the U.S. Military Academy in 1886, he was commissioned in the cavalry. He spent much of his early career serving on the western frontier in operations against the Plains Indians. As a member of the 6th Cavalry, he fought in an engagement against the Lakota Sioux on 1 January 1891, three days after the Battle of Wounded Knee. Pershing also served in Cuba during the Spanish–American War, fighting at the Battle of San Juan Hill in 1898. He spent several years as a white officer in the 10th Cavalry, manned by the black American troopers known as the "Buffalo Soldiers." His nickname, "Black Jack," derived from that assignment. In 1905 and 1906 Pershing was one of the official American military observers in Manchuria during the Russo–Japanese War. One of his German counterparts was Captain Max Hoffmann, who in 1914 would be Hindenburg's and Ludendorff's chief of operations at Tannenberg, and later the chief of staff of the German command on the Eastern Front (*Oberost*). From 1909 to 1913 Pershing commanded the Department of Mindanao during the Philippine Insurrection.

Between 1891 and 1895 Pershing served as a professor of military science and tactics at the University of Nebraska. He took advantage of that assignment to earn a law degree in his spare time. In 1897 he was assigned to West Point as a tactical instructor, where he acquired a reputation as a stern disciplinarian. In 1904 he graduated from one of the first classes of the newly established U.S. Army War College.

In December 1913, Pershing assumed command of the 8th Brigade, headquartered at The Presidio in San Francisco. But just four months later the 8th Brigade redeployed to Fort Bliss, Texas, in response to increasing tensions along the American–Mexican border. Pershing intended to relocate his family to Fort Bliss, but on 26 August 1915 a fire swept through his home at The Presidio. His wife, Helen Frances Warren, and their three young daughters were all killed in the blaze. Only his six-year-old son, Warren, survived. Despite the personal tragedy, Pershing carried on in command. In 1916, at about the same time that the European armies were fighting it out on the Somme, he commanded the unsuccessful Mexican Punitive Expedition to capture Pancho Villa. By the time America entered the Great War, Pershing was the most combat-experienced officer in the U.S. Army.

Pershing and U.S. national politics

Long before he was being considered for command of the AEF, Pershing was no stranger to the world of national politics. His late wife's father, Senator Francis E. Warren of Wyoming, had earned the Medal of Honor during the Civil War. Warren was the chairman of the Senate Committee on Military Affairs when in 1906 President Theodore Roosevelt promoted Pershing from captain directly to brigadier general, bypassing 835 more senior officers. At the time, there was grumbling in some quarters about political influence, but such fast-track promotions were not completely unprecedented. In 1902, for example, Tasker Bliss had been promoted from major directly to brigadier general. Within the officer corps itself, most of Pershing's contemporaries thought that his accelerated advancement was based on merit.

Pershing was not the only candidate for command of the AEF. A serious alternative was Major General Leonard Wood, who had earned the Medal of Honor during the Indian Wars, and had served as chief of staff of the U.S. Army from 1910 to 1914. However, his active affiliation with the Republican Party and reputation for insubordination made his selection less likely in a Democrat presidential administration. Secretary of War Newton D. Baker nominated Pershing, and President Woodrow Wilson immediately confirmed the appointment. Pershing first learned that he was being considered for the command when he received a telegram from his late wife's father saying, "Wire me today whether and how much you speak, read, and write French." Although Senator Warren at that point was no longer a member of the Military Affairs Committee, the appearance of political influence once more arose. Secretary Baker later stated definitively that Warren "had no part, and sought no part in the selection of General Pershing for the overseas command..."[4] The historical evidence generally confirms that Warren had no direct influence in Pershing's rapid rise in rank or selection for command. Before he left for France Pershing had only a very rudimentary command of French, but he worked hard to improve it.

When Pershing met with Baker and Wilson on 24 May 1917, the President gave the new AEF commander only cursory guidance that the AEF should be organized and fight as an independent American army. Wilson and Pershing did not meet again until after the end of the war. Baker was not much more specific in his own guidance and said to Pershing: "I will give you only two orders – one to go to France and the other to come home. In the meantime, your authority in France will be supreme."[5] Thus, Pershing received what amounted to a blank check from his political superiors. The political and military leaders of Britain and France, however, had far different expectations for the AEF and its (in their eyes) neophyte commander-in-chief.

At the national political level, the management of America's war effort was much different than it would be during World War II under President Franklin D. Roosevelt. As noted above, President Wilson was a failure as the manager of America's industrial mobilization. Rather than the "Arsenal of Democracy" America was to become in World War II, the Doughboys of the AEF fought the Great War armed almost completely with French- and British-supplied weapons. American-made rifles and sidearms were the exceptions. Secretary Baker likewise was reluctant to get involved in "purely military matters," and thus failed to manage the expansion of the Army.

Most of the expansion and mobilization effort was left in the hands of the U.S. Army General Staff, which itself was a relatively new and inexperienced organization. Only established in 1903, the General Staff 13 years later was still groping its way toward an effective organizational structure. The Army's chief of staff had no real command authority and had to jockey for power with the powerful chiefs of the individual branches – Infantry, Cavalry, Artillery, Signal, Ordnance, Quartermaster, Medical, etc. to accomplish any task. When America was thrust into the middle of World War I, it provided the catharsis that ultimately imposed some sense of order on the chaos that was the U.S. Army General Staff. By the time the Great War ended in 1918, both of America's other two four-star generals, Tasker Bliss and Payton March, had served as chief of staff of the U.S. Army and played differing roles in this position. Their respective relationships with Pershing also were distinctly different.

Pershing's relations with the Army's chiefs of staff, Bliss and March

Sixty-three-year-old Major General Hugh Scott was the chief of staff when America entered the war in April 1916. He retired in September 1917. Although not much progress was made during his tenure in bringing organizational order to the General Staff, Scott did play a key role in winning broad-based acceptance for the necessity of conscription, which America had not had since the Civil War.

Scott was succeeded by Major General Bliss as chief of staff on 23 September. Thirteen days later, Bliss was promoted to four-star general in the National Army. On 17 November 1917, Bliss was appointed as the American Permanent Military Representative (PMR) to the newly established Supreme War Council (SWC) at Versailles, France. For the time being, however, he remained in Washington, concurrently serving as the U.S. Army chief of staff. On 31 December Bliss was forced to retire upon reaching the maximum service age of 64. The following day President Wilson recalled him to active duty at his four-star rank and sent him to France, where he could serve more effectively as PMR. He remained the American PMR until the end of the war. Bliss was Pershing's most important American military ally. As chief of staff he never considered himself to be Pershing's military superior. Until he went to France, Bliss saw his job as doing everything possible to make sure the War Department supported the commander in the field. Once Bliss was in Paris, he steadfastly supported Pershing in his many clashes with the British and French political and military leaders. He loyally supported Pershing during the amalgamation controversy (the appeal by the French and British leaders to integrate American soldiers directly into their existing armies), although he personally thought that Pershing could have shown more flexibility in temporarily attaching larger American units to the French and British for training purposes. Despite his firm support for Pershing, Bliss established a reputation among the Allies for sound judgment and a steady hand.

On 20 May 1918 Bliss was succeeded as Army chief of staff by Major General Peyton C. March, who that same day was promoted to full general in the National Army, making him the third American four-star general during World War I. March had very different ideas about relative rank seniority and the chain of command, and he viewed himself as the U.S. Army's senior-ranking general officer. All other general officers, therefore, were subordinate to him, including and especially the AEF commander in France. But Pershing refused to admit subordination to another American general. For one thing, until March was recalled to Washington, he had been Pershing's direct subordinate in France as the artillery commander of the U.S. First Army. Pershing believed the chain of command ran directly from him, to Secretary Baker, to President Wilson. The chief of staff of the Army's job was to give the AEF commander what he wanted, when he wanted it. Neither Baker nor Wilson ever stepped in to clarify the situation. Sadly, this clash between Pershing and March continued well after the war ended.

With Bliss still the official chief of staff from January through May 1918, but physically in Paris, the War Department was in a state of chaos until March took over. March proved to be a strong and effective manager and forced through many long overdue organizational changes in both the War Department and the General Staff. He reorganized the structure of the Army, and abolished the distinctions between the Regular Army, the Army Reserve, and the Army National Guard during wartime. He established centralized control over supply operations, as opposed to the so-called "stovepipe" supply systems controlled by the individual branches. He also established new branches and technical services, such as the Army Air Corps, Tank Corps, Transportation Corps, and the Chemical Warfare Service. And when the war ended, he managed the demobilization of the 2-million-man Army. Despite the animosity between the Army chief of staff and the commander of the AEF, March played the second most important role for America in the war. The AEF owed its existence almost as much to March's "push" as it did to Pershing's "pull." Ironically, when Pershing became U.S. Army chief of staff in 1921, he not only continued March's innovations, but also moved to establish the chief of staff as the nation's senior Army officer and the top of the chain of command.

Pershing as an administrative commander

For most of Pershing's 17 months in command of the AEF, his time was devoted to planning, administration, logistics management, and training. American units only fought under his direct command for the first time with the start of the Saint-Mihiel offensive on 12 September 1918.

Pershing, along with a small advanced party staff, sailed for Europe on the RMS *Baltic* in May 1916. During the crossing they spent almost all their time planning the organization and deployment of the AEF main body. An operations planning team headed by Lieutenant Colonel Fox Conner, Pershing's assistant chief of staff for operations, studied the best sector for the main force to deploy as it reached Europe. The positions of the French ports centering on Saint-Nazaire that would be available to the Americans, combined with the existing rail lines running from those ports, made it almost impossible for the Americans to take up a position between the British and the French. Conner's team recommended the Lorraine sector, between the Argonne Forest and the Vosges Mountains. Conner also identified the elimination of the Saint-Mihiel salient, just south of Verdun, as the best option for the first large-scale American operation of the war.

Pershing arrived in London to a hero's welcome, and his reception in Paris was even more enthusiastic; but the buoyant atmosphere quickly wore thin. Within weeks Pershing was reporting to Washington that the French and British wanted to take control of U.S. forces even before America fielded an army. The AEF commander also was frustrated by the lack of coordination between the French and British. Until the establishment of the Allied Supreme War Council in November 1917, there had been very little synchronization between the two principal Western Allies. As a result, French and British instructors assigned to the AEF were teaching the Doughboys far different combat methods. What infuriated Pershing even more, the Allied instructors were teaching the new troops how to fight in static trench warfare, which ran counter to Pershing's passionate belief in the efficacy of maneuver-based "open warfare."

The last time America had fought a war with allies was in 1783. When the United States declared war on Germany in April 1917, it declined to become a party to the 1915 Treaty of London, which was the legal basis of the Entente. Rather than an Allied Power, America declared itself an "Associated Power." As soon as Pershing arrived in Europe, he made it clear to everyone that President Woodrow Wilson had personally ordered him to field and command an independent American army, one that would operate in coordination with, but would not be subordinate to, the Entente. Thus, he also made it clear that American troops would not serve as a replacement pool of company- or battalion-sized augmentations for French and British divisions, let alone as individual replacements. Before Pershing landed in Europe, British Expeditionary Force commander Field Marshal Sir Douglas Haig had recorded in his diary on 3 May 1917 that French Army commander General Phillippe Pétain wanted the Americans to send individuals over to France to enlist in the French Army. Haig realistically noted that he thought there was very little chance of that happening. Pershing's firm stance on the amalgamation issue was a source of constant friction throughout the war. At the height of the crisis of the first major German offensive in March 1918, however, Pershing did offer temporary amalgamation of American units.

On 1 September 1917 Colonel Conner and Pershing's aide, Captain George S. Patton, went to Chaumont to set up the AEF's General Headquarters (GHQ). Initially, Pershing's headquarters was overstaffed and top-heavy, with 15 heads of departments, bureaus, and services, as well as miscellaneous elements, such as a press bureau and various welfare agencies like the American Red Cross. Because of his tendency to micromanage, Pershing at first dealt with many of these entities directly, which consumed large amounts of his time. The Army General Staff in Washington was similarly chaotically organized. Despite his reluctance to learn from the Allies tactically, Pershing studied closely the French and the British staff organizations, and finally adopted the simpler four-bureaux French model for the American Expeditionary Forces:

- G-1 Personnel and Administration
- G-2 Intelligence and Security
- G-3 Operations and Training
- G-4 Logistics and Supply

Shortly, however, the AEF split operations and training, with the latter becoming the fifth General Staff branch: G-5 Training. When Pershing became chief of staff of the Army following the war, he adopted the AEF staff-structure army-wide, an organizational structure still used today.

In October 1917, Pershing and the War Department clashed over the assignment of general officers to key command positions in the AEF. He sent a cable to Secretary of War Baker objecting strongly to the standard practice of assigning general officers solely on the basis of seniority. Many of the older senior officers were well beyond the age where they were physically and psychologically capable of dealing with the stresses of brigade and divisional command in combat. Quite correctly, Pershing argued that combat command assignments should go to younger officers strictly on the basis of proven ability.

Despite March's efforts, the training of hundreds of thousands of new soldiers suffered from a shortage of stateside training camps, equipment, and qualified instructors. To compensate for the low level of training of the American troops sent to Europe, Pershing was forced to add three additional months of training once the units arrived in France. Of the more than 20 AEF schools that were established, one of the most critical was an American General Staff College at Langres. This tied-in closely with Pershing's running battle with the War Department over what he considered the lack of emphasis on "open warfare" training. A statement in a War Department training manual issued in December 1917 particularly drew his ire: "… in all the military training of a division, under existing conditions training for trench warfare is of paramount importance."[6]

Despite the AEF's battlefield experiences in October and November 1918, Pershing clung to his belief. In his postwar memoirs he wrote: "Most of our officers were firm believers in the soundness of our [i.e., Pershing's] doctrines, although a few continued to defer to the opinions of the French instructors, who were generally committed to the theory that only trench training was necessary."[7] Training for trench warfare, however, did not equate exclusively with passive defense. Without a detailed understanding of the conditions and realities of trench warfare, it was impossible to plan and execute successful attacks against heavily fortified and echeloned positions, such as the Hindenburg Line (which the Germans called the "Siegfried Stellung"). During the final months of the war, the Doughboys paid a heavy price for having to learn those lessons through trial and error in actual combat.

The training issue was only one part of Pershing's resistance to the Allies' pressures for amalgamation. He had valid reasons for resisting amalgamation, especially at the level of the individual soldiers, including the language barrier with the French, and the deep-rooted Irish-American hostility toward the British. At the political level, the absorption of American soldiers as fillers in French and British units would discount America's contribution to the war and reduce American influence in the subsequent peace settlement. And finally, there most certainly would be a huge public outcry if Americans suffered disproportionately heavy casualties while serving under foreign commanders. On the other hand, amalgamation, although not necessarily on the individual soldier level, made sense to the Allies, who were scraping the bottoms of their manpower barrels, and continually pointed to the AEF's severe shortage of experienced senior commanders and trained staff officers as the major stumbling block for fielding large American formations.

The amalgamation issue was closely linked to the problem of limited American shipping, which consumed much of Pershing's time in 1917 and well into 1918. America in 1917 had only 1 million tons of transatlantic shipping. That was the same gross tonnage as it had in 1810, and less than Norway then currently had. Thus, much of the AEF would have to cross the Atlantic in British ships. But Britain's merchant fleet was already stressed to near its limit, and the pressure only increased with the February 1917 resumption of the German unrestricted U-boat campaign. If American combat units as battalions or even regiments were amalgamated with British and French divisions, it would reduce the requirement for support forces, which ultimately made up 45 percent of the AEF. But without those support forces, America could never field its own independent army.

Pershing's relations with the Allies

Pershing's relations with the Allied political and military leaders were anything but harmonious. British Prime Minister David Lloyd George and French Premier Georges Clemenceau quickly became exasperated with Pershing's staunch refusal to allow U.S. troops to be used as filler replacements in the British and French armies. In September 1917 Pershing had his first major clash with Clemenceau, when the AEF commander flatly refused Clemenceau's demand that he put American troops into the French line immediately, with or without training. Pershing was right on that point. In December David Lloyd George proposed that the United States send over separate companies and battalions to fill out British divisions. Pershing continued to stand his ground, and Washington supported him. On 18 December Secretary of War Baker sent Pershing a cable confirming that he and President Wilson "… do not desire loss of identity of our forces, but regard that as secondary to the meeting of any critical situation by the most helpful use possible of the troops at your command."[8] Yet, what actually constituted a "critical situation" was left up to Pershing to decide.

On 10 January 1918, Pershing and General Bliss, in his role as the American PMR to the newly established SWC, met in London with British Chief of the Imperial General Staff General Sir William Robertson. Following up on Lloyd George's suggestion, Robertson tried to convince the Americans to bring over 150 separate infantry battalions to feed into the divisions of the British Expeditionary Force (BEF). When the three met again in Paris on 25 January, Pershing rejected Robertson's proposal and instead insisted on enough British shipping to transport six complete American divisions. Bliss had seen a great deal of merit in Robertson's proposal, but he nonetheless supported Pershing. The various possible solutions to the combined shipping and amalgamation problems remained a contentious issue well into the summer of 1918.

When the AEF finally started conducting large-scale operations in September 1918, Clemenceau's criticisms of Pershing became even more heated. During the kick-off of the Meuse–Argonne offensive, Clemenceau tried to visit the American forward line, but he became stuck in a hopeless jam of military traffic south of Montfaucon. This experience convinced Clemenceau that the entire American high command was totally incompetent and he ordered Allied General-in-Chief Ferdinand Foch to write to President Wilson demanding Pershing's removal. President Wilson and Secretary Baker could not have helped knowing about the French and British criticisms of Pershing, but they remained aloof. Had the war dragged into 1919 with the casualty count increasing, they almost certainly would have had to become involved. Although Pershing and

General Ferdinand Foch did not get along, Foch continually deflected Clemenceau's fierce political attacks against him.

Pétain and Pershing, on the other hand, developed a close relationship. After the war Pershing even called Pétain, "the greatest general of the war."[9] Ironically, Pershing's tactical thinking was much closer to Foch's. When Pershing and Pétain met for the first time on 16 June 1917, they rapidly established a close personal bond, even though they had much different ideas on modern war-fighting. Pershing disagreed with Pétain's concept of limited objective attacks, writing in his memoirs: "The theory of winning by attrition, with isolated attacks on limited fronts, which was evidently the idea of the British General Staff, did not appeal to me in principle."[10] Pershing also was critical of French training, which emphasized the teaching of trench warfare combat methods. Of this, he wrote: "In order to avoid the effect of the French teaching it became necessary to take over and direct all instruction ourselves. For the purpose of impressing our own doctrine upon officers, a training program was issued which laid great stress upon open warfare methods and offensive action."[11]

When Pershing first arrived in France, Foch was chief of staff of the French Army, a purely advisory position to the French government, with no direct command authority. At that time, there was not an actual unified command structure for the Allies. Although Haig and Pétain tried to coordinate with each other to a degree, each was essentially an independent commander. After the Germans launched their massive Operation MICHAEL offensive on 21 March 1918 and almost split the French and British armies, the key Allied military and political leaders met at Doullens on 26 March and finally agreed to appoint Foch General-in-Chief of the Allied Armies. Pershing was not a party to that meeting, and it was strictly a British–French agreement. By 30 March, however, Secretary of War Baker agreed that Pershing too would act under Foch's overall operational direction. After nearly four years of war, the Allies were finally on their way to achieving real unity of effort and unity of command. Only by this could they blunt the German Spring Offensives and go over on the offensive to win the war in late 1918.

In April, the Germans launched their second great offensive, Operation GEORGETTE, and almost drove the BEF into the English Channel.

With a sense of crisis in the air, the next meeting of the Supreme War Council took place in Abbeville on 1–2 May. Present were Haig, Foch, Pershing, Pétain, Clemenceau, British Secretary of State for War Lord Alfred Milner, and the new Chief of the Imperial General Staff, General Sir Henry Wilson. Inevitably, the topic of amalgamation came up once again, and just as inevitably Pershing refused to allow American units to be broken up. In exasperation, Foch told Pershing: "I am commander-in-chief of the Allied Armies in France, and my appointment has been sanctioned not only by the British and French governments, but also by the President of the United States. Hence, I believe it my duty to insist on my point of view." Pershing did not flinch and wrote: "We all knew that no authority to dictate regarding such matters had been conferred upon General Foch."[12]

Pressing the attack, Foch demanded of Pershing: "Are you willing to risk our being driven back to the Loire?" But Pershing shocked all those present by shooting back: "Yes, I am willing to take the risk. Moreover, the time may come when the American army will have to stand the brunt of this war, and it is not wise to fritter away our resources in this manner."[13] Pershing defended his position by insisting that the morale of his American troops was very high, while that of the French and British was very low. He did not want his Doughboys to be exposed to the negative influences of French and British pessimism.

They continued to argue hotly for another 40 minutes, with Lloyd George, Clemenceau, Foch, and Milner all attempting to pressure Pershing to give in. Pershing finally banged the table and said: "Gentlemen, I have thought this program over very deliberately, and I will not be coerced."[14] Then he walked out of the meeting. Haig recorded in his diary for that day: "I thought Pershing very obstinate and stupid. He did not seem to realize the urgency of the situation." And a little further on: "He hankers after a '*great self-contained American Army*' [original emphasis] but seeing that he has neither Commanders of Divisions, of Corps, nor of Armies, nor Staffs for same, it is ridiculous to think such an Army could function alone in less than 2 years' time."[15] At that point, there were 429,375 Americans in France, but only four divisions deployed in quiet sectors of the front lines.

Pershing as a tactical and operational commander

Despite Pershing's overriding objective of fielding and fighting an independent American army, the divisions of the AEF initially fought under French and British overall command from May to September 1918. During the first American divisional attack against German positions at Cantigny on 28 May, the U.S. 1st Division fought under the command of French X Corps. A little more than a week later, on 6 June, the U.S. 2nd Division attacked at Belleau Wood as part of French XXI Corps. During the same period the 3rd Division fought at Château-Thierry as part of French XXXVIII Corps. During the French counteroffensive starting on 18 July, the 1st and 2nd Divisions fought in the battle for Soissons as part of French XX Corps, and the 3rd Division again fought in the Château-Thierry sector with XXXVIII Corps. Meanwhile, throughout July and August the 4th, 26th, 28th, and 32nd Divisions all fought in the Aisne–Marne sector under French corps. The U.S. 27th and 30th Divisions, comprising the U.S. II Corps, fought under the command of the British Fourth Army from August to the end of the war. The 33rd, 37th, 80th, and 91st Divisions all fought under British command from August through October.

Despite having been in Europe for more than a year, Pershing still refused to accept the lessons learned by the French and British since 1914. Right up to the end of November 1918, Pershing continued to place all his faith in American rifle marksmanship, "self-reliant infantry," and "open warfare," which all too often meant frontal attacks. Pershing never accepted that modern weapons like trench mortars and machine guns could be any serious hindrance to well-led attacking infantry. "Well-led" was the key. If the attack failed or faltered, then the reason had to be a failure of leadership. Thus, during the final 12 months of the war Pershing sacked two corps commanders, six division commanders, and four brigade commanders.

The attack at the Saint-Mihiel salient just south of Verdun on 12–15 September was the first army-level operation led by Pershing. On 24 July 1918 Supreme Allied Commander Foch approved the operation, and authorized the establishment of the U.S. First Army, effective

10 August. Pershing agreed that the First Army would be under the overall operational control of Pétain's French Armies of the North and Northeast. Intending to retain complete control of all the American forces, Pershing decided to assume direct command of the U.S. First Army, while simultaneously retaining command of the American Expeditionary Forces. The AEF's chief of operations, Brigadier General Fox Conner, advised against such "dual-hatting," which would result in a span of control too wide for any commander. When Pershing persisted, Conner tried to help him, reassigning his own highly capable AEF operations deputy, Colonel George C. Marshall, to the First Army's Operations Section, where he later became chief of the section.

The AEF's initial planning for the Saint-Mihiel operation was not limited to simply cutting the salient off at its base. Some of the American planners even envisioned continuing on to take Metz at a single bound, which if successful would collapse the entire German rail system in the northern Lorraine sector. Pershing recommended such a plan to Pétain, who for sound operational reasons refused to approve it.

When Foch approved the Saint-Mihiel offensive, he also was planning his great Allied General Offensive, in which all the Allied Armies from the Belgian coast to northern Lorraine would attack simultaneously, aiming for virtually all the critical German rail centers across the front. Haig, however, saw a key flaw in Foch's overall plan. While the three planned major attacks by the Belgians, British, and French all converged, the southernmost American attack toward Saint-Mihiel diverged from the other three. On 27 August, Haig suggested to Foch that the Americans should attack, instead of east into the Saint-Mihiel salient, north toward the major German rail center at Mézières. Such a thrust would converge with the BEF's own planned attack toward the German rail centers at Cambrai. The idea made a great deal of operational sense, as Foch quickly saw.

Pershing was less impressed. Foch wanted to cancel or at least reduce the scope of the Saint-Mihiel offensive, so the AEF then could get into position to attack in coordination with the other three prongs of the Allied General Offensive. Pershing, however, already had too much invested in Saint-Mihiel. When Foch and Pershing met at U.S. First

Army's headquarters on 30 August, the two almost came to blows. Pershing accused Foch of wanting to reduce the size of the coming attack so he could take away several American divisions and assign them to various French field armies. "Marshal Foch," Pershing said, "you have no authority as Allied Commander-in-Chief to call upon me to yield up my command of the American Army and have it scattered among the Allied forces where it will not be an American army at all."[16]

The meeting ended with neither general giving ground. The following day, however, Pershing wrote to Foch:

> If you decide to utilize the American forces in attacking in the direction of Mézières, I accept that decision, even though it complicates my supply system and the care of my sick and wounded; but I do insist that this American army be employed as a whole, either east of the Argonne or west of the Argonne, and not in four or five divisions here and six or seven there.

Pershing concluded by telling Foch that even if the AEF conducted only a smaller-scale attack against the Saint-Mihiel salient, it would still be impossible to redeploy by 15 or even 20 September the 12–16 American divisions that Foch wanted committed in the direction of Mézières.[17]

Foch was running out of patience. On 1 September he wrote to Pershing: "If you think – as you let me know in your letter of 31 August – that you cannot make the Saint-Mihiel operation before [the Mézières attack] or simultaneously – even if reduced – I think we need to renounce it."[18] The following day, Foch, Pétain, and Pershing met, with Pétain brokering a compromise. Foch still wanted to cancel the Saint-Mihiel offensive and concentrate on the attack toward Mézières. Pershing argued that it was important to cut off the salient first, to eliminate any potential threat to the American rear. Pétain backed Pershing, and the final compromise was a reduced attack only to the limit of the base of the salient. Foch also accepted Pershing's arguments about the time needed to redeploy his forces after Saint-Mihiel, and he agreed to a projected start date of 20–25 September for the Meuse–Argonne offensive, with a force of 12–14 American divisions.

Pershing's victory in holding on to the Saint-Mihiel offensive came at a steep price. Conducting closely sequential attacks in two widely separated sectors was far beyond the capabilities of the AEF. The Americans' limited transportation assets meant that more than half of the total force of 600,000 troops and 2,700 guns would have to move by horse or by foot more than 60 miles over poor roads and often during the hours of darkness. The U.S. First Army staff had no experience in planning and conducting such a large-scale and complex movement. Moreover, on the very day that Foch, Pétain, and Pershing reached the final agreement, none of the staff officers at First Army headquarters had any idea that they would shortly be faced with such an immense task on such a short order. Furthermore, Pershing intended to commit his most experienced divisions at Saint-Mihiel, and it would be impossible for them to refit, redeploy, and be in position in time for the start of the Meuse–Argonne attack. Thus, almost all of the divisions in the first line when that attack finally jumped off on 26 September were inexperienced, and some of them were not even fully trained. Three of the first echelon divisions were not even supported by their own organic artillery brigades, which were still strung out along the line of march from the Saint-Mihiel sector. Pershing tried to explain this decision, by writing, "It was thought reasonable to count on the vigor and the aggressive spirit of our troops to make up in a measure for their inexperience."[19]

The start date for the Meuse–Argonne offensive was set for 26 September. At one-day intervals following, the other three attacks of the Allied General Offensive would jump off. Pershing assumed command of all Allied forces in the Meuse–Argonne sector on 22 September, with General Henri Gouraud's Fourth Army under his operational control. The Fourth Army's mission, advancing north along the western side of the Argonne Forest, was to cover the U.S. First Army's left flank. On 20 September First Army issued Field Order 20 for the operation. Three corps were to attack on line, but no main effort was designated. Nor did the distribution of forces indicate any weighing of the main effort. Each of the corps had three divisions in the first line, and one division in reserve. First Army had three divisions in general reserve, one behind each corps. The artillery and mortars also were evenly distributed across the front. Thus, the forces were deployed as if for a single massive frontal attack.

V Corps in the center was generally assumed to be the main effort, because of the high ground they were ordered to seize held by the Germans at Montfaucon, which gave observation dominance over much of the battlefield. The way the unit boundaries were established, however, made a difficult tactical problem even more difficult. The coordination of fire and maneuver across unit boundaries is one of the most difficult and complex of all combat tasks. The Butte de Montfaucon, rather than being in the center of the V Corps sector, was only about a mile away from the boundary with III Corps, on the right of V Corps. That severely limited V Corps' ability to maneuver against Montfaucon from both flanks. None of the inexperienced and partially trained attacking divisions was equal to such a task. To compound matters, the division tasked with the mission of seizing Montfaucon was the 79th, one of the least-trained units in the AEF.

Montfaucon was 4 miles from the American line of departure, and Pershing's plan required his Doughboys to advance more than 8 miles on the first day. In addition to taking the high ground at Montfaucon, he expected them to break through the first two German defensive belts, and finally the third and strongest of the German defensive belts of the Kriemhilde Stellung, and then capture the Heights of Romagne. Pershing's plan had no basis in reality, especially with inexperienced troops attacking into the deeply echeloned defensive systems the Germans had spent years reinforcing. Once the attack started, the American left flank was hit with heavy enfilading fire from German artillery in the Argonne foothills; while German guns on the high bluffs on the east bank of the Meuse River poured fire into the American right flank. Simultaneously, massive traffic jams along the poor roads of the American main supply routes prevented food and ammunition from moving up and the wounded from moving back. All the while blaming the failures and delays on inexperienced and timid officers, Pershing continually issued orders to "push on regardless of men or guns, night and day."[20]

By 30 September the offensive had run out of steam, and the Americans were forced into an operational pause in front of the as-yet unbroken Kriemhilde Stellung. When Phase II of the offensive resumed on 4 October, the experienced and refitted divisions from Saint-Mihiel had replaced most of the Phase I divisions in the line. The infantry-centered tactics did not change, however, and the AEF continued to make slow and costly progress. On 12 October Foch authorized the establishment of the U.S. Second Army, which when activated would attack the Germans northward along the east bank of the Marne. Relinquishing direct command of First Army, Pershing became the first American officer to command an army group. Now on an equal level with Pétain and Haig, he finally had his independent American Army.

General Hunter Liggett replaced Pershing as First Army commander, and the AEF's fighting tactics quickly changed for the better, with an emphasis on coordinated firepower and synchronized combined arms. Although little remembered today, Liggett arguably was America's best battlefield commander of the Great War. Pershing, however, had a hard time letting go, yielding to his tendency to micromanage. Lieutenant Colonel Pierpont Stackpole, Liggett's aide-de-camp, recorded in his diary on 16 October: "General Pershing is still around at his office on the train and butting into details, with numerous changes of mind." And, "An extraordinary spectacle is presented by Pershing… hanging around and worrying everybody with endless talk, rather than giving his orders and leaving the 1st Army to carry them out."[21]

By the end of October, the Americans had finally broken through the Kriemhilde Stellung, Pershing's objective for the first day. The AEF also cleared the Argonne Forest on their left, linking-up with the French Fourth Army at Grandpré, at the northern tip of the woods. The German positions on the Bois de Barricourt Ridge was the last significant obstacle before Mézières on the Meuse, as the river bent to the northwest. After another operational pause, Phase III of the attack started on 1 November. By the next day the Germans started withdrawing rapidly to the north. Pershing finally had his long-dreamed-of condition of "open warfare."

As the advance closed in on the Meuse and the town of Sedan, some 10 miles east–southeast of Mézières, the French Fourth Army started lagging behind. Sedan was where in 1870 French Emperor Napoleon III had been forced to surrender to Prussian King Wilhelm, who shortly would become Kaiser Wilhelm I. It was a psychologically important place for the French, and it was well within the boundary of the Fourth Army. But Pershing saw an opportunity to enhance the AEF's prestige by taking Sedan, and thereby mitigating the fierce criticism that the French and the British had been heaping on the tactical performance of the AEF. On the morning of 5 November, Pershing convinced French Army Group Center commander, General Paul Maistre, to agree reluctantly to let the Americans take Sedan if the Fourth Army continued to lag far behind.

By the end of 5 November, the Americans were a little more than 5 miles from Sedan when at 1600 hours Conner, as the G-3 of the AEF, walked into the office of the First Army G-3, George Marshall. After discussing the general situation, Conner said, "It is General Pershing's desire that the troops of the First Army should capture Sedan, and he directs that orders be issued accordingly."[22] After discussing the point a bit more, Marshall then drafted the initial message:

> Memorandum for Commanding generals, I Corps, V Corps.
> Subject: Message from Commander-in-Chief
>
> 1. General Pershing desires that the honor of entering Sedan should fall to the First American Army. He has every confidence that the troops of the I Corps, assisted on their right by the V Corps, will enable him to realize his desire.
> 2. In transmitting the foregoing message, your attention is invited to the favorable opportunity now existing for pressing our advantage throughout the night.[23]

Despite the fact that the order was coming directly from Pershing, Marshall was reluctant to issue it immediately. Neither Brigadier General Hugh Drum, the First Army chief of staff, nor General Liggett were present in the headquarters. Marshall finally agreed to send out the order no later than 1800 hours if neither of his bosses returned by then. Conner left about 1730 hours, shortly before Drum returned. Drum approved the release of the message, but he added a final sentence to the second paragraph: "Boundaries will not be considered binding." The message went out without Liggett's knowledge. The First Army commander did not learn of the order until about noon on 7 November.

The order broke just about every rule of tactical command and control. The last sentence, especially, added even more confusion. Many of the senior commanders on the AEF's far left flank concluded that it meant that not only was the boundary between the U.S. First and French Fourth Armies no longer binding, but also the boundaries of the American corps and divisions. Thus, the U.S. 1st Division, third in line from the American left, turned sharply to the left and headed straight for Sedan in the dark of night, cutting across the rear of the leading elements of the U.S. 77th and 42nd Divisions, and ultimately pushing the 42nd Division into the sector of the French Fourth Army. The resulting chaos brought the three American divisions and the French 40th Division to a dead halt, with their troops hopelessly entangled. All this took place under German observation from the far bank of the Meuse, while Allied troops shot at each other in the dark.

The real tragedy, however, was the 80 killed and 503 wounded soldiers the 1st Division suffered during just the two days of 6–7 November. They all paid the price for what General Liggett later called a "tactical atrocity."[24] There was no justification at all for what was little more than a glory grab by Pershing. As soon as Allied Supreme Commander Ferdinand Foch found out what was happening, he immediately ordered all the French and American units involved to remain in or return to their original boundaries. The French later generously shared the glory of liberating Sedan by inviting a company of Americans to take the city with their forces. Sedan was liberated after four years of German occupation by the French 40th Division and elements of the American 42nd Division on 9 November 1918.

Pershing later played down the whole sad incident, writing in his memoirs: "The troops of the 1st Division carried out this unnecessary forced march in fine spirit despite their tired condition." He did not, however, note the terrible casualty count. He also wrote: "Under normal conditions the action of the officer or officers responsible for this movement of the 1st Division directly across the zones of action of two other divisions could not have been overlooked; but the splendid record of that unit and the approach of the end of hostilities suggested leniency."[25] He never hinted that the blatant glory-grab had been his idea in the first place.

One hundred years later the Race to Sedan remains controversial. Conner and Marshall obviously were acting under direct orders from Pershing. It was simply a bad order to begin with, but could the message have been more clearly stated? The fatal sentence was the last one added by Drum, which only made it more confusing. Not only did Pershing gloss over the entire affair in his memoirs, in their own memoirs both Liggett and Harbord equivocated on pinning the responsibility. The animosities resulting from the Race to Sedan continued to ripple through the senior ranks of the U.S. Army during the inter-war years. Four of the six chiefs of staff of the U.S. Army during that period – Pershing, Summerall, MacArthur, and Marshall – had been involved in the incident to one degree or another.

Unlike his commandeer-in-chief counterparts in the British, French, and especially the German Army, Pershing's tactical and operational thinking changed little throughout that war. But a direct comparison between him and Haig, Foch, Pétain, or Ludendorff is somewhat misleading, considering the relatively short time he spent in command during the war. Pershing arrived in France with warfighting ideas little different than those of Haig in 1914–15. Like the British Army of 1914, the thinking of the U.S. Army of 1917 was still grounded in the notion of a human-centric battlefield, discounting the emerging military technologies of the new century. An infantryman was a rifleman, period. The American M-1903 Springfield was a superb battle rifle, but in American doctrine its long-range accuracy was far more important than its rate of fire. Thus, right through the end of 1918 Pershing continued to believe that "self-reliant infantry" and "open warfare" were the only means to fight wars. In the war's final weeks, however, the U.S. First Army under Hunter Liggett showed that it was beginning to learn how to fight a synchronized combined-arms battle.

Pershing's postwar service

Pershing returned to the United States a national hero. As early as 1918 he apparently had been harboring presidential aspirations. A movement to draft Pershing for the 1920 election campaign came to nothing, however. Appointed to succeed Peyton March as chief of staff of the Army in 1921, Pershing immediately consolidated the authority of the office to make it the senior position in the military chain of command. When he retired as chief of staff in 1924, he was appointed chairman of the American Battle Monuments Commission, responsible for the administration and maintenance of all of America's military cemeteries outside of the United States. He held that position until his death in Walter Reed Army Hospital in Washington, D.C. on 15 July 1948.

Pershing's war memoirs, *My Experiences in the World War*, were published in 1931. The book received a poor critical reception, and it did not sell well. This notwithstanding, the book was awarded the Pulitzer Prize, despite historian T. H. Thomas saying it was "in every way disappointing," citing its poor arrangement of subject matter, lack of adequate transitions between topics within chapters, and its excessive reliance on "swift generalizations, omissions, sweeping claims, [and] well-rounded covering statements."[26] The book also reignited many of the old wartime disputes. Peyton March took offense at Pershing's "damning him with faint praise," for his contribution to the war effort as Army chief of staff. The effects of the Pershing–March feud reached well into the World War II years, where many of the U.S. Army's most senior generals still considered themselves either "Pershing Men" (e.g., George Marshall, George Patton) or "March Men" (e.g., Douglas MacArthur, John Milliken).

The prevailing theme that runs throughout Pershing's memoirs is the substantiation of the claim he made in his 19 November 1918 preliminary report to the Secretary of the Army. Pershing wrote that the AEF under his command "had developed into a powerful and smooth-running machine."[27] Hunter Liggett, in his own 1928 memoirs, had directly contradicted that claim, but it nonetheless went largely unquestioned for many years in America. It was only in the final decades of the 20th century that historians began to examine it more critically.

Pershing also argued that he alone among the senior Allied military leaders was right about the supremacy of "open warfare," "self-reliant infantry," and "vigorous American manhood." Without a single shred of evidence, and contrary to the postwar writings of almost all the Allied senior commanders, Pershing wrote: "Ultimately, we had the satisfaction of hearing the French admit that we were right, both in emphasizing training for open warfare and on insisting on proficiency in the use of the rifle."[28] The French never admitted any such thing.

By the end of the war, many American generals had come to understand the importance of modern firepower and the necessity of tightly synchronizing fire and maneuver. Hunter Liggett was foremost among them, but they also included Marine General John Lejeune and General Charles Summerall, two of the AEF's most tactically innovative division commanders. To a large extent, they had been able to get away with significant departures from the Pershing doctrine because of the success they achieved on the battlefield.

As soon as the firing stopped on the Western Front, the AEF convened the Superior Board on Organization and Tactics to compile the lessons learned from the war. The members of the Board, however, tried to find a middle ground between support for the AEF's official "self-reliant infantry" dogma, and the realities of modern firepower and technology. In its final report issued in 1921, the Board recommended increasing the numbers of machine guns, automatic rifles, and mortars in the infantry units. The report even went so far as to recommend giving infantry commanders direct control over such "auxiliary weapons" as light field guns and tanks.

Pershing was not at all happy with the report. When he sent it on to the Secretary of War, he attached his dissenting assessment, arguing that the members of his board had been too influenced by the immediate past experiences of the static battlefield on the Western Front. Instead, he argued, they should have remained more focused on "the requirements of warfare of the character and the theater upon which we are most likely to be engaged."[29] The conclusions that Pershing refused to learn would be manifest in World War II, where, in fact, battles were far more fluid and less static – *because of* the firepower and mechanization that he had discounted two decades earlier. Machine- and technology-centric warfare was here to stay.

Pershing's lieutenants

Tactical innovation and the application of lessons learned in the AEF was far more a bottom-up than a top-down process. The burden of fighting the Great War on the battlefield ultimately fell on the shoulders of the subordinate leaders of the American Expeditionary Forces. It was they who had to contend with the lack of preparedness and the steep learning curve of 20th-century warfare against a skillful, determined, and vastly more experienced enemy. Rising out of this bloody epoch of 1918 emerged a new generation of leaders who would determine the composition, tactics, and focus of the United States armed forces during the interwar period as well as into World War II. The group of officers who served under Pershing in the AEF ultimately produced one president of the United States and one vice president; five chiefs of staff of the U.S. Army; two commandants of the U.S. Marine Corps; the inspiration of the U.S. Air Force; the organizer of the World War II Office of Strategic Services, the forerunner of the Central Intelligence Agency; and one of the pioneers of modern armored warfare. It was these leaders who shaped the U.S. military during the interwar period and developed the strategy that led to victory on a two-front war (the European Theater of Operations and Pacific Theater of Operations) during World War II. These rising American leaders would grapple with how to leverage new technologies, theories of war fighting, and rising threats from the old foe, Germany, and a former ally, Japan. Yet, the road to that uncertain future ran through the battle-tested German Army deployed along the Western Front in 1918.

Among these was future President Harry S. Truman, who served in the Meuse–Argonne as an artillery battery commander and who saw firsthand the cost of not preparing for war. The lack of strategic leadership during World War I by President Wilson was not lost on Truman during the final months of World War II; subsequently, during the dawn of a Cold War he applied the hard lessons of 1918 and 1919 in 1945.

Another was Colonel George C. Marshall, whose experience and vision would carry him from the Argonne in 1918, to chief of staff of the U.S. Army during World War II, where his leadership and strategic thinking helped propel the United States to victory. Other future leaders serving under Pershing in World War I included George Smith Patton, Douglas MacArthur, William "Wild Bill" Donovan, and Teddy Roosevelt, Jr. Patton's first experience in armored warfare was in a French tank on the Western Front and he would build on those experiences years later while facing German Panzers in North Africa, Italy, Belgium, Germany, and France.

Douglas MacArthur, living in the shadow of his Civil War hero (and Medal of Honor recipient) father, seemingly endeavored to prove himself by his reckless actions on the front in 1918. Yet, he was to find that heroism and bravado were nearly not enough to overcome a fortified German position on Côte de Châtillon in October 1918 where he nearly lost his Army career. Innovation and adaption by a subordinate officer saved the day and MacArthur would go on to serve as the Army chief of staff and as a key leader of American forces in the Pacific during World War II. Douglas MacArthur would receive the Medal of Honor in 1942 and be the first father-son recipient of this highest of American awards. Likewise, Teddy Roosevelt, Jr., had "big boots" to fill and would live up to the family name in 1918, going on to be awarded the Medal of Honor during the Normandy landings in June 1944, and the second father-son Medal of Honor recipient after the MacArthurs. Another rising star under Pershing was William "Wild Bill" Donovan, who proved his tenacity on the bloody fields of the Meuse Valley in October 1918 and would go on to lead the Office of Strategic Services (OSS) in World War II and help create the Central Intelligence Agency.

Pershing's rising stars included future important leaders in the Air Service as well as in the United States Marine Corps. The leader of Pershing's Air Service was William "Billy" Mitchell. Mitchell would be the leading thinker and voice calling for an independent United States Air Force. An independent USAF would not be achieved until after World War II; however, Billy Mitchell's theory of strategic bombing, based upon his experiences in 1918, shaped the way that the United States waged aerial warfare in both Europe and the Pacific between 1941 and 1945. Entire weapon systems were designed around his theory of strategic bombing. These included the B-17 Flying Fortress, B-24 Liberator, and many others. For the Marines, Pershing's lieutenants included John A. Lejeune and Wendell Cushing Neville, who would shape their U.S. Marine Corps into the premier force for the island-hopping campaign in the Pacific Theater of Operations in World War II.

Among the many other men serving as Pershing's lieutenants were leaders who influenced the United States Army across the generations by their mentorship, recommendations, and writing. Fox Conner is one of these strategic thinkers, whose greatest achievement was mentoring George Marshall, Dwight D. Eisenhower, and George S. Patton. Other important leaders rising to the forefront in 1918 and later shaping the course of the United States included Hunter Liggett, Leonard Hines, Robert Lee Bullard, Joseph T. Dickman, Hugh Drum, Malin Craig, Charles Dawes (future vice president), and many others.

Not all of Pershing's lieutenants were covered in glory. As expected in a new and evolving organization, there were controversies and clashes of personalities. General Pershing was a merciless boss, bent on micromanagement and firing subordinates for what at times seemed minor infractions. Among these was George H. Cameron, a corps commander sacked by Pershing, and Clarence Ransom Edwards, a fired division commander. There were likewise commanders that many observers thought that Pershing should have fired, such as the controversial commander of the 77th Division, Robert Alexander. Under his orders the famous "Lost Battalion" advanced alone deep behind German lines, only to suffer five days of siege. Yet, Alexander survived his controversies and returned home to a hero's welcome.

The experiences of the emerging leaders in the AEF during World War I shaped the history, not only of World War II, but across the generations and into the next century. Their experiences in a new organization, while facing a determined foe, were a "make or break" proposition. There was little room for error, although many were made. In the end, Pershing demanded results and expected his leaders to follow the spirit and letter of his commands and overcome the overwhelming odds they faced.

Some of Pershing's lieutenants came through the maelstrom with their reputations intact and the promise of another chance to prove their mettle in a second world war. Others did their job as best they could and adapted to the ever-changing operational environment to confront the enemy that lay before them and delivered acceptable results to remain in their positions of command or trust. Yet others did not succeed and either failed to adapt and deliver results fast enough, or fell into personal disfavor with Pershing, who quickly sacked them. In the end, personal relations mattered the most. If Pershing had the impression that a leader was lackluster or would not accomplish his vision, his time in command was brief. There were occasions when Pershing simply based such an assessment on an officer's personal appearance (e.g. not fit). The bottom line is that the hard-fought lessons of the successful, the survivors, and the failed hold resonance today, a century later.

The AEF was a new and expanding enterprise, in need of skilled men to command and plan the way forward against the highly skilled Imperial German Army. In this life or death struggle, the organization with the most adaptable leadership, applying its limited resources in the right time and place, prevailed. Indeed, "new things are old things happening to new people" rings true today. A look into Pershing's lieutenants will give us a glimpse into a past that still resonates in the present. In the end, what they did in 1918 mattered, and it echoes across the generations and into eternity.

PART ONE

THE FUTURE CHIEFS OF STAFF OF THE U.S. ARMY

CHAPTER 1

MAJOR GENERAL JOHN L. HINES

Tim White

In the office of the Walter Reed Army Hospital commander, a small group gathered on Labor Day 1967 to pay homage to former Army chief of staff John Leonard Hines, set to turn 100 years old on 21 May 1968. Cadets John Throckmorton and Thomas Burnette, ranking members of the West Point Class of 1968, and Colonel Horace M. Brown, Jr., were on hand to celebrate the general's achievement as the oldest living graduate of the academy. Participating as well were Army chief of staff General Harold K. Johnson, the commander of Walter Reed, Major General Philip W. Mallory, and General Hines' children and grandchildren.

What a century he lived! Born to Irish immigrant parents in White Sulfur Springs, West Virginia on 21 May 1868, Hines received an appointment to West Point and was commissioned into the infantry in 1891. His career spanned frontier duty, the Spanish–American War, service in the Philippines, the Mexican Punitive Expedition, and World War I. He witnessed the introduction of the machine gun, the devastating lethality of indirect artillery, the mechanization of the Army, and the rapid evolution of airpower. Entering World War I as a lieutenant colonel, Hines' accession in rank is unparalleled in Army history. Within a period of 15 months (15 May 1917–25 August 1918), Hines was promoted from lieutenant colonel to major general. In comparison, Dwight D. Eisenhower was promoted to colonel on 11 March 1941, after having served as a lieutenant colonel for nearly five years and pinned on his second star on 27 March 1942.[1] After the war, Hines followed Pershing as chief of staff of the U.S. Army, advancing ahead of other prominent Pershing lieutenants.

Notably absent from the birthday gathering at Walter Reed were Hines' contemporaries, the officers with whom he served in World War I. Pershing, Summerall, MacArthur, Craig, and Marshall – all former chiefs of staff and veterans of the Great War – were dead. Gone too were Liggett, Bullard, Dickman, Lejeune, Harbord, Drum, Patton, and Alexander, fellow officers from the 1917–18 campaigns in France. Hines had survived them all.

Army to the core and imbued throughout with the credo of his alma mater, Hines said to those assembled, "It is not so much what you do as how you do it. If you base your life on these three words, Duty – Honor – Country, you will be men of honor, men of character, men of integrity."[2]

When the United States declared war on Spain on 25 April 1898, Jack Hines had already been at Fort Harrison, Montana, for almost two years. For a young officer destined for war, his service to-date recommended little for what lay ahead. His assignments included several companies within the regiment and details such as the 1892 World's Fair in Chicago, regimental recruiting duty in Nebraska, railroad riots in Montana during the summer of 1894, and duty with the Pine Ridge and Santee Indian Reservations.[3] In an era of geographically based military departments and far-flung posts, there was little exposure to large-scale military maneuvers, training, or even command structures. These postings do not conjure up the image of an officer well trained for combat on a scale larger than companies or battalions.

Fort Harrison was a new post when Hines and two companies of the 2nd Infantry arrived in 1896.[4] Post commander Lieutenant Colonel

William Wherry nominated Hines for the position of constructing quartermaster, which Washington approved. Upon receiving the telegram that ordered his unit to the assembly area, Wherry informed Hines that he couldn't accompany the regiment, as constructing quartermaster was a non-regimental posting, and his appointment had come from Washington.

Determined to go to war, Hines negotiated with Wherry and found a qualified replacement to take over his responsibilities as constructing quartermaster. Traveling via Chickamauga and then Rossville, Georgia, the regiment finally arrived in Tampa, Florida, on 12 May. On the trip southeast, Wherry was promoted to colonel and the command of the regiment. Hines, after nearly seven years as a commissioned officer, was promoted to first lieutenant.

Mobilization for the conflict in Cuba was less than stellar. Although Tampa was close to Cuba, it was not equipped for the deluge of men and materiel that besieged the city. Tampa lacked a sufficient railroad infrastructure to readily accommodate the assembling forces. To make matters worse, the Army command was disjointed, inexperienced, and ill prepared for what was being asked. Those shortcomings were exceeded only by the War Department's lack of quality transport vessels for the voyage to Cuba.[5] Only through sheer determination, force of will, and initiative at the individual level was the expedition able to set sail. The order to embark came late on the night of 7 June with the stipulation that those not loaded by morning would not make the trip. Colonel Wherry, a combat veteran of the Civil War and a Medal of Honor recipient, was unconcerned about being left behind and went to bed awaiting rail transportation.

As regimental quartermaster, the job of getting the unit the final 9 miles to the Port of Tampa fell on Hines. Lacking his commander's intimacy with battle and very eager to experience combat for himself, Hines made sure that all the unit's baggage was packed and positioned along the tracks for easy and quick loading.

A train arrived at 0200 hours on the morning of 8 June designated to carry Teddy Roosevelt's Rough Riders, who were bivouacked near the regiment. Acting quickly, Hines told the conductor to park the train along the piles of baggage and "we'll be aboard in 20 minutes."[6] He awoke Colonel Wherry without letting him know that he had commandeered Roosevelt's train and had the regiment loaded in the allotted time. Roosevelt would later write, "we were ordered to be at a certain track along with our baggage at midnight, there to take the train for Port Tampa. At the appointed time we turned up, but the train did not."[7] The regiment arrived mid-morning in the Port of Tampa and loaded onto the *Yucatan* for transport to Cuba. From their perch aboard the *Yucatan*, soldiers of the 2nd saw the Rough Riders arriving in coal cars – dirty, tired, and disheveled from their trip. They, too, were loaded onto the *Yucatan*.

Hines' organization should not be overlooked in the chaos that surrounded the operation in and around Tampa. When the time came to move, Hines had the regiment ready and able to execute quickly. His decisiveness in securing and loading the train reflected not only his eagerness but also his focus on carrying out the regiment's orders. Hines provided the regiment with much-needed direction amid the corps' confusion and lack of overall leadership. Hines' talent was beginning to show.

Hines suffered yet another shock when the fleet arrived in Cuba. General William Shafter, the expedition's commander, ordered all quartermasters and regimental bands to stay on board to manage property. Committed to being with the regiment for battle, Hines went ashore and brought his case before General John Bates, who had commanded the 2nd Infantry before Wherry and had got to know Hines. After listening to Hines, Bates told him to "take your band and go join your regiment."[8] Once again, Hines demonstrated initiative and resourcefulness in fulfilling the unit's mission as well as his own. Hines wasn't afraid to confront superiors with whom he disagreed. Importantly, he proposed an alternative when he challenged authority. Hines did see battle and was awarded the Silver Star for gallantry on San Juan Hill on 1 July 1898.[9] Before the end of the year, Hines took leave to the United States, married Wherry's daughter, and returned to Cuba for the last year of the century.

During the intervening years, Hines served multiple tours in the Philippines as well as in New York and earned Pershing's trust in the Mexican Expedition. These years for Hines were a constant rotation between company and battalion assignments, quartermaster details and frequent responsibilities as adjutant. The regimental adjutant of the prewar army functioned as the principal staff officer for the unit alongside the quartermaster and the commissary officer. His many posts and years in the capacity of both adjutant and quartermaster honed his attention to detail, enhanced his understanding of the machinations of the service as limited as they were, and nurtured his understanding of soldiers.

Concurrent with his promotion to lieutenant colonel in May 1917, Hines was selected by Pershing for his staff and was soon en route to London to help establish the AEF headquarters. By now a veteran of 26 years, his only formal professional training since West Point was a three-month stint at the School of the Line at Fort Leavenworth in the winter of 1914. As the United States prepared to join the Allied war effort, Hines' career path exemplified the officer corps about to lead an ever-expanding army onto the modern battlefield. "We had line officers who could conduct elementary training, and who could command troops in small bodies; nothing more than this, as it turned out, was required of them."[10] The pace of the next 18 months had to be mind boggling to those frontier and guerrilla fighters as the total Army exploded from 203,964 soldiers and 9,693 officers in April 1917 to 3,687,831 soldiers and 203,786 officers by November 1918. This pace stood in stark contrast to the nearly two decades since San Juan Hill in 1898.

Major General Robert Bullard, who commanded Hines in several capacities during the war, wrote: "I have much difficulty in getting officers who know anything. All are untrained, and many of even our regular officers can never be worth anything in this war, unadaptable and immovable."[11] Bullard captured the essence of what the AEF needed: officers quickly able to adapt and willing to learn on the move. They needed to heed the advice of the battle-tested French and English as well as the instructors sent from the Army Service Schools at Fort Leavenworth. They needed to absorb those teachings and adjust to a battlefield unimaginable to them before they arrived in France.

Through the summer of 1917, Hines served as the assistant adjutant general for the AEF. He was promoted to colonel on 28 October and simultaneously assumed command of the 16th Infantry Regiment of the U.S. 1st Division attached to the French First Army. For Hines and the

16th Infantry, this was a period of training with limited exposure to combat. In solicited comments to Brigadier General Robert Alexander in a letter dated 10 March, he wrote how he prepared the regiment for what lay ahead. "I have found it imperative for a regimental commander to organize his work and distribute it to parts of his staff so that his time is free for supervision… I have the administrative work handled by my Lieutenant Colonel and my adjutant… with the adjutant, he runs the office leaving me rather free to get out with the troops."[12]

He continued by describing how officers were detailed to staff a training problem, such as laying wire or conducting patrols. One group handled the preparations for the training mission and liaison with the battalions and companies, and evaluated the execution of the training problem, while another group worked on the next assignment. By so organizing, Hines was able to optimize his resources and keep himself above the fray to monitor and lead.

Hines continued that he had a small team of officers detailed from the companies to serve as his operations staff. He was able to turn over the general orders from higher HQs to this group so that they could prepare the regiment's plans: "I would revise and change as necessary, but they would take care of the details that so often require so much time. I have just that much more time for getting around in my zone."[13]

Viewed from today's lens, when regimental tables of organization include operations staff, this approach is nothing novel. However, the regiment in that day was not organized in this way. Perhaps drawing on staffing structures being created on the fly and based on the British and French examples or from his many years serving as an adjutant, Hines established a logical and methodical process to train the 16th for combat. Hines commanded the 16th for less than six months, receiving his promotion to brigadier general on 2 May 1918, and command of the 1st Brigade, 1st Division on 5 May. Charles P. Summerall took over command of the 1st Division and Bullard moved up to command III Corps.

By mid-July 1917, the final German offensive had failed, leaving a salient extending south from the Aisne River–Vesle River line to the Marne River, anchored on Château-Thierry. Supreme Allied Commander General Ferdinand Foch determined to destroy the extended Marne salient as part of a broad Allied offensive across the length of the front. Two U.S. divisions, the 1st and the 2nd, were attached to the French XX Corps. The famous 1st Moroccan Division rounded out XX Corps. The corps order of battle, left to right, north to south, was the U.S. 1st Division, the 1st Moroccan, and the U.S. 2nd Division. Within the 1st Division, the 1st Brigade had the 18th and 16th Infantry Regiments (south to north) and the 2nd Brigade had the 28th and 26th Infantry Regiments (north to south).

On the morning of 18 July, Hines's 1st Brigade was deployed along a line that ran roughly from just north of Dommiers to Cutry. The plan called for a series of bounds east along phase lines[14] with the objective the Soissons–Château-Thierry highway. Much was required of XX Corps. For starters, the corps boundary to the north was dominated by German strength at Vauxbin. Moving west to east, the terrain along the corps' northern boundary was more difficult, especially around the Missy-aux-Bois and Ploisy ravines. Early rain made the going tough for the 2nd Brigade as the corps pushed east. Critically important for this operation was the need to maintain contact with the units on the flanks. For Hines, this required liaison with the 2nd Brigade to his left and the French on his right. Terrain, weather, local leadership, and German strength made coordination with the 2nd Brigade difficult throughout the operation.

As the action culminated on 21 July around Berzy-le-Sec, the liaison between the 16th and the 26th Infantry of the 1st Division broke down. Despite heavy artillery fire, Hines combed the battlefield to find the 16th's left flank and continued to traverse the field until he was able to re-establish contact with the 26th. All the while, the 18th was engaged with the Germans outside of Buzancy east of the Soissons–Château-Thierry highway. The 18th also had to secure and maintain contact with the French 87th Division, which only the night before had relieved the 1st Moroccan.

Several days later the 1st Division was relieved by the British 15th (Scottish) Infantry Division and was moved into reserve in the vicinity of Dammartin-en-Goële. During these two months in command of the 1st Brigade, Hines exhibited the energy and tenacity that Pershing demanded of his officers. The habits he had built into his training for the 16th

Infantry Regiment that allowed him to focus on the big picture carried forward to his tenure with the 1st Brigade. In these operations, Hines' ability to keep the units to his left and right connected was critical to the outcome of the battle. His focus on "getting out in his zone" allowed him a better feel for what was happening and to place himself where he was most needed.

For his efforts on 21 July, Hines received the Distinguished Service Cross. Summerall, his division commander, gave high praise to Hines for his command of the 1st Brigade during the Soissons operation: "He was distinguished by his masterful leadership, his unswerving loyalty, his indomitable courage, his wonderful endurance, and his skill as a technician."[15]

Less than two months remained in the war when Hines was promoted to major general and command of the 4th Division. He led this division in the mid-September Saint-Mihiel campaign before receiving command of III Corps for the final American operation in the Meuse–Argonne. Remarkably, for an officer whose first two and half decades of service were almost wholly characterized by regimental duty, Hines commanded more than 150,000 soldiers in III Corps when the guns fell silent on 11 November 1918.

Not long after assuming command of III Corps, Hines sacked Major General John E. McMahon, a West Point classmate of Pershing's, for his lack of tactical skill and his division's lack of discipline. This involved fighting in mid-October as the Meuse–Argonne campaign ground ahead. In contravention to directives from Pershing, McMahon "eventually pushed the entire 9th Brigade, irrespective of any means by which he could keep in touch with its elements or their ability to maneuver in the forest."[16] Later, McMahon pulled the 9th Brigade back from its hard-won ground around Bois de Rappes. Hines, like Pershing, had little tolerance for officers who did not meet his expectations. McMahon was relieved and was back in the United States by the end of October.

Following the cessation of hostilities, Hines remained in France until September 1919. Upon returning home, he commanded VIII Corps at Fort Sam Houston, Texas, until his appointment as Pershing's deputy chief of staff in 1922. Pershing wrote of Hines around this time, "An exceptionally fine officer in every respect... No. 1 on list of general officers known to me."[17] On 14 September 1924, President Coolidge appointed Hines U.S. Army chief of staff on Pershing's recommendation, ahead of officers senior to him.

Marked by an administration and a public not willing to invest in the military, Hines' tenure as chief, beyond the austerity of the era, had several highlights. Most notably and famously was the court-martial of Brigadier General Billy Mitchell. Close friends and onetime next-door neighbors, Hines and Mitchell could not have been more polar opposites in personality. Mitchell was flamboyant, rambunctious, outspoken, and egotistical; Hines was taciturn, efficient, steady, and more a steward than a visionary. In the end, Hines convened the court-martial board that, after a trial of seven weeks and a 30-minute deliberation, found Mitchell guilty of accusing senior leaders in the Army and Navy of incompetence and almost treasonable administration of the national defense. The verdict ended the pioneering aviator's career.

Despite inadequate funding, Hines did umpire two major maneuver exercises that tested the coordination of the Army and Navy. As deputy chief of staff, Hines oversaw a joint exercise in Panama in June 1924. This tested the ability of the Navy to utilize the canal and the strength of the Army's plan to defend it. Presciently, joint maneuvers were held in Hawaii in 1925 to test the validity of War Plan "Orange," the defense of Oahu in the event of a war with Japan. Unfortunately, the lessons learned were lost in the abyss of the Great Depression, leaving Oahu unprepared for the Japanese attack 16 years later. A point that did not go unnoticed and was eventually corrected was the rank disparity between the Army chief of staff (major general) and the chief of naval operations (admiral). During these combined exercises, Hines was outranked by chief of naval operations Admiral James Eberle, which made for an unlevel playing field.

There were, however, advancements during Hines' tenure that helped prepare the Army for the future. Officers continued to be schooled at the Army War College. Signal communications were significantly enhanced via cable linkage between Seattle and Seward, Alaska, creating the world's largest radio network.[18] Also, Major General James Harbord, close friend and World War I peer, was president of Radio Corporation of America (RCA) from 1922 to 1930. This relationship, foreshadowing the military-industrial complex of later years, enhanced the Army's radio communications. And it should be noted that Hines supported the idea of women serving in the American military.

Army strength by 1926 had fallen to 11,871 officers and 118,242 enlisted men with the administration looking for ways to reduce those numbers.[19] In contrast, Hines had commanded over 150,000 at the helm of III Corps in the Meuse–Argonne in the fall of 1918. When his tenure as chief of staff ended in November 1926, Hines accepted command of IX Corps in San Francisco. His successor was Charles P. Summerall, his former commander. Hines' duties at IX Corps included inspecting the National Guard units within his command. In May 1929, as part of an inspection tour of Montana, he revisited Fort Harrison, where 30 years earlier he had prepared to leave for war in Cuba.[20] He remained in San Francisco until 1930, when he replaced Douglas MacArthur as commander of the Philippines Department, before finally retiring on 31 May 1932.

Hines would spar with at least two of Pershing's lieutenants in later years. Of no major consequence, these episodes do speak to the egos of the men involved. In 1925, Major General Bullard, who commanded Hines when he moved to the 4th Division, penned his memoir of the war, *Personalities and Reminiscences of the War*. During the fight around Bois de Fay in early October 1918, Bullard wrote that Hines asked to have his division relieved. Bullard responded that they could not be relieved, that they could not give up ground. "Your division has done magnificent work and show wonderful courage," Bullard said to Hines. The 4th stayed put.

Hines took offense at the suggestion that he had requested to be relieved, and wrote Bullard asking for a public correction. He also corresponded with Colonel Christian Bach, his 4th Division chief of staff, in July 1927: "I think this reference does me an injustice as I know I had no idea of withdrawing troops from the Bois de Fay."[21] Hines asked Bach for his recollection of Bullard's visit to 4th Division headquarters on 5 October. Bach responded that Bullard had it wrong and that "the men had worked too hard to get the Bois de Fay for anyone to consider for a moment the possibility of giving it up."[22] Bach also thought that Bullard would correct his statement when confronted with their rebuttal. In a subsequent letter, Bach wrote, "I may say further that I don't believe that you ever considered the thought of voluntarily withdrawing from the Bois de Fay."[23] For the officer for whom integrity meant so much, setting the record straight was important for Hines.

Hines also clashed with Summerall after the latter succeeded him as Army chief of staff. Summerall attempted to force Hines to retire in 1930 to free up the command of the Philippines Department for his World War I protégé General Frank Parker. Hines refused to retire prematurely, and Parker had to wait until 1932 to assume command in the Philippines.

In retirement, Hines enjoyed his family, occasional golf, and horseback riding. He applied for active duty when World War II started, but was declined: he was well past 70. In a press release dated 7 February 1925, Secretary of War John Weeks said, "General Hines… is one of the finest commanders of combat troops ever developed in the history of our country."[24] Charles Bolte, often an aide to Hines, wrote of the general that he had "gained the reputation for sagacity, tact, and dependability which made him ever an outstanding leader."[25] He looked the part and had a presence that encouraged others to follow. Another aide, Charles Kilburn, saying good-bye to the "Old Man" as he left for the Philippines, felt "a deep sense of affection and respect for a great and good man."[26] Hines died in Washington D.C., on 13 October 1968. He was buried in Arlington National Cemetery.

CHAPTER 2

MAJOR GENERAL CHARLES P. SUMMERALL

Jerry D. Morelock

Charles Pelot Summerall's distinguished 43-year-long career notably featured World War I brigade, division, and corps command, culminating in his being U.S. Army chief of staff from 1926 to 1930 (the last Spanish–American War vet holding the Army's highest office). Tall and handsome, fit and ramrod straight, Summerall epitomized "command presence," possessing superb martial bearing and a forceful personality exuding competence and confidence. Fearless, he led from the front, fighting Filipino *insurrectos* (1899), China's Boxers (1900), and Germany's armies (1917–18). His well-earned reputation for being a tough, iron-willed, and, when necessary, ruthless leader is reflected in his mentor, Robert L. Bullard's, judgment: "[Summerall] did not have to have a hammer to drive a nail."[1]

Yet, Summerall suffered human frailties: "[His] strong will, fortitude, and conviction that his tactical decisions were flawless, revealed a troubling authoritarian streak."[2] The daring combat leader could not ignore criticism. Instead, Summerall internalized and resented it, seeking "consolation in his belief that he had always been right, and that those who had opposed him had always been wrong [driven] by less than honorable motives."[3] Summerall was "a man of strong convictions and decided opinions [using his 1950] memoir [written aged 83] to reiterate them, often to validate his actions, and to make clear who his friends and perceived enemies were and why."[4]

Like John J. Pershing – who rated Summerall World War I's "top commander" – he was old school, "a demanding taskmaster who drove his men hard." His uncompromising "sharp tongue [and] hard and rigid discipline" prompted "martinet" claims.[5] Nevertheless:

> What he required of his officers and men was obedience and conformity to his high standards of behavior and performance. Whether they liked him did not matter. What he really desired, and what he fully believed he had earned, was their respect for his leadership and their confidence in his expertise and ability.[6]

George C. Marshall likened him to Civil War genius Stonewall Jackson, deeming Summerall "one of the greatest living exponents of the principle that much more can be done than ever seems possible, if one has the will to do it."[7] Douglas MacArthur, a World War I comrade, considered him "a great fighting soldier."[8] Theodore Roosevelt, Jr., Summerall's combat-hardened regimental commander in his 1st Division (and World War II Medal of Honor recipient), claimed he "was the biggest troop leader we had in the American army."[9] Summerall's biographer, W. Gary Nichols, concluded he was "the premier battlefield commander of the AEF... [given his] hard-driving, relentless, and exhausting pursuit of the enemy."[10] Getting a corps command in October 1918, he was slated by Pershing for army command, but the war ended. Of all Pershing's lieutenants, "as a combat commander... Summerall rivaled any American general in terms of [AEF] service."[11]

Summerall was born on 4 March 1867 in rural Blounts Ferry, Florida, on the Georgia border, a region impoverished by the Civil War and Reconstruction. After attending Porter Military Academy in Charleston, South Carolina, his mother's home state, he entered West Point in 1888, two years after Pershing graduated. Summerall sought "the promise of a career, instead of hopelessness, [the] opportunity had opened up for me and I could not fail."[12] He graduated on 11 June 1892, 20th of 62 classmates; notably, his leadership stood out – he was Cadet First Captain, top in leadership, like fellow World War I generals Pershing (1886) and MacArthur (1903): "[T]his [First Captain appointment] was the proudest moment of my life... I believe that the experience laid the foundation for my future career."[13]

Summerall wanted Artillery or Cavalry branch commissioning, but settled for Infantry branch to ensure his assignment to San Francisco ("where I wanted to go").[14] Yet, in January 1893, Summerall used his friendship with the 5th Artillery Regiment commander, Colonel William M. Graham, to pull strings in the War Department and transfer to Artillery branch. In 1898, when Graham was promoted to major general and II Corps commander as the Spanish–American War began, he made Summerall his aide-de-camp: "I had the opportunity to attract attention to my work... [Graham] was an uncompromising disciplinarian [who] demanded the highest efficiency [and] was greatly feared by officers and soldiers, but he always treated me kindly... I owe General Graham much for his favor and esteem."[15]

During the short war, II Corps remained stateside, but in 1899 First Lieutenant Summerall (promoted in March) deployed to the Philippines, commanding an artillery battery platoon fighting nightly *insurrecto* attacks. There, Summerall made the most important contact of his entire career when his heroic combat exploits won him the lasting admiration and staunch support of the 39th Volunteer Infantry Regiment commander, Colonel Robert Lee Bullard: "In the Philippines I came in contact with... [Colonel] Bullard...We immediately had some fighting with the insurgents, and Colonel Bullard became very friendly. Before the campaign was ended, I was bound to him for life."[16] Next joining the 1900 China Relief Expedition subduing the Boxers, Summerall's artillery blasted open the Imperial City's gates on 15 August: "[S]ervice in the Philippines and China, [was] where I got my head out of the crowd. From then on, I had an individual reputation and standing in the army... and my work became widely known."[17]

Post-China, Summerall notably was West Point's senior artillery tactics instructor (1905–11), where one of his admiring cadets was George S. Patton, Jr. (Class of 1909). Summerall was promoted to captain (July 1901), major (March 1911), and lieutenant colonel (July 1916). He supervised National Guard artillery summer camps (1912–14), then was assistant chief of the Militia Bureau (1915–17) under bureau chief Major General William A. Mann.

When the U.S. declared war on Germany in April 1917, Summerall was selected by Secretary of War Newton D. Baker (prompted by Baker's ambitious protégé, Douglas MacArthur) to command the National Guard 42nd "Rainbow" Division's artillery brigade under his militia bureau boss, division commander Mann. Promoted to colonel (May), Summerall advanced to brigadier general on 5 September 1917, upon taking command of the 42nd's 67th Field Artillery Brigade forming at Camp Mills, Long Island. Previously, however, in June 1917 as a Baker Commission member studying AEF and Allied artillery types and employment, he nearly ruined his World War I chances. Summerall claims he ran afoul of Pershing's GHQ staff by vigorously recommending U.S. divisions receive more and larger caliber artillery (105mm and 155mm howitzers as opposed to the then-standard 75mm field guns):

> I was at once viciously attacked, personally and officially by officers of [Pershing's GHQ] staff [Fox Conner apparently led the criticism]… I replied with equal resentment. I told them that the infantry would pay in losses for lack of artillery… General Pershing then asked me to step out on the porch and said, "Summerall, I want you to get together with my staff." I replied: "General, no one wants your success more than I. Your staff was wrong, and I am going to Washington and fight for what I know is best for our artillery." He seemed to be furious and returned to the house without a word… I felt that I would not be allowed to return to France and that my part in the war was ended.[18]

Actually, although Summerall was proven right about the need for larger caliber artillery fire support, his claimed numbers of Allied guns per divisional front were wrong – Conner's numbers, as usual, were correct. Summerall's decades-later recollection of his alleged "Pershing confrontation" also is questionable, since Pershing subsequently praised Summerall's Baker Commission contributions: "[Summerall] very wisely concluded to work in conjunction with the Operations Section of my staff... to evolve and perfect a complete scheme of organization and armament for all combat units."[19] Casting further doubt on Summerall's "confrontation" allegation is the fact that Pershing subsequently promoted Summerall to ever-higher AEF command levels – hardly something Pershing would do had he actually been "furious" with the allegedly impertinent colonel.

Pershing's true personal relationship with Summerall is clouded by the latter's self-serving memoir – unlike Summerall's immediate post-World War I comments, unfailingly trumpeting all of Pershing's numerous accolades. Prior to the war, Pershing and Summerall barely knew each other personally. Summerall recalled their brief contacts consisted of "[their being] ushers at a wedding when [Pershing] was a first lieutenant and I was a second lieutenant, and he and his wife [calling] on us at Fort Myer when I was a captain."[20] Importantly, Pershing clearly relied on the advice of his trusted subordinate Bullard – who consistently championed Summerall – to guide his actions propelling the meteoric World War I rise of Bullard's protégé.

Upon arriving in France in December 1917, Summerall was one of the rising stars of the 42nd who immediately were transferred to more prestigious AEF positions. As 42nd Division Chief of Staff MacArthur recalled, "Of the thirty-three of the [division] staff all but two were ordered away [by GHQ]."[21] Certainly, Summerall benefited from Bullard's support, writing: "When [Bullard] was assigned to command First Division, he had me transferred from the Forty-second Division... to the First Field Artillery Brigade of the First Division. This gave me my start in the AEF. [Bullard's] confidence and loyalty to me never wavered."[22]

After the AEF's first major combat action, the May 1918 Battle of Cantigny, Pershing praised Summerall's magnificent handling of the artillery support that proved critically important to that victory. Notably,

Pershing singled out the artilleryman by name in his World War I memoir:

> It was a matter of pride to the whole AEF that the troops of this [1st U.S. Infantry] division, in their first battle, and in the unusually trying situation that followed, displayed the fortitude and courage of veterans, held their gains, and denied to the enemy the slightest advantage. It is interesting to record that of the officers of the 1st Division to participate in this battle... Summerall [later received] corps [command].[23]

Summerall earned his World War I rapid rise by his masterful command of the artillery support paving the way for American battlefield victories. Yet, other U.S. brigade commanders also achieved outstanding results. The key factor setting Summerall above his, arguably, equally qualified peers was the high esteem in which he continued to be held by Bullard. The latter had, in effect, progressed from being simply Summerall's friend and mentor to serving as the artilleryman's enthusiastic champion and booster. In July 1918, Summerall's obvious accomplishments, prominent position, and fortunate timing – but above all Bullard's recommendation – once again proved paramount to his success. Summerall rightfully acknowledged: "[W]hen he was promoted to the command of [III] corps, [Bullard,] no doubt, did what he could to have me promoted and assigned to the command of the First Division. I owe to him more than anyone else my advancement in the AEF."[24]

Pershing gave artilleryman Summerall command of 1st Division in July 1918, corps command three months later, and slated him for army command had the war continued. Regardless of how Summerall later chose to characterize their relationship, the AEF commander consistently supported the artilleryman for his stunning battlefield achievements – regardless of casualties incurred. Pershing, who seldom exaggerated his subordinates' accomplishments, later described Summerall in glowing terms:

> An exceptionally able man in all respects. Possesses soldierly qualities instinctively. Thorough in his knowledge of his profession. Most loyal

> and reliable. Very energetic and determined. Inspires the highest ideals of service in his subordinates, and makes them feel that nothing is impossible. Brilliant in handling a command, none better... The highest type of man and soldier worthy of every confidence and able to fill any position.[25]

Pershing's World War I memoir is a workmanlike – albeit dry – account of the AEF's operations; but it clearly reveals that he remained impressed by Summerall, whose achievements in command did not disappoint. Summerall excelled in 1st Division command, particularly during the September Battle of Saint-Mihiel. Pershing wrote:

> On the left of the army, the I Corps was very successful. The 1st Division [commanded by Summerall], in a fine display of power on October 4th, drove a deep wedge into the enemy's line which was of great value in affording space for the attack toward the Argonne which was to be launched later. The fighting here was characterized by the stubborn nature of the German resistance and the offensive spirit of [Summerall's] division.[26]

Colonel George Marshall, Pershing's gifted protégé, was equally impressed by Summerall's leadership and achievements:

> When a fresh attack jumped off on October 4, the veteran 1st Division, under command of Major General Charles P. Summerall, did particularly well in the Aire valley… Summerall… was the nearest approach to the [Civil War's Stonewall] Jackson type that I saw in the war. And he was a wonder to watch when the fighting was on… I never saw anything to beat him on a battlefield. I remember once he took around the British division commander who was going to relieve him. And when he got through walking around and talking like a cathedral, as he did, with shells breaking all over the place, this Britisher – who was accustomed to pretty hard fighting – came back and said he never wanted to make another inspection with General Summerall. [Summerall] was really unconscious of any feeling of fear.[27]

Summerall's continued success and aggressive leadership prompted Pershing to promote him to V Corps command on 12 October during the war-ending Meuse–Argonne offensive (26 September–11 November 1918). Visiting his forward corps, which continued forcefully to push the offensive forward, Pershing singled out V Corps commander Summerall, who was "very aggressive in severe fighting during some of the most bitter fighting of the war, forcing [his unit's] way through dense woods, over hills and across deep ravines, against German defense conducted with a skill only equaled by that of the French in front of Verdun in 1916." Pershing particularly was impressed by how Summerall's V Corps, steadily and against strong enemy resistance, advanced its lines, "capturing elements of the [German] Hindenburg Line."[28] Moreover, Summerall's "always lead from the front" reputation and ruthless commitment to success at any cost was confirmed by "Rainbow" Division's 84th Infantry Brigade commander, Brigadier General Douglas MacArthur, whose memoir recalled a dramatic frontline encounter with the V Corps commander:

> Major General Charles Pelot Summerall, the V Corps commander, entered the candle-lit C.P. [brigade command post]. He was tired and worn, and I made him drink a cup of steaming black coffee, strong enough to blister the throat. "Give me Châtillon, MacArthur," he suddenly said, his voice strained and harsh. "Give me Châtillon, or a list of five thousand casualties." His abruptness startled me. "All right, General," I assured him, "we'll take it, or my name will lead the list."... That is the way Côte de Châtillon fell.[29]

Not just his military comrades recognized Summerall's superb, grimly determined leadership. War correspondent Thomas Johnson effusively praised Summerall, even echoing Marshall's comparison of Summerall to Civil War Icon Stonewall Jackson: "To command the V Corps... came the epitome of a military leader, daring and careful, ruthless and inspiring... whose officers and men worshipped him, Maj. Gen. Charles P. Summerall... spiritually a Civil War corps commander, mentally a scientific modern soldier, a twentieth-century Stonewall Jackson."[30]

Pershing remained impressed by Summerall's rapid progress as the war's final offensive played out, noting "[by] dint of the superior determination of our troops, the enemy's lines were broken at a vital point by [Summerall's] V Corps."[31] Then, on 1 November 1918, "the V Corps, in the center [of AEF's advance] drove a wedge into the German defenses, swept through the zone of their artillery, and by night… the enemy's lines had been decisively crushed."[32]

Yet, on 5 November, the relentless advance of Summerall's V Corps toward the famed fortress city of Sedan embroiled the unit and its commander in a bitter controversy that threatened to shatter his otherwise sterling reputation – while its lingering aftermath brought out the less-flattering aspects of Summerall's character. Pershing wanted his AEF to have the honor of capturing historic Sedan; but the order Marshall wrote launching the operation included an unfortunately worded final sentence, added by First Army Chief of Staff, Brigadier General Hugh Drum: "Boundaries will not be considered binding" (see Introduction, pp. 51–53). Marshall explained what predictably transpired: "General Summerall, not one to hold back when invited to dash forward," seized upon what he saw as his chance to get V Corps into Sedan before any AEF or French unit. Summerall "took his orders in person" to 1st Division commander Brigadier General Frank Parker, who then ignored unit boundaries and entered I Corps' zone into the path of other U.S. divisions' advances, and thereby created chaos that risked friendly-fire casualties. Justifiably, the I Corps commander, Major General Joseph T. Dickman, took offense, "exploding with rage… fed by the suspicion that the dashing V Corps commander [Summerall] was trying to grab some additional glory at his expense."[33]

Eventually, the First Army commander, Major General Hunter Liggett, intervened. As his temper flamed, Liggett sent an order to his corps commanders to get their divisions back in their own zones at once. He then ordered an investigation of the whole affair. With the end of the war, the inquiry was dropped… but tempers never cooled. "The fight between Summerall and Dickman," Marshall commented long afterward, "was very intense and it went back to all sorts of jealousies… [I]t kept on in a senseless way for almost the rest of their service. It started from jealousy: They were jealous of General Summerall's great reputation which he had made in the hard fighting. The whole thing to my mind was out of place... [and] I didn't have much patience with it. But I wasn't the one [i.e. Summerall] receiving the animosity."[34]

Pershing briefly summarized the incident in his memoir: "V Corps' misconception of the exact intent of the [Sedan advance] order" caused "considerable confusion [and a] race for the honor of capturing Sedan." However, he concluded dismissively, the "splendid record of" the units involved "and the approach of the end of hostilities suggested leniency" in assigning any blame, thus ending further official investigation and any possible reprimands.[35] Although Pershing "officially" closed the book on the Sedan incident, he didn't forget about it. Sitting next to Summerall at a December 1918 post-Armistice luncheon, Pershing asked, "Summerall, tell me about that advance of the First Division at Sedan." According to Summerall, at the end of his detailed explanation of orders, troops involved, battlefield terrain, and his units' routes of advance – which he sketched out on their tablecloth – Pershing "showed every evidence of being entirely satisfied." Yet, typically, Summerall assumed his "GHQ enemies" were again at work: "I knew then that he had been told lies about confusion in the First Corps," adding, "afterward I marveled that he could receive so many false reports."[36]

After Sedan – ultimately captured by French troops – during the period 7–11 November 1918, Summerall continued pushing V Corps forward against retreating Germans, despite mounting casualties and rampant rumors of an armistice. "Of course, I knew nothing of an [impending] armistice and was obeying the most urgent orders from the high command," he later wrote.[37] Indeed, Pershing – urged on by Allied Supreme Commander, Marshal Ferdinand Foch's 5 November message, "Let no one cease hostilities of any sort" – was pushing all AEF commanders to press the enemy aggressively.[38] Summerall, therefore, claims the Armistice came as a surprise: "At 8:30 a.m., November 11, I received an order to cease the advance at 11:00 a.m. as an Armistice had been declared. I was greatly amazed and regarded it [at the time] as only a delay gained by the Germans."[39]

Post-Armistice, after a year of commanding occupation troops, escorting Congressional committees, and accompanying the official U.S.

officer delegation that witnessed the 28 June 1919 signing of the Treaty of Versailles, Summerall returned from France in September 1919. Deservedly, he had won numerous valor and service awards, notably the Distinguished Service Cross; the Distinguished Service Medal; and four Silver Stars.[40]

Although Pershing generously bestowed high praise upon Summerall, the latter's memoir pettily denigrated Pershing and, especially, his GHQ staff for perceived personal slights. Summerall particularly resented Pershing's failure to fully exonerate his "aggressive" thrust to Sedan, and he feuded with Dickman (died 1927) about it the rest of his life:

> [Summerall's] conviction of his own infallibility was to earn him many enemies in the future as it had in the past. As he reflected in his old age on the high commands that he had held, he rejected any criticism of his actions. To his dying day, he believed that those who disagreed with him such as [Maj. Gen] Liggett, [Maj. Gen. Dickman and Col. Conrad S.] Babcock, and those who later served in the War Department, were doing so out of personal animosity.[41]

Postwar, Summerall's commands notably included the Hawaiian Department (1921–24), enmeshing him in a scandal that eventually became more notorious than the Sedan incident. In November 1923, airpower advocate Colonel Billy Mitchell visited. Summerall, assuming Mitchell's visit was "entirely unofficial,"[42] extended his former comrade every courtesy – providing Mitchell an army aircraft (DH-4 bomber), which the airman crashed on Kauai. Mitchell, however, repaid Summerall's hospitality with a blistering report claiming that Hawaii's air defense was totally inadequate. Summerall characteristically exploded, denouncing Mitchell's report as "untrue, unfair and ignorant," calling Mitchell a "showman… irresponsible, eccentric and vain." Predictably, Summerall personalized the criticism: "Now it's all over. We're enemies Mitchell and I."[43] Mitchell subsequently was court-martialed for publicly calling the War and Navy secretaries' administration of the national defense "almost treasonable" after airship USS *Shenandoah* crashed on 3 September 1925. Although Mitchell's defense counsels justifiably blocked Summerall's

Map 1: Major German Rail Lines on the Western Front: 1918

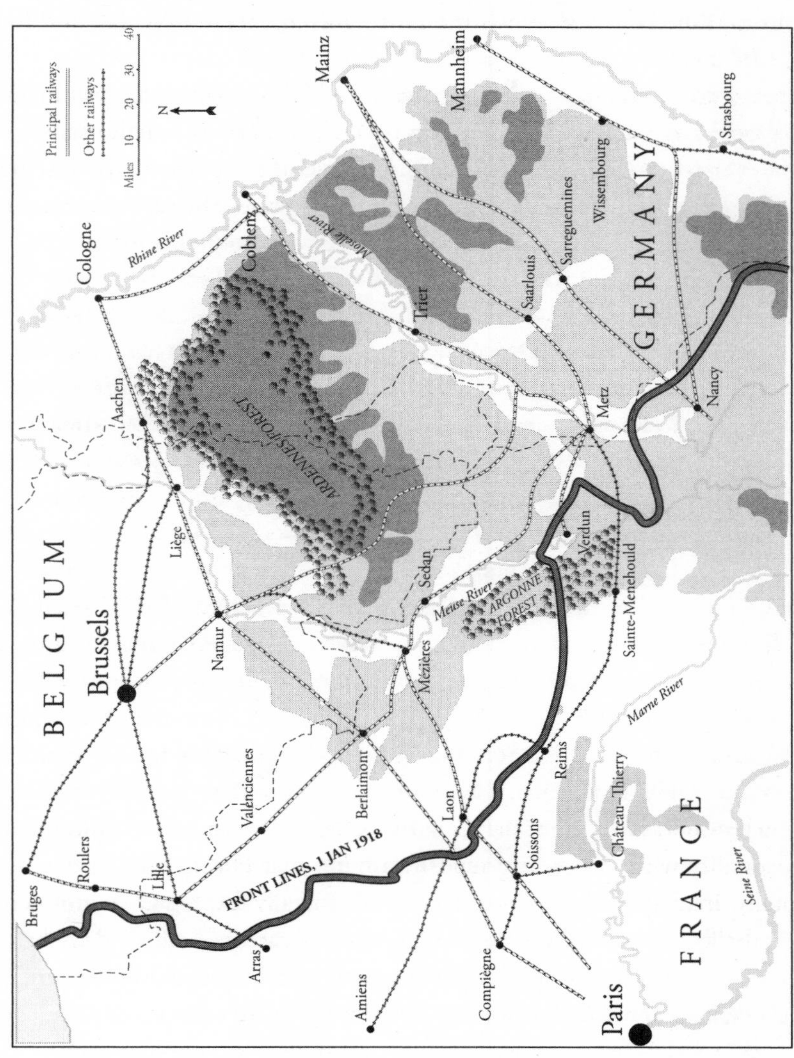

eagerly sought appointment as court-martial president, the enraged general testified damningly for the prosecution. After Mitchell's 17 December 1925 conviction, Summerall judged Mitchell "[that] damned kind of soldier who's wonderful in war and terrible in peace."[44]

On 21 November 1926, Summerall became Army chief of staff (promoted temporary four-star general in 1929, permanently in 1931). Hobbled by minuscule budgets, he nevertheless championed a modernized, mobilized, mechanized force of combined arms (tank, artillery, engineer, and quartermaster units) – visionary insight created in World War II. He also successfully resurrected his 1917 Baker Commission recommendation, upgrading field artillery to the excellent 105mm howitzer, the World War II American artillery's "workhorse" cannon. Yet, Ordnance Department procrastination delayed his effort to "expedite the manufacture of a semiautomatic infantry rifle" until 1936 when John Garand's famed M-1 rifle finally was adopted.[45] Summerall achieved considerable success despite a penny-pinching Congress and an isolationist, apathetic American public.

But Summerall's chief of staff tenure was marred by his long-festering World War I grudges. To then-Major Dwight Eisenhower Summerall was "dour" and "contentious," indulging in "petty bickering" creating a "poisonous atmosphere… rife with internecine squabbles and rivalries."[46] In his self-serving 1950 memoir, Summerall self-righteously complained:

> I realized [many General Staff senior officers] held the prejudice of [World War I] GHQ against me as being only a "combat officer," and I did not expect full loyalty from them... [O]ne chief of branch served notice on me, naming others who would help him, intending to fight me and discredit me in every way possible… Although I had… regarded them as my friends, with one exception all became my enemies… [But] I was far more satisfied to have done my duty and made enemies than I would have been if I had failed in my duty and retained their friendship.[47]

Despite Summerall's inexcusable pettiness, his former West Point cadet protégé Patton called him "a close friend [and] trusted mentor."[48] Indeed, Patton singled out Summerall as one of the interwar Army's visionary senior leaders, along with Pershing, MacArthur, Fox Conner, Marshall, and Eisenhower, who "kept afloat" the Army "despite appalling living conditions, reductions in rank to prewar levels, miserable pay, and no incentives whatsoever to remain soldiers."[49]

On 20 November 1930, Summerall passed the chief of staff torch to his younger successor and World War I subordinate, General Douglas MacArthur (Eisenhower, who had only observed Summerall's "petty, bickering" nature, cheered this exchange as "a breath of fresh air").[50] At age 64, Summerall mandatorily retired in March 1931. He became President of The Citadel, the Military College of South Carolina, his mother's beloved state, serving until 1953. Seventy-four when America entered World War II, Summerall was beyond active duty recall age; but from The Citadel he sent 10,000 cadets into military service (1941–45). The Citadel's Summerall Field (main drill field), Summerall Chapel, and elite cadet drill team, Summerall Guards, are named in his honor. At Fort Sill, Oklahoma, the Field Artillery Center's Summerall Hall appropriately bears the name of this famed artilleryman.

On 14 May 1955, Charles P. Summerall died aged 88 in Washington, D.C.

CHAPTER 3

BRIGADIER GENERAL DOUGLAS MACARTHUR

Jerry D. Morelock

General of the Army Douglas MacArthur is always a lightning rod for historians – admired and lionized by some, mocked and criticized by others. His half-century-long career in uniform (1899–1951) has provoked wildly contradictory assessments of his complex character: eloquently inspiring vs. irritatingly bombastic; distinctively individualistic vs. ostentatiously showy; graciously charming vs. maddeningly arrogant. In combat, MacArthur was often a sincere "soldiers' general," arousing his troops' unswerving devotion and incredible sacrifices; yet, many peers and superiors judged his relentless pursuit of victory as merely posturing by a self-aggrandizing careerist manipulating his subordinates for personal gain.

Possessing a verbal style mimicking his 19th-century predecessors, MacArthur's overly loquacious manner of expression proved double-edged: he delivered memorable, compelling, and dramatically enthralling speeches; but he also could sound imperious, egotistical, and overly theatrical. In a nation that prefers humble, modest, and self-effacing heroes, MacArthur sounded pompous, vain, and aloof. Few historians are neutral regarding MacArthur – they either love him or loathe him.

Born on 26 January 1880 in Little Rock, Arkansas, Douglas MacArthur was raised a "military brat" on Southwestern Frontier Army posts as the Indian Wars smoldered (until Geronimo's 1886 surrender). His father, Arthur, was a military prodigy. As an 18-year-old lieutenant in the Civil War's 24th Wisconsin Volunteer Infantry Regiment, teenaged Arthur propelled a crucial 25 November 1863 Union victory at Chattanooga, when he "seized the colors of his regiment at a critical moment and planted them on the captured works on the crest of Missionary Ridge."[1]

Later, General Arthur MacArthur fought Filipino guerrillas and was on the fast track to Army commanding general – until running afoul in 1901 of the Philippines governor-general, future President William Howard Taft. Nevertheless, war-hero Arthur retired a lieutenant general in 1909. He died in 1912 aged 67 of heart failure during a reunion of the Grand Army of the Republic, the national veterans' organization of Civil War Union soldiers.

Douglas's mother, Mary Pinkney "Pinky" Hardy, was an ambitious woman from an old Virginia family with aristocratic pretensions. Pinky not only bequeathed her ambitious nature to Douglas, she used family connections to promote his career until her December 1935 death (after Douglas had reached chief of staff, the Army's highest-ranking position). Bizarrely, Pinky lived in the West Point Hotel, located then on The Plain at the academy, purportedly monitoring Douglas's first two years' progress. Apparently, it worked. On 11 June 1903, Douglas graduated number one in his class – tops in academics and, as Cadet First Captain, leadership. Not even Robert E. Lee achieved this rare double distinction.

Great expectations accompanied Engineer-branched Second Lieutenant Douglas MacArthur into the Army – from his war-hero father, his supremely ambitious mother, and, most of all, from himself. His following half-century military service featured his rise to the Army's pinnacle through personal bravery, brilliant generalship, and remarkable grasp of complex strategy. Yet, MacArthur exhibited a few less flattering aspects of his unfathomable character: a prickly sense of honor unable to bear any criticism; single-minded pursuit of awards and public acclaim; and an unwillingness to share the limelight with subordinates.

Notably, MacArthur's pre-World War I service included his daring, highly dangerous one-man reconnaissance behind enemy lines during the April–November 1914 U.S. occupation of Veracruz, Mexico. This "preview" of his later World War I battle heroics resulted in the 34-year-old captain's (promoted 1911) first of three Medal of Honor nominations. Although Major General Leonard Wood and Brigadier General Frederick Funston (both Medal of Honor recipients) recommended MacArthur for the medal, War Department bureaucrats disapproved: "[It] might encourage any other staff officer, under similar conditions, to ignore the local commander, possibly interfering with reference to the enemy."[2]

Although an "incensed"[3] MacArthur scribbled futile, indignant protest letters, including to Chief of Staff Major General Hugh L. Scott, his unworthy fit of pique merely branded MacArthur "a supercilious special pleader."[4]

By spring 1917, Major Douglas MacArthur (promoted 1915) was on the War Department staff in its Bureau of Information – essentially the Army's official "press officer," showcasing his talents as a superbly articulate service spokesman. It also provided him access to manipulate high-level contacts, achieving influence beyond his junior rank. Importantly, MacArthur forged a personal relationship with Secretary of War Newton D. Baker, rapidly advancing his career. When Congress declared war on Germany on 6 April 1917, MacArthur quickly capitalized on this golden opportunity.

Two months before the war declaration, MacArthur claimed, he recommended then-Major General John J. Pershing to President Wilson and Secretary Baker as American Expeditionary Forces (AEF) commander. Although on 19 February, Major MacArthur, indeed, informed Baker (hosting a presidential dinner) that the designated AEF commander, Funston, had died suddenly and, when asked, told Wilson and Baker, "the choice [to lead the AEF] would unquestionably be General

Pershing."[5] MacArthur merely confirmed the obvious: Pershing was everyone's choice.

In America's last "great war" – the Civil War – Arthur MacArthur had achieved stardom. Douglas, undoubtedly, realized that the Great War was his chance to win his own "star." Characteristically, Douglas ensured his chance to capitalize on battlefield success by creating the means to accomplish it – 42nd "Rainbow" Division, comprising National Guard units from 26 states and the District of Columbia (MacArthur eloquently noted, it would "stretch over the whole country like a rainbow").[6]

MacArthur and "Rainbow" Division are so closely linked that many mistakenly assume he was the division's wartime commander. Actually, MacArthur was 42nd's chief of staff (August 1917–July 1918), then from July 1918 commanded the division's 84th Infantry Brigade, and only briefly (for 12 days) held temporary division command at war's end. Yet, "MacArthur" and "Rainbow Division" remain inextricably linked in popular memory – exactly his intention.

In contrast to MacArthur's specious insinuation that he ensured that Pershing received AEF command, he genuinely was indispensable in creating, training, and deploying the 42nd. After MacArthur appended his strongly worded non-concurrence to the General Staff study recommending the AEF be "500,000 strong" and "all regulars"[7] (i.e. no National Guard units were needed nor wanted), Baker summoned him to explain. The eloquent major not only convinced Baker to champion activating National Guard divisions to fight in France, but he persuaded Wilson to concur.

MacArthur also lobbied Baker to appoint Brigadier General William A. Mann, the nearly 63-year-old Militia Bureau Chief, as Rainbow Division commander; Baker approved (fully aware that 64 was mandatory retirement age). Baker (and, naturally, MacArthur) realized that Mann must "have the best colonel of the General Staff as his divisional chief of staff"[8] (i.e. the brains, energy, and competence backing-up the elderly commander). Baker, predictably, appointed MacArthur Mann's chief of staff and full colonel (promoted August 1917, skipping lieutenant colonel).

From its formation at Camp Mills, Long Island in August 1917, MacArthur was the division's key sparkplug, prime motivator, and individual most responsible for its creation. Competent, efficient, innovative, highly intelligent, and tirelessly energetic, as division chief of staff MacArthur appeared everywhere, at all hours – badgering, cajoling, inspiring, intervening, and attending to every detail, large and small. The indispensable colonel shipped out, along with 42nd's first echelons, across the Atlantic from Hoboken, New Jersey, on 18 October 1917, heading for Saint-Nazaire aboard USS *Covington*.[9]

The 42nd "Rainbow" Division, like all World War I U.S. divisions, was a robust "square division": two infantry brigades (83rd and 84th), each comprising two infantry regiments (165th and 166th, 167th and 168th respectively); a large field artillery brigade (67th Field Artillery Brigade containing one 155mm and two 75mm field artillery regiments – 149th, 150th, and 151st); and support units (engineers, signalers, transport, supply, medical, etc.) – totaling 27,000 soldiers. This was over *twice* the size of British, French, and German divisions.[10]

Once transport to France completed on 1 November, 42nd's major components entrained to training/assembly areas: division headquarters to Vaucouleurs, Lorraine; infantry regiments to Toul; and 67th Field Artillery Brigade to Coëtquidon, Brittany, to receive its artillery pieces and further training. Although MacArthur had judiciously prepared his division for six months' combat, he hadn't anticipated Pershing's AEF General Headquarters (GHQ) in Chaumont expropriating much of it:

> Except for artillery pieces, we had been completely equipped at Camp Mills – new machine guns, new uniforms, a full set of blankets, tin hats, gas masks, rolling kitchens, food and ammunition and I had brought with us sufficient clothing and supplies to last for six months. But a large part of these maintenance items which I had so carefully garnered, including 50,000 pairs of heavy marching shoes, were promptly taken over by G.H.Q. to supply deficiencies in other divisions. We suffered greatly later on from a lack of replacement equipment and supplies.[11]

Worse, shortly after MacArthur arrived in France a disaster – followed by a barely avoided catastrophe – occurred, nearly shattering his careful preparations. Pershing's GHQ also gutted 42nd's senior leadership by peremptorily requisitioning, for AEF headquarters and to create a corps headquarters for previously deployed divisions, all but *two* of the division's 33 senior staff officers. MacArthur described these officers as "carefully selected [from] the flower of the regular service"[12] – given his direct line to Baker, this rings true. Yet, he put on a brave face while, typically, emphasizing his own prescience: "I had, however, from the beginning provided understudies for all important positions and these younger officers met the emergency flawlessly."[13] Nevertheless, understudies are not lead actors – these younger officers' skill development required hard-earned battle experience.

MacArthur, however, "was not prepared," he admitted, "for the heaviest blow,"[14] Pershing's order to dismember the 42nd. Although narrowly avoided, MacArthur's reaction to the near-catastrophe destroyed his personal relationship with Pershing forever. Heavily pressured by the British and French to get U.S. troops into immediate combat, and proving incapable of devising a less draconian means to fill-out frontline divisions, GHQ:

> [D]ecided their most experienced divisions of Regular Army troops – the First, Second [with one USMC brigade] and [National Guard] Twenty-sixth – would go up into the line as soon as possible. The rest already in France, including the National Guardsmen of the Forty-second, would be used as replacements for those divisions, and would be fed in, battalion by battalion.[15]

Pershing was inflicting on his *own* U.S. divisions the same fate he successfully fought his Allied counterparts tooth and nail to prevent befalling the AEF as a whole – i.e. dismantled and parceled out as frontline fillers. MacArthur's beloved *personal* creation, the "Rainbow" Division, "was to be broken up as replacements,"[16] fed piecemeal into frontline divisions.

MacArthur was "appalled and furious," and not about to let "*his* division"[17] be callously destroyed – he pulled every possible string. MacArthur appealed to "Pershing's chief of staff, my old Manila friend,

Brigadier General James G. Harbord."[18] That personal appeal might have worked; but, just in case, MacArthur played *all* his political cards, including his ace-in-the-hole – he directly cabled his powerful mentor, Secretary Baker (and "virtually anyone else [with] a Washington, D.C., address"[19]). Pershing, naturally, was incensed by a colonel's string pulling. MacArthur admitted, "my action was probably not in strict accord with normal procedure" (indeed, it was outrageously insubordinate), adding, "it created resentment against me among certain members of Pershing's staff"[20] (notably omitting that Pershing himself most resented it!).

Despite MacArthur's dragging Baker into an obviously internal AEF issue, the always-astute Harbord saved "Rainbow" Division from dismemberment. Harbord bluntly explained the political facts of life to an enraged Pershing, perceptively noting that the 42nd was an extremely well-trained unit that would excel in combat, and dismantling "the first division to arrive [in France] complete"[21] would be an egregious military and political mistake. Tellingly, Harbord reminded Pershing, the "Rainbow" Division "has figured more in the press and has more friends to resent the matter."[22] Pershing reluctantly swallowed his pride, following Harbord's wise counsel; but he never forgot – nor forgave. In fact, Pershing later found several opportunities to exact revenge against his string-pulling upstart.

Arguably, this incident and its unorthodox resolution was the pivotal moment of MacArthur's career, profoundly propelling his eventual rise to the top. Without the "Rainbow" Division as his stage to demonstrate his battlefield heroics that set him above his contemporaries, MacArthur likely would have ended World War I as just one of many anonymous colonels: no general's star; no important post-World War I assignments; no rise to Army chief of staff; no World War II Supreme Command; no stewardship of post-World War II Japan; no rescuing of South Korea in September 1950. MacArthur's future legacy hinged upon preventing his division's 1917 dismemberment.

MacArthur's bold defiance of Pershing also taught him a lifelong leadership lesson: he would treat orders from superiors merely as "suggestions" if they didn't support his judgment of the situation.

MacArthur concluded, "'Sometimes it is the order one disobeys that makes one famous" – words he would make into a career.[23]

On 19 December 1917, MacArthur got a new boss – Mann, failing his physical exam, was replaced by Major General Charles Thomas Menoher. MacArthur wrote of Menoher:

> A regular colonel in the field artillery, who had been a [USMA 1886] classmate of General Pershing's at West Point. He was an able officer, an efficient administrator, of genial disposition and unimpeachable character. He preferred to supervise operations from his command headquarters, where he could keep in constant touch with the corps and army, relying on me to handle the battle line... We became great friends ...[24]

Clearly MacArthur "damned" Menoher "with faint praise," noting that Menoher was "an able administrator" with a "genial disposition," preferring "command headquarters" to frontline trenches where MacArthur "handle[d] the battle line." Translation: "I, not Menoher, personally commanded 'Rainbow' Division from the front." Although Menoher led 42nd Division during nearly all its World War I combat (until 7 November 1918), the heart and soul of the unit, MacArthur obviously implied, was himself.

Truthfully, *none* of "Pershing's lieutenants" endured more sustained combat or exposed themselves to more German fire and poison gas than MacArthur. *None* risked death or wounds on more occasions than twice-wounded MacArthur. *None* won more valor medals than MacArthur. *None* deserved the Medal of Honor more than MacArthur. Perhaps MacArthur actually believed he was invincible, allegedly declaring in typically melodramatic prose: "All of Germany cannot fabricate the shell that will kill me!"[25] But, whether believing that outrageous hyperbole or not, from his first trench raid (a minor French night action he insisted on accompanying on 26 February 1918) until the war's final shots, MacArthur *always* led from the front, recklessly exposing himself to shot and shell and deadly gas. He wanted "everyone in the Forty-second [to] know that their chief of staff was with them not just in spirit but in the flesh – even when the shells were falling and the machine-gun bullets were flying."[26] MacArthur's risk-taking prompted Menoher to write Pershing:

> MacArthur is the bloodiest fighting man in this army. I'm afraid we're going to lose him sometime, for there's no risk of battle that any soldier is called upon to take that he is not liable to look up and see MacArthur at his side. At every advance MacArthur, with just his [cloth service] cap and his riding crop, will go forward with the first line. He is the greatest possible inspiration to the men of this division who are devoted to him.[27]

Menoher also wrote Pershing about MacArthur's unsurpassed ability to evoke from soldiers what Abraham Lincoln called "the last full measure of devotion." He described how MacArthur personally movingly inspired a battalion commander in his brigade to successfully assault a formidable German position:

> MacArthur had just been placed in command of his [84th Infantry] brigade [July 1918]. He went forward to the battalion that was to lead the way. He said to the Major in command, "Now, when that barrage lifts, I want you to go forward with your men and lead the way. Don't stand back. They will follow you. You can't take it by standing back and telling them to go ahead, but you show the way and you can take it – right up to the top. You do this and I will see that you get the Distinguished Service Cross." Then MacArthur stepped back and looked at him and said, "I see you are going to do it. You've got it now," and took off his own Distinguished Service Cross decoration and pinned it on him as the barrage lifted. It is one of the greatest cases of intelligence, psychological leadership and direction I have ever encountered.[28]

Later historians who delight in denigrating MacArthur's personal leadership abilities as simply pompous grandstanding fail to understand what actually motivates soldiers to place unit, mission, and comrades above self-preservation – but MacArthur clearly understood.

The most visible physical manifestation of MacArthur's distinctive World War I personality was his premeditatedly crafted, studiously eccentric combat dress. He obviously intended his outlandish appearance to set him apart from other senior officers, his carefully chosen combat uniform consisting of: a leather-billed "crushed" service soft cap (its crown-stiffener removed for a distinctive look – precursor of his famed World War II, tarnished-gold-braided "crushed" cap); a bulky West Point athletic sweater with an Army letterman's "A" (his academy baseball team letter) sewn on it; an outlandish, 4-foot-long woolen neck scarf (knitted by Pinky); ostentatiously carrying neither gas mask nor weapon – only a riding crop; wearing spit-polished, ankle-high boots with knee-high leather gaiters. A sight to behold, to MacArthur's soldiers he looked like a fancified "dude," awarding him the well-deserved nickname "The Fighting Dude." This nickname "expressed a certain amusement but also a growing respect, as it became clear that MacArthur's outlandish costume was backed by the real goods."[29]

Not everyone appreciated MacArthur's outlandish outfit and recklessly brave actions: in mid-1918 he was subjected to an AEF investigation of his unorthodox, non-regulation dress and conduct. Although exonerated – all "Rainbow" Division witnesses, including Menoher, praised his conduct and combat leadership – MacArthur's own explanation seems self-servingly unconvincing:

> [T]hat I failed to follow certain regulations prescribed for our troops, that I wore no helmet, that I carried no gas mask, that I went unarmed, that I always had a riding crop in my hand, that I declined to command from the rear, were reported to G.H.Q. All of this was entirely specious, as senior officers were permitted to use their own judgment about such matters of personal detail. I wore no iron helmet because it hurt my head. I carried no gas mask because it hampered my movements. I went unarmed because it was not my purpose to engage in personal combat, but to direct others. I used a riding crop out of long habit on the plains. I fought from the front as I could not effectively manipulate my troops from the rear.[30]

On 21 June 1918, Pershing found an opportunity to extract some measure of revenge against this impertinent upstart. Appearing unannounced at the 42nd's loading ramp at Charmes for a surprise inspection, Pershing publicly confronted MacArthur, viciously "ream[ing] out the Fighting Dude inch by inch":[31]

> "This division is a disgrace" [Pershing] barked. "The men are poorly disciplined and they are not properly trained. The whole outfit is just about the worst I've seen."… "I'm going to hold you personally responsible for getting discipline and order in this division… I won't stand for this. It's a disgrace!" Reddening with shame and rage, MacArthur barked back, "Yes sir!" and flung out his hand in salute. Pershing turned and stomped away.[32]

Tellingly, the AEF commander held *MacArthur* – not *Menoher* – "personally responsible," revealing Pershing's ostensibly spontaneous outburst as a deliberately calculated attack on the 42nd's chief of staff, the unit's supposed "disgrace[ful]" condition merely a convenient occasion for the intentionally public dressing down. Moreover, since Pershing consciously ignored the hallowed military leadership maxim "Praise in public; punish in private," MacArthur clearly understood his public humiliation was intentional… and extremely personal. Like a West Point plebe being "hazed" by an upperclassman, MacArthur could only helplessly stand at rigid attention, enduring Pershing's verbal abuse. This wasn't the last time Pershing would wreak revenge on his string-pulling subordinate.

In July 1918, five months after the 42nd's February combat entry, Pershing forwarded his list of colonels recommended for brigadier general. Pershing deliberately left off MacArthur's name. However, his effort to deny MacArthur a well-deserved "star" hadn't considered Pinky and, above all, the power since 20 May 1918 of the Army's new chief of staff – Pershing's bitter rival, General Peyton C. March (Arthur MacArthur's 1899 Philippines' aide). Although Pinky wrote pleading letters to Baker, Wilson – and, incredibly, Pershing! – March himself "attached MacArthur's name to the list [of 43 new brigadier generals]… after crossing out five names Pershing had put forward. Pershing… acquiesced, but… seeth[ed] over March's interference."[33] With a 26 June 1918 date of rank, at age 38 "MacArthur was… the youngest general in the AEF, remaining so until

October, when two thirty-five-year-old [artillerymen], Lesley McNair and Pelham Glassford, became brigadiers."[34] Despite back-channel manipulations to secure his first general's star, any assessment of MacArthur's war record verifies he had earned the promotion. His heroics garnered him a chest-full of medals: two Distinguished Service Crosses; the Distinguished Service Medal; the French Croix de Guerre; seven Silver Stars; and two Purple Hearts.[35]

Although MacArthur's name topped the list of nine "Rainbow" soldiers recommended by Menoher for Medals of Honor, it was disapproved... by Pershing (possibly more MacArthur revenge; yet, Pershing in principle opposed *any* general receiving that medal – in fact, none did).[36] "It was Pershing, and Pershing alone, who finally blocked the award [despite] a board of officers from the Forty-second Division unanimously [putting] MacArthur at the head of the list of their men who deserved [it]."[37] Nevertheless, Pershing recommended MacArthur for major general (a short-lived two-star "promotion" aborted when "the day after the [11 November 1918] Armistice, March canceled all promotions"[38]), and appointed MacArthur "Rainbow" Division's temporary commander (10–22 November 1918).

MacArthur's beloved Rainbow Division served in France from 1 November 1917 through May 1919, spending 176 days in combat sectors and posting advances totaling 34 miles. Capturing 1,317 German prisoners of war, it lost only 112 captured. The division fought in four major 1918 campaigns/battles: Champagne–Marne (15–18 July); Aisne–Marne (16 July–6 August); Saint-Mihiel (12–15 September); and the Meuse–Argonne offensive (16 September–11 November). Thanks overwhelmingly to MacArthur's inspiring frontline leadership, the division finished second only to 2nd Infantry Division (half Army, half Marines) in combat effectiveness. The 27,000-man division received 17,253 replacements during the war after suffering nearly 15,000 casualties: 2,810 battle deaths/died of wounds and 11,873 wounded.[39] Importantly:

> MacArthur had risked being among them many times, but somehow emerged unscathed. Soldiers had a nickname to describe him: "Bullet Proof." As MacArthur made clear to others, he believed it was a sign of his destiny, even God's guidance. It had carried him through safely and made

> him [temporarily] a major general at thirty-eight. But would that destiny now carry him forward in peace as it did during war?[40]

MacArthur returned in May 1919 aboard USS *Leviathan* (the German liner *Vaterland*, seized 1917) after commanding 84th Brigade's Army of Occupation tour near Coblenz, Rhineland-Palatinate. A war hero with a nationwide reputation, MacArthur emerged the brightest-shining of Pershing's lieutenants' rising stars. Secretary Baker acclaimed MacArthur, "the greatest American field commander produced by the war," having earlier called him "[AEF's] greatest fighting front-line officer."[41]

Yet, Pershing had a long memory and was not inclined to forgive. In a 1922 fitness report as Army chief of staff (1921–24), Pershing ranked MacArthur merely "above average," placing him 38th of 46 brigadier generals. The officer he'd previously recommended for major general in October 1918 "should serve some years in present grade before promotion to next higher," and he noted that "[MacArthur] [h]as an exalted opinion of himself"[42] – undoubtedly a perceptive assessment of MacArthur's character, but unnecessarily petty in an official fitness report (likely exacerbated by Pershing's former mistress, socialite Louise Brooks, becoming "Mrs. Douglas MacArthur" on Valentine's Day that year). Yet, Rainbow Division's officers and soldiers who fought alongside MacArthur knew the truth – upon leaving the division, "he received a gold cigarette case, emblazoned 'Bravest of the Brave,' which he carried with him the rest of his life."[43]

MacArthur's post-World War I service is legendary. As U.S. Military Academy Superintendent (1919–22), his Herculean labors to bring that stagnated academy into the 20th century achieved mixed results, facing fierce opposition from entrenched fossils on the all-powerful Academic Board and from cadets who hated his elimination of hazing (a practice Pershing enthusiastically approved of). In November 1930, at the age of 50, MacArthur became chief of staff of the U.S. Army, serving five years (until 1 October 1935 – only George Marshall's six-year World War II term exceeded it). Confronting the Great Depression and isolationists, MacArthur shepherded the Army through its darkest period since Valley Forge. Although pilloried by the press for his ill-advised "strutting" before newsreel cameras at the July 1932 "Bonus Army" riots[44] dispersal (his aide, Major Dwight Eisenhower, had wisely cautioned him to remain in his office), the efficient, bloodless show of force MacArthur led masterfully dispersed the marchers without fatalities. Presidential candidate Franklin D. Roosevelt blasted MacArthur, but extended his chief of staff tour after taking office.

Upon retiring in 1935, MacArthur became a Philippine field marshal, creating that U.S. commonwealth's military force. Recalled to active duty in 1941, MacArthur led U.S. and Australian forces to victory as Southwest Pacific Area Supreme Commander – notably fulfilling his "I Shall Return" pledge in October 1944 at Leyte after his brilliant leapfrogging campaign conquered New Guinea with minimal Allied casualties. On 2 September 1945 he accepted Japan's surrender aboard USS *Missouri* in Tokyo Bay, then reconstructed Japan as a modern democracy and economic powerhouse.

As U.S./United Nations commander (1950–51), he defeated North Korea's attempt to overrun South Korea through his brilliant September 1950 Inchon landing, launched despite the vehement opposition of the Joint Chiefs of Staff. However, after the massive Chinese intervention in October–November 1950, President Harry Truman judged his support of MacArthur a political liability. Above all, the President and his strong-willed general increasingly clashed over the Korean conflict's strategic goals, their irreconcilable differences eventually becoming embarrassingly public. On 11 April 1951 Truman controversially relieved MacArthur of command, replacing him with General Matthew Ridgway.

On 19 April 1951, in his moving, heartfelt farewell to a Congressional joint session, MacArthur dramatically referenced an old barracks ballad, promising to just "fade away." MacArthur did just that, and on 5 April 1964 the old soldier died aged 84 in Washington, D.C. – but not before he had delivered one last oratory masterpiece: his famous 1962 "Duty, Honor, Country" speech at West Point.

CHAPTER 4

BRIGADIER GENERAL MALIN CRAIG

Douglas V. Mastriano and David T. Ząbecki

Malin Craig was the chief of staff of U.S. I Corps, under Major General Hunter Liggett, and then under Major General Joseph Dickman. Immediately following the war, he was the chief of staff of the U.S. Army of Occupation in Germany. He later served as the chief of staff of the U.S. Army from 1935 to 1939. His efforts to prepare the U.S. Army for the next world war were significant, but are largely forgotten today.

The son of an Army officer and West Point graduate, Malin Craig was born in St. Joseph, Missouri, on 5 August 1875. He graduated from the U.S. Military Academy at West Point in 1898 with his classmate Fox Conner. Initially assigned to the 4th Infantry upon commissioning, he transferred to the 6th Cavalry. During the Spanish–American War he served in Cuba during the Santiago campaign, and then he served with the 4th Cavalry in Oklahoma and Wyoming. He was posted to the Philippines during the Philippine–American War, and from there he took part in the 1901–02 China Relief Expedition to rescue the foreign legations in Beijing during the Boxer Rebellion.

When Craig returned to the United States, he attended the Infantry and Cavalry School at Fort Leavenworth, Kansas, and the following year he attended the second-year course at the Staff School. Promoted to captain in May 1904, he was assigned to the 10th Cavalry Regiment and then to the 1st Cavalry Regiment in 1905. After further cavalry assignments in the American West and the Philippines, Craig graduated in 1910 from the Army War College in Washington, where one of his instructors was Fox Conner. Another graduate of the Class of 1910 was Lieutenant Colonel Hunter Liggett, who was senior to both Conner and Craig in rank and experience. While working on one particularly complex tactical exercise, Conner assigned Craig to work with Liggett as his assistant. It was the beginning of a professional working relationship that would bear great fruit just a few years later.

Craig remained at the War College as an instructor the following year, working under Conner. Craig simultaneously was assigned to the Army General Staff as the chief of staff of the Maneuver Division. From 1912 to 1916 he served in various cavalry assignments in the west, including on the Mexican border where he served under John Pershing. In 1916–17 Craig was assigned as an instructor at the Army Service Schools at Fort Leavenworth. In 1917 he was detailed to the General Staff Corps.

When America entered the war in April 1917, Craig was one of the Army's few trained and experienced staff officers. Promoted to major in the Regular Army in May, the following August he was promoted to the temporary wartime rank of lieutenant colonel in the National Army and assigned as the chief of staff of the 41st Division, composed of National Guard units from the western states. The commander of the division, Liggett, had not specifically requested Craig, but he was more than happy to get his War College classmate. As Liggett noted in his memoirs: "I gave [Craig] a free hand and charged him with the responsibility in selecting his section chiefs and otherwise building the machine."[1] Craig's immediate tasks included organizing and training the divisional staff, and reorganizing and training the various and disparate National Guard units assigned to the division.

The 41st Division deployed to Europe in late November 1917 as part of the American Expeditionary Forces (AEF). Upon arriving in France, however, the 41st Division was designated as a replacement division, and it never saw combat. On 20 January 1918, Liggett was assigned to command the newly established U.S. I Corps and Craig went with him as the corps chief of staff. In his memoirs, Liggett later said of Craig that through his diligent study and native ability, he had made himself one of the most accomplished officers in the Army, regardless of rank. Liggett also wrote, "In two years in Europe he never had a day's rest, and he never saw Paris except the one night we slept at a hotel there on our way to the British front."[2] Craig was promoted to colonel in the National Army in February 1918.

In January 1918, U.S. I Corps consisted of the 1st, 2nd, 26th, 32nd, 41st, and 42nd Divisions. The line divisions were attached for training to various French corps in the Champagne and Alsace sectors. I Corps, with its newly established headquarters at Neufchâteau in the Vosges Mountains sector, exercised administrative command over the divisions. The total size of the corps, including its support units, was some 200,000 troops. As with the 41st Division, Liggett gave Craig a free hand in organizing the corps headquarters and staff. Liggett and Craig also made some significant changes to the way an American corps was organized. As Liggett described it in his memoirs:

> But almost immediately we adopted the French system of corps command under which an army corps consists of its staff, certain technical troops, the corps artillery and such divisions as happen to be on the lines at the point to which the corps is assigned – a more mobile and adaptable organization than our own.[3]

Relations were not especially good between the corps headquarters and the commander of the 26th Division, Major General Clarence R. Edwards. As early as 27 January, Liggett's aide-de-camp, Lieutenant Colonel Pierpont L. Stackpole, recorded in his diary a conversation he had with Craig following Liggett's visit that day to the division: "I detailed to Colonel Craig the experiences of the day, including General Liggett's remarks about General Edwards being always late, his fondness for wind-pudding, good dinners, etc., and the bad management in wasting the time of 1,500 men at a futile show."[4] ("Wind pudding" was a euphemism of the day for "nothing," dating back to the Civil War.)

In February the 26th Division was attached to the French XI Corps on the Chemin des Dames ridge in the Champagne sector. Edwards continued to clash with the I Corps staff, especially with Craig and the corps G-3, Colonel Stuart Heintzelman. Craig and Heintzelman were critical of Edwards for not being fully engaged with his subordinate units and failing to visit even his brigade command posts in the field. When the 26th Division was deployed to Seicheprey in the Toul region at the start of April to relieve the 1st Division in the line, the transition did not go smoothly. Edwards blamed 1st Division commander Major General Robert Bullard for the problems. When the clash between the two elevated to Liggett's level, Craig and Heintzelman supported Bullard. Criticism continued to build within the AEF chain of command over Edwards' leadership of the 26th Division. In mid-October 1918 Pershing finally relieved Edwards of his command. Curiously, Liggett in his memoirs never mentioned the running conflict between Craig and Edwards; for that matter, he never mentioned Edwards at all.

The Germans, meanwhile, conducted five major offensives on the Western Front between 21 March and 18 July. Although they managed to capture a great amount of ground, all five attacks ultimately failed operationally and strategically. Redeploying from Alsace, I Corps units began fighting at the divisional level against the Germans in May. The following month Craig was promoted to brigadier general in the National Army. On 4 July U.S. I Corps assumed tactical command from the French III Corps of the La Ferté-sous-Jouarre sector, between Paris and Château-Thierry. The divisions under the corps' operational control were the U.S. 2nd Division and the French 167th Division. It was the start of the first American corps-level operation since the Civil War, and the first time French troops served under American tactical command since the American Revolution.

When the Allies launched the Aisne–Marne counteroffensive on 18 July, I Corps' 1st and 2nd Divisions attacked toward Soissons under the operational control of French XX Corps. On 21 July, Craig established a corps advanced headquarters at Montreuil aux Lions, and I Corps assumed an operational role in the battle. Commanding the French 167th Division and the U.S. 26th, 4th, and 42nd Divisions, I Corps helped push the Germans back north to the Vesle River by 6 August. As Liggett later commented, "In the fighting just ended, the staff had functioned without a hitch in its first test, mainly due to the ability and energy of the Chief of Staff, Malin Craig."[5]

Following the end of the Aisne–Marne offensive, I Corps assumed defensive positions in the Champagne sector for the remainder of August. In early September, I Corps deployed to the Lorraine sector, just south of Verdun, to prepare for the first major American-led operation of the war. The mission was to reduce the Saint-Mihiel salient. The attacking forces included Liggett's I Corps, the French II Colonial Corps, and the newly formed U.S. IV and V Corps. Attacking on 12 September, I Corps had the mission of reducing the eastern flank of the salient. As the corps chief of staff, Craig's job was to develop the operations plan and oversee the day-to-day operations of the corps during the battle itself. Craig coordinated the operations and logistics staffs, and supervised the distribution of orders to the subordinate divisions, to give Liggett a free hand to focus on fighting the Germans. The attack was an overwhelming success, and the Americans pushed the Germans back to the base of the salient by 15 September.

Immediately after Saint-Mihiel, I Corps headquarters on 18 September was ordered to redeploy rapidly 60 miles northwest, to the west of Verdun, to assume its jump-off position for the Meuse–Argonne offensive, scheduled to start on 26 September. With three corps attacking, I Corps was on the left of the line, with V Corps in the center and III Corps on the right. Thus, I Corps had the farthest distance to travel to get into position, and much of that movement had to be made at night. In preparation for the massive movement, Craig worked closely with Colonel George Marshall, the U.S. First Army's chief of operations, G-3. The corps headquarters could do it in the time allotted, but it would take the divisions that had fought at Saint-Mihiel considerably more time. Thus, none of those experienced divisions would be available for the start of the offensive. Instead, I Corps had to put the 77th, 28th, and 35th Divisions in the first line, with the 92nd Division in corps reserve. The 77th and

28th Divisions were experienced, but they had sustained heavy casualties during the fighting that summer, and both had been refilled with thousands of green replacements. The 35th and 92nd Divisions had little experience. Furthermore, I Corps had the most difficult terrain to attack through. The Argonne Forest and the Aire River Valley comprised classic defenders' geography, full of deep ravines, artesian wells, steep cliffs and thick clusters of trees, and the Germans had been dug in there for more than four years.

The relative ease of the Saint-Mihiel operation had created misleading expectations among the Americans. The Meuse–Argonne was a far more difficult problem. The first several days of the operation fell far short of what AEF commander General John J. Pershing wanted. On 28 September, Pershing arrived at I Corps headquarters while Liggett was out with the units. Pershing ordered Craig to call the division commanders and order them to push on, regardless of men or guns, night and day.

When the 77th Division's "Lost Battalion" (see Chapter 17) was cut off and isolated deep in the Argonne Forest, Liggett and Craig on 7 and 8 October planned a bold flank attack with one brigade of the 82nd Division that would force the Germans to fall back all along the fronts of the 77th and 28th Divisions. It was a risky maneuver, with the flank of the attacking brigade exposed to converging German fire from the steep and rugged cliffs dominating the Aire River Valley. The attack, during which the 82nd Division's Corporal Alvin York earned the Medal of Honor, broke the ring around the Lost Battalion, allowing it to be relieved. All of the French liaison officers attached to I Corps headquarters had opposed the plan, as did every member of Liggett's corps staff. As Liggett later wrote, "only the chief, Malin Craig, supported me."[6] By 10 October the attack forced the Germans completely out of the of the Argonne Forest.

When Liggett assumed command of U.S. First Army on 16 October, Craig remained as chief of staff to the new I Corps commander, Major General Joseph Dickman. During the final days of the war the incident known as the "Race to Sedan" (see Introduction, pp. 50–53) resulted in some tension between Liggett and his old I Corps staff. The directive for the Americans to take Sedan had been issued by Pershing, without Liggett's knowledge. As an outcome, U.S. V Corps' 1st Division crossed the boundary into the I Corps sector without coordination, and the result was chaos on the ground. When Liggett reached the I Corps command post on 8 November to restore order, "First Corps headquarters was buzzing like a hornet's nest when I arrived, and as the first victim to hand, I was the sufferer. Although this was my own old corps, they were inclined to hold me personally responsible for the 1st Division's 'atrocity,' as they termed it."[7]

In the aftermath, Dickman and Craig largely blamed V Corps' commander, Major General Charles P. Summerall, for the debacle. The result was lifelong animosity between the two corps commanders. When Summerall, who could hold a grudge forever, became chief of staff in the U.S. Army in November 1926, he still bore lasting enmity toward the now-retired Dickman, along with his former I Corps chief of staff. Fortunately for Craig, he already had been promoted to major general in the Regular Army eight months before Summerall was appointed chief of staff. (In the 1920s major general was the highest rank in the U.S. Army, with the exception of the chief of staff, who was a four-star.)

After the war ended in November 1918, Dickman and Craig took over the newly formed U.S. Third Army, the major element of the U.S. Army of Occupation in Germany. Another large-scale and long-distance transfer of forces was required to get the American occupation troops into position for the beginning of the movement to the Rhine, scheduled to start on the morning on 17 November. But the order establishing the Third Army was not issued until 13 November, which left Craig with little time to get his new field army headquarters organized, let alone plan, coordinate, and direct the divisions marked for occupation duty in Germany. On the evening of the 13th Craig visited Marshall at First Army headquarters, requesting his help in getting the divisions moving, while Craig pulled together the new Third Army staff. Marshall also helped Craig by detailing officers and clerks from his own First Army Operations Section to Craig's new Third Army, which now had the AEF's primary mission. During the subsequent interwar years, Craig would remember George Marshall as the consummate team player.

In May 1919 Craig was reunited with Liggett, when the latter assumed command of Third Army from Dickman. For his service as a divisional, corps, and army-level chief of staff, Craig was awarded the Distinguished Service Medal. He also was decorated with the Companion of the Order of the Bath by the United Kingdom; the Commander of the Legion of Honor and the Croix de Guerre with Palm by France; and the Commander of the Order of the Crown by Belgium.

In August 1919, Craig reverted to his Regular Army permanent rank of major, and was assigned as the director of the Army War College. In January 1920 Craig joined the tour already in progress that Pershing – at the direction of Secretary of War Newton Baker – was making of army camps throughout the United States. George Marshall at the time was Pershing's aide-de-camp, and Craig and Marshall during the tour cemented a close relationship that would continue for the next 25 years.

In July 1920 Craig was promoted to the permanent rank of colonel in the Regular Army, and assigned command of the District of Arizona. The following year he was promoted to brigadier general and assigned as the commandant of the Cavalry School at Fort Riley, Kansas, where in 1923 one of his students was Major George S. Patton. Later in 1923 Craig assumed command of the Coast Artillery District of Manila, and in 1924 he was promoted to major general and assigned as the U.S. Army's chief of cavalry. In October 1923, when Pershing was still chief of staff of the Army, George Patton had taken the liberty of writing a personal "cavalryman-to-cavalryman" letter to Pershing strongly supporting Craig for the chief of cavalry position.

In 1924–26, Craig was the Army's assistant chief of staff for operations and training, G-3. In 1926 he added his support to deputy chief of staff of the Army Fox Conner's unsuccessful effort to get George Patton assigned as commandant of cadets at West Point. After another officer was given the appointment, Craig wrote to Patton: "I regret very much that circumstances existed as they did, as you are the one fellow for whom I am always ready to go to the bat."[8]

Craig assumed command of the IV Corps Area in 1926; the Panama Canal Division in 1927; the Panama Canal Department in 1928; and the IX Corps Area in 1930. While he was the commander of IX Corps, Craig in 1934 was a member of a promotion board that nominated George Marshall for brigadier general. Marshall, however was not selected for promotion. Craig later complained to Secretary of War George Dern that the Army's flawed promotion system resulted in too many deadwood senior colonels being promoted, while officers of Marshall's caliber were passed over. Craig said that Marshall should have become the Army's next brigadier general that year.

In 1935 Craig returned briefly to the U.S. Army War College as the school's commandant. Promoted directly from major general to general, Craig succeeded General Douglas MacArthur as chief of staff of the U.S. Army on 2 October 1935. George Marshall was promoted to brigadier general 11 months later, and in July 1938 Craig brought Marshall to Washington as chief of the War Department's War Plans Division. Only three months later, Craig made Marshall the deputy chief of staff of the U.S. Army. (The deputy chief of staff at the time was the equivalent of today's vice chief of staff of the U.S. Army.)

As chief of staff, Craig sought to convince Congress of the Army's great weaknesses in manpower and materiel, and he fought to reform the Army against the severe budgetary and other constraints. His efforts, although largely unheralded at the time, were extremely important in preparing the army for World War II. Craig modernized army equipment and he introduced realistic training maneuvers that involved large numbers of troops. In November 1937, Craig told the Army and Navy Joint Board that the current JB325 version of the 1928 Basic War Plan Orange for war with Japan was obsolete and should be completely revised. The result was an updated War Plan Orange adopted in May 1938. The following October, that version, along with all the other "color" war plans, was superseded by the five Rainbow Plans, developed to meet the threat of a two-ocean war against multiple enemies.

In December 1937, Craig established a board to make the final recommendation on the reorganization of the U.S. Army's future divisions. The main decision was over retaining the huge "square" division structure of the World War I era, or adopting a smaller and more flexible "triangular" division structure. The three members of the board were Fox Conner, George Marshall, and Lesley McNair. Marshall later referred to it as a "stacked deck" for the triangular division. In December 1938 the War Plans Division issued the results of a study directed by Craig that called for increases in army manpower, and the formal establishment of five infantry divisions, which at that point only existed on paper.

Perhaps Craig's greatest contribution to the coming World War II was the Protective Mobilization Plan of 1939, which the War Plans Division completed at Craig's direction in December 1938. It provided for a two-stage expansion: 1. an Initial Protective Force of about 400,000, consisting of most of the active Army and the National Guard, to be operational by 30 days after mobilization; and 2. an expansion to 1,150,000 active troops by 240 days after mobilization. Supported by a $575 million arms program, it was only a very small effort compared with the later reality of World War II. But compared to the state of the U.S. Army in 1939, it was a bold step forward in the face of political and bureaucratic gridlock. It became the Army's basic prewar expansion plan. In February 1939 Craig sent Marshall to Congress to argue for an increase of Army end strength by 40,000, and the pressing need to equip the Regular Army and National Guard with modern equipment, especially new artillery and a semi-automatic rifle. The authorized increase, however, was only 17,000.

Near the end of Craig's tenure as chief of staff, he frequently found himself caught in the middle of a power struggle between Secretary of War Harry Woodring and Assistant Secretary of War Louis Johnson. Woodring was very cautious about risking involvement in Europe, to the point of being a borderline isolationist. Johnson, on the other hand, was a staunch advocate of rapidly expanding American military capabilities, and he had the strong political backing of the American Legion. This political crossfire between the two ultimately compromised Craig's effectiveness in dealing with Congress and thereby limited his ability to secure what was needed to better prepare the U.S. Army for war.

As Craig's mandatory retirement date approached, he and Secretary of War Woodring lobbied hard with President Franklin Roosevelt to appoint Marshall as the next chief of staff, although Marshall was junior to 32 other general officers. Marshall succeeded Craig when he retired on 31 August 1939, the day before Germany invaded Poland to start World War II in Europe. In his final "Annual Report of the Chief of Staff" in June 1939, Craig urged the United States to strengthen its military forces by reorganizing its five geographically scattered standing divisions to defend the Western Hemisphere; establish a war reserve with equipment for 1 million men; and establish an outpost line from Alaska to Hawaii to Panama to Puerto Rico. Craig also accurately warned that because of the time lag in industrial production, the modest appropriations that had already been approved for increased military equipment would not "be fully transformed into military power for two years."[9]

In September 1941 Craig was recalled to active duty in the retired rank of general to head Secretary of War Henry L. Stimpson's War Department Personnel Board, which was responsible for selecting senior-level civilian specialists for direct commissions in the Army. The most senior of those direct commissions went to William "Big Bill" Knudsen, a native of Denmark who in 1940 was the president of General Motors. In January 1942, Knudsen was directly commissioned as a lieutenant general, and appointed director of production, Office of the Under Secretary of War. Under Knudsen's direction, American production of machine tools for the manufacture of war materiel tripled.

During his tenure as chief of staff of the Army, Malin Craig established much of the critical foundation from which the U.S. Army expanded from 174,000 troops in 1939 to more than 11 million in 1945. Today, General George C. Marshall is rightly remembered as America's "Architect of Victory." But thanks to Craig, Marshall did not have to start from ground zero, a lesson hard learned by the United States Army and Craig in 1916. And it was also thanks to Craig that the relatively obscure Colonel Marshall of September 1936 replaced him as chief of staff of the U.S. Army just three years later. Although Craig and Marshall had once met briefly as company grade officers in the American West in 1905, it was their close working relationship in France during World War I that paid great dividends for the United States in World War II.

During World War II, Craig's younger brother, Major General Louis A. Craig, Jr., commanded the U.S. 9th Infantry Division in 1944–45. Malin Craig died at Walter Reed Army Hospital in Washington, D.C. on 25 July 1945. He was buried in Arlington National Cemetery.

CHAPTER 5

COLONEL GEORGE C. MARSHALL

Mark Grotelueschen and Derek Varble

George Catlett Marshall is best known for his enormous contributions to the United States, and the world, as U.S. Army chief of staff during World War II, Secretary of State from 1947 to 1949, and Secretary of Defense from 1950 to 1951. However, Marshall's first impact on American national security occurred decades earlier in the American Expeditionary Forces (AEF) during the Great War, when he served as the assistant chief of staff for operations (G-3) for the 1st Division, then as the assistant G-3, AEF General Headquarters (GHQ), and subsequently in the Operations Section of the First Army. After the Armistice Marshall served briefly as chief of staff, VIII Army Corps, before returning to the Operations Section at GHQ.

During his service in France, Marshall came into regular contact not only with General John J. Pershing, but with other leading U.S. Army officers as well, such as Robert Bullard, Charles Summerall, John Hines, Hugh Drum, Fox Conner, John M. Palmer, Lesley McNair, George Patton, and Malin Craig, among others, which had a significant impact on his professional development. While the records suggest that Marshall impressed all who worked with him during his wartime service at division, corps, army, and GHQ levels, he developed a remarkable rapport with Pershing in the fall of 1917. These extensive interactions with Pershing led the AEF commander to promote Marshall to positions of increased responsibility during the war, and ultimately to select Marshall to serve as his personal aide-de-camp after the Armistice, a position he held from May 1919 until July 1924.

Pershing and Marshall both spoke their minds, and expected the same of others. In 1917, candor brought Marshall into Pershing's circle of trust upon their first substantive conversation, marking Marshall as a valuable leader whose counsel Pershing would seek whenever possible. Marshall later commented about Pershing, "I've never seen a man who could listen to as much criticism, as long as it was constructive criticism. You could say what you pleased as long as it was straight, constructive criticism. He did not hold it against you for an instant. I never saw another commander that I could do that with."[1] Marshall's peers, superiors, and subordinates all recognized this quality in Marshall. In fact, Marshall not only shared Pershing's appreciation for candor, he demanded it. General of the Army Omar Bradley, who served on Marshall's staff during World War II, wrote of one particular instance when Marshall called his team together to tell them, "I am disappointed in all of you... You have not disagreed with a single thing I have done all week." Bradley concluded that "what made General Marshall an outstanding leader" was that, like Pershing before him, "he did not want a staff of 'yes men.'"[2]

Marshall was born in Uniontown, Pennsylvania in 1880. He followed his older brother to the Virginia Military Institute, where he served as the Class of 1901's first captain. After obtaining a U.S. Army second lieutenant's commission as an infantry officer the following year, Marshall sailed to the Philippines for his first military assignment. In Manila and other locations throughout that archipelago, Marshall participated in various occupation duties, such as leading patrols to restore law and order in the wake of the Philippine Insurrection, for nearly two years. Great Plains garrison duty followed Marshall's initial assignment to the Philippines. While participating in a topographical surveying expedition of the Southern Plains, Marshall met Captain Malin Craig, who, 33 years later as U.S. Army chief of staff, chose

Marshall to serve as his deputy chief of staff and then supported Marshall's accession to the chief of staff position upon Craig's retirement. Marshall remained in the Great Plains for his next assignment at Fort Leavenworth, Kansas, where, in June 1907, Army chief of staff and former U.S. Infantry and Cavalry School commandant Major General J. Franklin Bell took note of Marshall's success as top graduate at the School of the Line, as the Infantry and Cavalry School had been renamed. Marshall's retention for a second year of Leavenworth coursework at the Army Staff School led to his selection for the faculty, on which he served for two years. Marshall's achievements made him a favorite of Bell, while affording him opportunities to make acquaintance with those he would later work with in World War I. Beyond his classroom duties as student and teacher, Marshall participated in militia mobilization exercises with National Guard units from several states, including those of his home state of Pennsylvania. Training alongside citizen-soldiers proved to be excellent preparation for Marshall's whirlwind of assignments over the next six years that saw him travel throughout much of the United States, and Philippines, while leading Regular Army and National Guard maneuvers and mobilization exercises. With both Bell and fellow Pennsylvanian Major General Hunter Liggett, Marshall also continued the association he had begun with these men while at Leavenworth. He served as an aide to both general officers, a position he held on Bell's staff in April 1917, upon U.S. entry into World War I.

Shortly after the United States declared war on Germany in April 1917, Marshall moved to Governors Island, New York, with Bell, who took command of the Eastern Department. While there, he had his first interaction with Pershing, as he and Bell accompanied the new AEF commander to the ship that took him and his initial staff to Europe. In June, Major General William L. Sibert selected Marshall to serve as the operations officer for his newly established 1st Division. Marshall travelled to France with one of its lead elements, sharing a berth with Lesley McNair, who became a lifelong friend and colleague. Although this division was supposedly composed of U.S. Army "regulars," most of the officers and men were inexperienced, not just in waging modern industrial war, but in doing any kind of fighting at all, as well as in training, staff work, and logistical operations. More than half of its soldiers were new recruits. Only a few of its non-commissioned officers had been in the Army for two years or more, and nearly all of the lieutenants had been commissioned for less than six months. Despite these statistics, the 1st Division was the first American division to arrive in France, and served as pathfinder and showcase unit for the 33 other American divisions that subsequently joined the AEF.

In France, Marshall had to solve the extraordinary array of administrative, logistical, personnel, and training problems involved with getting this completely inexperienced unit ready for combat in the shortest possible time. This led to an unsatisfactory training event that Pershing himself observed. Pershing "just gave everybody hell" – including Sibert and his top staff officers. Marshall decided to make what he called a "sacrifice play" and step in to explain the situation. When Pershing responded dismissively and attempted to walk away, Marshall put his hand on Pershing's arm "and practically forced him to talk." Admittedly "mad all over" at Pershing's unjust public rebuke of his boss and colleagues, Marshall let Pershing have it, explaining how the turbulence caused by decisions at GHQ was negatively affecting the division. When Pershing responded by saying, "Well, you must appreciate the troubles we have [at GHQ]," Marshall shot back, "Yes, general, but we have them every day and many a day, and we have to solve every one of them by night." Marshall's commander and colleagues "were horrified," and assumed his career was over. But they couldn't have been more wrong. From then on, whenever Pershing visited the division, he took Marshall "away from the others" to get the straight story on the current "condition of affairs."[3]

The winter of 1917–18 was a difficult one for Marshall, the 1st Division, the AEF, and indeed, the entire coalition. Marshall later referred to it as "the most depressing and gloomy period of the war."[4] Nevertheless, the division completed extensive training, much of it under French tutelage, including time in the trenches along the Saint-Mihiel salient. By mid-April 1918, the division was deemed ready to be given command of its own portion of the front near Montdidier, at the apex of the bulge created by the first German offensive that year.

Before the 1st Division headed into the line, Pershing gave an inspirational address to the division's officers; Marshall reported that it "made a profound impression on all those present."[5] They needed all the encouragement they could get, as the conditions near the German-held village of Cantigny were horrific. Artillery fire was almost constant in this new sector, which lacked trenches or bunkers. The men were dispersed in foxholes, and told to hold the line. Casualties mounted, despite the lack of any infantry attacks.

By mid-May, the division's leadership, with the support of their French corps commander, decided it was time to seize the German-held high ground in and around Cantigny. Marshall worked 16–18 hours a day developing what proved to be a superb attack plan. This assault, though supported by French artillery, tanks, and aircraft, was the first American attack of the war, and it was a clear, though costly, success. Marshall's plan, which fully integrated all the various weapon systems at his disposal, shattered the German defensive system and enabled the attacking infantrymen and tankers to kill, capture, or drive out every defender in the village, on schedule. American casualties in the initial assault were surprisingly light, except on the flanks where German resistance was more formidable. Intense German counterattacks followed and continued for many hours. The French had to withdraw most of their artillery to meet a new German breakthrough to the south, which left the attacking American infantry, now exposed in their new positions in and around the village, without much counter-battery support. Nevertheless, after three brutal days of fighting and a casualty list that exceeded 900 men from just the one attacking regiment alone, the Germans gave up. Marshall proudly wrote, "We held Cantigny. The Germans never afterwards reoccupied the village."[6]

Marshall's division held the Cantigny sector until July, when two French divisions finally relieved it. Within a week of leaving the front lines, Marshall received orders re-assigning him to the Operations Section of GHQ at Chaumont. There, under the supervision of General Fox Conner, Marshall demonstrated his genius for planning and organizing operations on a truly massive scale. While his work with the 28,000-man 1st Division was impressive, he demonstrated an ability to plan, arrange, and shape the complex details, movements, and operations of army corps and field armies of hundreds of thousands.

Marshall's first major task at GHQ was to develop a concrete plan for the soon to be formed American First Army's first attack of the war, along the Saint-Mihiel salient. As early as the summer of 1917, GHQ had identified the reduction of the salient as a likely operation for the AEF, but no detailed planning had been completed thus far. As Marshall began to design a specific plan for this crucial mission, the fluidity of the strategic and operational situation in July and August forced unforeseen adjustments. With only six divisions at his disposal, Marshall's first scheme called for a limited attack on the south face of the salient to free an important east–west railway. But just as he was finishing this plan, Conner informed him that ten divisions would be available. Marshall promptly reworked the plan. Just as he completed that version, the improved Allied situation suggested that a total of 14 divisions would be in the offensive, which led Marshall to conclude that "a much more elaborate operation became possible," and he reworked the plan again.[7] For each successive plan, Marshall had to arrange for the concentration of the required force, and calculate the amount of artillery, tanks, and engineers to request from the French. Just as that plan was nearly completed, Marshall was told that 16 American and six French divisions would be able to take part, which meant the upcoming offensive could now aim at "the complete reduction of the salient by heavy attacks on both flanks and the advance of our lines to the outskirts of the famous fortifications of Metz."[8]

Marshall completed this plan, and forwarded it to the new First Army headquarters, just then being organized at Neufchâteau. As tens of thousands of troops began to flood into the Saint-Mihiel region, the Germans showed signs of being aware of the approaching attack. Therefore, Marshall began work on a new plan for a large American attack some 150 miles to the south, through the Belfort Gap near the Swiss border. Marshall later admitted that his "state of mind at this period is impossible to describe."[9] While a ruse in the Belfort Gap served to distract the Germans and even divert a few enemy divisions to that sector, arrangements for the Saint-Mihiel offensive worked their way toward fruition.

On 20 August, without any warning, Conner ordered Marshall to proceed directly to First Army headquarters, where he was "attached" to the chief of staff to help execute the plans he had developed at GHQ.[10] At First Army, he double-checked the arrangements the First Army staff had made, worked with Colonel Walter Grant to draft the attack order, and developed a set of tactical guidelines for the First Army based on his experiences with the 1st Division, "the dictums of GHQ," and, he later admitted, "copies of Ludendorff's most recent tactical instructions for German Army."[11] In the end, the First Army's attack in mid-September caught the German defenders by surprise and drove them completely out of the salient within four days. Total German losses approached 20,000, while the Franco–American attackers suffered less than half that figure.

Even before the Saint-Mihiel offensive had begun, Marshall's duties at First Army had shifted to planning for the next great attack, scheduled to commence just two weeks after the Saint-Mihiel attack was to start, but located some 50 miles northwest, between the Argonne Forest and the Meuse River. Marshall was given the daunting task of planning the movement of forces from Saint-Mihiel to the Meuse–Argonne sector. Marshall admitted that "this appalling proposition… disturbed" his "equilibrium."[12] He continued:

> [I] could not recall an incident in history where the fighting of one battle had been preceded by the plans for a later battle to be fought by the same army on a different front, and involving the issuing of orders for the movement of troops already destined to participate in the first battle, directing their transfer to the new field of action.[13]

He later wrote that the hours wrestling with this dilemma – "the hardest nut" he "had to crack in France"[14] – stood out to him "as the most trying mental ordeal" he experienced during the war.[15] Although he initially felt that his solution was "far from satisfactory," time constraints demanded he submit the order immediately. The very next day General Hugh Drum, the First Army chief of staff, told him that the order was "a dandy," and that Pershing "thought it was a fine piece of work." Marshall concluded that the order, which enabled the Meuse–Argonne offensive to begin on time, constituted his "best contribution to the war."[16]

Writing a complex order was one thing; ensuring its successful execution was another. While the Saint-Mihiel offensive continued, Marshall focused on preparations for the Meuse–Argonne, which involved the movement of more than 500,000 men, 2,000 guns, and 900,000 tons of supplies and ammunition. Executing such an order involved constant coordination not only with American units ranging from corps to regiment, but with multiple

French headquarters, combat units, and logistical organizations as well. He soon realized the enormity of the approaching battle – which involved not only the American First Army, but multiple French, British, and Belgian field armies attacking all along the Western Front. Focused exclusively on successfully executing the force concentration, Marshall did not see the actual attack plan until the night before the jump-off. For the first weeks of the battle, he served in the First Army's Operations Section, handling all movements of divisions into or out of the battle, as well as "special jobs" assigned by Drum. In mid-October, after initial successes had given way to slow progress and heavy casualties, Pershing handed command of First Army to Hunter Liggett, and Marshall was appointed the First Army's assistant chief of staff for operations. He then directed a series of small operations to secure a suitable line for the Army's next major push, and led the effort to develop the plans for that new attack, which began on 1 November, and proved to be the most successful of the entire campaign.

The Armistice of 11 November brought no rest to Marshall, who had to implement the ceasefire, prepare forces for a march to the Rhine for occupation duties, and move the rest of the First Army from the battlefield to billeting areas. Despite involving the movement of more than 600,000 men, Marshall reported that these activities were "carried through without a hitch."[17] Within a week, Marshall became chief of staff of the new VIII Corps, which was to prepare units for occupation duties. After getting that command on its feet, he moved back to GHQ to develop contingency plans should Germany reject the treaty terms. Marshall recommended a minimal use of military force, and suggested that the Allies send food into Germany to stabilize the situation. Marshall next worked on Pershing's Final Report, travelled from camp to camp assessing troop morale, lectured on the AEF's accomplishments, and briefed visiting members of the House Military Affairs Committee. In April, Marshall traveled to Metz to receive the French Legion of Honor, and while there, accepted an offer to serve as Pershing's aide – a commitment that continued for the next five years. Marshall assisted Pershing as he inspected occupation forces in Germany; visited the great battlefields of the Western Front; completed a grand victory tour with celebrations in Paris, London, and Italy; closed-down Pershing's headquarters; and travelled back to the States with the last contingent of troops on the USS *Leviathan*.

Pershing's ten-year-old son Warren clamored aboard *Leviathan* when that vessel made landfall in Hoboken, New Jersey in September 1919. Warren brought the happy news of Pershing's promotion as the first-ever General of the Armies in U.S. history. Showers of flowers greeted Pershing, Marshall, and thousands of other AEF veterans as their victory parade took them through the streets of Manhattan. These celebratory blossoms soon faded, leaving Pershing to decamp for Washington and issues there that would preoccupy him for the remainder of his active Army service, which culminated in 1921 with a three-year assignment as Army chief of staff. Demobilization now fully underway, Pershing and other national leaders faced hard tradeoffs regarding the U.S. military's ideal size, composition, organization, and budget. Anticipating countless Congressional appearances of his own later in life, Marshall helped Pershing prepare for testimony on Capitol Hill that addressed these topics.

Marshall's other duties as aide to the chief of staff included overseeing revisions to the AEF final report, as well as making recommendations about the utility of military installations that had opened in the course of wartime mobilization. As time permitted, Marshall stood beside Pershing throughout the general's public duties, providing him with personal introductions to many of the era's leading men, including U.S. President Warren Harding, when Pershing served as marshal for the new President's 1921 inauguration ceremonies. When Harding died two and a half years into his presidential term during a West Coast tour, U.S. Secretary of Commerce Herbert Hoover joined Pershing and Marshall aboard the railcar Superb as the funeral cortège rolled eastward to the nation's capital.

Pershing's connections also linked Marshall with Great War heroes Charles Dawes and Bernard Baruch. Dawes received the 1925 Nobel Peace Prize for his contributions to European economic recovery, while Baruch led U.S. industrial mobilization during World War I, a role he reprised when the country entered World War II.

Upon concluding his assignment as Pershing's aide, Marshall proceeded to Tianjin, China, for three years' duty with the 15th Infantry Regiment, where he reunited with fellow Saint-Mihiel planner Joseph Stilwell, an intelligence officer who in 1918 had served with Headquarters IV Army Corps. Marshall's Tianjin assignment coincided with tumultuous events in Asia. Revolutionary leader Sun Yat-sen died in 1925. Two years later and 600 miles south of Tianjin, the Nanking Incident precipitated the outbreak of civil war in China. Marshall and Stilwell, who later attained Army four-star rank as the general commanding U.S. military forces in World War II's China–Burma–India Theater, witnessed the first waves of disorder and unrest that soon engulfed China. The resulting chaos in the decades that followed frustrated both men's effort toward that country's peaceful unification.

The tragedy of the death of Marshall's wife Lily in 1927 shortly after the Marshalls returned from China resulted in reassignment from the National War College to Infantry School duty at Fort Benning, Georgia, where for four years he helped lay a foundation for subsequent Army success in World War II. Pershing and Marshall maintained the close ties they had developed while in the AEF and Washington, D.C. Pershing also regularly offered career advice as Marshall weighed various opportunities that emerged as his professional responsibilities increased.

Subsequent assignments in the American South, Middle West, and Pacific Northwest demonstrated Marshall's remarkable breadth, with the versatile officer commanding large units during weeks-long maneuver exercises involving thousands of Regular Army and National Guard soldiers. Marshall also organized and trained volunteers in the Civilian Conservation Corps, a Depression-era recovery program emphasizing civilian efforts at infrastructure enhancement and natural resource development. Two years after a 1936 promotion to flag rank in the grade of brigadier general, Army chief of staff Major General Malin Craig – formerly a corps chief of staff and close colleague of Marshall during the Great War – assigned Marshall to lead the General Staff's War Plans Division at the War Department. Later that year Craig designated Marshall deputy chief of staff.

Through the Allies' 1945 victory in World War II, Marshall served as U.S. Army chief of staff, holding that office the longest in Army history while leading a force of more than 8 million soldiers and airmen, a forty-fold expansion in its size across Marshall's six years as Army Chief. After Marshall left active service, President Harry Truman, himself a veteran of the Meuse–Argonne, selected him for several important assignments. As Special Ambassador to China, Marshall sought in vain to help the

Map 2: The Allied Counteroffensive on the Marne: 18 July–6 August 1918

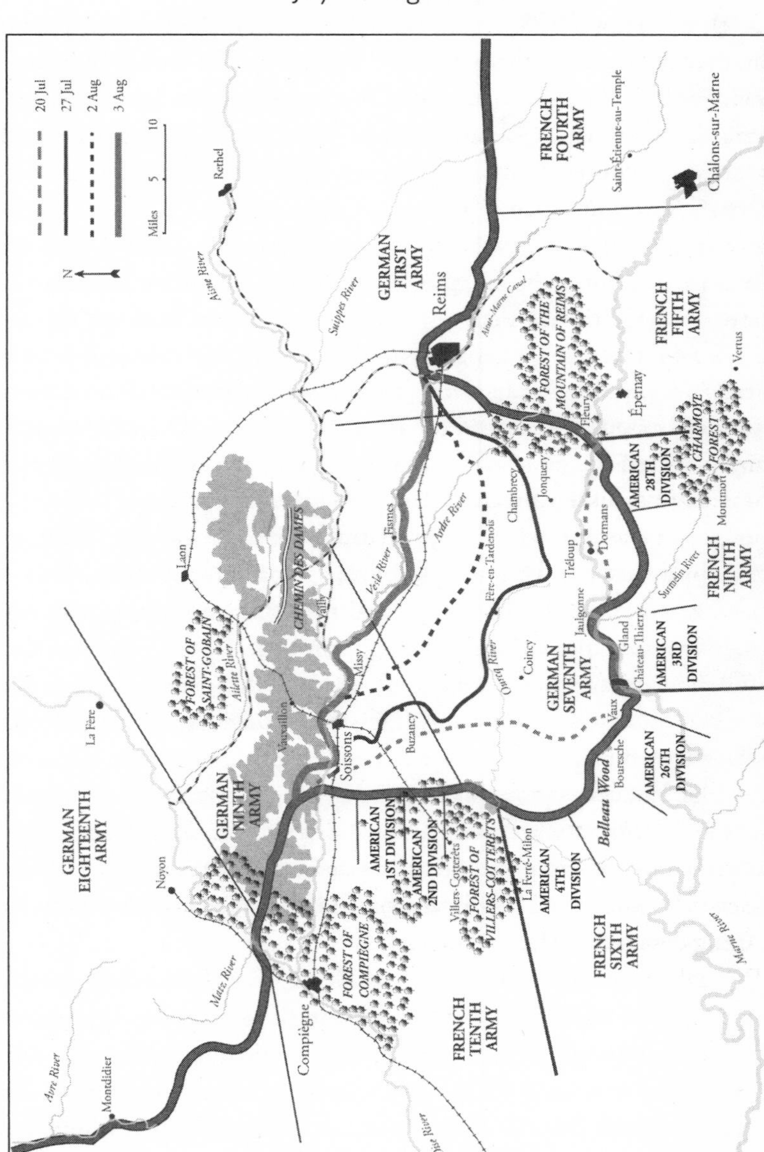

Communist Party of China and the Nationalist Party of China resolve their differences peacefully and end the Chinese Civil War, a conflict that, more than 60 years after Marshall's death, has yet to reach an official conclusion.

Marshall then took office as U.S. Secretary of State. While Secretary, he helped the U.S. and its allies implement a foreign policy of Cold War containment through initiatives such as the 1947 doctrine bearing Truman's name, and the North Atlantic Treaty Organization, as well as the 1948 European Recovery Program that unofficially bears Marshall's name and provided billions of U.S. dollars for postwar European reconstruction. Another cabinet position soon followed these achievements, with Marshall appointed Secretary of Defense the same year his Foggy Bottom[18] assignment ended, and three months after the United States commenced military operations supporting United Nations Security Council Resolution 83 in Korea. Marshall's nearly yearlong tenure as secretary saw United Nations military forces liberate previously occupied areas of the Korean Peninsula, withstand attacks by hundreds of thousands of People's Volunteer Army troops in the course of Communist Chinese intervention there, and stabilize a front line just above the 38th parallel, where it remains to this day as the northern border of a sovereign, independent, and prosperous Republic of Korea.

When Marshall died in 1959, he was the U.S. Army's senior ranking officer and he was laid to rest in Arlington National Cemetery, just a half-mile north of Pershing's grave. President Dwight Eisenhower, who served under Marshall throughout World War II, praised Marshall as "one of the distinguished military and civilian leaders of our century."[19] Eisenhower's commendation remains an apt appraisal of a revered soldier-statesman who orchestrated victory in two world wars and whose legacy endures into the current century.

Of all his lieutenants, Pershing's relationship with Marshall may have been the most significant and far-reaching. In selecting Marshall for crucial staff positions, as well as modeling both strong leadership and an appreciation for candor, Pershing not only permitted Marshall to help him win the Great War, but helped create a soldier-statesman who enabled the United States to win the next world war, and set it on a course to avoid a third world war while prevailing in the Cold War.

PART TWO

THE FUTURE COMMANDANTS OF THE U.S. MARINE CORPS

CHAPTER 6

MAJOR GENERAL JOHN A. LEJEUNE

G. K. Cunningham

The outbreak of World War I in 1914 presented the United States Marine Corps (USMC) with a peculiar challenge to its ethos, mission, and modes of operating. Accustomed to service with the fleet, Marines had largely deployed as security detachments ashore or onboard Navy ships, sometimes as landing forces, hastily assembled for crisis response and committed for limited durations. Yet, as the war in Europe unfolded, it was clear that the 20th century would bring a new kind of warfare, far larger in scope than the Marines were used to, involving millions of men and mountains of materiel, in land-based struggles far from the littorals and the seas.

Thus, when the United States entered the fray in Europe in April 1917, Marine commandant Major General George Barnett pressed Secretary of the Navy Josephus Daniels to include Marines in the American Expeditionary Forces (AEF). Despite the misgivings of senior U.S. Army commanders, one of whom referred to the Marines as "a bunch of adventurers, illiterates, and drunkards,"[1] two regiments of the Marine

Corps, the 5th and 6th Marines, were formed as the 4th Marine Brigade for service with the U.S. Army in Europe. Barnett viewed this initiative as so important to the future of the Marine Corps that he detailed his most trusted officer, Brigadier General John Archer Lejeune,[2] to oversee the formation and training of this expeditionary brigade.

Lejeune came from a well-established Southern family. He was born at the end of the U.S. Civil War on 10 January 1867 at the family plantation near Lacour, Louisiana after his father, Confederate States Army Captain Ovide Lejeune, returned from the American Civil War. An 1888 graduate of the U.S. Naval Academy, Lejeune served as a Navy midshipman for two years until he obtained a commission as a second lieutenant in the U.S. Marine Corps on 25 July 1890, subsequently serving in a number of Marine Corps assignments, worldwide. He served with distinction in assignments ashore and at sea, which included Panama, the Philippines, Cuba, and Mexico. He graduated from the U.S. Army War College in 1910, where he established relationships with many U.S. Army officers, including Hunter Liggett and Fox Conner. While in Guantanamo Bay, Cuba, Lejeune helped found and became the first director of the Marine Corps Association. He was promoted to colonel on 25 February 1914 and served in the occupation of Veracruz, Mexico, with notable fellow Marines Smedley D. Butler, Wendell C. Neville, and Littleton W. T. Waller. In December 1914 he returned to Washington, D.C. to become assistant commandant of the Marine Corps under Major General Barnett. Lejeune subsequently was promoted to brigadier general on 29 August 1916. There was no intent on Barnett's part to place Lejeune in command of the Marine brigade. Rather, he was Barnett's choice to succeed him as commandant.

The 4th Marine Brigade consisted of the 5th and 6th Marine Regiments and the 6th Machine Gun Battalion. Each 250-man training company had two French and four Canadian officers assigned to it as advisers. Training was arduous and unrelenting. Newly enlisted Marines underwent basic training at Parris Island. Meanwhile, newly commissioned officers fresh from officer candidate school, and seasoned officers and non-commissioned officers all arrived incrementally at Quantico for advanced training. The 5th Marines were the first unit to deploy, beginning on 27 June 1917, where they were initially assigned to the U.S. Army's 1st Division. The 6th Marines joined them on 5 October 1917, and the 6th Machine Gun Battalion arrived in France on 28 December 1917. All units were then assigned to the newly formed 2nd Division, where they would remain until 8 August 1919. Then as now, medical and morale support personnel were provided by the U.S. Navy for medical and dental officers, chaplains, and 500 medical corpsmen. Other units in the 2nd Division included the Army's 3rd Infantry Brigade, the 2nd Field Artillery Brigade, the 2nd Engineer Regiment, and various service and support troops.

At first, General John J. Pershing assigned the 5th Marines to securing lines of communication and guarding supply depots. As the rest of the Marine brigade arrived in France, piecemeal, they were assigned similar duties. As units arrived and were incorporated into the 2nd Division, senior commanders found themselves shuffled between Army and Marine units as others arrived, a practice which would continue throughout the war. The brigade did not reach its full fighting strength, with 280 officers and 9,164 enlisted men, until 10 February 1918, under the command of Brigadier General Charles Doyen.

The 2nd Division was soon detailed to shore up the Allied defenses near Verdun. As British and French units redeployed in reaction to the German 1918 Spring Offensives, the 4th Marine Brigade expanded its sector to fill lines vacated by a French division. Despite the performance of the Marines in driving off German secondary attacks near Verdun, Brigadier General Doyen was relieved by General Pershing, ostensibly for failing health. He was replaced by Pershing's chief of staff, Army Brigadier General James A. Harbord. While Harbord was an excellent officer and the Marines served under him loyally, the perception was that Pershing's animosity toward Marines had gotten the best of him, and that the brigade would eventually be relegated to rear-echelon duties. When the German Operation BLÜCHER of 27 May–4 June appeared to threaten Paris, American 2nd and 3rd Divisions were committed to the Château-Thierry sector of the Marne River.

Harbord and his Marines were assigned to drive the Germans from a hunting preserve about 9 miles west of Château-Thierry, called Belleau Wood. In the early morning of 6 June 1918, advancing across a wheat field, the Marine brigade seized key terrain at Hill 142 and held it against repeated German counterattacks after stopping a German assault largely through well-aimed, well-timed rifle fire. As John W. Thomason recounted:

> The Boche wanted Hill 142; he came, and the rifles broke him. All his batteries were in action, and always his machine-guns scoured the place, but he could not make head against the rifles. Guns he could understand; he knew all about the bombs and auto-rifles and machine-guns and trench mortars, but aimed, sustained rifle-fire, that comes from nowhere in particular and picks off men – it brought the war home to the individual and demoralized him. And trained Americans fight best with rifles.[3]

But the thick woods remained a tangled inferno of mutually supporting German positions, skillfully organized by Major Josef Bischoff, a proficient woodsman with ample experience in expeditionary operations in German colonial Africa. The Marine brigade, joined by the Army's 7th Infantry Regiment and elements of 2nd Engineers, took two weeks of bloody, hand-to-hand fighting to secure the woods on 26 June 1918. The cost was high – 9,800 Marine and Army casualties. The astonished French renamed the woods from Bois de Belleau to Boise de la Brigade des Marines, and the impressed Germans gave the Marines their cherished nickname, "*Teufelshunde*" – Devil Dogs – which has long since been transformed into the grammatically incorrect "*Teufelhunden.*"

Lejeune, meanwhile, chafed under a sense of guilt. He repeatedly sought assignment to France, but was resisted by Barnett, who wanted him in Washington, D.C. Worse, he was not wanted in France by Pershing, who had advised Barnett that General Harbord had the 4th Marine Brigade well in hand, and any U.S. Marine general sent to France would not be assigned to any other frontline unit. Undeterred, Lejeune continued to agitate for transfer and suggested that he would take his chances in France. Barnett finally relented, and Lejeune quickly left for France on the USS *Henderson*, to arrive on 8 June 1918.

True to his word, Pershing refused to assign Lejeune to any forward command, and the Marine found himself relegated to observer duties with the U.S. 35th Division. The 35th Division was adjacent to the 32nd Division, commanded by Major General William G. Haan, and with Lejeune's friend from the U.S. Army War College, Colonel W. D. Connor, as chief of staff. Lejeune was asked by V Corps commander Major General William M. Wright to accompany him on an inspection tour of the 32nd Division. Much to his surprise, Haan asked Lejeune during the visit if he would like to command the 64th Infantry Brigade, to which he readily assented. General Wright agreed with the appointment, as he no doubt felt he would be able to placate his former West Point roommate, General Pershing. Events now moved rapidly for Lejeune. General Harbord was promoted to command the 2nd Division, and Lejeune replaced Harbord on 25 July 1918. He finally achieved his dream of commanding the 4th Marine Brigade – but only for three days. Lejeune had no sooner issued an assumption of command letter when he was called to see Harbord at 2nd Division headquarters on 28 July. He was stunned to learn that Harbord had been reassigned by Pershing to command the AEF's Services of Supply. Pershing approved that Lejeune, as the next senior officer, would temporarily assume command of the 2nd Division. As a brigadier general, the assumption was that Lejeune would only be a short-term placeholder for an Army major general. However, after a flurry of cables to the Navy Department, Lejeune was promoted to major general on 7 August 1918, to be followed in command of the 4th Brigade by his old friend, Wendell C. Neville, who also was promoted to brigadier general the same day.

After Belleau Wood and the 18–22 July Battle of Soissons during the Allied Second Battle of the Marne counteroffensive, the 2nd Division received a respite in the Marbache sector. On 2 September 1918, the division was ordered to the Saint-Mihiel salient sector, southeast of Verdun. That bulge in the lines had been an irritant to the Allies since the beginning of the war. Pershing recognized it as a proving ground for the AEF, and his planners, among them Colonel George C. Marshall, had been working on plans for reducing it since July 1918.

Lejeune's 2nd Division was assigned to I Corps on the southern flank of the salient. It took up positions on the left of the line, adjacent to the 89th Division of IV Corps. With its Army and Marine infantry brigades, field artillery brigade, engineer regiment, and support units, the 2nd Division totaled 979 officers, 27,080 enlisted men, and 6,636 draft animals. Its equipment included 1,078 wagons, 676 motor vehicles, 74 cannon, 260 machine guns, and 48 mortar-type weapons. Lejeune trained his Marines and soldiers hard, and at the commencement of the campaign, he considered the division ready for battle.

The Franco–American plan was a simple one: on the early morning of 12 September 1918, to commence simultaneous attacks on the exposed flanks of the salient from the south and west, close on the heels of a powerful artillery preparatory barrage. The Germans already had plans for an orderly withdrawal from the salient to tighten their lines and occupy more favorable terrain. The only surprise the Germans experienced was the timing and speed of the American offensive. Nonetheless, the operation was a viable proof of concept for the AEF. Not only could the AEF react swiftly as a reinforcing or counterattack force, as the Americans had done at Château-Thierry, but it could also coordinate and conduct large-scale fire and maneuver against an entrenched enemy. On 17 September, Lejeune sent a congratulatory order to the division: "I desire to express to the officers and men my profound appreciation of their brilliant and successful attack in the recent engagement. Our Division maintained the prestige and honor of our country proudly and swept the enemy from the field."[4]

Subsequent to the success at Saint-Mihiel, Lejeune was surprised to find the 2nd Division detached from Liggett's I Corps and assigned to IV Corps, to shore up the new Allied lines while I Corps redeployed to fight in the Meuse–Argonne sector. Lejeune's disappointment, however, lasted only two days, when he received orders detailing the 2nd Division to a move to the Aisne Valley, to the west of the Argonne Forest, to report to General Henri Gouraud, commanding the French Fourth Army. As part of the general offensive along the entire Western Front, the French had been stalled by heavy fortifications atop Blanc Mont Ridge, and Foch had appealed to Pershing for assistance.

At first, Gouraud intended to split up the two American brigades and assign them as replacements for the weary French 61st and 21st Divisions. Lejeune insisted that, if left intact, the American division could take Blanc Mont. When Gouraud stressed the criticality of the key terrain there,

Lejeune simply became more emphatic, a reaction that favorably impressed the old French campaigner. He forwarded Lejeune's intention to Foch and Pétain, who approved the operational approach. On 2 October, Lejeune, Gouraud, and the French XXI Corps commander, General Stanislaus Naulin, developed a plan for the U.S. 2nd Division to attack the German fortified hill on a narrow front, behind a creeping barrage of American and French artillery.

French units would conduct supporting attacks on both flanks. By attacking in column, carefully linked to the creeping artillery barrages, and skillfully passing reinforcing troops through the forward lines, Lejeune was able to sustain a rapid advance, even when his flanks became exposed. After two days of fighting, the Americans seized the strongpoint that was the key link in the German defenses west of the Argonne Forest. By 10 October, the Americans had pushed the Germans off Blanc Mont Ridge and turned over the sector to the French 26th Division. The cost had been high – the casualty count included 209 officers and 4,771 enlisted men – but the resistance at Blanc Mont had been broken and the Germans were forced to withdraw north to the line of the Aisne River.

Despite heavy losses, Lejeune and the 2nd Division had little time to rest. The U.S. First Army chief of staff, Brigadier General Hugh Drum, had allowed the French to retain certain 2nd Division AEF units, intending to replace them eventually with other American units. Lejeune wanted his division to remain intact, and he appealed directly to the First Army commander, Lieutenant General Hunter Liggett, who was his old friend from the Army War College. Liggett supported Lejeune, and by 1 November 1918, the 2nd Division was reassembled, just in time for it to rejoin the AEF in the last great offensive in the Meuse–Argonne. The 2nd Division was now attached to the First Army's V Corps, under the command of Major General Pelot Summerall.

In the early morning of 1 November 1918, the 2nd Division took up its assembly positions preparatory to conducting the V Corps main attack to seize its first objective, the village of Landres-et-Saint-George. Artillery preparation fires began at 0330 hours, and the division moved out two hours later, accompanied by 18 tanks. The Marines by this time had perfected small-unit envelopment tactics, using sustained rifle and machine-gun fire to cover the maneuver of small elements to the flanks of enemy positions. Some German positions were surprised to find themselves attacked from the rear. By the end of the first day, the 4th Marine Brigade had advanced to Bois de la Folie, where they halted for the night, unable to continue the advance. Army brigades from adjacent units were equally aggressive and soon caught up to the 2nd Division's lead elements.

The Germans were not prepared for the suddenness of the 1 November assault. The German Fifth Army commander, General Max von Gallwitz, approved a withdrawal to the rearward Freia defensive position, just north of Buzancy. Unknown to him, the Americans had already breached that trench line, and the German situation was worsening rapidly. Lejeune pressed on during on 2 and 3 November, leading with his Army 3rd Infantry Brigade, consisting of the 9th and 23rd Infantry Regiments. The German forces had begun to retreat across the Meuse River, but their covering forces put up stubborn, effective rear-guard actions, exploiting their knowledge of the terrain. Lejeune ordered the 3rd Infantry Brigade to advance 5 miles to clear Belval and Forêt de Dieulet and ultimately seize Beaumont. Colonel Robert Van Horn, commander of the 9th Infantry, had been in command for only one day, but he had a distinguished career in the Spanish–American War and in the Philippines. He proposed a daring night march using deception to capitalize on the inevitable confusion generated by the German withdrawal. The 3rd Brigade commander, Colonel James Rhea, readily approved the plan, and Lejeune attached the 2nd Battalion, 5th Marines as the brigade reserve, and also a battery of 75mm guns to move with the lead battalion. With the 9th Infantry in the lead, Van Horn's point element was heavily weighted with German-speaking Americans to confuse the German defenders. The steady rain and obscure light aided the deception measures, which resulted in large numbers of Germans captured and disarmed. By midnight, Van Horn had infiltrated 4 and a half miles behind the forward German positions. On the following day, the U.S. 89th Division advanced west of the 2nd Division. In the north, meanwhile, British and French forces had successfully driven the Germans out of their trenches and back toward Germany, just as Supreme

Map 3: The American Saint-Mihiel Offensive:
12–19 September 1918

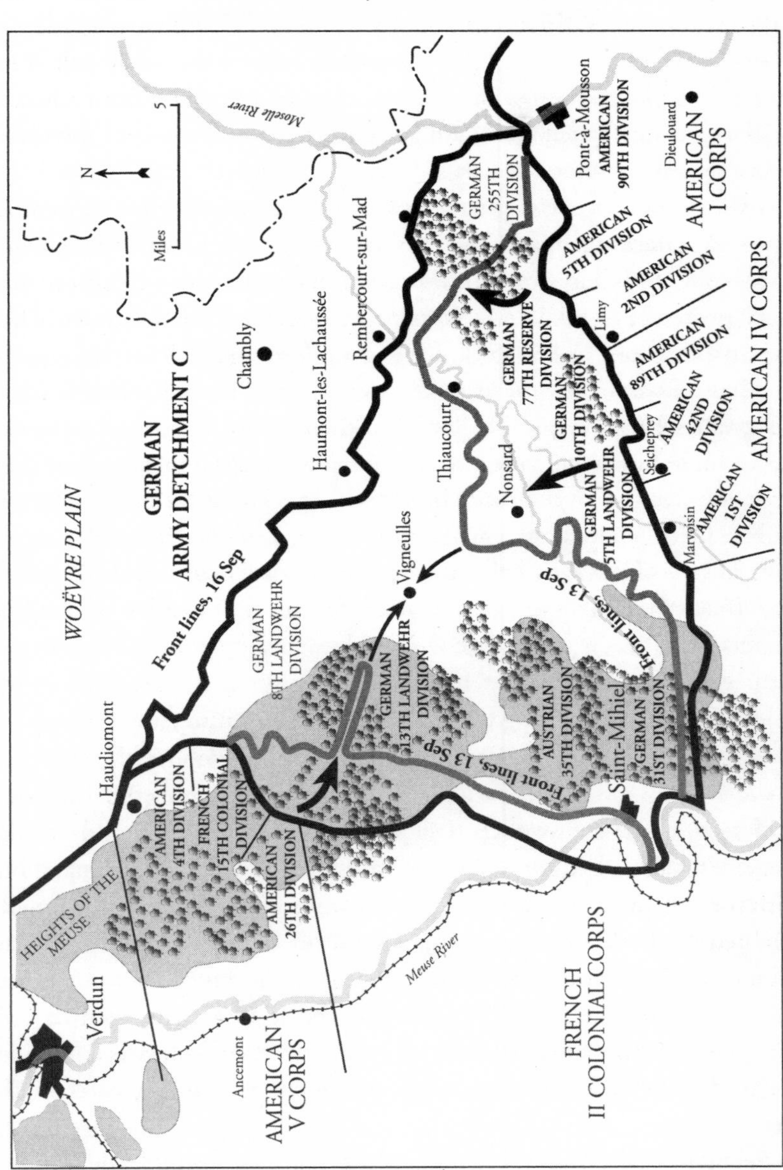

Allied Commander Marshal Ferdinand Foch had planned. American artillery exploding around his headquarters and massive air attacks on his withdrawing forces convinced Gallwitz of the inevitability of defeat. On 4 November, the German high command ordered the Fifth and Third Armies to withdraw across the Meuse.

The Germans called for an armistice to go into effect on 11 November 1918. The Allied senior leaders – Pershing included – seemed convinced that the Germans were capable of a counterattack, and resolved to continue attacking until the last moment. V Corps commander Summerall, smarting over a misdirected and vainglorious 7 November attack on Sedan by his 1st Division under Brigadier General Frank Parker (see Introduction, pp. 50–53), decided to drive the 2nd Division across the Meuse River before the armistice could take effect. The 89th Division was given similar orders. The lack of bridging and extremely congested supply lines, however, made any attempt at crossing problematic, and the effort was delayed several times before V Corps could make the attempt.

The Germans had prepared a stiff resistance, planning to use the Meuse as an obstacle to delay the advancing American forces and cover the retreat of the main German formations. The 2nd and 89th Divisions' soldiers and Marines had been badly battered by the fighting in the Meuse–Argonne sector, but had no intimation that an armistice was pending, Thus, they fought on dutifully, attempting the crossing on 10 November. The main assault, just south of Mouzon on the east bank of the Meuse, failed. The withering heavy German machine-gun and artillery fire, and the swollen river with its exceptionally muddy banks, effectively made any unprotected attempt at bridging the river impossible. The crossings farther south, originally conceived as supporting attacks, then became the main effort of the 2nd Division. Even there, the crossing points were well covered by German fires, and the engineers and infantry had an extremely difficult time effecting the seizure of the far bank. By the morning of 11 November, the day the Armistice took effect, both the 2nd and 89th Divisions had a firm foothold on the east bank of the Meuse River.

Following the Armistice, the tired and battle-worn 2nd Division was assigned to occupation duties on the Rhine. It began a long, arduous, cold and wet march on 17 November, through Belgium and Luxembourg, crossing into Germany on 25 November and reaching the Rhine on 10 December 1918. Sometime during the long, weary march General Pershing had occasion to drive past the 2nd Division as its soldiers trudged along in the freezing rain. Pershing apparently stormed into III Corps in a rage, opining that Lejeune's command was ragged, slovenly, and ill-led.

Lejeune's old Army War College classmates were quick to apprise him of Pershing's hostility. Lejeune was incensed, as his requests for a period of rest and refitting before being ordered to march into Germany had been rejected. He smarted under the affront in silence, until the 2nd Division reached its assigned sector east of Luxembourg. He then turned his attention to discipline and morale among his men, and he requested a general officer-level inspection of the division. Major General André Brewster, the AEF inspector general, arrived personally and visited every unit. Brewster reported back to Pershing that the 2nd Division was in superb shape. Lejeune finally received orders to move his division on 15 July 1919 to Brest by rail, preparatory to embarking for home.

John Archer Lejeune became the thirteenth commandant of the Marine Corps, serving from 30 June 1920 to 5 March 1929. His memoirs are silent on those eight-and-a-half years, for he apparently considered his service with the American Expeditionary Forces and the 2nd Division the highlight of his professional life. But, clearly, Lejeune's tenure as commandant was greatly influenced by his World War I service.

Along with Major General Charles P. Summerall, who like Lejeune became a service chief, Lejeune is credited with being among the best of the division commanders in the AEF. However, the two men had very contrasting leadership styles. Summerall had a reputation for aggressive action in the extreme and is often described as a vainglorious driver rather than a leader. Lejeune, in contrast, was a humble leader with great respect for the Marines and soldiers he led. His leadership style was enlightened for his time, and he had genuine compassion for the men who might be killed or maimed as a result of his orders. His personally written paragraphs from the *Marine Corps Manual* (1921 edition) reflect his dissatisfaction with the demanding, belittling leadership style of Pershing and Summerall and remain quoted as fundamental Marine Corps leadership guidance today:

> Comradeship and brotherhood. – The World War wrought a great change in the relations between officers and enlisted men in the military services. A spirit of comradeship and brotherhood in arms came into being in the training camps and on the battlefields. This spirit is too fine a thing to be allowed to die. It must be fostered and kept alive and made the moving force in all Marine Corps organizations.
>
> Teacher and scholar. – The relation between officers and enlisted men should in no sense be that of superior and inferior nor that of master and servant, but rather that of teacher and scholar. In fact, it should partake of the nature of the relation between father and son, to the extent that officers, especially commanding officers, are responsible for the physical, mental, and moral welfare, as well as the discipline and military training of the young men under their command who are serving the nation in the Marine Corps.[5]

Lejeune's men responded to his authentic leadership style not only with loyalty and respect, but also with love. Lejeune's leadership style has become enshrined as the standard for which all Marine Corps officers should aspire.

The Department of the Navy had insisted on sending a Marine brigade to serve with the AEF at a time when the future role of the Marine Corps was in doubt and widely debated. It was clear from the onset that General Pershing did not want the Marines. Lejeune came away from World War I convinced that service with U.S. Army units was not the best option for the Marine Corps. The animosities were too great, the approaches to command too different, to be synchronized easily. As commandant, Lejeune was tireless in his advocacy of a role for the Marine Corps closely tied to the U.S. Navy, centered on seizure and security of advanced naval bases. This role required the Marine Corps not only to expand in size, but also to retain mastery of military art and tactical skills.

Moreover, to reinforce its uniqueness from the U.S. Army, the Marine Corps needed to perfect a new form of warfare – amphibious operations launched in large formations from the sea. In reference to his operational approaches as 2nd Division commander, Lejeune was convinced that such operations needed to be combined arms in nature, and he pursued the incorporation of armor, artillery, aviation, communicators, and engineers along with Marine light infantry. These units would require specialized equipment, landing craft, and tactics. Lejeune became his own publicist for these pioneering innovations, lobbying Congress, the American public, disapproving U.S. Navy officers, and recalcitrant officers among his own service. His writings in the *Marine Corps Gazette*, the magazine of the Marine Corps Association, describe his vision of the amphibious and expeditionary nature of the future Marine Corps.

It is no accident that Pershing's lone Marine division commander's name adorns the largest amphibious training base on the east coast, Camp Lejeune, North Carolina. And it is no small honor that, every 10 November on the anniversary of the founding of the Marine Corps, John A. Lejeune's 1921 birthday address to his Marine Corps is read, word for word, at every Marine Corps birthday ceremony held by Marines, in units as small as an embassy security detachment or as large as the I Marine Expeditionary Force:

> From the battle of Trenton to the Argonne, Marines have won foremost honors in war, and in the long eras of tranquility at home, generation after generation of Marines have grown gray in war in both hemispheres and in every corner of the seven seas that our country and its citizens might enjoy peace and security.
>
> In every battle and skirmish since the birth of our Corps, Marines have acquitted themselves with the greatest distinction, winning new honors on every occasion until the term Marine has come to signify everything that is highest in military efficiency and soldierly virtue.
>
> … So long as that spirit continues to flourish Marines will be found equal to every emergency in the future as they have been in the past, and the men of our nation will regard us as worthy successors to the long line of illustrious men who have served as "Soldiers of the Sea" since the founding of the Corps.[6]

CHAPTER 7

BRIGADIER GENERAL WENDELL C. NEVILLE

Carl O. Schuster

On 26 March 1930, a stroke took down Major General Wendell C. "Buck" Neville, the fourteenth commandant of the U.S. Marine Corps, partially paralyzing his right side. The Washington Naval Hospital's electrocardiogram revealed significant myocardial damage. The doctors also discovered that his blood pressure had reached 210/130. A courageous fighter by nature, the Medal of Honor recipient faced his condition with determination and humor. He moved to his daughter's home in Edgewater Beach, Maryland, to convalesce. It was there that he suffered the second stroke that killed him on 8 July 1930. The stress of defending the Marine Corps from budget cuts and threats of dissolution had taken the life of a man who had survived over 20 combat engagements against his country's enemies. He had commanded the Marines' first Mobile Advanced Base Battalion, precursor to today's Battalion Landing Teams, leading it into combat at Veracruz in 1914. But he is best known for commanding the legendary 4th Brigade of Marines in France. Neville was an advocate of combined arms over independent infantry assault.

His division commander in France, and predecessor as commandant, Major General John A. Lejeune, attributed much of the 2nd Division's brilliant successes to Neville's courage and leadership.[1] Ironically, nothing in General Neville's early life suggested he would become one of General Pershing's top brigade commanders in the American Expeditionary Forces (AEF).

Wendell Cushing Neville was born in Portsmouth, Virginia, on 12 May 1870 to a lower-middle-class family. His father, William Henry Neville, was a carpenter who died of dysentery in 1883, leaving Wendell's mother, Mary Elizabeth Cushing, to raise six sons and one daughter with the assistance of her oldest sons, especially George, who funded Wendell's education at the Norfolk Academy. Completing high school at a time when the South's adult illiteracy rate hovered at 70 percent placed Wendell far above his contemporaries. With few job prospects available for those lacking connections, Wendell, like many poor Southerners, chose to enter the military. His high school diploma gave him a chance at a military service academy appointment, in his case from Virginia's 2nd Congressional District. At the time, academy acceptance was conditional upon the appointee convincing the academy's examiners that he had the mental and physical capacity to face the rigors of academy life. He reported to the U.S. Naval Academy on 10 September 1886 and made it past the examiners despite some academic shortcomings. Only 34 of the 81 midshipmen who entered with him that day made it to graduation. He claimed later in life he gained the Naval Academy appointment because no one else wanted it.

Neville entered the Naval Academy at a critical period in U.S. Marine Corps history. Stung by criticism of the Marines' performance during the Civil War (Fort Fisher aside) and postwar ill-discipline, the Marine Corps' eighth commandant, Colonel Charles G. McCawley, had initiated a series of reforms to tighten discipline and improve morale, focusing first on leadership. He also recognized that the late 19th century was a time of rapid technological change in both naval and land warfare tactics and weapons, placing a premium on an officer's ability to adapt to the changing warfare environment. McCawley responded by raising educational standards, commissioning only Naval Academy graduates during his

15-year tenure as commandant. McCawley's efforts defeated calls to remove Marines from naval ships.

Neville was popular at the Naval Academy and was given the nickname "Kid." The curriculum focused on engineering, navigation, and science, but graduation did not guarantee commissioning. More an athlete than a scholar, he graduated 24th in his class and reported to the 28-year-old steam-powered sloop-of-war USS *Kearsarge* of Civil War fame for a year at sea, spent primarily in the Caribbean. That tour was followed by a year aboard the newly commissioned protected cruiser USS *Newark* (C-1), operating out of Norfolk, Virginia, as part of the Atlantic Squadron. Then, like his classmates, he returned to the academy for the professional qualification exams required for commissioning.

He didn't do well and was given the choice of either discharge from the Navy or a commission in the Marine Corps. He chose the latter, being commissioned as a second lieutenant on 8 July 1892 and joining the second group of Marine officers to attend the Marine Corps School of Application, established in 1891 by the ninth commandant, Brigadier General Charles Heywood. General Heywood established the school to give Marine officers and non-commissioned officers the leadership skills to instill *esprit de corps* in their Marines, as well as develop and test their tactical acumen under demanding conditions. The School of Application later evolved into today's Marine Corps Officers' Basic School.

As at the academy, Lieutenant Neville's performance was not exceptional. He graduated in the middle of his class on 24 April 1893, but he demonstrated a talent for training. The school retained him to instruct non-commissioned officers. Promoted to first lieutenant on 4 February 1894, he deployed that summer for a three-year sea tour as commander of a ship's Marine detachment, spending a year each in that role aboard the protected cruisers USS *Cincinnati* (C-7), and USS *Raleigh* (C-8); and the recently commissioned second-class battleship USS *Texas*. His sea tour ended on 2 June 1897 with his detachment for duty as a guard officer at the Washington, D.C. Marine barracks. It was there that he met Francis Adelphia Howell, the daughter of the navy yard commander, Rear Admiral John Adams Howell. Neville and Francis were married on 4 January 1898. Three months later, the United States declared war on Spain and Neville was one of the Marines who joined Lieutenant Colonel Robert Huntington's expeditionary battalion in New York which would establish a camp at Guantanamo Bay, Cuba, in May 1898 that remains a U.S. naval base to this day.

With his camp under constant threat and his water supplies uncertain, Huntington ordered future Marine Corps commandant, then-Captain George S. Elliot, to destroy the Spanish water point at Cuzco Well. Neville commanded the detachment that seized a key road junction in the valley south of the camp and then joined Elliott's assault. It was Neville's first combat action, earning him a "mention in dispatches" (roughly the equivalent to today's Silver Star) and a brevet promotion to captain. Neville later received the Marine Corps Brevet Medal. Awarded only 23 times, the now obsolete Brevet Medal was rated above the Navy Cross and just below the Medal of Honor. Neville demonstrated his penchant for courage and rapid decision-making under fire.

Neville returned to the United States in September 1898 to take charge of the Marine Corps Recruiting Office in New York, celebrating promotion to captain on 3 March 1889 and the birth of his daughter and only child on 6 June. One year later, he joined Major Littleton W. T. Waller's expeditionary battalion in the Philippines. From there he accompanied Waller's advanced detachment ordered to China to protect American lives and interests threatened by the Boxer Rebellion. The detachment landed at Taku on 19 July 1900, four days before China's Imperial government ordered its forces to join the "Society of Harmonious Fists" in driving the foreigners out of China. The international legations in Peking (today's Beijing) were under siege. Under U.S. Army Major General Adna Chaffee, Waller's battalion participated in the Allied drive to relieve the foreign legations in Peking. Neville led his company in assaults on Tianjin, Beicang, and Huangcun as well as in the fighting in and around Peking. His bravery was mentioned in Major Waller's dispatches.

After China, Neville served two years in the Philippines, including time as the military governor of Basilan Province from June to September 1902. Although his forces saw little combat, he adopted the civic action practices established by previous Marine contingents, which improved relations with the Philippine population and facilitated the end of insurgency in Basilan. He returned to New York in 1903. During a stint of temporary duty at Marine Corps headquarters, he applied for an adjutant and inspector's position in the Marine Corps inspector general's office, but he was not accepted. He was, however, assigned as an umpire at the 1904 Naval War College war games. Promoted to major on 1 June 1904, he assumed command of the small Marine barracks at Narragansett Bay, Rhode Island.

He returned to the fleet in August 1905, serving one-year tours each as the Marine contingent commander on the pre-dreadnought battleships USS *Maine* (BB-10) and USS *Connecticut* (BB-18). It was in that capacity that he led the battalion of Marines and sailors formed from ships of the Atlantic Fleet that landed at Havana, Cuba, on 1 October 1906 to protect American lives and property during that city's civil unrest. He returned home in 1907 to take command of the Marine barracks in Washington, D.C. In June 1909, he was one of four Marines who testified before Congress in opposition to President Theodore Roosevelt's executive order that removed all Marines from U.S. Navy ships. They argued that the order would harm Marine and Navy combat readiness, have a negative impact on their knowledge of all aspects of naval warfare, and reduce the Navy's ability to respond rapidly to events ashore that might threaten U.S. interests. Congress agreed, convincing the President to rescind the order.

Neville left Washington in November 1909 to command the Marine battalion sent to Panama and then Nicaragua. Departing Nicaragua on 30 April 1910, he spent the next four years commanding successive Marine Corps barracks, first establishing the one at Pearl Harbor, and then commanding the one at Charleston, South Carolina. Promoted to lieutenant colonel on 25 February 1914, he took command of the 1st Provisional Battalion, 2nd Marine Mobile Advanced Base Regiment. The battalion was embarked aboard the naval transport USS *Prairie*. The regiment, commanded by Colonel John A. Lejeune, was headquartered in Washington, D.C. Neville's battalion was structured as a combined-arms unit to conduct amphibious operations under the newly established Advanced Base Concept, making it the forerunner of today's Marine Expeditionary Units (MEUs). The battalion deployed to Veracruz, Mexico in response to General Victoriano Huerta's overthrow of the Porfirio Diaz government and the resulting tensions with President Wilson's administration.

On 21 April 1914, believing a major arms shipment was en route to Veracruz aboard the German-flagged steamer *Ypironga*, President Wilson ordered Navy Secretary Josephus Daniels to order the seizure of the Vera Cruz customs house and port. Admiral Frank Friday Fletcher received the order six hours later. Lieutenant Colonel Neville commanded the provisional Marine regiment that consisted of his battalion and the Marine contingents from the battleships USS *Florida* (BB-30) and USS *Utah* (BB-31). A battalion of sailors from those same battleships rounded out the Naval brigade landing force. Neville landed shortly before 1130 hours, seizing Pier 4 and the adjacent buildings. The landing itself met no resistance and Neville moved quickly to occupy the rail terminal and stockyard, as well as the telegraph station, and to secure the American Consulate. The naval battalion was the first to come under fire as they neared the customs house. Neville took the offensive, advancing toward the city center until ordered to halt by Captain William Rush, the Naval brigade commander. Neville was reinforced the next day by a Marine battalion drawn from the contingents aboard the four battleships that arrived on 22 April. Placing that battalion in reserve, Neville advanced to the city center against growing resistance. Despite the Mexican garrison's withdrawal, the fighting intensified, becoming house-to-house as local residents rallied to their city's defense. Colonel Lejeune's arrival that day brought a second Marine regiment, but the fighting ended before it completed disembarkation. Neville earned the Medal of Honor for his actions that day. He was one of only three Marines officers to have earned both the Medal of Honor and the Brevet Medal. Ironically, he also received a negative fitness report from the USS *Prairie*'s commander for his aggressive but accurate criticism of the poor state of that ship's berthing and sanitation spaces.[2]

Neville's next posting came in December 1915, as commander of the Marine contingent at America's Beijing Legation. Promoted to colonel on 29 August 1916, his reputation made him a natural choice to command the 5th Marine Regiment deploying to France. Leaving Beijing in October

1917, Neville assumed command on 1 January 1918. He found regimental command somewhat frustrating since the command and control practices of the era required him to remain at headquarters to coordinate troop movements. He used his deputy, Lieutenant Colonel Morgan Feland, as his forward liaison officer with his subordinate units. Because the commander of the 4th Marine Brigade, U.S. Army Brigadier General James Harbord, tended to bypass his regimental commanders and order the battalions directly, Feland's overly optimistic reports shaped the brigade's actions during the key battles of Belleau Wood and later Soissons. Neville's contribution consisted primarily of moving ammunition and other supplies forward and casualties to the rear. He was more directly involved in the regiment's seizure of Hill 142 on 5 June 1918, outdistancing the French division on his flank. The regiment held against determined counterattacks by larger German forces, suffering 55 percent casualties in the process.

When Harbord was promoted to command the 2nd Division, Brigadier General John A. Lejeune assumed command of the 4th Marine Brigade. When Harbord was reassigned as the commander of the AEF's Services of Supply, Lejeune moved up to command the 2nd Division on 25 July 1918. Neville replaced Lejeune as the 4th Brigade commander the same day. The division consisted of the 4th Marine Brigade and the U.S. Army's 3rd Infantry Brigade.

During the fighting in the Champagne sector during the Allied general counteroffensive that started on 18 July 1918, Neville exhibited ingenuity in deploying his battalions, especially in situations where higher headquarters ordered multiple units along the same transport routes. Neville moved his forces in echelons to reduce traffic density, employing parallel routes and cover whenever possible.[3] Instead of using the overcrowded main roads assigned to other divisions, Neville and his Army counterpart moved their troops along minor roads and paths paralleling the primary roads.[4] His planning also facilitated the brigade's logistics support, enabling the Marines to receive a higher level of food and ammunition supplies than other AEF units involved. During the after-action review of the Battle of Saint-Mihiel he stated that he wanted his Marines to "rely more on auxiliary arms in future battles"[5] – that is, artillery and other supporting arms. In emphasizing firepower and maneuver, his views contrasted sharply with Pershing's rifle and bayonet approach to battle.

Neville commanded the 4th Marine Brigade during the 2nd Division's capture of the heavily defended German positions on Blanc Mont Ridge on 3 October 1918. The attack was arguably the most ingenious and skillfully conducted American divisional attack of World War I. The 2nd Division was deployed in the sector of the French Fourth Army, some 20 miles west of the main sector of the U.S. First Army. The American main force was heavily engaged in the Meuse–Argonne sector. Attacking on the American's left flank, the French Fourth Army under General Henri Gouraud had the mission of clearing the German positions from the relatively open country on the west side of the Argonne Forest and screening the U.S. First Army's flank. After four days of fierce fighting, Gouraud's troops by 30 September were stalled about 2 miles south of Blanc Mont Ridge. Gouraud was forced to ask Pershing for the temporary loan of fresh American forces to help take the ridge. Understanding the importance of keeping the French closed up on his own left flank, Pershing reluctantly agreed to detail his 2nd Division to Gouraud.

Rather than the attempt to achieve instant "open warfare" that was the bedrock of Pershing's AEF tactical doctrine, Lejeune and his brigade commanders, Neville and U.S. Brigadier General Hanson E. Ely, planned instead a methodical, set-piece attack, with the supporting artillery moving forward with each phase to provide the infantry with a constant artillery umbrella. The scheme of maneuver called for the two brigades to start from their lines of departure with a thousand-meter gap between them, and then make converging attacks toward the top of the ridge that would pinch out the triangle of open space between their inner flanks. It was a bold but risky maneuver by the standards of World War I.

The attack worked brilliantly, although the battle was hard-fought and both the Marines and the Army infantry suffered heavy casualties in taking their objectives. The French were ecstatic in their praise of the 2nd Division. Neville praised "the excellency of the rolling barrage and the accuracy of the special fire."[6] Nonetheless, the 2nd Division was later subjected to official criticism by the AEF's inspector general, Major

General Andre W. Brewster, for failure to follow approved American tactical doctrine – regardless of the actual battlefield success.[7] The 2nd Division was refitted and reverted back to Pershing late in October where it participated in the breakout in the Meuse–Argonne. The 2nd Division's success was the result of Lejeune and his brigade commanders acting independently and occasionally in contravention of official orders. On 1 November 1918, the AEF's First Army attacked across the Meuse Valley in an attack that was so well coordinated that it finally broke the German grip on the region. The 2nd Division was part of V Corps' push, with the Marine and Army brigades superbly leapfrogging past each other every two–three days. Neville eagerly supported the Army 3rd Brigade's stunning march through the German lines in early November, and, with that, ensured the rout of the enemy until the end of the war.

In the war's final offensive, the 2nd and 89th Divisions were ordered to attack across the Meuse near Létanne and Mouzon.[8] The crossing was initially repulsed near Mouzon. However, the Marines and soldiers of the 2nd Division, backed up with the 89th's highly contested crossing nearby, facilitated a successful crossing at Létanne. In the waning hours of the war, the 2nd Division slugged it out to cross the Meuse River and the Meuse Canal, and then up the high ground east of the river. The German defenders tenaciously fought the Americans to a crawl. Runners sent forward to alert the Americans that the Armistice was going into effect at 1100 hours were cut down trying to cross the Meuse River. However, when the Armistice went into effect, the Germans shifted their fires after 1100 hours to spraying bullets in front of the Americans to stop them, rather than killing them. This enabled the runners to finally reach the Marines to tell them to stop. Thus, fighting till the end, the war came to a close.

In recognition of Neville's service in France, he received the Army and Navy Distinguished Service Medals; the Legion of Honor Grand Cross; and three Croix de Guerre. The Secretary of the Navy accepted General Lejeune's recommendation for Neville's promotion to major general, promoting him on 26 March 1920 and appointing him assistant to Marine Corps Commandant Major General George Barnett. In 1923 Neville assumed command of the Marine Corps' Pacific Department in

San Francisco, and in 1927 he returned to Washington as deputy commandant under Lejeune. When Lejeune retired in 1929, Neville succeeded him as commandant. Neville intended to continue Lejeune's vision and policies for the Marine Corps. Unfortunately, the Great Depression intervened, cutting funds without reducing Marine Corps commitments. Neville fought Congress and the Secretary of the Navy to improve his Marine facilities, housing, and other quality of life issues. His advocacy of these issues irritated Navy Secretary Charles F. Adams and many members of Congress.

Neville tried to end the Marine presence in Haiti, but neither Congress nor the State Department was willing to determine a withdrawal date. He was able to reduce the force size there but the commitment remained. Moreover, the President simply dispatched the released battalion to Nicaragua, gaining Neville no respite from his manpower crunch. He convinced the President to remove two brigades from China, but the Navy Secretary reduced those units to cadre status and discharged most of their personnel. Lejeune had established Marine Corps field artillery, but most were being employed as infantry. Neville's Marines were stretched thin, overworked and under-supported.

Its officer corps was getting old as well. Like Lejeune, Neville went before the House and Naval Affairs Committee, urging promotion reforms lest he have 50-year-old lieutenants commanding companies. The House passed the legislation but it stalled in the Senate. The same results followed his efforts to increase the Marine Corps' budget and personnel strength. Navy Secretary Charles Adams provided only lukewarm support. Despite Neville's best efforts, his officer corps was becoming older with only slightly more than half his field grade officers fit for deployed service, and their continued presence in the ranks prevented him from promoting his best company-grade officers.

The long hours and constant in-fighting inflicted a toll on Neville's health. Suffering chronic hypertension, he had ignored doctors' advice to get his blood pressure down, triggering the stroke that felled him on 30 March 1930. Although his short tenure as commandant limited General Neville's impact on the Marine Corps, his leadership and defense of the Corps budget and support for key future leaders sustained General

Lejeune's initiatives into the 1930s and ensured its leadership was positioned for success in World War II. Neville was not the visionary of his predecessor, but his involvement in virtually every pioneering Marine Corps action of the late 19th and early 20th century gave him an appreciation for what was required to succeed in the next world war. In that regard, he should be viewed as the man who transformed Lejeune's vision on the battlefield and died trying to sustain it in peace. His planning and command of the Marine Advance Force Regiment in Veracruz demonstrated the wisdom behind the Marine Advanced Force concept and unit structure. In that regard, perhaps Neville should best be remembered as the first commander of a Marine Battalion Landing Team and the operational father of what became the Marine landing teams and expeditionary forces of the modern era.

PART THREE

THE SENIOR STAFF OFFICERS

CHAPTER 8

MAJOR GENERAL JAMES G. HARBORD

David T. Ząbecki

James Guthrie Harbord was General John J. Pershing's first chief of staff in the American Expeditionary Forces (AEF), from May 1917 to May 1918. During June and July 1918, he served briefly as a combat commander, first in command of the 2nd Division's 4th Marine Brigade, and then as commanding general of the 2nd Division itself. From late July 1918 until the end of the war he commanded the AEF's Services of Supply. He was a forceful and effective organizer, administrator, problem solver, and senior manager, upon whom Pershing placed great reliance. Harbord's brief period as a combat commander, however, is a different story. Although in his memoirs Pershing called Harbord a "brilliant leader,"[1] his record as a battlefield commander does not hold up well to close examination.

Like Pershing, Harbord came from the American heartland. Harbord was born in Bloomington, Illinois, on 21 March 1866. He grew up in Manhattan, Kansas and graduated from Kansas State Agricultural College in 1886. He worked as an instructor at the college for two years, but he found teaching unrewarding. Harbord enlisted in the U.S. Army in 1889 and rose rapidly to the rank of quartermaster sergeant. On 31 July 1891 he received a direct commission to second lieutenant in the 5th Cavalry. In 1895 he completed the Cavalry and Infantry School at Fort Leavenworth, Kansas, as the distinguished honor graduate. During the Spanish–American War Harbord was assigned to the 2nd U.S. Volunteer Cavalry in May 1898 as a major of volunteers. His unit was not sent to Cuba, and was disbanded after only five months. Harbord reverted to the Regular Army rank of first lieutenant, and was assigned to the 10th Cavalry, which was then in Cuba on occupation duty. The 10th Cavalry was one of the "Buffalo Soldier" regiments, composed of African-American troopers and white officers. That was where he had his first contact with Pershing, who was a captain in the 10th Cavalry. While in Cuba, Harbord served as quartermaster and commissary officer of the 10th Cavalry, and later as adjutant general of the Department of Santiago and Puerto Principe.

In January 1899 Harbord married Emma Overshine, the daughter of Brigadier General Samuel Overshine. In February 1901, he was promoted to captain and assigned to the 11th Cavalry. In 1902 Harbord was transferred at his own request to the Philippines, where he served for the next 12 years. During the early part of his tour he had frequent contact with Pershing. From 1903 to 1909, and again from 1910 to 1913, Harbord was the assistant chief of the Philippine Constabulary. Returning to the United States in 1914, he assumed command of a cavalry squadron guarding the U.S.–Mexico border at Calexico, California. In 1916 Harbord's unit participated in the Mexico Punitive Expedition, under the command of Brigadier General Pershing.

Harbord was a student as a major at the U.S. Army War College in May 1917 when President Woodrow Wilson selected Pershing as commanding general of the AEF. On 15 May Harbord was ordered to report to Pershing at the War Department. Unaware that Pershing had been selected for overseas command, Harbord was taken by surprise when the general told him that he wanted him as the AEF's chief of staff. During the course of the ensuing discussion, Harbord admitted that he spoke almost no French, although he was proficient in Spanish. Since Pershing's

French was only marginal, he concluded that he would have to think about the chief of staff assignment, although he definitely wanted Harbord to come with him to France as part of his staff. Several days later Pershing decided on Harbord, despite his lack of French proficiency.

Harbord never returned to the War College to complete the course of instruction. On the same day of their first meeting, Pershing and Harbord set up an office in Room 223 of the War Department to assemble a staff. Initially, the two had only the vaguest notions about how to establish a headquarters and general staff for the AEF. The U.S. Army itself had only established a general staff in 1903 and by 1917 there were only about 200 trained General Staff officers. Although some had experience serving in Washington, none had experience at the divisional, corps, or field army levels of command and staff. Except for a very brief period during the Spanish–American War, the U.S. Army had not even had those echelons of command since the end of the Civil War. Nonetheless, the year-long Army Staff School at Fort Leavenworth, Kansas, was training a few handfuls of staff officers each year. Those younger majors and lieutenant colonels who had graduated from Leavenworth would become many of the chiefs of staff for the AEF's divisions and corps; but there were not enough of them. The lack of trained staffs was one of the reasons that AEF divisions were almost twice the size of the British and French divisions. The U.S. Army simply could not have staffed twice as many divisions.

In late May 1917, Pershing and his AEF advanced party staff sailed for Europe on the RMS *Baltic.* They spent the crossing planning the organization and deployment of the main force. With no experience upon which to base the organization of a general staff, Harbord and Pershing faced the daunting task of pulling together staff officers and NCOs who had almost no training and even less practical experience. Back in Washington, the Army General Staff was still going through its own early growth pains, and the deeply entrenched chiefs of the traditional War Department bureaus were not subordinate to it. Harbord was determined to avoid such a recipe for bureaucratic gridlock. Initially, then, the AEF staff was organized into three functional areas – operations, administration, and intelligence – each headed by a "chief of section." But Pershing and

Harbord seriously underestimated the number of officers and supporting troops it would take to run the General Headquarters of an organization that started out the size of a division, but would quickly expand to become the first army group in the history of the U.S. Army. When Pershing arrived in England, the British were surprised by the small staff that accompanied him. The American complement on the *Baltic* totaled only 190, including enlisted men and civilian clerks and interpreters – barely suitable for a combat brigade. As Brigadier General Dennis Nolan, Pershing's highly capable intelligence chief, later recalled, the British concluded that the Americans had very little understanding of the task they were facing.

In the summer of 1917, the fledgling AEF established its operational headquarters at Chaumont, France. Despite intense pressure from the British and the French to amalgamate small American units, and even individual soldiers, into their respective armies, Pershing was determined to field a separate-standing American Army that would have its own commanders and its own sector of the battlefield. Pershing also thought that the war had been fought wrongly. Completely rejecting the experiences of the previous three years, he believed that the stalemate of trench warfare could only be overcome by a return to mobile, "open warfare," based on "self-reliant infantry." Pershing put emphasis on traditional American rifle marksmanship and the bayonet and underestimated modern weapons like machine guns, barbed wire, flamethrowers, tanks, aircraft, and artillery. The Allies knew that Pershing was wrong, having learned the opposite lessons the hard way, but they could not convince him otherwise. As a fellow cavalry officer, Harbord was a staunch disciple of Pershing's tactical dogma. Harbord made sure that all officers serving at GHQ were true believers in the "Pershing Orthodoxy," and he was critical of officers like General Charles P. Summerall who argued for more artillery support for the AEF.

Despite the tactical/operational blinders he wore, Harbord took a "power down" approach to running the staff, one that was more similar to the German Army than to the British and French armies of the period. As he wrote after the war, he did not expect anyone working under him on the AEF GHQ staff to buck-up to any superior an issue that he was competent to decide at his own level. Powers not specifically reserved by higher authority would be vested in the subordinates. There were two key reasons behind Harbord's approach. As any good chief of staff, he protected his commander's time. Pershing had a strong tendency to micromanage and get bogged down in minor details. The second reason was that Harbord jealously guarded his relationship with Pershing, and he had no intention of allowing majors and lieutenant colonels direct access to the commander-in-chief.

The shortage of trained staff officers was a problem that continually handicapped the AEF. In August 1917 Pershing authorized the establishment of an American General Staff College at Langres, France. Starting that October, the "crash course" lasted only three months. The British and French were not supportive and argued that all AEF General Staff officers should be sent to them for training in the staff procedures for combined arms warfare. That was exactly what Pershing did not want. He did not want his AEF's staff officers to be "contaminated" with what he believed to be the Allies' failed concepts of trench warfare. When the French realized that the Americans would not be dissuaded from establishing their own staff school, they assumed that they would provide both the director and the majority of the instructors for the college. Harbord instead selected Brigadier General James McAndrew as the commandant, and he decided that the Americans only needed a small handful of French advisors and instructors.

The British and French, meanwhile, pressed Pershing hard on the issue of amalgamation, wanting to use the Americans as a replacement pool for their own depleted divisions. Pershing continued to insist on developing, fielding, and commanding a separate American army. But the amalgamation issue was tightly linked to the shipping problem. America did not have anywhere near the sealift capacity to move large forces across the Atlantic, and Britain's already stressed merchant fleet was coming under increasing pressure from the renewed German U-boat campaign. Amalgamation of combat units would reduce the requirement for support forces, which made up 45 percent of the AEF. Pershing and Harbord continued to wrestle with the shipping problem throughout the war.

On 24 April 1918, Pershing and Harbord met with British Secretary of State for War Lord Alfred Milner, and General Sir Henry Wilson, the

Chief of the Imperial General Staff. In what became known as the London Agreement, British and American shipping would, during May, transport six divisions of U.S. combat troops, without their heavy equipment or artillery. Those divisions would be attached temporarily to the British Expeditionary Force for training. Pershing was bending slightly on the amalgamation question, in exchange for increased sealift. Rather than entire divisions, the British really wanted battalions or even companies to level-out the depleted BEF divisions. Returning to France, Pershing met with General Ferdinand Foch and informed him about the London Agreement, to which the French had not been a party. The Allied commander-in-chief was not at all pleased, which only increased tension between the two.

Harbord had a keen eye for identifying and developing talented subordinates. One of them was Captain Hugh Drum, who was a member of the advanced party on the *Baltic*. Initially assigned to the Operations Section under Brigadier General Fox Conner, Drum handled a number of complex tasks, including participating in the study group to formulate AEF strategy on the Western Front, and working with the French on transportation problems. When the U.S. First Army became operational, Drum on Harbord's recommendation was selected as its chief of staff and promoted to brigadier general. Harbord also intervened in the career of Major William J. "Wild Bill" Donovan. As the AEF's divisions and corps established their own training schools in France, U.S. II Corps in February 1918 assigned Donovan to be an instructor in their schools. Donovan, who at the time commanded a battalion in the 42nd Division's 165th Infantry Regiment, tried to decline the transfer, wanting to remain with his battalion. Colonel Douglas MacArthur, the chief of staff of the 42nd Division, appealed directly to Harbord, and Donovan was allowed to stay with his battalion.

During the early months in France, when the AEF had almost no troop units on the ground, the GHQ staff structure that had been cobbled together on the *Baltic* seemed to work well enough. But as the combat units arrived in France, the staff structure started to break down under the increased strain. To remedy this, Harbord convened a board of officers at Chaumont under Colonel Johnson Hagood, which recommended a new general staff structure on 7 February 1918. After studying both the British and the French General Staff systems, the board recommended a modified version of the French system. AEF GHQ was reorganized into five sections, each headed by an assistant chief of staff. It was the forerunner of the current "G System": G-1 Personnel, G-2 Intelligence, G-3 Operations, G-4 Logistics, and G-5 Training. The assistant chiefs of staff would coordinate with each other as necessary, but all would be directly subordinate to Harbord as the chief of staff, who would "command" the staff and be the principal advisor to the commander-in-chief.

Brilliant staff officer that he was, Harbord like all good officers wanted to command troops, and after more than a year in France Pershing felt that he owed him the opportunity. In May 1918 Major General James W. McAndrew succeeded Harbord as AEF chief of staff. Pershing had second thoughts about losing Harbord, recording in his diary at the time, "Regret my promise to let him serve with troops."[2] Harbord was assigned to command the 4th Marine Brigade. Consisting of the 5th and 6th Regiments of Marines, the 4th Marine Brigade was the main U.S. Marine Corps contingent of the AEF. It was one of the two infantry brigades of the 2nd Division, the other brigade consisting of two Army infantry regiments. Although he was an Army officer, and although he had only previously commanded a cavalry squadron, Harbord was given command of the 4th Marine Brigade after its commander, 59-year-old Marine Brigadier General Charles A. Doyen, failed to pass a mandatory medical evaluation.

Harbord assumed command on 5 May. Although he held National Army temporary rank as a brigadier general, his Regular Army permanent rank was lieutenant colonel. Both of the Marine regimental commanders were permanent full colonels. Wendell C. Neville and Albertus W. Catlin were both tested combat commanders, and both recipients of the Medal of Honor for action at Vera Cruz in 1914. One of Harbord's brigade staff officers was Marine Major Holland M. Smith, the legendary "Howlin' Mad Smith," who during World War II would command V Amphibious Corps in the Pacific, and is still considered America's father of modern amphibious warfare.

On 26 May 1918 the Germans launched Operation BLÜCHER, attacking south from the Chemin des Dames Ridge to the Marne River.

Almost immediately the U.S. 2nd Division was redeployed to the sector just northwest of Château-Thierry, under the operational control of French XXI Corps. On 6 June the 4th Marine Brigade was ordered to attack the recently halted German lines in Belleau Wood. As a devoted disciple of Pershing's "open warfare" doctrine, Harbord planned minimal artillery support for the initial attack. The artillery order specifically stated that there would be no structured preparation fires, to avoid sacrificing the element of surprise, nor would there be there a creeping barrage to cover the advance. Harbord thought that with no long-established trench lines to his front, Belleau Wood was the perfect place to prove the AEF's "open warfare" doctrine. He was wrong. As military historian Richard Holmes put it, "The Marines attacked in long, straight lines, with the sort of tactical innocence that European armies had long since lost."[3] The leading ranks were cut down in droves by German machine-gun fire. But the Marines kept attacking.

By 8 June Harbord concluded that he had to make greater use of artillery. Brigadier General William Chamberlaine, commander of the 2nd Division's 2nd Artillery Brigade, visited Harbord and proposed a set-piece attack with heavy artillery support. Fortunately, Harbord saw the wisdom of this and issued the planning orders for such an attack starting on 10 June. When the advance resumed, all 160 guns in the sector fired in support of a single Marine battalion that attacked to secure the southern sector of the woods. Despite good results between 10 and 12 June, Harbord throughout the rest of the battle continually underestimated the German defenders and allocated insufficient artillery to support the attacks. It took the Marines until 26 June to secure Belleau Wood. Including the Army troops who supported the Marines, the attackers lost 1,811 killed, including 1,087 total casualties on 6 June alone.

On 15 July Harbord was promoted to major general and moved up to assume command of the 2nd Division. That same day the Germans launched Operation MARNESCHUTZ-REIMS, their fifth and final great offensive of 1918. The German attack stalled almost immediately. On 18 July the French launched a well-prepared counteroffensive into the German right flank. The French Tenth Army's XX Corps, which consisted of the U.S. 1st and 2nd Divisions, with the French 1st Moroccan Division between them, attacked toward the key German communications center at Soissons. Harbord and his staff had less than 24 hours to plan and prepare the 2nd Division attack. The infantry units had to march all night in a thunderstorm to reach their designated lines of departure on time. Over the next 24 hours the 2nd Division made three separate attacks, none of which were adequately supported by artillery. Nonetheless, the division achieved its initial objective of interdicting the Soissons–Château-Thierry Highway. Driving forward nearly 7 miles, it had advanced farther and faster than any other Allied division; but the casualty count of 4,319 was horrendous.

The Allies did not take Soissons until 3 August, but on 26 July Pershing ordered Harbord to relinquish command of the division to Marine Major General John A. Lejeune. Harbord had commanded the 2nd Division for less than two weeks. The reason for Harbord's reassignment was that Pershing desperately needed him to take command immediately of the AEF's chaotic and failing logistical command, the Services of Supply (SOS). Of the more than 1 million American soldiers in France by August 1918, almost one-quarter of them were involved in transportation, supply, maintenance, and other logistical functions. But even that number was stretched thin. Making matters worse, many of the functions and the decision-making responsibilities were fragmented among various headquarters. The result was all too often the wrong supplies, getting to the wrong places, and at the wrong times – or not at all. Pershing decided that he needed someone in charge who had command experience and knew what was needed on the front lines. Harbord was given total control of the procurement, reception, maintenance, and distribution of all supplies.

Taking over from General Francis Kernan, Harbord moved immediately to SOS headquarters at Tours. Rather than trying to run such a huge organization from a desk at the headquarters, Harbord spent much of his time at the various ports, railheads, and depots, personally identifying problems and issuing the orders to correct them. The SOS was a massive organization that managed all aspects of the AEF's logistics in theater. It was organized into seven base sections that operated the seaports; an intermediate section that provided storage and support services; and an advanced section that stored supplies and issued them to the line formations. The wide range of SOS units included port operations troops; rail and motor transport troops; quartermaster and supply troops; ordnance and maintenance troops; labor troops; medical units and medical facilities; replacement and convalescent centers; prisoner of war escort troops and guards; and laundry units.

By November 1918 SOS had 602,910 soldiers, 30,593 officers, and 5,586 Army nurses – totaling almost one-third of the entire AEF. Back in his natural element of organization and management, Harbord solved the most pressing problems and kept the system running to the end of the war. In doing so, Harbord forged a close working partnership with Brigadier General Charles Dawes, the chief of the AEF Purchasing Board. Nonetheless, the SOS system always operated under great strain and required constant tight control. After the war Harbord admitted that if the Armistice had not come when it did on 11 November 1918, the AEF would have had to stop fighting because its logistics system would have totally collapsed.

In 1919 President Woodrow Wilson designated Harbord to head a fact-finding mission to the Middle East, with the task of evaluating the implications of Britain's Balfour Declaration supporting the establishment of a Jewish state in Palestine. Harbord also filed a report on Turkish–Armenian relations and the Armenian Genocide. Upon his return to the United States, Harbord again assumed command of the 2nd Division. When Pershing was appointed chief of staff of the U.S. Army in 1921, Harbord joined him in Washington as the assistant chief of staff. At the time, it was only a major general's position, but it was still the Number 2 officer's slot at the War Department, the equivalent of today's four-star position of vice chief of staff of the U.S. Army. In that position, Harbord was instrumental in making the AEF's wartime G-staff system the standard model throughout the Army, and especially at the War Department. That finally broke the bureaucratic power-lock of the old bureau chief system.

Harbord retired from the Army in 1922 and accepted the presidency of the fledgling Radio Corporation of America (RCA). He retired from the presidency in 1930, replaced by David Sarnoff; but he remained chairman of the board of RCA until 1947. On 9 July 1942 an act of Congress promoted Harbord to lieutenant general on the retired list. Harbord died at his home in Rye, New York on 20 August 1947, and was buried at Arlington National Cemetery.

As a combat commander, James G. Harbord had serious shortcomings, but his brief time in command did not give him the time to learn and adapt that many other American commanders had in World War I. If there was any flaw in his approach to the AEF chief of staff job, it was that his extreme personal loyalty to his commander, Pershing, worked sometimes to the disadvantage of the U.S. Army overall. Harbord was a fierce partisan in the running conflict between Pershing and the U.S. Army chief of staff, General Peyton C. March. Pershing staunchly defended his own rights and responsibilities as commander of the AEF, but Harbord at times in defense of his boss influenced Pershing to higher than necessary levels of antagonism toward Washington. Nonetheless, with no formal staff training behind him, Harbord became the U.S. Army's first modern operational-level chief of staff in a combat theater, and he would be the model for all others who followed. He played a key role in developing the staff structure and organization used throughout the U.S. military to this day, as well as by most NATO countries. He was one of the most influential U.S. Army officers of the early 20th century.

CHAPTER 9

BRIGADIER GENERAL FOX CONNER

David T. Ząbecki

Although Major General Fox Conner never commanded troops in combat, he was among the most influential U.S. Army officers of the 20th century. As deputy chief of staff for operations (G-3) of the American Expeditionary Forces, he was one of General John J. Pershing's closest aides, and the principal planner for the AEF's Saint-Mihiel and Meuse–Argonne offensives of 1918. But along the way, Conner also mentored several future generals, who included George Marshall, Dwight Eisenhower, and George Patton. At different periods in his lifetime Conner was known as "The Brain of the American Expeditionary Forces" and "The Man Who Made Eisenhower." Pershing told Conner after the war, "I could have spared any man in the AEF better than you."[1] Ironically, he is not as well remembered today as he deserves, largely because he did not write his memoirs and after he died his papers and journals were burned on his orders. Only 28 of his letters survive. What we know about him comes mostly from the writings of Pershing, Marshall, Eisenhower, Patton, and Pershing's first AEF chief of staff, General James G. Harbord.

Conner was born at Slate Springs, Mississippi, on 12 November 1874. His father had been a Confederate soldier, and his great grandfather a Continental Army soldier. Although his parents were farmers, they also were schoolteachers who ensured that he received a solid basic education. Captivated by military history at a young age, Conner decided early on to become an Army officer. He entered the U.S. Military Academy in 1894. During his final year at West Point, Conner's company tactical officer was First Lieutenant Pershing. Conner had a towering intellect, but his overall academic record at West Point was only slightly better than average. Upon graduation he requested commissioning in the cavalry, but the needs of the Army assigned him to the artillery.

Conner initially was assigned to a coast artillery unit at Fort Adams in Newport, Rhode Island. In January 1899 he was posted to Cuba to serve with the U.S. occupation force following the Spanish–American War. While he was on the island he became proficient in Spanish. In November 1901 he assumed command of the 123rd Company, Coast Artillery, at Fort Hamilton, New York. He quickly established a reputation as a leading gunnery expert. In 1902 Conner married Virginia Brandreth, the heiress to a pharmaceutical company fortune, whose family and friends called her "Bug."

In June 1906 Conner graduated with honors from the U.S. Army Staff School at Fort Leavenworth, Kansas. Originally, the course was designed for infantry and cavalry officers. Before artillery officers could attend, they were required to attend the School of the Line. Conner, however, was among the first of a group of three artillery officers admitted directly to the Staff School. His next assignment was as adjutant of the artillery sub-post at Fort Riley, Kansas, where he was assigned the task of revising the curriculum for the artillery officer course to incorporate the lessons of the Spanish–American and Russo–Japanese wars.

Conner graduated from the U.S. Army War College in 1908, and was assigned to the Army General Staff in Washington. The War College at the time was in Washington, and like many of the members of the General Staff, Conner was also detailed to the War College faculty as an additional duty. He frequently found himself as a captain lecturing to majors and colonels. Among his students during the period was Colonel Hunter

Liggett, who in October and November 1918 would command the U.S. First Army during the final weeks of the Meuse–Argonne campaign. During his time on the General Staff, Conner also worked on the modernization of American artillery doctrine. In 1910 he wrote the influential pamphlet *Field Artillery in Cooperation with the Other Arms.*

While he was stationed in Washington, Conner devoted much of his off-duty hours to the study of French and German so he could read in their original languages the writings of the major European military theorists. His mastery of French was rewarded in 1911 when Conner was posted to France as an exchange officer with the French 22nd Artillery Regiment. By the time he returned to America two years later, he probably had more hands-on experience than any other American officer with the *Canon de 75 modèle 1897*, the famous "French 75mm" gun, the most advanced artillery piece in the world at that time. When the Americans deployed to Europe in 1917, one of Conner's tasks would be to develop the tables of organization and equipment for the direct and general support artillery battalions of the AEF's divisions. Virtually all the direct support battalions would be armed with the French 75, which was a far superior gun than anything the Americans could have brought to the fight themselves.

Upon his return to the United States in 1913, Conner was assigned command of Battery E, 6th Field Artillery Regiment at Fort Riley. That October, Conner first met Lieutenant George S. Patton, Jr. on a train while both officers and their wives were traveling from Kansas City, Missouri to Fort Riley. The two quickly discovered that they shared mutual passions for horses, hunting, deep-sea fishing, and especially military history. Their wives, who both came from wealthy and socially prominent families, also struck up an immediate and lasting friendship. Conner was the elder by 11 years, and for the remainder of their lives their personal relationship would be that of an older and younger brother, although Conner would also be Patton's direct military superior more than once. In June 1916, during Pershing's Punitive Expedition into Mexico, Conner served as the escort officer for the assistant chief of staff of the Army, General Tasker Bliss, as they traveled 150 miles into Mexican territory to visit Pershing's headquarters. Following the meeting, Pershing's aide, Patton, personally escorted Bliss and Conner back to Columbus, New Mexico.

After commanding his battery, Conner served as an instructor at the School of Fire at Fort Sill, Oklahoma. One of Conner's fellow instructors was Captain Lesley McNair, the future commander of U.S. Army Ground Forces during World War II. Conner also worked on a number of development and evaluation projects, including the testing of caterpillar tractors as prime movers for field guns, and procedures for adjusting fires by aerial observers. Following his tour as an instructor, Conner was assigned to the Army inspector general's office in Washington, as inspector of field artillery.

When America entered the war in April 1917, Conner's experience with the French, and especially his knowledge of French artillery, made him a natural choice for Pershing's advanced party staff. As a lieutenant colonel, Conner was assigned as the AEF's assistant inspector general, and the following month he sailed with Pershing and the advanced party for Europe on the White Star Line RMS *Baltic.* Patton, now a captain, was part of the group as the commander of the AEF's Headquarters Company. During the crossing Pershing and the senior members of his staff planned continuously for the organization and deployment of the AEF. Even before the *Baltic* docked, Pershing changed Conner's duty assignment to assistant chief of the operations staff, which at that point was headed by Lieutenant Colonel John Palmer.

Once they were in France, Pershing assembled a task group to analyze the strategic situation, and recommend the best place in the Allied line for the AEF to deploy. The team consisted of Conner, Palmer, AEF assistant chief of staff Lieutenant Colonel Hugh Drum, and Major Frank Parker. On 26 June 1917 the team told Pershing that based on the French ports that would be available to the AEF, it would be impossible for the Americans to assume a position in the line between the French and the British. The availability of France's western ports centering on Saint-Nazaire and the existing rail network south of the Marne River made the Saint-Mihiel sector the optimal location. Conner further recommended the elimination of the Saint-Mihiel salient, just south of Verdun, for the AEF's first major operation.

Pershing selected Chaumont, south of Verdun, as the location for the AEF's General Headquarters (GHQ). On 1 September Conner and Patton went to Chaumont to set up the headquarters. Initially, AEF GHQ was overstaffed and top-heavy. Some 15 heads of departments, bureaus, and services were based there, in addition to the five principal divisional chiefs of the General Staff. Also included were miscellaneous elements (e.g. a press bureau) and various welfare agencies (e.g. the American Red Cross). Because of his tendency to micromanage, Pershing dealt with many of these entities directly, which consumed great amounts of his time.

In November 1917 Conner replaced Palmer as the G-3 of the AEF. As American forces poured into France, he spent a great deal of time with the units, observing their training and their orientation tours in the quiet sectors of the front lines. During one such trip in February 1918 he had a close call. Patton described the incident in a letter to his wife, Beatrice:

> Col. Fox Conner got wounded last week. They were inspecting and came to a part of the trench full of water. They climbed out on the top and ran along to avoid the water when just as they were jumping in again a shell blew up and cut Col. C's nose and throat. He is alright again, and will get a Wound Badge, which is nice.[2]

In 1932 the Wound Badge was converted to the Purple Heart.

The first American divisional-sized attack of the war was made by the 1st Division on 28 May 1918 against German positions around the village of Cantigny. Monitoring the 1st Division's planning and preparations very closely, Conner spent one day each week at the divisional headquarters working closely with the divisional G-3, Lieutenant Colonel George Marshall. Conner was impressed by the quality of the 38-year-old officer's work. When the Cantigny attack succeeded, it proved to the enemy and Allies alike that the Americans were capable of mounting operations at the divisional level. Shortly thereafter, Conner arranged to have Marshall transferred to the AEF staff as his assistant G-3.

In Marshall, Conner recognized an officer whose grasp of operational planning and strategy was equal to his own. They worked as a close team to develop the operational plans for the Saint-Mihiel offensive. Marshall frequently ran the AEF G-3 shop on his own while Conner accompanied Pershing to coordination meetings with the French. In August 1918 Conner was promoted to brigadier general, and Marshall to full colonel. That same month the U.S. First Army became operational. Contrary to Conner's advice, Pershing decided to "dual-hat" himself as commander of the First Army, while also retaining command of the AEF. It was a bad decision, but Conner ensured close coordination between the two headquarters by arranging for Marshall to transfer to the First Army as its G-3. Thus, Conner and Marshal continued to coordinate the final preparations and planning for the Saint-Mihiel offensive, which was fought from 12 to 15 September. They then collaborated on the planning for the massive Meuse–Argonne campaign, which started on 26 September and lasted until the end of the war on 11 November.

On 12 October Pershing relinquished command of the U.S. First Army when Allied Generalissimo Ferdinand Foch authorized the activation of the U.S. Second Army. Lieutenant General Hunter Liggett assumed command of the First Army, as Pershing became a full-fledged army group commander. Pershing, however, had a hard time letting go. His tendency to micromanage continually got the better of him. That was a significant factor in one of the most controversial incidents of Fox Conner's career, during the final days of the war. As discussed on pages 50–53 of the Introduction, the French Fourth Army on the American left flank started to fall behind. Pershing then saw an opportunity for the AEF to get the glory for liberating Sedan, which was actually in the French operational sector. Thus, late in the afternoon of 5 November the memorandum, including the infamous "Boundaries will not be considered binding" clause, went out for the American advance on Sedan,

It was a poorly crafted message, and a recipe for disaster, no matter how it was interpreted. Unit boundaries that designate tactical areas of responsibility are among the most fundamental of all standard operational control measures. Writing after the war, General James Harbord, Pershing's earlier AEF chief of staff, noted:

> The test of an order is *not* can it be understood, but *can it be misunderstood*? [emphasis in the original] By this test the Memorandum Order of

> November 5th is bound to be condemned. Yet it was drawn by experienced officers and issued to others equally experienced – all of them supposed to be familiar with at least the elementary principles of warfare.[3]

Major General Charles P. Summerall, who had only recently relinquished command of the 1st Division to assume command of V Corps, either misread the order or read more into it. Summerall passed the directive on to the new commander of the 1st Division, Brigadier General Frank Parker, telling him, "I expected to see him in Sedan the next morning."[4]

On 6 November Liggett was still unaware of the order that had gone out from his headquarters, as he was in the process of reorienting the First Army to wheel to the east to operate in coordination with the U.S. Second Army on the east side of the Meuse. But Parker believed he was following Pershing's directive and Summerall's orders when on the night of the 5th he turned the 1st Division hard left to the west, sending his already tired troops on a forced march directly across the front of the 77th Division, and deep into the sector of the 42nd Division. As the 1st Division drove forward throughout the day and the night of the 6th, American troops continued to shoot at each other in the dark. The lead elements of the 77th Division that reached the Marne River about 3 miles southeast of Sedan on the 7th were cut off by the 1st Division units marching across their rear.

The French Fourth Army, meanwhile, had finally broken free in their sector. They were now moving forward again, and by the 7th had pretty much caught up with the Americans. But the U.S. 42nd Division on the American far left flank had been pushed by the 77th and 1st Divisions into the French sector. Thus, the 1st and 42nd Divisions and the French Fourth Army were now in a neck-and-neck race to reach Sedan. For the better part of a day, three American frontline divisions remained stuck and powerless as their commanders tried to untangle them. Among those trying to restore order on the ground was Brigadier General Douglas MacArthur, the acting commander of the 42nd Division.

When the normally unflappable Liggett finally learned what was happening on his left flank, it was the only time in the war that he lost his temper completely. He had intended to hold the 1st Division in reserve as an exploitation force for after the First Army crossed the Meuse in force. This sad episode could have been an even greater disaster if the German Army had possessed any significant combat power left with which to mount a counterattack. The three American divisions would have been just so many fish waiting to be shot in a barrel. As MacArthur wrote: "[this] precipitated what narrowly missed being one of the great tragedies of American history."[5] MacArthur's comment notwithstanding, it was a great enough tragedy for the 583 American soldiers killed or wounded during the Race to Sedan. Their names are listed on a bronze plaque attached to a monument erected by the 1st Division after the war. To this day, that monument, which never should have been there in the first place, stands on the west bank of the Meuse, just opposite Sedan.

Conner was present with Pershing at the signing of the Versailles Treaty on 28 June 1919. He was appalled by the harsh punitive terms imposed by the Allies, which made even less sense because the German Army had been allowed to march back home to Germany carrying their weapons and with colors flying. Conner later told Marshall that the Allies almost certainly would have to fight another war in the future, in the same place, against the same enemy. Knowing only too well what was coming, Conner spent the remaining 20 years of his Army career identifying talented young officers and grooming them for positions of high responsibility in the war he knew they would have to fight.

When they returned to Washington later that summer, Pershing, Conner, and Marshall sequestered themselves at Conner's farm in upper New York, preparing Pershing's testimony before the Congress on the reorganization of the Army based on the experiences of the world war. Pershing appeared before a joint session of Senate and House Military Committees on 31 October. Throughout the three days of his testimony, Conner and Marshall were seated on either side of him. A few months later, both Conner and Marshall accompanied Pershing on a long inspection tour of Army posts in the United States.

Conner was not through testifying before the Congress. In January 1920 he appeared before a House of Representatives subcommittee investigating why the AEF had suffered more than 3,000 casualties on

11 November, the last day of the war, when the Armistice was scheduled to go into effect at 1100 hours that morning. Pershing himself had testified earlier before the committee, unapologetically stating that it had been necessary to keep the pressure on the Germans because they could not be trusted to comply with the ceasefire terms. During Conner's testimony Congressman Oscar E. Bland of Indiana heavily criticized the AEF's former G-3 in particular for not halting the scheduled attacks in General Robert Bullard's U.S. Second Army. Brigadier General John Sherburne, the former divisional artillery commander of the 92nd Division, also singled Conner out as the AEF General Staff officer most responsible for allowing the attacks to continue right up to 1100 hours. In the end, however, the other committee members refused to concur with Bland's and Shelburne's accusations against Conner, and the final committee report did not assign blame for the high losses that day.

Pershing became chief of staff of the U.S. Army in July 1921, with Marshall as his aide. Conner, meanwhile, was assigned command of the 20th Infantry Brigade at Camp Gaillard in the Panama Canal Zone. Based on a recommendation from Patton, who was then at the Infantry Tank School at Fort Meade, Maryland, Conner offered the job of his brigade executive officer to Patton's friend, Major Dwight Eisenhower, who was stationed with Patton at Meade. Ike reported to Panama for duty in January 1922. As Eisenhower later told it, the next two years under Conner were the most intense period of military education he ever experienced. Conner recognized that Ike had a great but underdeveloped talent, which Conner set out to fix.

Conner ingrained in Eisenhower the principles of methodical and systematic military planning, tasking him to produce a standard five-paragraph operations order for everything the 20th Infantry Brigade did. Conner also assigned military history readings to his executive officer, requiring him to discuss each book in detail and explain the relevant lessons for modern warfare. Ike had to read Clausewitz's *On War* – more than once – and Conner extended the limits of Eisenhower's intellectual horizons by requiring him to read such varied authors as Shakespeare and Nietzsche. Conner also made sure Eisenhower understood thoroughly three very important lessons of modern warfare: 1. Never fight unless you have to; 2. Never fight alone; and 3. Never fight for long.

In 1925 Conner pulled strings to get Eisenhower into the Command and General Staff School. Thanks to Conner's tutelage in Panama, Eisenhower graduated first in his class in 1926. From that point on, Ike's career took off, and although Eisenhower spent the remaining 46 years of his life among the greatest men of the 20th century, he continually described Fox Conner as "the ablest man I ever knew."[6]

In 1925 and 1926 Conner served as the deputy chief of staff of the U.S. Army, a position today called the vice chief of staff of the Army. In 1927 he commanded the 1st Infantry Division and the following year assumed command of the Hawaiian Department and the Hawaiian Division, the forerunner of today's 25th Infantry Division. One of his principal staff officers was Patton, an officer with a piercing intellect and deep passion for the profession of arms. Conner's influence on Patton was essentially the inverse process of his influence on Eisenhower. Rather than lighting a fire under Patton, Conner more than once stepped in to restrain him and prevent his aggressive and abrasive nature from damaging his career.

When Conner returned to the United States in 1930, General Charles P. Summerall was on the verge of retiring as chief of staff of the Army. The two leading candidates to replace him were Conner and Douglas MacArthur. Although Pershing had been retired for several years, he was still a major voice in U.S. Army circles. No real admirer of MacArthur, Pershing supported Conner for the job; but MacArthur got it. According to some sources, Conner took himself out of the running. He hated Washington, and he did not want to go back there. Nonetheless, one can only speculate how differently the course of U.S. Army history might have run if Conner rather than MacArthur had replaced Summerall.

Throughout the 1930s Conner held a series of high-ranking assignments, culminating with command of the U.S. First Army. He retired in 1938, just a few months before George Marshall was sworn in as the 15th chief of staff of the Army. Marshall wrote to his old mentor: "I am deeply sorry, both personally and officially, to see you leave the active list, because you have a great deal yet to give the Army out of that wise head of yours."[7]

Conner retired quietly, but as Marshall predicted, the U.S. Army was still not through with him. Throughout World War II all three of his star pupils wrote to him regularly, quite often to ask his advice or his opinion on plans in progress. Couriers from Washington frequently brought classified files full of war plans to Conner's New York farm for him to review, sent by Marshall or Eisenhower. After careful analysis, Conner sent the plans back accompanied by extensive notes. Fox Conner died on 13 October 1951, a little more than a year before his most famous protégé became the 34th President of the United States. Fox Conner never wore more than two stars, but his three most famous understudies accounted for a cumulative total of 14 stars.

CHAPTER 10

BRIGADIER GENERAL HUGH A. DRUM

Patrick Gregory

Hugh Aloysius Drum was in a literal sense born for the army, and it was to the army that he would devote 45 years of his life. Born the youngest of six children to Captain John Drum and Margaret Desmond Drum on 19 September 1879 at Fort Brady in Michigan, he grew up traveling with his family in New Mexico and Texas, living in military outposts. After nearly 30 years of service in these lands, Drum senior was appointed military instructor at St. Francis Xavier College in New York in 1894 where Hugh enrolled as a student: a rare opportunity for him to enjoy public school, as his education until then was largely at the hands of his parents. Hugh performed well academically and excelled in military studies, rising through the ranks of the cadet force. With the outbreak of the Spanish–American war in 1898 his father shelved retirement plans to rejoin his regiment, sailing for Cuba. But within two days of his arrival, John Drum was dead, killed at the Battle of San Juan Hill. After mourning his father, Hugh determined to pursue a commission in the Army and, with this in mind, petitioned President William McKinley, who responded positively to his request, decreeing that the children of deceased Army officers be permitted a direct commission for service. Drum was offered his commission on 19 September 1898, his 19th birthday.

By early 1899, Drum was assigned to Manila on the first of three tours of duty during and after the Philippines Insurrection, serving with 12th Infantry and subsequently the 25th, 27th, and 23rd Infantry Regiments. In August–November 1899, he participated in operations deep into the hinterland, including the main Luzon offensive of late 1899 to root out insurgent strongholds. This resulted in the capture of a sizable number of rebel leader Emilio Aguinaldo's forces, an operation in which Drum played a significant part. The young lieutenant would garner further credit during the so-called "pacification" program of 1900.

On an extended furlough in the United States 1901–02, Drum met his future wife Mary Reaume, but he was to return to duty in the Philippines and service on the island of Mindanao (where he met Captain John Pershing). Relations with the ethnic Moros tribe had deteriorated, triggering more U.S. Army operations in the region. Drum's part in a successful attack against the rebel stronghold of Fort Bayan caught the eye of his commanding officer Colonel, later Brigadier General, Frank Baldwin, a double Medal of Honor recipient. Baldwin awarded him a brevet captaincy, and Drum would serve as Baldwin's aide-de-camp for the next three years, following him back to the U.S. During this time Hugh and Mary married.

After a final tour of duty in the Philippines (1908–10), Drum was ordered to the School of the Line at Fort Leavenworth, Kansas – the fulfilment of a long-held ambition to study at such a military institution. He believed it would go a long way to rounding him off as qualified for higher assignments in later years. He graduated from the school with honors, third in his class, moving swiftly on to the second year of study at the Staff School. He was already identified as having the qualities needed for a staff officer. He subsequently returned to the Army Service Schools at Fort Leavenworth as an instructor from 1914 to 1916.

Drum was chosen by Major General Frederick Funston – whom he had known at Leavenworth – to join his Veracruz Expedition, occupying the Mexican port city in 1914. He served briefly as Funston's aide and assistant chief of staff in the Southern Department, until Funston died suddenly in February 1917. Funston's replacement was John Pershing, fresh from his Punitive Expedition in Mexico. Drum was kept on by Pershing, who saw that he had talent as a staff officer. James Harbord, whom Pershing had selected as chief of staff for the American Expeditionary Forces in May, put a staff together in the fortnight before departure of the advanced party, with Harbord recalling, "One of his [Pershing's] first remarks was 'we have got to take Hugh Drum along', and we did."[1]

Drum was delighted after joining the General Staff to discover that he was to serve in the Operations Section under James McAuley Palmer. It was an area which held special appeal for him, he told Mary, where he believed he could make a contribution. Hugh equipped himself with manuals from Leavenworth and a number of European military handbooks for the trip. However, on board the S.S. *Baltic* as it left New York, he was tasked with something further removed from the work he had been expecting: a study of French ports which could be used by the AEF. He set to work with three other officers under the direction of Colonel Daniel McCarthy, settling into the routine of 16- to 18-hour days, which was to become the hallmark of his working life in France.

McCarthy's group weighed which ports might work best as depots, trying to estimate the tonnage each would need to handle and how best to use the French railroad system to move men and materiel to potential future American areas of operations. Key to all this was to avoid encroaching on any sectors already being used by the Allied armies. The Atlantic ports presented the best options, notably Saint-Nazaire, Nantes, Brest, Bordeaux, and La Pallice. Leaving Pershing's advanced party behind in England when the *Baltic* arrived on 8 June, the port study group traveled ahead to France to begin their inspection tour. Drum was satisfied by what they saw at Saint-Nazaire in particular, and within a fortnight the first contingent of 14,000 American 1st Division troops had arrived there.

It was the first of a number of studies and reports Drum undertook in his early months in France, going on to work with Lieutenant Colonels

Fox Conner and LeRoy Eltinge and Major Alvin Barber on a number of others. One such effort was the July 1917 "Committee on Organization of Forces," assessing a range of topics from the organization of their own Operations Section to examining where incoming divisions could best train; and, crucially, assessing the optimal size and organizational structure of American divisions. Key here was the establishment of what became the AEF's standard divisional structure, the so-called "square division," an outsized two-brigade, four-regiment formation totaling around 28,000 men. It would, they believed, help compensate for the shortfall in the number of officers qualified for command positions; and, possibly more tellingly, the larger division could allow the Americans to conduct the "open warfare" advocated by Pershing, rather than the trench-based fighting of the Allies. Simply put, the larger divisions could stay in the line longer and maintain momentum through their large number of troops.

From July through September came two further reports. One was a study on the establishment of an AEF school system and instruction program on the Leavenworth model. The next important study in September was a 21-page estimate of the situation on the Western Front, produced by Conner, Drum, and Eltinge. Among its recommendations, "A Strategical Study of the Employment of the AEF Against the Imperial German Government" recommended the cutting off of the Saint-Mihiel salient bulging into Allied lines southeast of Verdun: an attack which could itself pave the way for a thrust on the German stronghold of Metz and the important Briey iron and coal area.

Over the next several months, Drum – now a lieutenant colonel – worked on operational matters, ensuring that incoming divisions were properly billeted and moved into appropriate training areas with Allied forces. He went on two inspection tours with the AEF's 1st Division and an observation tour with the British 29th Division before spending four weeks in February–March with the 42nd Division, then training in the Lunéville sector.

For a time Drum wanted to be assigned as a line officer; but twice – following endorsement by AEF chief of staff James Harbord and his successor James McAndrew – his requests were denied by Pershing.

Indeed, Drum, promoted to colonel in April, had become a key member of Pershing's inner circle, embracing and amplifying his mentor's views. The start of Ludendorff's Spring Offensives in March 1918 caused the French and British to demand priority shipments of American men and machine-gun units, without accompanying support units. But whatever the immediate need to throw men into the field, Drum echoed Pershing's concerns against amalgamation: "We must have an American army here to win the war... The British and French are down and out. They can fight defensively but have no punch left in them."[2]

Following the U.S. 1st Division's offensive at Cantigny in late May 1918 and the 2nd Division's actions of Belleau Wood and Vaux in June–July near Château-Thierry, Pershing asked Drum to turn his attentions to the establishment of a new field army staff and headquarters that would become the U.S. First Army. Heavy fighting still lay ahead for the AEF divisions, contributing significantly to repelling Ludendorff's final MARNESCHUTZ-REIMS offensive in mid-July, and the Allies' subsequent Aisne–Marne counteroffensive. Throughout this period, Pershing pushed for the establishment of a distinct American field army with responsibility for its own sector of the front; and he wanted Drum to be its chief of staff.

The new field army, comprising U.S. I and III Corps, officially came into being on 10 August at La Ferté-sous-Jouarre on the Marne. Forty-eight hours earlier the British had launched their attack against Amiens. German forces were in retreat and the final, dynamic phase of the war had begun. "The time appeared propitious," Pershing recalled, "for activity farther east."[3] Accordingly, plans were advanced for the American reduction of the Saint-Mihiel salient.

The U.S. First Army took up its new headquarters at Ligny-en-Barrois, then Souilly, south of Verdun, from where it would lead the final U.S. operations of the war. The General Staff assembled there by Drum included Willey Howell as his G-2 Intelligence chief; Alvin Barber, G-1 Personnel; John DeWitt, G-4 Logistics; Lewis Watkins, G-5 Training; and most significantly, George Marshall, G-3 Operations. It was the latter who would come to the fore particularly under Drum, planning the final two campaigns of the war: Saint-Mihiel and Meuse–Argonne.

Following discussions with Foch in August, Pershing finally committed his forces to fighting two major battles in quick succession, barely a fortnight apart and with a distance of approximately 60 miles separating them. Drum knew it was a huge undertaking, but for Pershing the reduction of the Saint-Mihiel salient was a long-cherished ambition, one he was unwilling to relinquish, even with the much larger Meuse–Argonne operation to come. Accordingly, on 8 September, Drum tasked George Marshall to come up with an integrated plan to fight the two battles in succession. The plan he came up with was "a dandy" in Drum's view.[4] It required moving troops northwest to the Meuse–Argonne sector even while the Saint-Mihiel operation was still in play, yet without jeopardizing this first offensive. The lead elements – U.S. I, IV, and V Corps – were en route to the Meuse–Argonne sector on 13 September, only 24 hours into the Saint-Mihiel attack. During the following days a total of 600,000 men, with accompanying artillery and supply trains, moved under cover of darkness. On the eve of the Saint-Mihiel attack and again a fortnight later before the Meuse–Argonne, Drum was joined in his offices at Souilly by U.S. Secretary of War Newton D. Baker, who was in France making a frontline tour. Baker was impressed by what he saw of Drum in action, making decisions as he dealt with incoming reports and his staff. The functioning of the U.S. First Army, through its General Staff and in its dealings with the corps headquarters, worked in an orderly manner and allowed Pershing (and later Hunter Liggett) to spend more time meeting Allied commanders, or in the field. Drum "ran the First Army,"[5] remembered Douglas MacArthur.

During the waning days of the war the "Race to Sedan" incident in early November resulted in a blemish on Drum's World War I record. A memo, issued in Pershing's name by AEF Operations Chief Fox Conner, passed down through George Marshall and authorized for release by Drum, gave the green light for divisions of U.S. I and V Corps to advance ahead of adjacent left-flank French forces to liberate the key railway center of Sedan (see Introduction, pp. 50–53). The directive informed the corps commanders that "the honor of entering Sedan should fall to the First American Army."[6]

As he read through the initial draft, Drum was pretty sure he knew what Pershing wanted. But Drum then tried to clarify the order further by adding a final sentence to the second paragraph: "Boundaries will not be considered binding."[7] That latter appendage, however, caused much of the confusion that resulted in V Corps' 1st Division wheeling west across the front of the 77th and 42nd Divisions of I Corps and into French territory. Liggett, the First Army commander, who was not consulted about the directive, considered the whole incident a "military atrocity."[8] Yet, in the weeks that followed the matter was glossed over to Drum's advantage.

Drum remained in Europe until June 1919, serving in different capacities, including as deputy chief – and briefly chief – of staff of the Services of Supply, helping organize the large troop withdrawal effort back to the United States. Upon his return to the United States Drum reverted to his permanent rank of major, having risen to brigadier general in the last weeks of the war. By late 1921, however, he was quickly promoted through the ranks of the Regular Army to brigadier general.

Drum was assigned again to Fort Leavenworth, first as director of military training at the School of the Line and then as its overall commandant. There, he took care to build on lessons of the AEF in France. He wrote and edited a clutch of textbooks and manuals covering everything from combat orders to topography, tanks, and signaling. He was determined to press home "open warfare" doctrine, noting with satisfaction in one lecture: "For the first time [in an instructional sense] all our doctrine was inculcated with the offensive spirit."[9]

After brief stints in New York inspecting state National Guard units and commanding the Second Coast Artillery District, Drum was assigned to Washington in 1923 as assistant chief of staff of the U.S. Army, serving under General John Hines. Drum's time there was challenging, dominated by the controversy surrounding the Air Service and its spiky assistant chief, Billy Mitchell. The pair had crossed swords before in France, and they were to find themselves adversaries once more. Mitchell had kept up a determined campaign to promote the need for an independent air force as well as consideration of his developing ideas of strategic bombing. But Mitchell's criticism of colleagues and disregard for military processes had culminated in his court-martial in late 1925. Drum had already been involved in a number of investigations involving the Air Service and he delivered a detailed rebuttal of Mitchell's arguments to uphold the Army's case against an independent air force. Mitchell was found guilty of insubordination and resigned his commission, and Drum's testimony carried forward to a subsequent inquiry whereby the Army retained control of the service as the newly styled U.S. Army Air Corps.

Drum left Washington in spring 1926 for the 1st Infantry Division in New York, first as commander of its 1st Brigade, and then as divisional commander. In January 1930, he was promoted to major general and assigned as U.S. Army inspector general. In November 1931 he assumed command of U.S. V Corps in Ohio. He returned to Washington in early 1933 as deputy chief of staff to General Douglas MacArthur. Yet it was around this time that Drum's hopes of reaching the summit of the Army profession began to drift away from him. MacArthur's term as chief of staff was extended for an additional year, and then he was succeeded in 1935 by Malin Craig, who served in office until 1939. During those years Drum held a range of other commands, including the Hawaiian Department; VI Corps Area; and First Army in New York.

Drum suffered a disappointment in 1939 when his old AEF subordinate, George Marshall, succeeded Craig as U.S. Army chief of staff. It came as a blow to Drum, who felt bitterly let down by his old mentor Pershing with whom he had remained in regular contact during the 20 years since France, even helping proofread his memoirs; and he believed that Pershing could have and should have done more to promote his candidacy.

The curtain gradually began to come down on Drum's career. His last position was that of First Army commanding general, a posting he coupled with the Eastern Defense Command in 1941–43. He retired from the U.S. Army as a lieutenant general in October 1943, moving with Mary to New York. There he became president of the New York Empire Corporation. He also served as commander of the New York National Guard until 1948. On 1 October 1951 Drum died suddenly while working in his office at the Empire State Building. Following requiem mass in St. Patrick's Cathedral, New York, he was buried at Arlington National Cemetery, Virginia.

Hugh Drum's contribution to the American Expeditionary Forces has been largely forgotten and today he is remembered mostly as an efficient military administrator of Pershing's plans in France. Nonetheless, Drum's building of the First Army and his guidance of it through the battles of September–November 1918 represented a considerable logistical achievement in the most testing of circumstances: an exercise in the harnessing of officer talent, both staff and in the field; the coordination of a huge array of manpower; careful liaison with the Allies; and the efficient use of resources. He did not underestimate the scale of the task ahead of the First Army in the Meuse–Argonne ("the most ideal defensive terrain I have ever seen or read about"[10]) and he was careful and painstaking in his approach to it. He maintained discipline and secrecy so great that he only briefed corps staff officers six days before operations began.

But even when difficulties were encountered in the early days of the Meuse–Argonne, with AEF forces falling short of their initial objectives, he remained phlegmatic: "The gaining of ground counts for little, it is the ruining of his [the enemy's] army that will end the struggle," he wrote in a letter to his wife.[11] It was a hard, but accurate, reading of the situation, as however high the cost in American battlefield casualties, German forces were being sucked deeper and deeper into an area which they could ill afford to defend.

It is clear that Drum was highly regarded by his fellow AEF officers. Pershing said the First Army had been "rapidly whipped into shape under the able direction"[12] of his chief of staff. Other senior AEF officers agreed. Liggett thought Drum "accomplished and most capable" and Conner spoke of "an excellent and well-trained general officer."[13]

Although higher ranks and command positions awaited him in later life, just as he had hoped in 1917, in many respects it was that position of chief of staff of the First Army which represented the apogee of Drum's military career. "He had been the Chief of Staff of an army which numbered at one time over a million men," said Marshall. "General Drum had carried a vast burden of responsibility. In a veteran army his task would have been heavy, but the complications and difficulties involved in organizing and fighting, at one and the same time, an abnormally large army beggars description."[14]

CHAPTER 11

BRIGADIER GENERAL CHARLES G. DAWES

William H. Van Husen

Charles Gates Dawes was born on 27 August 1865 in Marietta, Ohio. His father, Rufus Dawes, was a Union Army officer in the Civil War, fighting at Gettysburg, the Wilderness, Spotsylvania, and Cold Harbor, ultimately becoming a brevet brigadier general on 13 March 1865. Rufus Dawes is most remembered for his heroism at the railroad cut, Gettysburg, on the first day of that battle. Charles Dawes graduated from Marietta College and received his law degree from Cincinnati Law School in 1886. After law school, Dawes relocated to Lincoln, Nebraska, to practice law. There he met Lieutenant John Pershing, who was there teaching military science at the University of Nebraska, and began a lifelong friendship. Pershing at the time was working on his own law degree while at the university.

In 1894, Dawes moved to Chicago and invested in gas companies in Wisconsin and Illinois. This caught the eye of the Republican Party and he was asked to manage William McKinley's campaign for President in Illinois. With McKinley's successful election, Dawes was appointed the Treasury

Department's Comptroller of the Currency, supervising, chartering, and regulating all national banking institutions and foreign banks operating in the U.S. In 1901, Dawes decided to run for senator, hoping to get McKinley's endorsement. However, on 14 September 1901, McKinley was assassinated and his vice president, Theodore Roosevelt, became President. Roosevelt, instead, endorsed his Republican rival Albert Hopkins.

Disillusioned, Dawes left politics to manage the Central Trust Company of Illinois, a banking and financial institution. He remained its president until 1921. In 1915 Dawes was instrumental in securing a $500 million loan to France and Great Britain for the funding of the war through the Anglo–French Financial Commission. As this was the largest single loan from private U.S. institutions in history, a syndicate was established led by J. P. Morgan, Dawes, and other bankers. The loan was not extended to Russia, as Jewish bankers refused to deal with Russia because of its strong anti-Semitic pogroms. Germany tried to stop the transaction, but its efforts proved fruitless. The United States went from a debtor to a creditor nation.

On 6 April, President Woodrow Wilson requested Congress to pass a declaration of war against Germany. In mid-April, Dawes travelled to Washington, D.C. to meet with his longtime friend John Pershing to request a commission. Dawes, coming from a long line of military officers, felt it was his duty to participate in the Great War. By this time, Dawes was 51 years old, his bank was flourishing, and the family holding company, Dawes Brothers, Inc., was doing very well.

While attending law school in the 1880s, Dawes had supported himself as a surveyor for the railroad. With this experience he hoped to get a commission as an engineer. When meeting with Pershing, the general was not overly impressed by his engineering knowledge; however, he knew of his business knowledge and experience and felt that those would be of use to the AEF. On 27 May 1917, Dawes received his commission as major and proceeded to Atlanta, Georgia for training with his commanding officer Colonel John S. Sewell, 17th Engineer Regiment. With training completed on 26 July, Dawes and the rest of the 17th Engineer Regiment departed for New York and sailed to Liverpool on the troopship RMS *Carmania.*

When Dawes arrived in London, he immediately met with the head of J. P. Morgan's British affiliate, Morgan, Grenfell & Co. Upon arriving in Paris, Dawes met with J. P. Morgan's French affiliate, Morgan Hartjes. These were not merely courtesy calls. Both offices were clearing houses under the Anglo–French Financial Commission for armament procurements and handled transactions between their respective militaries and American suppliers. With the U.S. in the war, the AEF would be competing for armaments the Allied Powers had purchased over the previous two years and would continue to purchase for the remainder of the war. His background in negotiating the Anglo–French Financial Commission and knowledge of banking institution structures proved key in procurements for the U.S. forces.

When the U.S. entered the war, the Army was woefully unprepared. Prior to departing for Europe, Pershing had conducted an inventory of armaments: 285,000 Springfield rifles, 400 light and 150 heavy field guns, 1,500 machine guns of various makes with parts that were not interchangeable, and shortages in uniforms, boots, and winter gear. In aviation, the Army had only 55 training airplanes and 56 rated pilots, none of whom had any experience with attack tactics. To cap that all off, the Army did not have any plans for sending an army to Europe.

To overcome these shortages, Pershing established the General Purchasing Board on 20 August 1917 and appointed Lieutenant Colonel Dawes as chief of the Purchasing Board. At first Dawes was reluctant to accept the position but he was persuaded by Pershing. Dawes coordinated procurement for not only the Army, but also the Red Cross and the YMCA (Young Men's Christian Association) in France. Working under Pershing's chief of staff, Brigadier General James G. Harbord, Dawes had:

> unlimited discretion and authority to go ahead and devise a system of coordination of purchases; to organize the board; to arrange the liaison connections between the French and English army boards and our own; to use any method which may seem wise to me to secure supplies for the army in Europe which to that extent will relieve our American transports in their enormous burden.[1]

One of Dawes' first challenges was to resolve a critical shortage of coal needed by France and the AEF; 50,000 tons was required right away and, by 1 February 1918, 150,000 tons per month would be required. Dawes, through his British liaison, secured the coal but the British were unable to provide transports. Vice Admiral William Sims, commander of U.S. naval forces in Europe, was unable to provide the necessary shipping. Dawes then turned to Major General Richard M. Blatchford, commander of the AEF's Line of Communications, who loaned him Army Captain H. B. Moore, an expert on shipping. Moore knew that Sims had at least one collier which could be used, and he devised a plan to refit roughly 20 ships from the Great Lakes for sea voyages. They would soon be ice-bound during the winter months, and could be better used bringing coal from America. To accommodate the influx of 50,000 tons of freight (including the coal) per day, new piers at Saint-Nazaire would be needed. This task fell to the 17th Engineer Regiment.

In October, Dawes established a French line of credit through the Federal Reserve Bank of New York to the amount of $50,000,000 for procurement of ordnance and aviation materiel. The French for their part estimated that they would provide $60–100 million in supplies per month. France needed the credits for American purchases and the settlement of balances would be worked out at a later date. Dawes' British counterpart was Major General Sir Evan E. Carter. Through him, Dawes coordinated the continental purchasing and handling of supplies among the Allies, including the French. By 3 November, French and British contacts, including Belgian Minister of Finance Aloys Van de Vyvere, were established. Pershing placed the securing and purchasing of materiel for the AEF through Dawes' office. On 8 January 1918, Pershing cabled to Washington his recommendation for Dawes' promotion to colonel. On 16 January, Pershing officially pinned the "eagles" marking Dawes' promotion. It was a promotion well deserved; by the first week in February, AEF had purchased 2,690,000 tons of materiel.

On 5 February, Pershing ordered Dawes to establish a labor bureau under his (Dawes') authority with the immediate procurement of 50,000 men, ultimately having 100,000 workers to free up AEF troops better used for combat operations. A ready source of labor would come from Spain and Dawes worked with Maurice Ganne, chairman of the French Mission in charge of French relations with the AEF. Unloading and distributing more than 300,000 tons of materiel per month was labor intensive. In April, 5,000 more laborers were added, many of whom were German prisoners of war. Also, at this time, Dawes established a Board of Contracts and Adjustment to settle complex business contracts, and business questions with the French and British governments. With his background in business and banking, Dawes excelled.

Throughout April and much of May, Dawes developed plans to integrate the distribution of materiel among the American, British, French, and Italian forces – an Allied Services of Supply. The idea was to reduce waste and the unnecessary building of warehouses where vacant Allied facilities were available. Additionally, materiel unloaded from the docks was then transported where the immediate need existed, saving time – and of course lives – versus warehousing it for later distribution. Central distributing depots for joint use were established. Management and allocation of locomotives and freight cars expedited delivery of materiel to the front, reducing the need for waiting in a queue for available railroad stock. Pershing presented the detailed proposal to French Prime Minister Georges Clemenceau, who endorsed it on 22 May with the desire to submit the agreement to the British and Italian governments.

The British War Office was, at first, against it; Dawes went to London in late May to convince the War Office to sign off on the proposal. Dawes met with Prime Minister David Lloyd George, who himself was for the proposal. British Secretary of State for War Lord Alfred Milner convinced the War Office, and in particular Lieutenant General John Cowans, British quartermaster-general, to endorse the proposal. On 3 June, Milner, representing the British government, signed the letter of acceptance with a recommendation to include the Belgians on the committee. The Military Board of Allied Supplies (MBAS) was established for allocating materiel and supplies, and its unanimous decisions, which were given the force of orders, were to be carried out by the respective supply agencies. There was some pushback from Allied Supreme Commander General Ferdinand Foch, who detested the idea of a "services of supply board" that he had no control over. However, Clemenceau informed Foch of this arrangement, and the Prime Minister arranged for the board staff to be billeted in a 16th-century château once occupied by the sister of Louis XIV. Assigned to MBAS were Brigadier General Charles Payot, representing the French government, and Major General Reginald Ford for the British.

The board's first meeting was on 28 June. Coalition warfare is difficult, at best, to prosecute. Still, the MBAS managed successfully to allocate the limited resources as well as assign railway stock to deliver needed armaments and materiel to the frontline forces – soldiers were fed and Allied operations progressed, often with greater intensity. The board's duties also included mail delivery; at its peak in October 1918, MBAS handled over 64 million letters per week for all Allied soldiers. The MBAS was short-lived and one can only speculate how more or less effective it might have been had the war progressed into 1919. Still, the MBAS laid the groundwork for future wars involving multinational forces.

The MBAS existed because of the coordinating efforts of Dawes in getting the French and British on board with the idea of a joint logistics command. However, as the French liaison was a brigadier general and the British a major general, Dawes was at a disadvantage. In a long memo to Pershing in August, detailing the accomplishments of the MBAS, Colonel Dawes proposed that the AEF chief of staff act as the American liaison. Upon learning of this, Payot pleaded with Dawes not to leave of his own volition. He stated that it was Dawes who had got the French on board and it was Dawes' personal relationship with the British that had also got them on board. Dawes was the glue that held the MBAS together, particularly in the face of the opposition to the organization by Marshal of France Ferdinand Foch.

On 3 October, the newly appointed German Imperial Chancellor Prince Max von Baden, through the Swiss government, notified President Woodrow Wilson of his desire to open negotiations for a ceasefire. Two weeks later, Dawes received his promotion to brigadier general (effective 15 October). As negotiations proceeded, the fighting continued with no lessening of the duties of the MBAS. On 3 November, negotiations continued with indications that an armistice was imminent. The priority for MBAS was the procurement of vehicles and horses to prevent a rapid retreat of German forces east; 12,000 vehicles were immediately available and another 12,000 sought. On 11 November, the Armistice was signed at 1100 hours Paris time, and the guns fell silent for the first time in over four years. The job of MBAS was not over, however. There was the task of feeding Belgians and Germans, and helping the Italians with over 1 million Austrian prisoners of war. Dawes authorized the shipment of flour to Italy and $3 million worth of food stuffs to Belgium. Germany was also critically short on food; however, France was unwilling to permit food shipments to Germany. The head of the U.S. Food Administration, Herbert Hoover, would not exclude any nation, including Germany, from receiving needed food. Dawes would manage this distribution.

As the shooting war in Europe ended, a new enemy was rearing its head – the influenza pandemic or Spanish Flu. The flu killed more soldiers than war wounds and it spread rapidly throughout the barracks and the trenches. The pandemic spread as returning soldiers infected their home areas. Dawes authorized the use of his hotels in Boston and Chicago as infirmaries.

However, Dawes' tour in Europe was not over. Secretary of War Newton Baker appointed him as the military member of the U.S. Liquidation Commission tasked with disposing of movable and immovable properties. Immovable properties were permanent structures to include barracks, hospitals, warehouses, and docks. Movable materiel included items that could be shipped back the U.S. There was, however, a problem with that: priority transport was given to the nearly 2 million troops, and at a rate of 250,000 soldiers per month the redeployment would not be completed until the end of 1919. Additionally, flooding the market with surplus goods would affect the economy by reducing domestic manufacturing. France bought much of the surplus of goods in bulk and agreed to pay $400 million for property valued at close to $1 billion and another $423 million for other properties. The Liquidation Commission settled claims with Allied governments and nongovernmental agencies totaling $873 million.

With these sales nearly completed, Dawes resigned his military commission on 26 July 1919 and returned stateside. Before leaving, France awarded him the Croix de Guerre and made him a Commander of the Legion of Honor. On 9 January 1919, Dawes was awarded the Distinguished Service Medal. The citation reads:

> He rendered most conspicuous services in the organization of the General Purchasing Board, as General Purchasing Agent of the American Expeditionary Forces, and as the representative of the United States Army on the Military Board of Allied Supply. His rare abilities, sound business judgement, and aggressive energy were invaluable in securing needed supplies for the American Armies in Europe.[2]

Dawes visited his friend Aloys Van de Vyvere in Belgium, and while there, King Albert I of Belgium personally conferred upon Dawes the Commander of the Order of Leopold. Upon arriving in Chicago, Dawes assumed his previous position of president of the Central Trust Company of Illinois.

On 2 February 1921, Dawes was called to testify before a Congressional Select Committee on Expenditures in the War Department, which took all day. He was called back the next day with the committee repeating the same questions. The questioning focused on expenditures dealing with outside sources, and addressed price gouging, unnecessary purchases, etc. At one point, Dawes became angry, thumped the table, and raised his voice: "For every mistake made in the AEF, you have been making the same mistake here in Washington for a hundred years. Hell Maria, we weren't trying to keep a set of books. We were trying to win a war."[3] Congressional members considered censure for his use of profanity. The expression stuck and for the remainder of his life, he would occasionally be referred to as "Hell and Maria Dawes."

Later that year, in June, Dawes was appointed director for the newly formed General Accounting Office (now the Government Accountability Office or GAO). The Budget and Accounting Act of 1921 required the director to: "investigate, at the seat of government or elsewhere, all matters relating to the receipt, disbursement, and application of public funds, and... make to the President... and to Congress... reports [and] recommendations looking to greater economy or efficiency in public expenditures."[4]

The Treaty of Versailles of 28 June 1919 saddled Germany and its allies with the collective guilt clause and a huge reparations bill totaling $15 billion, plus an additional $482 million to Belgium for four years of occupation. By June 1922, owing to high inflation, Germany could not meet its payment obligation. France wanted no alteration to Germany's payment schedule; Great Britain tended to be more lenient. France and Great Britain had outstanding loan obligations, not only to the U.S. but also to each other, and the bankers refused to write down any loan values, demanding full payment. Investment on the Continent suffered and Germany's economy was severely strained. Germany missed a reparation payment and, as a result, on 10 January 1923, France and Belgium occupied the Ruhrgebiet (Ruhr region), the center of Germany's steel production. France used the occupation to take control of Germany's coal production. This severely depressed Germany's economy, resulting in hyperinflation and currency devaluation. Discussions took place in 1923 among the European powers, with little accomplishment; by October Germany's economy was sliding toward collapse. In early 1922, the exchange rate in Germany was 320 Reichsmark to one U.S. dollar. When the currency finally collapsed in late November 1923, the exchange rate was 4.2 trillion Reichsmark to the dollar.

The British government cabled U.S. Secretary of State Charles Evans Hughes for assistance. In December, two committees were formed: the first committee of experts was chaired by Dawes and tasked to balance Germany's budget and stabilize the currency; the second committee of experts was chaired by Reginald McKenna, a board member of Midland Bank. They determined how much capital had left Germany and how to return the funds. On 23 December 1923, Dawes and the committee sailed for Europe and arrived in Paris on 8 January. The first task was to establish a security currency – the Rentenmark – and peg the exchange rate at 4.2 gold Rentenmark to the dollar to encourage foreign investment in Germany. The next step was to set a realistic reparation payment framework to meet Germany's ability to pay. The plan called for an annual percentage based on total state revenues – the higher the income the greater the reparation payments. Finally, Germany needed an infusion of funds. This included $200 million in bank loans, half of which came from

General John J. Pershing arriving at Boulogne, France on 14 June 1917. This photo first appeared in the pages of the French weekly newspaper *L'Illustration*. (Bettmann/Getty Images)

General Philippe Pétain (French Army), Field Marshal Douglas Haig (UK), Marshal Ferdinand Foch (Supreme Allied Commander), General John J. Pershing (USA). The photo was taken at Foch's headquarters in the Chateau de Bombon on 24 July 1918. (NARA)

General Peyton C. March, chief of staff of the U.S. Army during most of 1918. Despite his fractious relationship with Pershing, the establishment of the AEF owed almost as much to March's "push" as to Pershing's "pull." (NARA)

General Tasker Bliss, former chief of staff of the U.S. Army, and Pershing's ally as American Permanent Military Representative on the Allied Supreme War Council. (NARA)

Major General John L. Hines, photographed outside 4th Division Headquarters during the Meuse–Argonne campaign on 1 October 1918. He later succeeded Pershing as chief of staff of the U.S. Army. (AHEC)

Major General Charles P. Summerall commanded the 1st Division, and then V Corps during the final month of the war. He is photographed (left) with Brigadier General Frank Parker late in October 1918. Summerall succeeded John L. Hines as chief of staff of the U.S. Army. (NARA)

Brigadier General Douglas MacArthur (second from left), photographed during the Saint-Mihiel offensive with Lieutenant Colonel Walter Bare, the commander of the 167th Regiment (right of MacArthur) and a French liaison officer (left). MacArthur later succeeded Charles P. Summerall as chief of staff of the U.S. Army. (AHEC)

Lieutenant Colonel George C. Marshall (standing right) as operations officer G-3 of the 1st Division, shortly after the Battle of Cantigny. Also pictured are Colonel Campbell King (standing left), 1st Division chief of staff, and Brigadier General John L. Hines, commander of the 1st Infantry Brigade. Marshall succeeded Malin Craig as chief of staff of the U.S. Army. (NARA)

Brigadier General Malin Craig, chief of staff of I Corps Headquarters, in October 1918 near the Argonne Forest. He served superbly as the chief of staff at the division, corps, and army levels. Craig later succeeded Douglas MacArthur as chief of staff of the U.S. Army. (AHEC)

Marine Major General John A. Lejeune (right), upon assuming command of the 2nd Division from Army Major Omar Bundy on 28 July 1918. The 2nd Division comprised both soldiers and Marines. After the war Lejeune became the commandant of the U.S. Marine Corps. (AHEC).

Colonel James Harbord (far right) arriving in France with Pershing in 1917. Harbord served as the AEF's first chief of staff, briefly commanded the 2nd Division, and ultimately led the AEF's Services of Supply (SOS). (NARA)

Colonel Wendell C. Neville commanded the 4th Marine Brigade during the final months of the war. He later succeeded John A. Lejeune as commandant of the U.S. Marine Corps. (NARA)

Major General Fox Conner served as the operations officer for the AEF and shaped the next generation of U.S. Army officers. (NARA)

Brigadier General Hugh Drum, First Army's chief of staff in 1918. (NARA)

Major General Joseph T. Dickman commanded the 3rd Division, IV Corps, I Corps, and Third Army during the Army of Occupation. (NARA)

Brigadier General Charles G. Dawes was appointed to serve as the AEF's chief of the Purchasing Board and later served as the vice president of the United States. (NARA)

Lieutenant General Robert Lee Bullard, Second Army commander in France, October 1918. (NARA)

Major General Hunter Liggett (right), photographed with Major General Clarence R. Edwards in May 1918. Liggett commanded I Corps, First Army, and Third Army. (NARA)

Major General Clarence R. Edwards (left), commander of the 26th Division, photographed with Brigadier General John Sherburn of the 92nd Division near Verdun in October 1918 shortly before Edwards was sacked. (NARA)

Major General George H. Cameron, commander of V Corps for the first phases of the Meuse–Argonne offensive. (NARA)

Below Major General Robert Alexander, the controversial commander of the 77th Division, pictured (seated left) with members of his staff in 1918. (AHEC)

Brigadier William "Billy" Mitchell served as the AEF's chief of air service during the latter half of the Meuse–Argonne campaign. Immediately following World War I, he was America's leading advocate of airpower. (NARA)

Lieutenant Colonel George S. Patton, pictured with a Renault tank, commanded the 304th Tank Brigade late in the war. During the interwar years, he was one of America's leading advocates of armored warfare. (AHEC)

Lieutenant Colonel William J. Donovan commanded the 1st Battalion, 165th Infantry Regiment of the 42nd Division in 1918 and would go on in World War II to lead the Office of Strategic Services (OSS), which after the war became the foundation of the Central Intelligence Agency. (AHEC)

The son of a former president and cousin of a future president, Lieutenant Colonel Theodore Roosevelt, Jr. (center) commanded the 1st Division's 26th Regiment in 1918. During World War II he earned the Medal of Honor on Utah Beach on D-Day. (AHEC)

Captain Harry S. Truman commanded Battery D, 129th Field Artillery of the 35th Division during the war. He later retired from the U.S. Army Reserve as a colonel of field artillery. He succeeded Franklin D. Roosevelt as President of the United States. (NARA)

Official U.S. Army Signal Corps photo of General Pershing taken during the war. This picture appeared as the frontispiece in the 1931 edition of Pershing's memoirs. (NARA)

U.S. banks, sale of railway stocks, and sale of industrial bonds. The Reparations Committee and Germany accepted the Dawes Plan in April 1924. The plan was implemented on 30 August; the first reparation payment was made on 1 September. The occupation of the Ruhr ended on 22 October. For this accomplishment, Charles Dawes was awarded the 1925 Nobel Peace Prize, shared with Sir Austen Chamberlain, for facilitating reconciliation between Germany and France. Dawes was unable to travel to Oslo to receive his award. He, instead, sent the following telegram on 10 December 1926:

> This award, which is in recognition of the work of the First Committee of Experts, Reparation Commission, of which I was chairman, is gratefully acknowledged. The committee was composed of Owen D. Young, Sir Josiah C. Stamp, Sir Robert M. Kindersley, Jean Parmentier, Edgard Allix, Alberto Pirelli, Frederico Flora, Emile Francqui, Baron Maurice Houtart, and myself. It was the endeavor of the experts to found their plan upon the principles of justice, fairness, and mutual interest, relying for its acceptance thus prepared upon that common good faith which is the enduring hope for the universal safeguarding of peace. That the results achieved under it have merited in your judgment this high recognition is a tribute to the united efforts of the committee.[5]

Dawes' success in Europe garnered fame stateside. In the 1924 presidential election, incumbent President Calvin Coolidge easily captured the Republican nomination. After some back and forth at the Republican convention in Cleveland, Dawes was nominated for vice president. It was an interesting pairing, as the taciturn Coolidge preferred to continue running the country as President (he had assumed the presidency after the death of Warren G. Harding from a heart attack) and left the campaigning up to Dawes, who crisscrossed the country travelling over 15,000 miles and delivering 180 speeches. During the campaign, the Democratic team of West Virginia's John W. Davis and his running mate, Nebraska governor Charles W. Bryan, attacked the Dawes Plan as "sinister," accusing it of merely enhancing the wealth and power of bankers while impoverishing further the German people. Still Coolidge/Dawes won overwhelmingly with 54 percent of the popular vote and capturing 382 electoral votes to Davis/Bryan's 136.

At Dawes' swearing in, he took the opportunity to admonish the Senate for their conduct, at times shouting and pounding (the furniture) and further reminding them that it was he as the vice president who presided over the Senate. Coincidentally, just a few days later, Dawes was absent when a crucial tie-breaking vote was needed over a cabinet appointment. By the time Dawes arrived, one senator had changed his vote to "nay," scuttling the appointment. This angered Coolidge and left Dawes hounded by the press for much of his term in office. Dawes would ruffle feathers with many of the senators concerning the cloture and filibuster rules which he believed contributed to the Senate's gridlock in passing legislation. Still, by 1927, he began developing personal and respectful relationships with many of the senators, which became instrumental in getting key pieces of legislation passed. One of his last successes was getting the Versailles Treaty ratified on 15 January 1929, nearly ten years after its signing.

In 1927–28, there was widespread support for Dawes to run for President. Coolidge had decided not to run for reelection. The frontrunner for the Republican Party was Herbert Hoover. Dawes was determined not to run and instead supported Hoover, who proved victorious in November. On 9 April 1929, Dawes was appointed ambassador to the Court of St. James, an ideal choice given Dawes' personal relationship with Great Britain, which went back to his role in securing the $500 million Anglo–French loan in 1915 and his time serving on the MBAS during the war. He resigned as ambassador in February 1932 and returned to Chicago serving as chairman for City National Bank and Trust Company for the remainder of his life. Charles Gates Dawes died of a heart attack at his home in Evanston, Illinois on 23 April 1953.

PART FOUR

THE ARMY COMMANDERS

CHAPTER 12

LIEUTENANT GENERAL HUNTER LIGGETT

Douglas V. Mastriano

Hunter Liggett was the personification of a soldier-scholar. He studied the character of war and considered its ramifications on the future. Liggett studied campaigns of old, constantly reading books of history that highlighted the campaigns of Grant, Lee, Stonewall Jackson, and Napoleon, and endeavored to pass this knowledge on to his subordinates. His keen eye and understanding were evident in a staff ride that he led in 1914 in Luzon, Philippines, where he intuitively identified the Lingayen Gulf as the best location to conduct an invasion. This beach would be used by Japanese Lieutenant General Masaharu Homma in 1941 and by General Douglas MacArthur in 1945 during World War II. Such foresight would serve Liggett well in World War I, especially in the Meuse–Argonne campaign of 1918.

Liggett was born in Reading, Pennsylvania, on 21 March 1857. He graduated from West Point in 1879 and was assigned to the 5th Infantry Regiment, serving along the frontier in the Dakota and Montana territories, pursuing groups of Lakota Indians. Most of the frontier was secure in July 1881 after the surrender of Sitting Bull (the Apache Wars continued in the southwest for several more years). After this, Liggett and the 5th Regiment served in Texas and Florida. He deployed briefly to Cuba during the Spanish–American War and then to the Philippines. While there, Liggett met John J. Pershing, an acquaintance who would play an important role in his life during World War I.

In 1903, Liggett returned to the U.S. as a staff officer at the Department of the Great Lakes in Chicago and then held battalion command at Fort Leavenworth, Kansas, in 1907. Although not officially a student, Liggett furthered his military education at Leavenworth by monitoring classes at the School of the Line and the Staff School, thanks to the help of Lieutenant George C. Marshall. In 1909, Liggett reported to the U.S. Army War College as a student and was subsequently selected to serve as a member of the faculty. Liggett updated the curriculum with historic studies in the context of the changing character of war, as well as developing war plans for regional interventions.

Liggett's career continued to prosper when he was selected to command the Department of the Great Lakes in 1913. This was followed by brigade commands in Texas and the Philippines. In 1916, Liggett was given command of the Department of the Philippines and by that time was one of the most experienced officers in the United States Army. When war was declared in April 1917, Hunter Liggett was quickly given command of the 41st Division and would rise rapidly to corps and army command.

On 22 September 1917, a group of 14 American division commanders, including Hunter Liggett, sailed from Hoboken to France to get a firsthand view of the war. After a tour of the British and French lines, they reported to Pershing's headquarters at Chaumont where he briefed them on his vision for fighting the war. Pershing commented on the quality of the senior officers in the group, writing in his memoirs, "Quite a number of the division commanders… were either physically unfit or had reached the age when new ideas fail to make much of an impression and consequently, I recommended that both classes be left home for other duty or retired."[1]

Liggett, very overweight and 60 years old, seemed to fit into this class of officers. However, Pershing knew him from the Philippines and saw that, even in 1917, he was both an innovative thinker and a tireless leader. Nonetheless, the group of officers returned to Bordeaux for transport back to the States to prepare their divisions for deployment to France. However, Liggett's 41st Division was soon to arrive and he remained in France to await them. When the unit arrived in December 1917, it was broken up and the men assigned largely to the 1st and 2nd Divisions. (The 41st was a designated replacement division.) Liggett later took pride in the performance of the 1st and 2nd Divisions, knowing that he had trained many of the men.

Pershing personally selected Liggett to command I Corps on 15 January 1918. His excellent character as an officer, and his reputation as a critical thinker and a brilliant student of history, continued to bless his career with success. I Corps was comprised of the 1st, 2nd, 26th, 32nd, 41st, and 42nd Divisions. The corps deployed to the Vosges, with the remnants of the 41st assuming training duties. The units assigned to Liggett's I Corps were spread across France in various French training areas or supporting Allied operations. He organized his staff and did all that he could to ensure that they would be ready to plan and conduct corps-level operations.

Liggett's chief of staff when he commanded the 41st Division was Colonel Malin Craig, a future chief of staff of the U.S. Army. They had met at the Army War College. Due to their friendship, Craig announced to Liggett that he would serve as the chief of staff, to which Liggett readily agreed. Liggett said that he "gave [Craig] a free hand and charged him with responsibility in selecting his section chiefs and otherwise building the machine." Liggett diverged from Pershing's penchant for micromanagement, and instead demanded that the staff sections "relieve [him] of all detail… permitting [him] to concentrate entirely on [his] job as commander."[2] Liggett's guidance to his staff was that he wanted a "harmonious family" and that any troublemakers would be removed. This gave Liggett time to contemplate how best to employ his troops in the ever-changing environment without getting bogged down into unnecessary details.

Hunter Liggett also disagreed with Pershing's cult of the bayonet view on how to fight in 1918. Pershing believed that the French and

British had become flaccid during the years of trench warfare. To overcome this, he believed that the Americans should not train for trench warfare and rather focus on open "maneuver" warfare. This led to the over-emphasis on bayonet and rifle training, in the belief that once the American solider arrived, the AEF would break out of the trenches and drive the Germans back. This resulted in Pershing issuing orders to not heed the lessons learned from the Allies' experience, as he feared this would take the aggressive fighting spirit from his Doughboys. Liggett disagreed with Pershing on this. Although he supported the idea of training the men in maneuver, he also thought it foolhardy to ignore the realities of the trenches. Liggett rightly believed that it was essential that the Americans were trained in both areas and used his position as commander to make this happen. The French and British were happy to accommodate this and eagerly accepted the rotation of American units into the trenches.

The collapse of the Russian Empire in November 1917 gave Germany an opportunity to knock the French or British out of the war before the late-arriving American Army could swing the balance against them in mid-1918. Ludendorff wrote of this:

> With the American entry into the war, the relative strengths would be more in German favor in the spring than in late summer… unless we had by then gained a great victory… Only a far-reaching military success which would make it appear to the Entente powers that, even with the help of America, the continuation of the war offered no… prospects of success, would provide the possibility of rendering our embittered opponents really ready to make peace. This was the political aim of the Supreme Command in 1918.[3]

With that in mind, Ludendorff transferred nearly a million men to the Western Front over the winter of 1917–18 to participate in a series of offensives that began in March 1918. The German hammer blows achieved some deep penetrations into the Allied lines, but never achieved a breakthrough. In the end, Ludendorff's offensives failed to achieve the strategic success needed to win the war.

Liggett rushed his units to various parts of the Western Front to backstop British and French divisions as well as to occupy large segments of the line to free up additional troops to deploy to threatened sectors. As the American 1st Division launched an impressive attack against the Germans at Cantigny, the fourth German offensive (Operation BLÜCHER) kicked off north of the Marne, driving a 30-mile wedge south into the Allied lines at Château-Thierry. Liggett's American I Corps joined the French Sixth Army to blunt the German attack and then drive them back in an audacious counteroffensive in July. The legacy of this campaign is still with the United States Army and Marine Corps. During the defense of the Marne River, I Corps' 3rd Division absorbed a series of fierce German attacks and then drove their enemy back, earning the moniker "Rock of the Marne." Meanwhile, the 2nd Division, comprised of one Marine brigade, dashed into Belleau Wood and drove the Germans back; earning the moniker "Devil Dogs."

As the last of the German attacks faded in July, Liggett was ordered to support the French to drive the Germans back from the Marne. Liggett was given tactical command of the French III Corps in addition to his own I Corps – the first time that French soldiers served under American command since the 1781 Battle of Yorktown. The attack kicked off on 18 July 1918 and the Franco–American attack drove the Germans back. Liggett's force included nearly 200,000 men from nine American divisions. The debut of the first American corps-level attack since 1865 showed immense promise. Liggett remarked, "Our officers, with very few exceptions, had measured up the most exacting requirements of modern warfare in the open."[4] With this impressive start of large American operations, Liggett's corps was moved south of Verdun to prepare for the reduction of the Saint-Mihiel salient.

The Saint-Mihiel salient had existed since 1914 and was 25 miles wide and 16 miles deep. This wedge gave the Germans several advantages, chief of which was threatening the vital French Paris–Nancy rail network. Pershing planned this operation, with the approval of Foch, to test the American First Army. Liggett's I Corps would fight here with two other American corps (the IV and V) and the French II Colonial Corps. The operation kicked off on 12 September and included 550,000

Americans, 110,000 French, 1,481 aircraft, 3,000 pieces of artillery, and 400 tanks.

Liggett's I Corps was responsible for reducing the eastern flank of the salient and he appealed to Pershing for a more aggressive attack to cut off the Germans before they were able to escape. He also pushed for the element of surprise with a less lengthy preparatory barrage. Unfortunately, Liggett's proposals were disregarded, denying the opportunity for what might have been an even more successful operation. B. H. Liddell Hart remarked on Liggett's astute understanding of war:

> Liggett's early perception of the essential value of methods which the best of his allies only reached after years of trial and error, and which many of his contemporaries never arrived at, is a testimony to the superiority of study and reflection over mere experience, and to the value of a mind nourished on military history.[5]

This reduction of the Saint-Mihiel salient was an astounding success, as Pershing remarked:

> The rapidity with which our divisions advanced overwhelmed the enemy, and all objectives were reached by the afternoon of September 13. The enemy had apparently started to withdraw some of his troops from the tip of the salient on the eve of our attack, but had been unable to carry it through. We captured nearly 16,000 prisoners, 443 guns, and large stores of materiel and supplies. The energy and swiftness with which the operation was carried out enabled us to smother opposition to such an extent that we suffered less than 7,000 casualties during the actual period of the advance… After seventeen months… an American army was fighting under its own flag.[6]

As the attack ended, Liggett's I Corps, and most of the other American units, began a 60-mile move west to be ready for the Meuse–Argonne campaign, slated to kick off on 26 September 1918. The Meuse–Argonne campaign would be the largest battle in American history, and over the course of its 47 days included 1.2 million Americans and several hundred thousand French troops. The initial attack would include three American corps. Liggett's I Corps was on the left third of the Meuse–Argonne area of operations; in the center was V Corps (under General George Cameron); and on the right, III Corps (under General Robert L. Bullard).

This area of operations was not new to Liggett's staff; he had ordered them to study it eight months before as the best place for the American Army to attack. His thinking was precise; it was the narrowest part of the line along the Western Front where a successful offensive could threaten the vital German rail network at Sedan–Mézières. Germany had an extensive lateral rail network behind the lines along the Western Front, where it could shuttle some 20 reserve divisions to blunt Allied breakthroughs. Foch needed the German strategic reserves committed to fighting the Americans in the Meuse–Argonne region to open the way for a British and French breakthrough in the north. After the American attack in the region commenced on 26 September 1918, three other Allied Army converging attacks would follow in sequence.

Liggett's I Corps was given difficult terrain to attack through. With a sector about 10 miles in width (west to east), the western half encompassed the entire Argonne Forest along the American boundary with the French Fourth Army. The Argonne is one of the rare ancient forests in Western Europe that withstood time, empires, and the industrial revolution. It is simply too rugged to navigate or exploit. The forest juts up above the western flank of the Meuse Valley along a north–south axis. It is filled with deep ravines, artesian wells, steep cliffs, and thick groups of trees. Control of the Argonne affords the occupant extensive observation and control of the Meuse Valley to the east, and was therefore considered key terrain for both the Germans and Americans in 1918. Everything about this forest gave the defender the advantage.

The eastern portion of I Corps' sector was in the western Meuse Valley, intersected by the narrow L'Aire River and a series of hills and ridges running west to east (favoring the German defenders). The key terrain in the Meuse Valley facing Liggett's men was the devastated hill of Vauquois. The hill once had a village on top of it, but it was completely destroyed as French and German engineers exploded more than 500 subterranean mines under the hill in an effort to drive each other off of it. A massive scar split the hill along what became no man's land as a result.

Liggett had three divisions in his corps for the main attack. The 77th Division occupied the western half of the Argonne with its western boundary along the French Fourth Army area of operations. The 77th was a National Guard division mostly recruited from New York City; the division had the nicknames of "Metropolitan Division" and "Liberty Division." It was commanded by Major General Robert Alexander who had a reputation for pushing blame down the line to his brigade and regimental commanders when things went wrong. The 77th was one of the AEF's most experienced divisions, but had suffered heavy casualties and was in the midst of incorporating 4,000 new soldiers into the unit.

Given the mission of clearing the eastern half of the Argonne and the western edge of the Meuse Valley was the 28th Division. The 28th was also a National Guard division, had an excellent reputation in the AEF, and was commanded by Major General Charles Muir. The 28th likewise had suffered significant casualties earlier in the summer and was integrating green replacements before the attack kicked off. The 35th Division occupied the eastern third of I Corps' area of operations and was given the daunting task of liberating Vauquois. The 35th was also a National Guard division comprised of men mostly from Kansas and Missouri. Captain Harry S. Truman commanded a battery of artillery in the 35th. The division was commanded by Major General Peter Traub and was one of the most inexperienced in the AEF.

As the Meuse–Argonne attack kicked off, Liggett's men pushed ahead, meeting stiff German resistance especially in the Argonne Forest, where American gains were negligible at best. The forest was defended by the German 76th Reserve Division and the 2nd Landwehr Württemberg Division. The Württembergers spent most of the war in the Argonne and said that it was like a second home to them. They made the Americans pay dearly in blood and held them at bay in the Argonne. However, the 28th Division had success in driving the German 1st Prussian Guards back in the valley east of the Argonne, forcing the Württembergers in the Argonne to fall back to avoid encirclement.

The inexperienced 35th Division managed to secure Vauquois in just a few hours. This was due largely to the heroic action by several small-unit leaders, such as a battalion commander Major James Rieger, and a squadron of tanks led forward by Lieutenant Colonel George S. Patton. But the 35th began to fall apart as German resistance stiffened when the strategic reserves arrived. A series of German counterattacks threatened to punch a hole into the 35th Division, but this was averted by several of the unit's chaplains who took command of broken units and the swift arrival of the 110th Engineer Regiment. The 1st Division arrived on 30 September to take over the 35th's area of operations.

Meanwhile, things were not going well in the Argonne. Neither the 77th nor the 28th Division had made significant headway in the forest. To make matters worse, a joint push of the French Fourth Army to the west of the Argonne and I Crops in the Argonne failed on 2 October 1918. However, a mixed command of just under 700 Americans from the 77th Division found a gap in the German lines and penetrated about half a mile behind the enemy. Under the command of Major Charles Whittlesey, this element would be called the "Lost Battalion" by the Americans and endure a five-day siege, with every frontal attack by the 77th Division trying to save them being driven back. Liggett saw his opportunity. Borrowing a page from Stonewall Jackson's brilliant flanking maneuver at Chancellorsville in 1863, Liggett ordered the 82nd Division to advance up the Meuse Valley, and, together with the 28th Division, attack in a westerly direction to cut off the Germans in the Argonne from the rear. If this worked, the Lost Battalion would be saved.

The American attack kicked off in earnest on 8 October 1918 and initially failed to make headway, until Corporal Alvin C. York from Pall Mall, Tennessee, rose to the occasion. Alvin was a Christian from a pacifist denomination and struggled with the morality of killing for one's country. However, facing a hail of German bullets, and in an endeavor to save the lives of his fellow soldiers, Alvin York eliminated a German machine gun, fought off a bayonet attack, killed 25 of the enemy, and captured 132. His actions helped to break the German control of the Argonne and triggered their withdrawal from the forest.

Although making small gains in mid-October, the American First Army was facing stalemate and stagnation. Pershing was too caught up in the details of running the First Army and dealing with the Allied leaders as AEF commander-in-chief. Additionally, he planned on establishing a U.S. Second Army, and therefore decided to relinquish command of First Army to Hunter Liggett on 16 October 1918. The First Army was in bad shape after three weeks of continuous attacks and Liggett accepted command contingent on being given a free hand in reorganizing it, putting off the next major offensive until 1 November (in conjunction with the French Fourth Army), and not having constant interference from the AEF commander. To his credit, Pershing agreed, knowing that Liggett was the best man for the job.

The plan was for First Army units already in the line to maintain pressure on the Germans until the 1 November push. Liggett ordered integration of artillery, aviation, and tanks in the big push. He called for troops to use small-unit tactics to bypass enemy strongpoints and to maneuver to their designated objectives. Liggett wrote of this:

> There was a lull of two weeks in the major operation while we tightened up. My staff and I traveled constantly among the troops, making every effort to profit from my past mistakes and to encourage the fighting spirit of the army for the impending attack on the enemy's main positions, and never was the response more immediate or effective.[7]

His view of Pershing's handling of the First Army was not a positive one: "The defects of the American operation in this battle were such as were humanly inescapable in a not yet fully seasoned army…"[8] Reflecting on the first large battle of the American Civil War, Liggett wrote, "I know that [Union General] McDowell had a perfect plan of battle at the First Bull Run [1861], but that he made the mistake of assuming that he had an army instead of a well-intentioned mob…" Liggett's First Army attack, which began on 1 November 1918, progressed superbly. Artillery fire was maximized, coordination with aviation improved, and the use of tanks was brilliantly executed. He managed to do in one day what the AEF had not been able to do over the previous five weeks – drive the Germans back into open warfare. For the next ten days Liggett's First Army was largely in pursuit of the enemy. Pershing's dream of open warfare had at last arrived.

Liggett's more flexible leadership style had the added benefit of encouraging risk and individual initiative. In one case, the Army brigade in the 2nd Division used its native German speakers to advance on the flanks and in front of the unit at night to tell the enemy to "join the formation" whereupon they were captured. This ruse enabled the 2nd Division to advance 4 miles behind enemy lines and drive them off the last defensible terrain in the area.

The waning days of the war were not without its controversies. First Army issued orders to continue the attack on 11 November, and these orders were not rescinded when word of the Armistice going into effect at 1100 hours arrived. This resulted in men falling in the final minutes of the war and costly river crossing operations over the Meuse River and Meuse Canal. Then there was the disastrous order to seize Sedan that resulted in the 1st Division countermarching across the I Corps sector and thereupon stopping the advance of a third of the First Army. Liggett's reaction was nothing short of furious, calling the entire affair a "tactical atrocity."[9]

After the war, Liggett took command of the U.S. Third Army during its brief occupation of the German Rhineland. He retired from the U.S. Army in 1921. He died on 30 December 1935 in San Francisco, after writing two noteworthy books on his experience as a leader in the AEF. Of his experiences, Liggett wrote, "I took command of the First Army on the sixteenth [October 1918]. It then consisted of seventeen American and four French divisions… a total of more than 1,000,000 men," and "The war was a succession of lost opportunities on both sides."[10]

Despite Liggett's advanced age and ponderous appearance, Pershing recognized a leader who had a brilliant mind, and whose grasp and understanding of history was unmatched in the AEF. Indeed, Liggett was a model of what a scholar-soldier could do as a senior leader. His keen mind was quick to apply the lessons of history in the context of modern warfare. His leadership and vision perfected the First Army and he was responsible for its superb performance in the waning days of the war.

CHAPTER 13

LIEUTENANT GENERAL ROBERT L. BULLARD

Sebastian H. Lukasik

Lieutenant General Robert Lee Bullard belonged to a small circle of U.S. Army officers, which also included Hunter Liggett and Joseph Dickman, who rose to field army command during or immediately after the Great War. Bullard established a reputation as one of the senior officers upon whom Pershing could rely to implement the standards the AEF's commander-in-chief expected of American troops in France. A devotion to Pershing's emphasis on discipline and offensive-mindedness helped propel Bullard through the AEF's hierarchy at a rapid pace, elevating him to the command of a brigade, a division, a corps, and a field army in less than a year. He played a major role in some of the AEF's pivotal engagements, including Cantigny, the Aisne–Marne offensive, and the climactic fighting in the Meuse–Argonne. Overshadowed by more flamboyant officers and largely forgotten today, Bullard nonetheless emerged as a mainstay of the AEF's combat leadership structure, and typified both the strengths and weaknesses of the officers that dominated the AEF's higher-echelon combat commands throughout the war.

Born on 15 January 1861 near Opelika, Alabama, into a struggling farming family, Bullard sought to overcome his circumstances through higher education. He attended the Agricultural and Mechanical College of Alabama (today Auburn University) for one year, but his family's inability to pay for additional studies prompted him to seek and accept admission to the U.S. Military Academy at West Point in 1881. Bullard graduated with a second lieutenant's commission in 1885, placing 27th in a class of 39 graduating cadets. Assigned to the 10th Infantry Regiment in New Mexico, Bullard participated in the campaign to capture the Apache leader Geronimo. After this, Bullard's career settled into the routine of peacetime garrison duties on the Western frontier. Desperate to escape the stasis into which his career appeared to be sinking by the mid-1890s, Bullard attempted to obtain a transfer from the line to one of the U.S. Army's powerful staff bureaus, a move that promised faster promotion, an increase in pay, and proximity to the Army's centers of institutional power and influence in Washington.

Bullard's efforts paid off with his appointment to the Subsistence Bureau, but before he could take up his duties as a staff officer, the outbreak of the Spanish–American War dramatically altered the course of his career. Commissioned a major in the wartime U.S. Volunteers, Bullard organized and trained a battalion (subsequently expanded into a regiment) of African-American volunteers from Alabama. Although the regiment was disbanded without ever being deployed overseas, Bullard gained experience as a troop leader, sufficiently impressing his superiors to warrant further promotion and to gain command of another regiment of U.S. Volunteers that he led in the Philippine War in southern Luzon, and in the Moro Insurgency in Mindanao. Returning to the United States after an assignment as an administrator of a district in the Philippines, Bullard reverted to duty with the infantry. Over the next few years, he served in a variety of assignments that included temporary duty with the Provisional Government in Cuba, command of a Regular U.S. Army infantry regiment, and a year as a student at the Army War College (1911–12).[1]

Over the next five years, Bullard's military career was bound up with events on the Mexican border. The political instability during the Mexican Revolution (1910–20) prompted the Wilson Administration to maintain a military presence in the Southeast for much of the decade. Bullard took command of one of the infantry regiments deployed to the Mexican border. By 1916, with the crisis in Mexico threatening to spill over into U.S. territory, Wilson ordered the mobilization of the National Guard for deployment to the southern border. As an officer with command experience, Bullard was a natural choice to lead one of the National Guard brigades.

While on the Mexican border, Bullard had given little thought to the possibility of the United States actively intervening in the war that had been ravaging Europe since 1914. All of that changed in April 1917, when the United States entered that war. Confronted with the need for a massive expansion of the peacetime U.S. Army into a force capable of making a meaningful impact on the course of the war, the War Department authorized the organization of several officer training camps to produce a cadre for the wartime army. Within a few days of America's declaration of war against Imperial Germany, Bullard was assigned the task of organizing and commanding one such facility, at Little Rock, Arkansas. In May, he was promoted to brigadier general, and assigned to command the 2nd Brigade of the 1st Division, the formation that comprised the nucleus of what would become the American Expeditionary Forces (AEF).

Arriving in France in mid-June 1917, Bullard spent several months overseeing the establishment and operation of the AEF's school system. That assignment reflected Pershing's high estimate of Bullard as an officer capable of implementing what the AEF chief envisioned as a key element of his command's future success on the Western Front.[2] Pershing viewed AEF schools as crucial to imbue his subordinates with the offensive spirit he believed America's European partners lacked. In spite of the AEF high command's determination not to emulate French or British warfighting methods, Bullard took care to inspect and observe the French Army's approach to organizing instructional facilities. His responsibilities were subsequently narrowed down to establishing four schools for training infantry platoon leaders. While willing to observe his hosts' best practices, Bullard was careful not to imitate their tactical precepts, thus remaining well within the parameters of Pershing's guidance concerning military instruction in the AEF.

Notwithstanding his contribution to setting the foundations of the AEF school system, Bullard's work in that sphere soon came to an abrupt end.

Determined to restrict the AEF's higher command echelons to officers who conformed to the strictest standards of professional competence, mental agility, and physical fitness, Pershing proved uncompromising in culling the ranks of his divisional and corps commanders of officers he believed failed to measure up to those standards, and replacing them with men of greater promise. Among the first to fall short of the mark was Major General William Seibert, commander of the 1st Division, whose unsatisfactory performance resulted in his being sent back to the United States. Pershing designated Bullard as Seibert's replacement.[3]

Given the privileged place that the 1st Division – "Pershing's Pets," as its soldiers became known in the AEF – occupied in Pershing's mind, Bullard's assignment spoke volumes about the professional regard the AEF's commander had for the erstwhile brigadier general. But it also placed on Bullard a considerable burden of responsibility. As commander of the 1st Division, Bullard became a key player in Pershing's efforts to transform it into an organizational template for the AEF as a whole, a formation whose high standards of discipline, training, and combat effectiveness would serve as a benchmark for all American combat divisions. Bullard threw himself into the task of molding the 1st Division into an organization capable of operating effectively in the challenging combat environment of the Western Front. Toward that end, Bullard supervised the implementation of an AEF-prescribed training program designed to get his division ready to take its place in the front line.

By January 1918, Bullard's division was proficient enough to enter the line in a "quiet" sector of the front located in the Saint-Mihiel salient. Here, the troops honed their tactical skills by conducting raids against German positions and learning infantry–artillery cooperation and aerial observation in support of ground operations. In addition, this helped Bullard address lingering deficiencies in staff work and communications with his command, while providing valuable experience in working with French commanders.

Although much work remained, events unfolding on the Western Front ensured that the 1st Division would never complete its training regimen. The onset of Operation MICHAEL, the first of the great offensives that the German high command launched in the spring of 1918, forced the AEF to commit its partially trained units to battle. Accordingly, Bullard received orders to proceed with his division from the Saint-Mihiel salient to Picardy, where it could assist the French in stopping the German advance. In late April, the 1st Division took up positions opposite the German-occupied village of Cantigny, northwest of the town of Montdidier. Although the expected German hammer blow against the sector did not materialize, Bullard's troops remained in place. Both the American and French high command had something more ambitious in mind for the 1st Division, however. In early May, the division began preparations for the first major American offensive operation of the war: a well-rehearsed attack to capture and hold Cantigny to improve the Allies' tactical position in the sector, but also to show to America's French and British allies the AEF's maturation as a military force.

Preceded by elaborate and carefully rehearsed preparations intended to minimize the possibility of failure, the attack consisted of a limited operation by a single regiment of the 1st Division heavily supported by French artillery and aerial reconnaissance assets. Determined that nothing be left to chance, Bullard delegated the burden of developing the plan to liberate Cantigny to his G-3 (operations chief), Lieutenant Colonel George Marshall. Marshall's brilliance shone forth with his singular ability to develop complex plans and present them in a manner that subordinates could execute them. Such acumen caught the attention of not only Bullard, but General Pershing as well. Bullard's trust in Marshall paid off, and on 28 May, the 28th Infantry Regiment captured Cantigny with only about a hundred casualties. Consolidating the gains and defending the village from German counterattacks proved significantly more problematic, however, with the 28th Infantry losing a third of its strength while fighting off repeated German counterattacks before being relieved by the 18th Infantry. A relatively minor engagement by the standards of the Western Front, Cantigny was the first American offensive victory of the war, and provided Pershing with the evidence he needed to demonstrate that his troops were capable of operating effectively on the Western Front.[4]

In early July Bullard was elevated to command the AEF's newly established III Corps. Bullard was tasked with coordinating the preparations of the 1st and 2nd Divisions for the Franco–American counterattack at Soissons, but critical shortages of staff meant that Bullard had to delegate effective tactical control of the two AEF divisions to the French XX Corps, while Bullard and his staff observed the attack from the sidelines. Only a few days later, however, III Corps received control of three AEF divisions (3rd, 28th, and 32nd) operating in the Aisne–Marne sector as part of the French Sixth Army.

Bullard's experiences in July and August 1918 proved among the most challenging and frustrating of his time in command. For several weeks, his divisions were bogged down in the vicious fighting focused on the valley of the Vesle River, where they fought to dislodge the retreating Germans from their defensive positions along the northern bank. In addition to the tenacity of the German opposition, Bullard had to contend with an array of problems that constrained his ability to exercise effective command. Serious friction characterized Bullard's relationship with General Jean Degoutte, commander of the French Sixth Army, with the latter professing impatience with what he saw as his American divisions' deficient aggressiveness. Bullard also clashed with Colonel Alfred W. Bjornstad, his abrasive and at times insubordinate chief of staff. Poor staff work, compounded by logistical and communications problems, exacerbated Bullard's frustrations. These issues culminated in the painful episode at Fismette, a small hamlet on the north bank of the Vesle that became the focal point of some of the bitterest fighting that American troops endured that summer. Convinced that retaining the small bridgehead his troops held in Fismette in the face of fierce German counterattacks was futile, Bullard ordered the bridgehead evacuated, only to have his orders countermanded by Bjornstad and Degoutte, resulting in the killing, wounding, or capture of the better part of a company of the 28th Division clinging to Fismette.[5]

The impasse along the Vesle came to an end in early September, when the Germans abandoned their positions because French successes further to the northwest had made their positions untenable. Bullard's troops followed the retreating defenders for a few days, but on 8 September, III Corps turned its sector over to a French headquarters and proceeded east to join the U.S. First Army. Bullard's men did not participate in the reduction of the Saint-Mihiel salient (12–15 September), but would play a key role in the great offensive that Pershing intended to launch between the Argonne Forest and the Meuse River later that month. The plan for what would become the Meuse–Argonne offensive envisioned III Corps operating on the right of the line, its eastern boundary along the Meuse itself. Bullard's task was to advance alongside and protect the eastern flank of General George Cameron's V Corps. The latter, positioned in the center of the U.S. First Army's three-corps front, had the decisive task of capturing the dominant German defensive position at Montfaucon. Bullard's orders lacked clarity. While they required III Corps to advance against and capture German defensive positions east of Montfaucon and subsequently take the latter terrain feature under enfilade fire, they provided little indication about whether Bullard's units were expected to turn Montfaucon from the east by crossing into the V Corps zone of advance. In the absence of explicitly articulated guidance, Bullard and his staff elected to treat divisional and corps boundaries as binding, a decision that would have profound implications for the attack's execution.

When the Meuse–Argonne offensive began on the morning of 26 September, Bullard's attack initially went well. All three of his frontline divisions (from west to east the 4th, 80th, and 33rd) moved forward despite suffering from enfilading artillery fire directed at them from the German batteries on the east bank of the Meuse. Problems soon developed on Bullard's left, where the 4th Division's initial rapid advance to the corps objective soon slowed down when it became clear that the German defenders of Montfaucon were holding out against the attacks of V Corps' 79th Division, while pouring enfilading fire into the 4th Division's left flank. General John L. Hines, commander of the 4th Division, sought permission from Bjornstad to swing his division west, into the V Corps sector, to link with the 37th Division north of Montfaucon, thus enveloping the troublesome strongpoint and severing its defenders from sources of supply and reinforcements. Bjornstad balked at the audacity of Hines' proposal, but in Bullard's temporary absence from headquarters, authorized the 4th Division commander to make a limited advance into the V Corps zone beyond Montfaucon. Before the movement could begin in earnest, however, Hines received orders from III Corps headquarters countermanding this limited attack.

The cancelation of the order remains one of the most controversial episodes of the Meuse–Argonne offensive, not in the least because the person on whose authority it was issued has never been conclusively identified.[6] Historians have variously singled out both Bullard and Bjornstad as responsible for the revocation of the order. Regardless of who bore the blame, III Corps continued to attack straight ahead toward the First Army's objective line, instead of maneuvering to support the 79th Division. The strongpoint did not fall until the following day, slowing down the First Army's advance and contributing to its loss of momentum, while allowing the Germans to bring up reinforcements that further slowed the tempo of the offensive as a whole.

Over the next few days, III Corps continued to push against rapidly hardening German defenses. Typical of the conditions all along the American line, Bullard's troops found their progress hampered not only by the enemy but also by deteriorating weather and the logistical gridlock that threatened to overwhelm the sparse road network upon which the entire First Army depended for its sustainment. Even so, Bullard's command advanced farther than either V Corps or I Corps (the latter on the extreme left of the line), reaching the second German defensive line by the time Pershing called an operational pause on 30 September. When the offensive resumed on 4 October, III Corps focused its efforts on capturing German positions between Cunel and Romagne, sustaining 8,000 casualties in two days of fighting in exchange for relatively limited gains. For nearly a week thereafter, Bullard's attacks conformed to a similar trend. By 12 October, III Corps had pushed through the Kriemhilde Stellung, the mainstay of the German defensive network in the Meuse–Argonne sector, but at the cost of mounting casualties, with Bullard and Pershing increasingly compelled to goad unit commanders into action they perceived as inadequately aggressive.

On 10 October 1918 Pershing activated the U.S. Second Army, with Bullard in command as a lieutenant general. Once the new formation was ready for combat, its mission would be to advance up the eastern bank of the Meuse, screening the right flank of the U.S. First Army. Arriving at his new headquarters at Toul in mid-October, Bullard threw himself into the task of preparing his new, and still largely notional command for a major attack. With the Meuse–Argonne offensive in full swing, Bullard did not have much to work with. The Second Army's order of battle never exceeded six divisions, including units that had suffered heavy losses in the Meuse–Argonne or, conversely, had little to no combat experience. Bullard's army also lacked a sufficient number of specialized combat support and transport units, though in contrast to his previous experience as a corps commander, it did have an efficient staff, including a chief of staff, Colonel Stuart Heintzelman, whose professionalism offered a refreshing contrast to Bjornstad's controlling tendencies.

Apart from organizational and logistical considerations, Bullard's tenure as Second Army commander embroiled him in the controversy surrounding the treatment of the 92nd Division, an African-American formation assigned to his sector. Like many other detractors of black troops, Bullard exaggerated the substandard performance of one of the division's four infantry regiments in the Meuse–Argonne, while overlooking the impressive combat records of its other elements. He also ignored the role that the racist mindsets of the division's white officers played in hampering the unit's ability to function effectively in combat. Bullard's own racial outlook may also have contributed to the jaundiced view he expressed on the division's combat effectiveness in particular, and African-Americans' soldierly qualities in general.[7]

The Second Army finally went on the offensive on the morning of 10 November, when Bullard ordered his divisions to make limited attacks against German positions in preparation for a general offensive that Pershing directed Bullard to commence the following day. The Armistice put an end to that operation before the Second Army had had a chance to make more than limited advances along its front, although Bullard insisted that his troops press on with their attacks even after he had learned, early on the morning of 11 November, that a ceasefire would take effect later in the day. The decision reinforced Bullard's reputation, in the eyes of contemporaries and future historians alike, as a commander whose dedication to Pershing's insistence on aggressiveness in battle bordered on a callous disregard for his soldiers' lives.

The anticlimactic conclusion of Bullard's Great War experience foreshadowed the remainder of his long life. Returning to the United States in March 1919, he was attached to the Office of the Chief of Staff of the Army, General Peyton March, and participated in discussions about the postwar structure of America's defense establishment. In October 1919, he received command of the Eastern Department (designated the II Corps area in 1920) with headquarters on Governors Island in New York harbor. Rapid demobilization soon stripped Bullard's command of troops and units to a point where his duties became largely ceremonial. Though he continued to influence debates related to national defense policy and advocated universal military training, the decline of popular interest in such matters rendered his proposals moot. Following his retirement from the Army at the mandatory age of 64 in January 1924, Bullard struggled to find a useful role. The following year he became president of the National Defense League, a civic organization dedicated to the promotion of causes close to his heart, including higher defense budgets, universal military service, and patriotic instruction in the nation's schools. A prolific writer, he authored three books, including his own wartime memoir, intended to highlight the American contribution to the Allied victory in 1918, as well as newspaper articles on military subjects. In spite of his knack for publicity and tireless involvement in veterans' organizations, Bullard slipped out of public consciousness within a few years of his retirement. He died on 11 September 1947 in New York City, World War II having erased from popular memory what little recognition he may have once had.

A century after the Great War, historians remain ambivalent about Bullard's legacy. His biographer Allan R. Millett views Bullard's significance largely in terms of his stature as the archetype of a senior U.S. Army officer whose career reflected in microcosm that institution's transition from a "frontier constabulary" to a professional military serving an industrialized world power.[8] A more recent historiographical strain emphasizes Bullard's willingness to conform to Pershing's injunctions about leadership, organization, and operational and tactical doctrine as the key to his dazzling career trajectory during the war.[9] Whatever the verdict, there is no doubt that Bullard's consistent, and at times ruthless, commitment to acculturating his various commands to the spirit of Regular Army discipline and aggressiveness in battle was instrumental in shaping the AEF as a whole in the mold Pershing continually sought to impress upon it.

CHAPTER 14

MAJOR GENERAL JOSEPH T. DICKMAN

J. Mark Jackson

Joseph Theodore Dickman was a writer, thinker, chronicler, scholar, teacher, prophet, and soldier – the veteran of five American wars. He was born on 6 October 1857 in Dayton, Ohio to Theodore and Mary (née Weinmar) Dickman. The devout Catholic family moved to Minster, Ohio (near Wapakoneta, Ohio) when Joseph's father left for service in the Civil War as a lieutenant in the 57th Ohio Volunteer Infantry, fighting in the western theater of the Civil War. He saw action principally at Shiloh and Vicksburg, and thus the Dickman military dynasty began, encompassing four generations of Army officers.

Joseph attended school in Wapakoneta, St. Mary's Institute (now the University of Dayton), and the U.S. Military Academy. His education at West Point was interrupted by a suspension for involvement in a hazing incident. However, he was reinstated and graduated 27th of a class of 54 cadets in 1881. He was commissioned second lieutenant, 3rd Cavalry, and remained a cavalryman at heart throughout life. While training at Fort

Leavenworth, Kansas, he met Mary Rector and the two married on 26 September 1882.

Dickman was assigned to various posts with the 3rd Cavalry in Texas, Kansas, Arizona, and Illinois between 1883 and 1894. He participated in the capture of Geronimo and the suppression of public disorder during the Pullman Strike. After a stint at Fort Ethan Allen, Vermont, Dickman was assigned to Fort Leavenworth in 1895 as head instructor at the Infantry and Cavalry School. Dickman had the opportunity to study military arts and impart this knowledge to other officers. He also found his voice through the pen, writing numerous articles for newspapers and military journals. He became a military scholar at precisely the time the U.S. Army was about to need thinkers and strategists.

When war erupted with Spain in April 1898, First Lieutenant Dickman reverted to a cavalryman and served as adjutant general under General Joseph Wheeler. This position recognized Dickman's organizational capabilities. He later was promoted to captain and assigned as chief commissary, heading logistics and resupply for combat operations. Ever the cavalryman, however, Dickman participated in the Battle of San Juan Hill. He remained in Cuba until 1899 as part of the occupation force. Shortly after this, he was deployed to the Philippines, promoted to major in the 26th Volunteer Infantry in August 1899, then to lieutenant colonel in September, 1899. In 1900, he served in China as part of the American expedition to quell the Boxer Rebellion. He served on the staff of Major General Adna Chaffee.

In early 1901, Dickman was ordered back to the United States, mustered out of the volunteer infantry, and reverted to his Regular Army rank of captain. Nonetheless, during his brief time as a lieutenant colonel he had gained invaluable staff experience well beyond the level of his permanent rank of captain. He then returned to Fort Leavenworth as an instructor at the Infantry and Cavalry School, where he established a reputation as an accomplished writer and strategic thinker. His articles advocating a robust reserve component to augment the active component gained notoriety and he became a respected voice for the Army of the future.

Promoted to the permanent rank of major in March 1906, Dickman experienced a rapid succession of positions and promotions between 1906 and 1917, including commander of the 13th and 2nd Cavalry Regiments, inspector general of cavalry in the Philippines, and then for the entire U.S. Army. Dickman was promoted to lieutenant colonel in February 1912 and colonel in December 1914. While inspector general of cavalry, he made a grand tour of Russia, Germany, Italy, Austria, France, and Great Britain, observing their tactics. His experience with the future belligerents gave Dickman insights few American Army officers possessed.

Dickman waxed prophetic in an article for *Free Press* of Burlington, Vermont, exhibiting a strong grasp of European military affairs on the eve of the British declaration of war against Germany in August 1914:

> In the general conflagration impending the nations concerned can place in the field no less than 15,000,000 trained soldiers of various arms. It is likely that on the open fields of eastern Prussia and the north of France there will be battles in which a million men will be engaged in mortal combat at the same time. There will be fierce fighting in the air, underground in sieges, and beneath the waters of the ocean. The cheapness of human life is likely to be illustrated on an enormous scale. Extensive use will be made of aviation, and the relative merits of the dirigible balloon and the aeroplane will be shown. The vast armaments of modern field artillery will have ample opportunity to establish its claim to preponderating influence on the field of battle.[1]

America entered the war in April 1917. It then had the 17th largest army in the world and it was unprepared to enter a technologically advanced war. Dickman's military experience, coupled with his knowledge of the belligerents, made him an invaluable asset. He was promoted to brigadier general in May, 1917. The enormity of the task facing the United States daunted the Army as it was woefully short of leaders at all levels. Men were promoted at a dizzying and even alarming rate. Dickman was promoted to major general in August 1917 and given command of the 3rd Division. He, like his colleagues and superiors, operated in leadership roles at least two or three ranks in advance of their experience levels. The 3rd Division embarked for France in early March, 1918 and made first landfall in the United Kingdom. He held the naïve American belief that the battlefield problem and the war itself would be solved by the young and bold American soldier. Nonetheless, there was a sense of trepidation at the prospects of the situation that awaited the Americans. They also resented what they saw as a sense of arrogance among the Allies that viewed the Americans as backward upstarts. Writing after the war in his book, *The Great Crusade*, Dickman complained:

> A general air of pessimism and lack of confidence in the outcome of the war seemed to pervade the country [England]... Friction was also reported between the Americans and the English, the latter stating that the Americans had delayed coming across for fear of being licked, to which the Americans retorted that the British were already whipped, and that they had hurried over to help them out.
>
> The British army was... three hundred thousand men short and unable to obtain replacements, unless the home defense army of over one million men could be drawn upon. A plan advocated at this time was to utilize the American battalions immediately and, under pretext of necessity for training and experience, to incorporate them in the British divisions in order to bring them up to war strength. Our attaché reported that the French also were "all in."[2]

The 3rd Division arrived in France by the end of April 1918 and went into a two-month training phase: one month of training and one month in a quiet sector of the trenches. The 3rd Division's quiet sector was slated to be in the Vosges; however, the German Spring Offensives of 1918 diverted the division into the line about 25 miles west of Reims, near Château-Thierry. The 3rd Division was attached to the French XXXVIII Corps. As Dickman later wrote, "When the 7th Machine Gun Battalion of the 3rd Division arrived at Conde-en-Brie, at noon of May 31, the confusion of the general retreat was so great that it was difficult to locate the front and to find the higher commanders."[3]

With the support of the U.S. 1st, 2nd, and 3rd Divisions, the French managed to bring to a halt Operation BLÜCHER, the fourth of the five great German Spring Offensives. Dickman, however, expressed frustration with the parceling out of his division's units to plug gaps in the line. Although he disliked being the caretaker instead of the commander, Dickman supported the Allies. He later wrote, "In conformity with the French policy of giving the American divisions instruction and experience, our regiments and battalions were scattered, laterally, over a wide area… and they performed a variety of duties, such as occupying front line positions, guarding bridges and constructing trench systems and other defensive works."[4]

After the Allies halted Operation BLÜCHER, the French high command assigned the 3rd Division to a consolidated sector in the line centering on Château-Thierry. In a letter to his brother-in-law, Dickman described the 3rd Division's role in halting the German Operation MARNESCHUTZ-REIMS on 15 July, and the subsequent Allied counteroffensive starting on 18 July:

> The River Marne flows in a deep valley, the bluffs on each side being more than 300 feet high… In this deep valley there are two good roads and a railroad which would be indispensable to the enemy in an advance towards the south and eventually towards Pairs. This valley was held by the right of my division and became the principal objective for the great attack of the Crown Prince, which at midnight of July 14th and 15th at 12:10, he turned loose all the artillery he had within reach – calibers of 77[mm], 150[mm], 210[mm] and Minenwerfers, which, for two hours and forty minutes, bombarded the front-line of my position and chewed up the ground and the forest. At ten minutes of three in the morning of July 15th, he commenced crossing the Marne in boats and on foot-bridges. The attack extended from near the left on my position [Château-Thierry] nearly all the way east to Dormans.
>
> The artillery of my division immediately began its fire of counter-preparation directed against the north bank of the Marne and then against the bridges which he was trying to throw across the river. His troops were under fire as they approached the crossing, while in the boats and when they landed. I had over 200 machine-guns in selected positions, carefully camouflaged and protected, which opened a very destructive fire on the enemy as he came across.
>
> However, on the right of my position, which was held by the 125th French Division and other divisions of the French Army, and towards

> Dormans, the enemy was more successful. The whole thing gave way and by early morning the German troops had gained the high ground five miles south of the river, and my division was fighting the enemy's force five miles in the rear of its right flank. We lost a battery, which could not be carried off, as the French support disappeared early in the game. It was necessary to refuse the right flank a little to meet this attack, but the whole line held firmly and effectively stopped the invasion of the German forces, and as he was unable to gain possession of the Sumerlin Valley, he could make no headway.[5]

Dickman was kind in his description of the French units on his right flank. The French 125th Division unceremoniously pulled back, leaving the 3rd Division's flank completely exposed at the point of German penetration across the Marne. Swiftly, the 3rd Division "refused their right" by essentially forming a right angle, fighting along the Marne and on their right in the Surmelin River Valley. Tenacity more than expert execution enabled the 3rd Division to thwart the German advance. The attacks were disjointed and unsupported, resulting in high casualties. But the American propensity to fight tenaciously, almost to the last man, masked operational shortcomings. The 3rd Division held, and in the process earned the nickname it still bears, "Rock of the Marne." During the battle Dickman famously said, "*Nous resterons là*" ("We shall remain here"). In August 1918 Dickman was given command of the U.S. IV Corps, which included the 1st, 3rd, 42nd, and 89th Divisions – all battle-tested and experienced units. After a reprieve, IV Corps deployed in early September to participate in the Saint-Mihiel offensive. The German-occupied Saint-Mihiel salient protruded into the Allied line and threatened the French ability to support Verdun. The salient also represented a threat to the American right flank and rear for the planned Meuse–Argonne offensive. AEF General John Pershing therefore insisted on eliminating the Saint-Mihiel salient before launching the Meuse–Argonne attack.

Writing his brother-in-law on 11 September, Dickman described the plans and preparations for the Saint-Mihiel offensive:

> The command of a corps of over 100,000 men now under my control is a serious business. When orders are prepared the operation is prescribed for

> D day and H hour. These are kept secret as long as possible. It is just not D-1 and H-10hr. The artillery bombardment of 800 guns from my corps alone begins at H-4 and lasts until H hour at which time the infantry leaves the jumping off trench and starts for the enemy. In this case H hour is 5 in the morning of Sep. 12th. My corps, as you will have seen in the papers, is the 4th and consists of the 1st, 3rd, 42nd and 89th divisions. I also have several hundred tanks, 5 balloons, and it is reported that 1,700 airplanes are to take part in the show. All the preparations are made, the die is cast, I am waiting for the few remaining hours for the beginning of an affair, the effect of which will be felt around the world. If it succeeds, it must convince the German people that they cannot win this war.[6]

Dickman also described the uncomfortable situation a senior commander finds himself in just before the start of a battle: the plan is set, the orders are issued, and the corps commander can only wait. Dickman spent the hours prior to the attack playing the card game solitaire. Once the attack started, the combined American and French forces reduced the salient in just two days. At the time, it appeared to be a stunning feat of arms, but the Germans were already in the process of withdrawing from the Saint-Mihiel salient, and the attack caught them just as they were starting their retrograde action.

The Meuse–Argonne offensive kicked off on 26 September 1918. Most of the units that had fought in the Saint-Mihiel offensive were still in the process of redeploying, and were not available for the first phase of the Meuse–Argonne operation. Thus, mostly new, untested American divisions were committed, and the initial results were not good. The French had not been able to pierce the German first-line Kriemhilde Stellung in three years, yet Pershing required almost impossible objectives and accepted nothing less than success. But the Meuse–Argonne offensive stalled quickly and the casualties were exceedingly high. Pershing's determination to fight a maneuver battle of "open warfare" and reliance on the verve of the untested American soldier risked catastrophic failure. Pershing sacked officers who failed to meet their objectives, no matter the casualty rate or the impossibility of their missions. In a letter to his wife, Dickman expressed his concern: "So many generals are being reduced in

Map 4: The Allied General Offensive: 26 September–11 November 1918

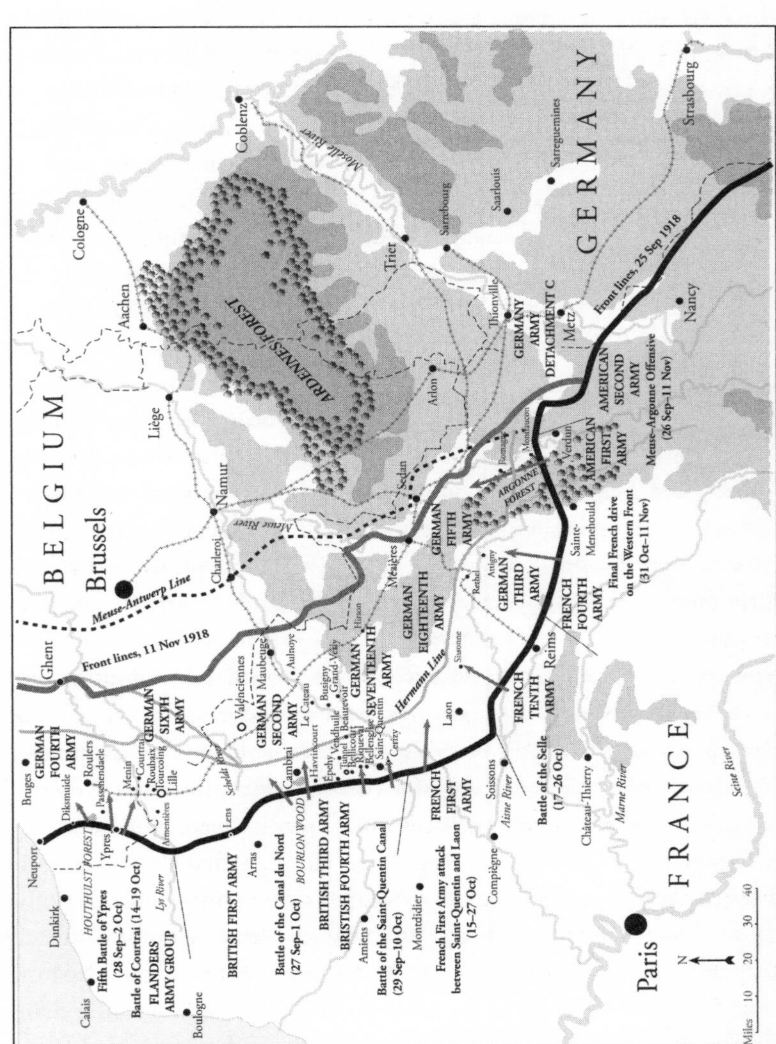

rank or sent home that I sometimes wonder when my turn is coming... As somebody says, all this may build up a back-fire and if anything should go wrong, somebody else's head might go into the basket."[7]

In a letter five days later, the possibility of being relieved of command still haunted Dickman, but he tried to remain optimistic: "Five more generals have been sent home. I am feeling in such good shape physically that they are not likely to get me, especially if my good luck keeps up."[8] As the American offensive stalled and restarted, Dickman in October was shifted from IV Corps to command of I Corps, on the American left. He replaced General Hunter Liggett, who replaced Pershing as U.S. First Army commander, although Pershing remained in command of the AEF. In a letter to his brother-in-law Dickman explained the situation on the Western Front at the time he assumed command of I Corps:

> The present situation of the German Army may be compared to that of a large crowd in a hall, trying to get out at the back door. The British, French and Belgian Armies are pushing against the crowd, while the Americans are trying to close the door by an advance to the north and west of Metz. Naturally the hardest fighting is at the door which must be kept open at all cost to prevent capture of the whole crowd. We find the troops in front of us are constantly reinforced by those withdrawn from the north and west. Those who follow the retiring German armies in Flanders and the north of France are making good progress whereas we are up against a very stiff proposition and do well to keep the enemy occupied. The greatly reduced German divisions still fight very well as our casualty lists will show when they are published.[9]

After regrouping, the American advance in the Meuse–Argonne continued, with Dickman's corps securing the heavily wooded Argonne Forest. Dickman described the heavy fighting in a letter to his brother-in-law:

> In the dense forest filled with a maze of barbed wire and loaded with machine guns commanding every path and opening as well as across the open fields swept by guns of all caliber directed by airplanes, the struggle goes on. The weather is cold, raw and wet and there is a very little shelter

> as all the towns and farms have been destroyed. The soldiers not actually on the line are living in ruins, caves, cellars & rude shacks or lean-tos.[10]

The American Army was close to Sedan when the Armistice went into effect on 11 November 1918. Two days later Dickman was named commander of the newly formed U.S. Third Army. The mission of this new army was to shadow the German Army back across the Rhine River, and ensure compliance with the terms of the Armistice, and assume occupation duties in the American Occupation Zone. Dickman was disappointed that the command did not come with promotion to lieutenant general. But with the end of combat, Congress was conferring no further high-level promotions. Maintaining discipline and morale of a new army, only four days old, that did not have the bonding experience of combat was no easy mission. Nonetheless, the Third Army started its advance to the Rhine on 17 November.

The Third Army passed through Luxembourg and arrived on the German frontier on 23 November. Relations between the Americans and the Allies, especially the French, had been strained enough throughout the war, but the situation became perhaps worse at this juncture. The Allies acutely and justly resented any implications that the Americans had won the war and the peace. Both France and Britain had lost too many lives and expended too much treasure to be upstaged by the late-arriving Americans. Yet, it was Pershing himself who was the lead pusher of just such a narrative. Further, American political leaders were more concerned about the future world order, based upon President Woodrow Wilson's Fourteen Points. The Allies wanted reparations and vengeance. Dickman's role required balancing American interests and values with those of the French. Dickman wrote: "While our troops no longer were indispensable to the Allies, they still needed our money."[11]

During the period leading up to the signing of the Versailles peace treaty, Dickman met with Allied Supreme Commander Marshal Ferdinand Foch, whom he described as, "A small dried up Frenchman of 67 [years old] and he looks it. He was very pleasant however and we had a nice talk."[12] Yet the French reduced and limited the Rhine River frontage which Dickman's Third Army occupied on 10 December 1918. Dickman relinquished command of the Third Army on 28 April 1919 and assumed the position of president of a board of officers to capture the lessons of the war and propose future organization and doctrine for the U.S. Army. Dickman embarked from Brest on 12 July 1919. Once back in America, Dickman continued serving as the president of the Tactics and Organization Board until his retirement on 6 October 1921. He was briefly recalled to active duty in 1922 to preside over the postwar-Army downsizing board. He died on 23 October 1927 of a heart attack in Washington, D.C. and was buried in Arlington National Cemetery.

PART FIVE

THE CORPS AND DIVISION COMMANDERS

CHAPTER 15

MAJOR GENERAL GEORGE H. CAMERON

Kenneth S. Shaw

George Hamilton Cameron commanded U.S. V Corps at the start of the Meuse–Argonne campaign in 1918. His relief from command by General John J. Pershing 12 days into the battle is one of the most controversial and least understood episodes in the history of the American Expeditionary Forces (AEF).

Cameron was born in Ottawa, Illinois, on 8 January 1861. He graduated from the U.S. Military Academy at West Point in June, 1883 with a commission as a second lieutenant of cavalry. He served his first tour of duty with the 7th Cavalry, followed by several tours with the 4th Cavalry at Fort Riley, Kansas, from 1887 to 1912, interspersed with multiple deployments to the Philippines and one tour as an instructor at West Point. In 1888, Cameron married Nina Tilford, the daughter of Brigadier General Joseph G. Tilford. He was promoted to lieutenant colonel in 1914, and served as an instructor and then director of the U.S. Army War College until 1916.

Cameron was promoted to colonel in July 1916. Three days before the United States entered the war in Europe, he was assigned to command the 3rd Brigade, 5th Cavalry Division, and then command of the 25th Cavalry Regiment. Promoted to temporary brigadier general, he assumed command of the 40th Division in September 1917. In December, Cameron was promoted to temporary major general and assigned to Camp Greene, North Carolina, to organize and command the newly formed 4th Division. From December until March 1918, the poor weather resulted in only 16 suitable days for outdoor military training, which severely limited the time for training on critical skills such as marksmanship until just a month before the division left Camp Greene for Europe on 18 April. New troops arrived continuously, and the majority remained nearly completely untrained until they reached France.

By 3 June, all elements of the division were training with the British and French. In July, two battalions of the 47th Infantry Regiment, fighting under the French VII Army Corps, got the first combat experience of the 4th Division, participating in the Allied counteroffensive that pushed the Germans back from the Marne. Some of the men engaged in this action had never fired a rifle before. From 3 to 12 August, the 4th Division, now fighting as part of the U.S. I Corps, advanced to the Vesle River, fighting through a well-planned German defense, and finally established a solid front line across the river. In its first combat experience, Cameron's new division advanced 10 miles, while losing 752 killed, 4,912 wounded, and 590 missing.

On 18 August, Cameron assumed command of U.S. V Corps, which was assigned a mission in the upcoming attack to reduce the Saint-Mihiel salient. Early in the war, the sector between Verdun and Nancy had been the scene of heavy fighting between the Germans and the French. The resulting salient was 20 miles wide, with a total perimeter of approximately 40 miles. For nearly four years the French attacked repeatedly, but every attempt failed, with great losses against a very strongly reinforced defensive network with excellent rail support, which facilitated reinforcement on interior lines.

Pershing had long planned for the reduction of the Saint-Mihiel salient to be the first major American offensive under U.S. command. Allied

Supreme Commander Marshal Ferdinand Foch wanted to cancel the offensive, to give the U.S. First Army more time to prepare and get in position for the coming attack into the Meuse–Argonne sector. This would be the American vector of Foch's Allied General Offensive, converging from four arms across the entire length of the Western Front. Pershing, however, insisted that the failure to eliminate Saint-Mihiel first would constitute a threat to the American rear when the U.S. First Army attacked into the Meuse–Argonne. Foch relented.

Cameron had less than a month to organize his newly formed corps and prepare it for battle. The plan for Saint-Mihiel had the French II Colonial Corps attacking against the nose of the salient, while U.S. I and IV Corps attacked the southern face of the salient, and Cameron's V Corps attacked the base of the salient from the west. The total force was comprised of 216,000 American and 48,000 French soldiers, with another 190,000 Americans in seven divisions in reserve. The German defenders numbered about 75,000, supported by very considerable artillery with large stocks of ammunition. Cameron's V Corps, consisting of the U.S. 26th Division, the French 15th Colonial Division, and the U.S. 4th Division, was assigned to attack Mouilly and Watronville. The 26th Division was commanded by Major General Clarence Ransom Edwards, another of the AEF's controversial commanders who was later relieved. Cameron and Edwards, who were West Point roommates and classmates, clashed during the Saint-Mihiel operation.

The American artillery preparation started at 0100 hours on 12 September 1918. The infantry on the south face advanced at 0500 hours, with the infantry to the west starting three hours later. The 26th Division on V Corps' right flank was the corps' main effort. By the afternoon of the first day Cameron was not satisfied with the slow progress of the French 15th Colonial Division. He ordered Edwards to take over part of the French sector. But as soon as that order went out, Cameron sent the 26th another order, this one originating directly from Pershing. The Germans had already planned to evacuate the salient, and were in the early stages of withdrawing when the Americans and French attacked. Pershing wanted the 26th to link-up with IV Corps' 1st Division attacking from the opposite direction, and close the pincer across the base of the salient near Vigneulles, thereby bagging much of the German artillery. That was a complete change in the scheme of maneuver. Cameron, nonetheless, told Edwards: "This is your chance, old man. Go do it... Try to beat the 1st Division in the race to clean up."[1]

By 0700 hours on 13 September, the 26th Division's 102nd Infantry Regiment had linked up with elements of the 1st Division near Hattonville, cutting the salient in two. They had accomplished their mission, but not without difficulty along the way. Inexplicably, Cameron was critical of the 26th Division in the V Corps after-action report filed on 25 September:

> ... the discipline of some units is very poor and a great improvement in this regard is to be insisted upon... the straggling of American units on the move is very great and it is believed this is due to a lack of discipline on the part of company officers... There was considerable straggling in the captured area during this operation by the 26th Division... It is noted that at times orders are not obeyed with the alacrity so necessary to complete military success.[2]

When V Corps later relinquished command of the 26th Division so that the corps headquarters could redeploy for the coming Meuse–Argonne offensive, Cameron told Liggett that he was glad to be rid of the Yankee Division, because its spirit was "rotten," and that failing originated at the top with Edwards. Many other AEF senior leaders seemed to agree with Cameron.

Saint-Mihiel was the final justification for Pershing's repeated demands that the Americans be allowed to operate in France as an independent army, rather than under French or British command. The drawback to Saint-Mihiel was that it was fought too close in time but too far in distance to the planned start of the Meuse–Argonne offensive, and Pershing had committed most of his experienced divisions at Saint-Mihiel. There was not enough time for those veteran divisions to refit and redeploy for the start of the Meuse–Argonne. Cameron's V Corps was assigned to the center of the American sector, with III Corps on the right, and I Corps on the left. V Corps now consisted of the (from left to right) 91st, 37th, and 79th Divisions, with the 32nd Division in corps reserve.

V Corps' initial objective was the German strongpoint at Montfaucon. Cameron planned for the inexperienced and only partially trained 79th Division to attack the high ground at Montfaucon on the east, and the equally inexperienced 91st Division on the west. Neither division had ever seen the front line when they arrived to take their positions for the attack. More than half of the infantrymen in the 79th Division had only been in the Army for four months.

Many historians have questioned the wisdom of assigning V Corps, with only its 37th Division having any combat experience, to the toughest mission at the start of the operation. Montfaucon was the dominant feature – key terrain – along the entire line. Pershing's plan called for the 79th Division not only to take it, but to advance several miles past on the first day. The commander of the French Army, General Philippe Pétain, warned Pershing that the Americans would not be able to capture Montfaucon before winter.

For inexperienced troops, the 79th Division performed far better than could have been expected. At the jump-off, German wire was thicker than anticipated, and cutting through took longer than the 25 minutes allotted. The artillery creeping barrage passed on ahead, and the German defenders were able to recover and resume their defensive positions, allowing them to inflict heavy casualties from machine-gun positions in Malancourt, Montfaucon, and Bois de Cuisy. Because of their lack of experience, the American troops did not know which enemy forces could be safely bypassed and which had to be completely eliminated. Follow-on elements came under fire from enemy units that had not been eliminated. The 79th Division's lead elements lagged behind the divisions on its flanks, and it found itself almost 2½ miles behind the III Corps' 4th Division on their right.

At about 1600 hours, the 79th Division finally reached the base of Montfaucon. Cameron had anticipated that the German defenders would abandon the position once it became obvious that they were being cut off. The Germans did not cooperate with his plans. Unknown to the Americans, the German 117th Division had arrived in the sector on 12 September, and 6,665 German soldiers now occupied the trenches and hardened dugouts. But Montfaucon could not be bypassed without considerable losses that would result from the dominating fields of fire. For the next two hours, the 79th Division fought its way to the foot of the great hill. The division's 313th Infantry Regiment attacked up the hill without artillery or armor support, and were driven back by German machine guns.

Meanwhile, the 4th Division on the right and the 37th Division on the left were forced to slow their advances to maintain contact with the 79th Division. Progress on 26 September averaged between 3 and 4 miles. The 91st Division on the V Corps left flank made the greatest advance, pushing through the Bois de Chepoy and Bois de Very. By 1700 hours, the 91st Division had advanced 6 miles and occupied the town of Épinonville. The 37th Division spent the day fighting through the dense woods to the west of Montfaucon. Despite German resistance, they achieved their objectives. The 37th Division's 145th Infantry Regiment actually came within striking distance of Montfaucon. Even though it was across the divisional boundary in the 79th Division's sector, they made an attempt to take it, but were driven back.

Things got worse for the Americans as the battle progressed. Each of the three corps had only a single, poor road for a main supply route. All movement on these roads became hopelessly snarled by huge shell holes and the ever-present mud. Engineers and infantrymen worked endless hours to fill in the holes, while trucks, horses, artillery, and wounded waited in maddening traffic jams for days. Meanwhile, III Corps' 4th Division had an opportunity to capture Montfaucon, but did not do so because it was not in their sector. Attacking across division and corps boundaries is a very complicated undertaking that would have to have been coordinated at First Army level. Considering the inexperience of the entire American Army, and in particular, the 79th Division, and the poor communications capabilities that existed at the time, losses from friendly fire would have been highly likely.

The 4th Division received ambiguous orders from First Army headquarters that urged it to support the 79th Division in taking Montfaucon, but the orders failed to provide any detail or cross-boundary coordination instructions. The 4th Division's chief of staff, Colonel Christian Bach, conferred with the III Corps chief of staff, and they agreed

Map 5: The American Meuse–Argonne Offensive: 26 September–11 November 1918

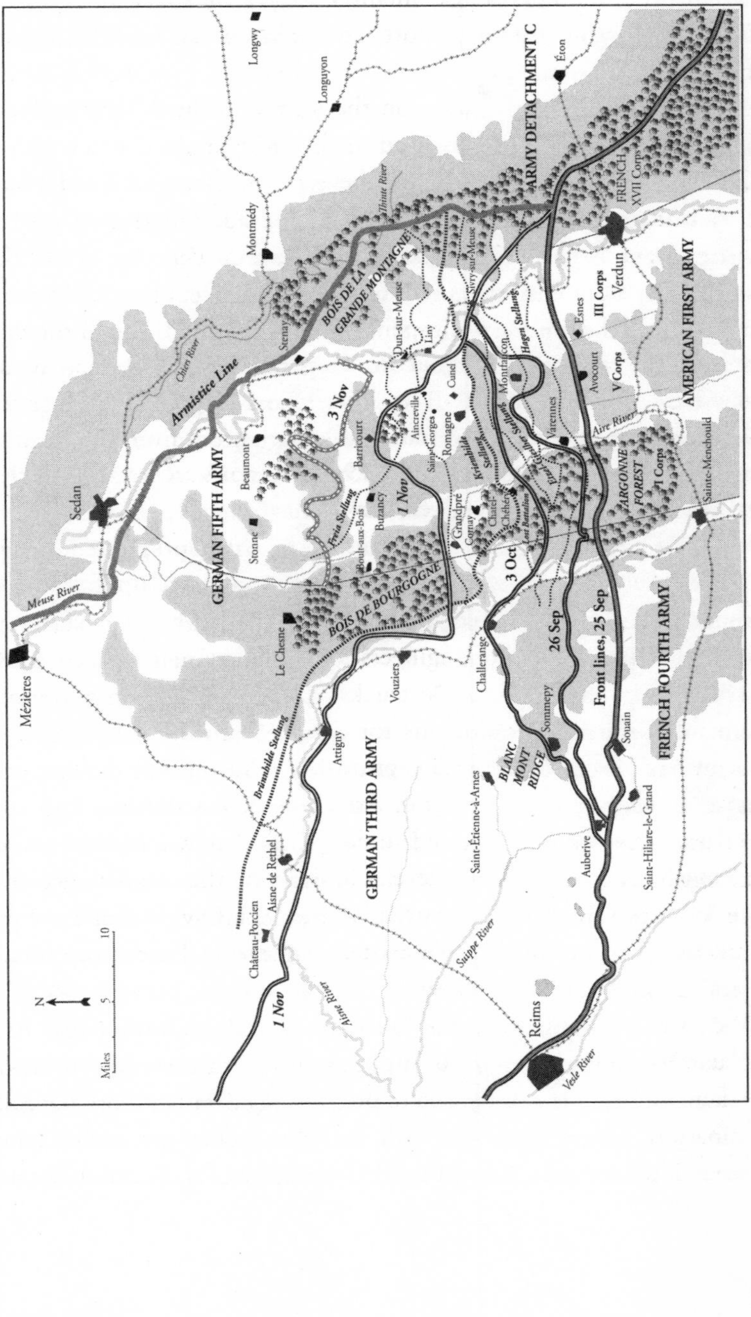

that the 4th Division could do no more than support the 79th Division by continuing to push forward, threatening an encirclement of Montfaucon, and thereby pressuring a German withdrawal. The next morning, the 313th Infantry Regiment again attacked up the slopes of Montfaucon into tremendous German artillery fire. A great effort over the next five hours culminated in the capture of Montfaucon, which gave the Americans the freedom of maneuver to continue advancing.

By the start of October, the offensive in the Meuse–Argonne sector had all but ground to a halt in front of the Kriemhilde Stellung, the German main defensive line. That line remained anchored on three strongpoints: from east to west, the Heights of Cunel, the Heights of Romagne, and the northern apex of the Argonne Forest. The strongpoints were mutually supporting. After a short operational pause, the American First Army launched Phase II of the Meuse–Argonne Offensive on 4 October. In the center, all of Cameron's original frontline divisions had been replaced with rested and refitted veteran divisions. He now had the 32nd Division and the 1st and 3rd Divisions in the line. Pushing steadily forward, V Corps on 9 October attacked the key high ground at Romagne.

On 11 October, three days before the Americans took Romagne, Pershing sacked Cameron as commander of V Corps. He replaced him with the 1st Division commander, Major General Charles P. Summerall, who had long been one of Pershing's favorites. Cameron reverted to command of the 4th Division, which was a very unorthodox assignment for a relieved senior commander. The 4th Division at the time was still fighting as part of III Corps. To this day, many questions linger over Cameron's relief from V Corps. Pershing in his memoirs only mentions the change of V Corps command in very matter of fact terms, offering no explanation for the decision. In his postwar memoirs, General Hunter Liggett merely states that Pershing told him that "he had other uses for General Cameron."[3] Major General William Wright, commander of the 89th Division, speculated in his memoirs that the reason for Cameron's relief was his failure to take Montfaucon on the first day of the Meuse–Argonne offensive. That seems to be the general opinion today. But if that was the case, why did Pershing wait until more than two weeks later to relieve Cameron? And why didn't he do it during the 1–3 October operational pause, rather than after the start of Phase II operations on 4 October? By 11 October V Corps had been heavily engaged for the last week. Nowhere in the discussion of Montfaucon in his memoirs does Pershing directly criticize Cameron or V Corps.

Cameron believed that he was relieved because of a sharp telephone confrontation he had with Pershing's First Army chief of staff, Hugh Drum, who was a colonel at the time. Drum had called Cameron during the fighting at Montfaucon and pressed him to accelerate his advance. Cameron took objection to Drum's tone of voice and said, "Look here, do you know that you are talking to a corps commander and a major general, and that there is only one man in the AEF who can talk to me like that and you are not that man?"[4] Cameron believed that Drum reported the conversation to Pershing, which turned the AEF commander against him from that point on.

Another possible explanation was that Pershing simply wanted to open up a corps command for Summerall. Pershing had a reputation for taking care of his favorites. He almost certainly considered Cameron more replaceable than either I Corps commander Major General Hunter Liggett, or III Corps commander Major General Robert Bullard. In fact, on 12 October, the day following Cameron's relief, U.S. Second Army was established. Pershing, who up until that point had been "dual-hatted" as both AEF commander and First Army commander, relinquished command of the First Army to Liggett, and Bullard was given command of the new Second Army. Major General Joseph Dickman moved laterally to I Corps from IV Corps, which was still in the Saint-Mihiel sector. Major General John Hines moved from the 4th Division to command of III Corps. That, then, left the command of 4th Division open for Cameron to revert to.

There are two key questions here. First, why would Pershing replace all three experienced corps commanders in the middle of a battle? Dickman, of course, was already an experienced corps commander. But although Summerall and Hines were excellent divisional commanders, the command of a corps is far more complex than the command of a division; and upon moving up to that echelon even the most competent general officer must experience a "learning curve" period. And second, if Cameron was an incompetent corps commander, why trust him with division command again, especially one in the middle of a battle? This certainly was not the procedure when Major General Lloyd Fredendall was relieved from the command of U.S. II Corps following the American failure at Kasserine Pass in 1942; or when Major General John Lucas was relieved from command in 1944, after his U.S. VI Corps had spent a month floundering on the beachhead at Anzio.

The official story at the time for Cameron's relief and reassignment was that he "wanted to go back to his old division, the 4th."[5] But this does not square with what Summerall had to say about Cameron on the day that he relieved him:

> The corps commander whom I was relieving had been one of my instructors in drawing when I had been a cadet at West Point. I had always liked him. When he had visited my command post during the battle, he said that he never interfered with his division commanders. From what I afterward learned, he had told the commander in chief, his classmate at West Point [sic], that his corps could not accomplish all that was expected, and orders were given to relieve him. When I arrived, he was alone and walking back and forth in the small dugout. He shook hands with me and said: "Good-bye, I hope you will do better than I have done." He entered his waiting car, and I never saw him again. He was a crushed and brokenhearted man.[6]

On close examination, V Corps' delay in taking Montfaucon on schedule cannot be laid entirely at the feet of Cameron. A large part of the problem was inherent in the basic operations plan, which was laid-out in First Army Field Order No. 20, issued on 20 September 1918. Despite the inexperienced divisions of V Corps being placed in the center of the American attack, the order did not designate a main effort. Nor did anything in the order of battle and the allocation of forces indicate any weighting of a main effort. Each of the three attacking corps was allocated three first-line divisions and one as a corps reserve. The First Army reserve consisted of three divisions, with one deployed in the rear of each of the three corps sectors. The artillery was likewise evenly distributed, with each corps being allocated around 650 guns and some 100–130 trench mortars. The deployment of the forces resembled one massive frontal attack.

Another flaw in the First Army plan was that Montfaucon was only a little more than a mile to the west of the boundary with III Corps, on V Corps' right. In V Corps' sector, Montfaucon sat almost directly on the inner boundary between the 79th and 37th Divisions. Even on the divisional level, then, each of the two attacking divisions could only maneuver against a single of the objective's flanks. It was an extremely difficult tactical problem, one that neither the 37th nor 79th Divisions were up to.

Cameron remained in command of the 4th Division for only 11 days, when on 22 October he was again relieved of command. Apparently, he was not informed of the cause of his relief. That day Cameron visited First Army commander Hunter Liggett to discuss the situation. Liggett's aide, Lieutenant Colonel Pierpont Stackpole, was no great admirer of Cameron. His personal diary entry that day presents a somewhat different picture of Cameron than does Summerall. Ironically, Stackpole also paints Cameron and 26th Division commander Edwards with the same broad brush:

> Cameron in my opinion is a treacherous eel. Later it appears that Cameron has been relieved from the 4th Division and is going home, but without reduction in rank. He wanted to learn from General Liggett why he had been relieved and the latter told him he did not know. Cameron told him many things about his talks with Pershing, including the allusion to the tired condition of the troops, and General Liggett told Cameron he thought he could find in his own utterances the reason, as even though what he said might be true, Pershing did not want to hear them. General Liggett said Cameron had a letter announcing the fact of his relief, and apart from his inquiry as to why he had been relieved gave no evidence of disappointment or disposition to complain or protest – and so far as I know, General Liggett did not commit himself as pro or con in the business and did not sign anything. And the sooner Cameron and Edwards, who thank God is also relieved, get out of reach, the better pleased I shall be.[7]

Three days after Cameron was relieved of command of the 4th Division, Edwards was relieved of command of the 26th Division. Cameron was ordered to return to Camp Gordon, Georgia, to assume a training command. Tragedy struck for the family on 3 November 1918, when Cameron's son, First Lieutenant Douglass Gilford Cameron, Battery D, 7th Field Artillery, 1st Division, was killed in action while directing fire west of the Meuse River, just a few days after his father left to return to the United States. Cameron commanded Camp Gordon until 1 May 1919. He returned to Fort Riley, Kansas, to command the Cavalry School. In May 1919 Cameron reverted to his prewar permanent rank of colonel. Cameron retired from the Army in 1924, after 41 years of service. In 1930, he was restored to the rank of major general on the retired list. He died in Staunton, Virginia, on 28 January 1944 and was buried at Arlington National Cemetery.

To this day Cameron's relief from command is still clouded in questions and controversy. Three factors seem to have played a role to one degree or another in his relief. The running personal animosity between Cameron and Drum was a source of intense friction within the U.S. First Army's chain of command. V Corps' failure to take Montfaucon on the schedule set by Pershing reinforced preconceptions of some key French leaders that the Americans were still incapable of conducting independent operations, increasing the already intense political pressure on Pershing. And finally, the establishment of a second American field army provided an opportunity for Pershing to promote some of his favorites and at the same time remove Cameron in the shuffle. Major General George H. Cameron remains one of the great enigmas of the AEF.

CHAPTER 16

MAJOR GENERAL CLARENCE R. EDWARDS

William H. Van Husen

Clarence Ransom Edwards was born in Cleveland, Ohio, on 1 January 1859, the son of William Edwards, a store merchant. During the Civil War, William, or Billie, was a member of the Cuyahoga County Military Committee responsible for voluntary enlistments. William would eventually recruit 100,000 men for military service, and as a result, he would be given the honorific title of "Colonel." Also in the family was an uncle, Oliver Edwards, who served in the Valley campaigns, the Battle of Gettysburg, and the Appomattox campaign of the Civil War, finishing his service in January 1866 as brevet major general.

Edwards attended Brooks Military Academy in Cleveland before entering West Point in September 1879. He graduated in 1883, 52nd out of a class of 52. His weakness in math and science contributed to his finishing last. Upon graduation, Second Lieutenant Edwards was assigned to Fort Union, New Mexico Territory, guarding the Santa Fe Trail. The following June, his company was reassigned to Fort Porter, Buffalo, New York, where he married Bessie Porter, a member of the prominent Buffalo family from which the fort was named, in June 1889. Edwards was promoted to first lieutenant in February 1891, while assigned as professor of military science at St. John's College (now Fordham University), New York. In November 1895, he was posted to Fort Clark, Texas, promoted to captain, and given command of a rifle company.

With the outbreak of the Spanish–American War, Edwards was promoted to major and served as adjutant general of IV Army Corps, Alabama. IV Corps was slated to deploy to Cuba but, owing to lack of transport, stayed behind and did not participate in any military action. In January 1899, Edwards was appointed adjutant general on Major General Henry Ware Lawton's staff and sent to the Philippines. He participated in all of Lawton's campaigns, earning three Silver Star citations for gallantry in action. A year later, in February 1900, Edwards was reassigned to the War Department as chief of the Division of Customs and Insular Affairs with the rank of lieutenant colonel. In 1902, he was promoted to colonel and named chief of the Bureau of Insular Affairs, where he would stay for the next ten years. In October 1912, Edwards, now brigadier general, was assigned to Fort D. A. Russell (later Francis E. Warren Air Force Base), Wyoming, and commanded the 6th Brigade. In February 1913, the brigade moved to Texas City, Texas, in response to the Mexican Revolution. One year later, he took command of the 1st Hawaiian Brigade at Schofield Barracks, and from February 1915 to April 1917, he commanded U.S. forces in the Panama Canal Zone.

With America's entry into World War I looming, the War Department reorganized and increased the regional Army departments from three to six. Edwards was given command of the newly formed Northeastern Department comprising the New England states. He arrived from the Canal Zone and took command at Boston on 28 April. In the ensuing months, Edwards toured the New England states to view the National Guard troops as well as selecting a suitable site for large-scale training of a division of draftees from New England which eventually became the 76th Division. A site near Ayer, Massachusetts, was selected for this and named Fort Devens, after Civil War Brigadier General Charles Devens.

In May 1917, with the formation of the National Army divisions, the need for new major generals arose. Edwards was disappointed in not being selected for major general, particularly since three officers junior to him were selected. He felt his Republican Party leanings played a part in this. Although he kept his feelings to himself while communicating with his political sponsors, Senators Henry Cabot Lodge and John Weeks, he wrote to his brother, Harry, of his bitterness for non-selection. All were Republicans and close to Theodore Roosevelt, whom President Woodrow Wilson despised. Edwards was eventually promoted major general in August 1917.

On 13 August, Edwards was ordered to form and assume command of the 26th Division and to be prepared to ship overseas in September. The officers comprising his staff and the brigade commanders were a mix of Regular and National Guard officers. The task was formidable, but by the time the first units of the "Yankee Division" sailed to France, the organization was complete. The remaining elements and staff sailed for France on 26 September and upon arrival became the first fully organized and operational American Expeditionary Forces (AEF) division in theater. Edwards arrived in Great Britain on 3 October and crossed the channel into France. He spent the next six weeks touring elements of British VI Corps in the frontline trenches. Several close calls provided his initial "baptism under fire."

In October, the 26th Division deployed to Neufchâteau (division headquarters) in northeastern France. As units arrived, they began training with veteran French and British armies. The winter of 1917/18 was particularly harsh and Edwards' soldiers lacked the proper clothing. Owing to slow logistics and transports, Edwards dispatched his staff to procure shoes, shirts, and underwear, and contracted with local suppliers for woolen items, boots, and firewood. Not surprisingly, this drew criticism from AEF General Headquarters (GHQ). Additionally, in late 1917 the early stages of the great Spanish Flu pandemic were spreading rapidly among the troops in Europe. Close quarters, particularly the trenches, accelerated the spread as did close confinements in army hospitals.

According to prevailing rumors within the AEF, Pershing was "not satisfied with his major generals," and if he wanted to see any of his divisional commanders, "he would send for them."[1] As a result, Edwards did not meet Pershing until 9 November at GHQ, Chaumont. Shortly after that meeting a lingering cold he had suffered after observing frontline

British formations developed into pneumonia. Edwards spent a week in late November at the Johns Hopkins unit hospital at Bazoilles-sur-Meuse, followed by two weeks of quarters rest.

Edwards' 26th Division came under I Corps, commanded by Major General Hunter Liggett. Edwards found him likable, but he had difficulties promoting officers under Liggett's command. Liggett's chief of staff, Lieutenant Colonel Malin Craig, seemed to detest Edwards and blocked his recommendations for promotions. Liggett tended to defer the day-to-day running of the corps to Craig. Edwards had problems keeping his officer positions filled. Pershing frequently poached staff officers for posting to GHQ. To be fair, all AEF divisions sacrificed officers to General Staff positions. Edwards, nonetheless, tried to retrieve some of his officers taken by GHQ, but he was blocked by Pershing's chief of staff, Brigadier General James G. Harbord.

Edwards purged 55 officers whom he felt were unfit for combat command. Many were either posted to the AEF's Line of Communications (later renamed the Services of Supply) or sent home. In January 1918 Edwards relieved Colonel Ernest L. Isbell as commander of the 102nd Infantry Regiment. As a replacement, Harbord sent Colonel John H. "Machine Gun" Parker. Edwards was skeptical at first, given Parker's reputation as an eccentric, but Parker proved to be what the unit needed to revive its morale and energy. Between January and November 1918, Parker received four Distinguished Service Crosses for valor, oftentimes leading his troops from the front.

The new year did not begin well for Edwards. Liggett observed that he was often late and was a bad manager of time. On one occasion Edwards forgot to schedule a machine-gun exercise which he had invited Liggett to observe; he was late for a meeting that same evening – both of which did not go unnoticed by Craig. On another occasion, Edwards retrieved two of his companies temporarily assigned to the Line of Communications. Although GHQ had scheduled the release of these companies back to the 26th Division, the formal order had not been issued. As Edwards had no authorization to transfer his units back, he was given a written admonishment by Brigadier General Benjamin Alvord, Jr., the AEF adjutant general. Also, in January, the AEF inspector general, Brigadier General Andre Walker Brewster, conducted a training inspection and delivered "an absurdly unfair and unjust inspection report" that "demanded the unobtainable."[2]

In February, the 26th Division was assigned to the French XI Corps on the Chemin des Dames ("Road of the Ladies") ridge for training under General Louis de Maud'huy. Craig, still having Liggett's ear, implied that Edwards was not fully engaged and failed to visit his units. Additionally, Craig overheard Colonel James L. Bevans, the division surgeon, complain of poor sanitary conditions to Edwards. These incidents were reported by Liggett to GHQ where they were noted and filed in Edwards' personnel folder. The training continued into March when Liggett reported to Pershing that the 26th Division's spirit and discipline were excellent, though Edwards remained in poor health – the lingering effects of his bout with pneumonia. Around this time, Edwards made critical comments of fellow officers which also got back to Pershing. When the AEF commander sent Harbord to talk to Edwards, the latter wrote to Pershing claiming to have been misquoted and assured Pershing of his full support. Pershing was close to relieving Edwards.

On 1 April, the 26th Division was sent to the Toul region to relieve the 1st Division. Edwards established his HQ at Boucq. He deployed his troops along an 11-mile line southeast from Apremont, with the French 10th Colonial Division on his left and the French 69th Division on his right. The relief was not a smooth transition; Edwards' report laid the blame on the 1st Division, which Major General Robert Bullard, 1st Division commander, took personally. Both Bullard and Craig blamed Edwards. Still the transfer was completed on 3 April. Liggett felt the transfer was adequate, noting that mistakes were bound to happen.

In mid-April, Edwards' chief of staff, Lieutenant Colonel Cassius M. Dowell, requested to be relieved and reassigned, because he felt he had difficulty working for Edwards. Reluctantly, Edwards agreed and requested a replacement from GHQ. Pershing sent Lieutenant Colonel Duncan K. Major, who previously had served as aide to Edwards in Texas. Major proved to be rigid and dogmatic and not well liked by the other officers. Additionally, he frequently back-channeled information to Pershing.

Activity in the region was heavy. During one particular raid at Apremont, the 26th Division's 101st Field Artillery Regiment not only stabilized the division's line but also helped stabilize the adjacent French line. As a result, the 101st Field Artillery became the first American regiment to be awarded the Croix de Guerre.

The war's first major engagement with American forces came on 20 April 1918, near the village of Seicheprey. Two companies of the 26th Division's 102nd Infantry Regiment were subjected to a German surprise attack which started with a heavy artillery barrage that disrupted the American communications and isolated the companies. The initial barrage was followed by a 3,000-strong attack by German infantry and *Stosstruppen*, supported by aircraft and trench mortars. By the time the Germans withdrew and the front line was restored, the 102nd Infantry had suffered 81 killed, more than 400 injured or gassed, and 197 prisoners captured. American reports of German casualties numbered over 1,200; but postwar German reports recorded only 82 killed and 270 wounded. Although initially overrun by the German attack, with the village lost, by nightfall the Americans had retaken their original positions. The inexperienced Doughboys had put up a better fight than the Germans had expected, and the interrogations of the captured Americans gave the Germans greater insight into their new enemies. Pershing, nonetheless, was furious that his forces had been caught by surprise. He blamed Edwards for the high casualty numbers, going so far as to accuse him of dereliction of duty. He also accused Edwards of sitting quietly in the trenches while allowing a surprise attack on his troops, further stating that such unpreparedness was inexcusable and would not be tolerated.

In June, the 26th Division was ordered north to the Aisne–Marne sector to relieve the 2nd Division. As the result of their Operation BLÜCHER offensive, the Germans drove a deep salient near Château-Thierry. Following the 6–26 June Battle of Belleau Wood, the U.S. 2nd Division was relieved in-place by the 26th Division, and once again, reports of a poorly conducted hand-off made their way to Pershing. On 15–17 July, the Germans tried to expand the pocket but failed. The next day, Allied forces, including the 26th Division, went on the offensive and forced the Germans into a "fighting withdrawal." On that same day,

Pershing sent a telegram to Secretary of War Newton D. Baker advising him of his intent to relieve Edwards. However, since the 26th Division was currently engaged, Pershing sent a subsequent telegram the next day, 19 July, putting Edwards' dismissal in abeyance.

Edwards' difficulties with his superiors continued. On 20 July, the 26th Division's right-most element, the 101st Infantry Regiment, was bogged down at Bois de Halmardiére. Liggett ordered Edwards to bypass the woods and to keep the counterattack going on schedule. Edwards ignored the order and kept on pressing through the woods. That decision resulted in far more casualties and delays. Also, at this time, Liggett ordered Edwards to move his divisional headquarters from his château at Méry-sur-Marne forward to Genevrois. Reluctantly, Edwards set up an operational forward HQ, thereby still allowing Edwards to live at the château. On the 24th, Liggett summoned Edwards and his officers to his headquarters. High on the agenda were Liggett's recommendations to relieve Colonel Edward L. Logan, commander of the 101st Infantry Regiment, and Colonel Frank Hume, commander of the 103rd Infantry Regiment; Edwards made excuses to keep them on. Liggett spoke to Edwards privately to discuss his reluctant attitude and his failure to obey orders or to force his subordinate officers to obey Edwards' orders. Liggett finally said that it wasn't for officers to exercise their own ideas, and called for only one thing – exact obedience.[3] In the end, Edwards relieved Colonel John Henry Parker, commander of the 102nd Infantry Regiment (succeeded by Colonel H. P. Hobbs) and Colonel Alfred Foote, commander of the 104th Infantry Regiment (succeeded by Lieutenant Colonel Duncan K. Major).

On 25 July, the 26th Division was relieved in the line by the 42nd Division, for rest and training. Some of the command changes that occurred did not go over well. As mentioned above divisional chief of staff Duncan Major was given command of the 104th. He did not take that well and told Edwards he did not have the authority to relieve him as chief of staff without permission from GHQ. Although the reassignment was initially approved by Liggett, Edwards received a telegram on 8 August from I Corps signed by Craig that said he had no authority to relieve Major and ordered his return as chief of staff. Edwards asked GHQ for Major John W. Hyatt as assistant chief of staff for intelligence. Major went over Edwards' head to GHQ and arranged for them to send instead Major

Hamilton R. Horsey. Upon his arrival at the divisional headquarters, Horsey went first to Major before reporting to Edwards. Between Major and Horsey at division and Craig at I Corps, the seeds of discord were sown and Edwards was being set up for failure.

Early September found the 26th Division at the town of Saint-Mihiel, south of Verdun at the western edge of a salient in a high wooded area overlooking the Meuse River. Edwards moved his headquarters to the commune of Rupt-en-Woëvre, near the Heights of the Meuse. Early on 12 September, the 26th Division launched an attack which went off flawlessly, having attained that day's objective in the morning. Pershing hoped to trap the Germans in the salient and ordered the 26th Division to close the gap and link-up with the 1st Division. The 26th Division was at its mark waiting on the 1st Division. The next day, Pershing railed about Edwards not closing the gap. Major General George H. Cameron, commander of V Corps, assured Pershing that Edwards had carried out the orders given, at which point Pershing merely laughed it off.

The first week of October, the 26th Division was ordered to the hills north of Verdun in relief of a French division. The objective was to clear the fortified rail and road lines and neutralize the German artillery. Weather and illnesses became the division's biggest enemy; influenza (now a pandemic) was taking its toll. At this time, AEF troops succumbed more to flu and pneumonia than to battle casualties. Edwards also learned that his daughter, Bessie, had died on 13 October, from pneumonia brought on by influenza; he took the news particularly hard.

Late October saw the end of Edwards' command. Pershing, with the approval of Secretary of War Newton D. Baker, signed the order relieving Edwards on 11 October, but this was not issued until 20 October. Edwards was notified on the 22nd. He did not see this as totally unexpected; he had seen this coming since July. In fact, Edwards often wondered why it took so long for Pershing to relieve him. When his replacement, Brigadier General Frank Ellis Bamford, arrived on the 24th, he found Edwards depressed and little was discussed on the handover of the division. The loss of his daughter and his command in just a few days was too much to bear. In Pershing's memoirs, he gave no reason for relieving Edwards; in fact, he didn't even mention it. Other sources mention Pershing's personal "vendetta," but merely speculate on the possibility that Edwards rose through the ranks under Republican patronage, thereby making this a political issue. Bamford was told by Pershing's assistant chief of staff for training, Brigadier General Harold B. Fiske, that he was getting the "worst division in the AEF." Considering the many achievements of the 26th Division since arriving in France, this remark seems to ring hollow. Although Edwards was a Regular Army officer, the 26th Division was a National Guard unit and Pershing had contempt for National Guard troops, often referring to them as "boy scouts," canceling leaves, and delaying necessary replacement troops.

Another possible reason for his relief was fraternization. Since the "Christmas Truce" of 1914, all commands – French, British, and later American – had been given strict orders against "friendly" contacts with the enemy. Still, periodically small, spontaneous gatherings among belligerents occurred from time to time, particularly in the waning days before the Armistice. One such incident occurred on 19 October when members from the 102nd Infantry met German soldiers from the 84th Landwehr Regiment; Edwards subsequently ordered his troops to, in no uncertain terms, cease any further fraternization and if approached by the enemy again to "shoot them up."[4] The incident was recorded and sent to Liggett, now commander of First Army, who put Edwards on further notice about the standing order against fraternization. Judging by the dates, this had little influence on Edwards' relief of command. However, it was the next day that Pershing issued the order to relieve Edwards. Remarkably, given Edwards' history of "speaking his mind," he didn't utter a comment or criticism regarding the dismissal; he took the action with dignity.

Edwards departed his headquarters on 25 October, and after a brief stay in Paris, made his way to Brest and departed for the United States on 5 November. On 1 December, he assumed command of the Northeast Department in Boston. In late 1919, Edwards was glad to learn that he would be one of 155 general officers to be retained by the Regular Army. However, on 1 July 1920, he reverted to his permanent rank of brigadier general and was given command of a brigade at Camp Dix, New Jersey. After some back and forth among various senators, Edwards' name was added to a list of brigadier generals selected for promotion to major general.

One of Edwards' backers was Senator Henry Cabot Lodge. The nominees, including Edwards, were approved by the Senate on 26 April with an effective date retroactive to 5 March 1921. Edwards returned to Boston to command I Corps on 30 June, where he remained until his retirement on 1 December 1922, completing 39 years of active service. After retirement, Edwards served as commanding general of the Military Order of Foreign Wars, one of the oldest veteran organizations for military officers.

Clarence Ransom Edwards died on 14 February 1931. His body was laid in the Hall of Flags at the Boston Statehouse, where more than 21,000 people passed through to pay their respects. The 26th Division casualties in the AEF theater included 1,587 killed and 12,077 wounded in actions in all campaigns throughout the 210 days in combat. Although a flawed commander, the harsh judgments and rigid command style of Pershing put Edwards in his crosshairs. Additionally, Pershing's dislike of National Guard troops may have clouded his judgment as was the case when he blamed the 26th Division and not his beloved 1st Division for failing to close the gap at Saint-Mihiel. In the end, Edwards fell into disfavor with Pershing and this led to his ultimate relief as commander of the 26th Division (the Yankee Division). Yet, despite this, Edwards and his division accomplished the missions given to them in the waning months of World War I.

CHAPTER 17

MAJOR GENERAL ROBERT ALEXANDER

Robert J. Laplander

From the beginning, it seemed that Major General Robert Alexander was meant for greatness and obscurity. As a commander, he was haughty and hard to get along with, and there was a Texas-sized chip forever on his shoulder. At the same time, the units he commanded during his military career performed exceptionally well. Yet he was destined never to be one of World War I's remembered or respected leaders. This is not because he wasn't capable or didn't execute his duties well. It was because of the manner in which he did it, as well as his handling of the one incident for which he is most remembered, popularly known as the "Lost Battalion."

Robert Egbert Alexander was born on 17 October 1863 in Baltimore, Maryland. His father William was a justice on the Court of Appeals for the State of Maryland, and a member of the circuit court for Baltimore. Well respected in his community, Justice Alexander placed enormous pressure on his young son to live up to a high standard of ideals. Like his father, Robert was expected to enter public service. This meant emulating his father and becoming a lawyer. However, after passing his bar exam,

Robert Alexander enlisted in the Army's 4th Infantry Regiment in April, 1886, as a private soldier.

A long and successful military career followed, marked by dogged determinism and *esprit de corps*, peppered with large doses of arrogance and egoism. During his first year in uniform he had attained the rank of first sergeant, and after a little more than three years he was a second lieutenant. He spent his early years at duty stations in the west, and participated in virtually every campaign the U.S. was involved in through the end of World War I. He was cited three times for gallantry during the Spanish–American War and the Philippine Insurrection, during which he was wounded, and held nearly every rank from private to major general. Along the way he befriended or made the acquaintance of virtually all those who were to be the major players in the AEF during the war. It was while serving as a major on the Mexican border in 1916 that he met General John Pershing and became a devoted follower of "Black Jack."

Unlike many of his fellow officers, Alexander was not a graduate of the U.S. Military Academy at West Point. He did attend the School of the Line and then the Staff School at Fort Leavenworth, Kansas, completing the two years of instruction in 1910. Nonetheless, he resented the attitude of many of his fellow officers who believed he could never stand on a level field with those who had attended West Point. Alexander thus worked twice as hard to prove himself worthy of all he accomplished. Along the way he developed an inherent defensive arrogance which was to further mark him as unprofessional in the eyes of many West Point officers. As his career progressed, he came to be known as a glory seeker, a self-serving individualist, and a bootlicker *par excellence* by many field-grade officers who came in close contact with him.

As a colonel, Alexander went to France in December 1917 with the 17th Infantry Regiment. Pershing, who well remembered the efficient Alexander, made him the inspector of the AEF's Line of Communications (later named the Services of Supply). Pershing next placed him at the head of the 1st Depot Division (a depot division being army vernacular for a replacement pool), which under his firm hand became a model for later depot divisions that served the AEF. Pershing was so impressed with Alexander's performance that on 3 August 1918 he moved him to command of the 63rd Infantry Brigade of the 32nd Division, while it was fighting in the Vesle sector, near Château-Thierry. It was there that Alexander's troubles started.

Alexander replaced Brigadier General William D. Conner at the head of the brigade – something the decorated Conner and the 32nd Division's commanding general, Major General William G. Haan, could not fathom or accept. Hann made no effort to hide his disdain for Alexander, and Alexander's long-inbred arrogance began to show in full force. While he made it a habit to visit the front often and know his junior officers and men firsthand, he consequently was frequently out of contact with Haan, setting a dangerous precedent and giving the division commander ample reason to complain. Nevertheless, Alexander did do much good with the 63rd Brigade, which was then suffering from the experience of too much training in trench warfare, as opposed to Pershing's preferred emphasis on "open warfare." Almost immediately upon arrival, Alexander threw himself into training his junior officers and NCOs in Pershing's cherished "open warfare" tactics.

On 13 August, Alexander watched as the 77th Division came into the sector alongside the 32nd to relieve the 4th Division on its left. The 77th originally had been raised from the greater New York City area; its enlisted ranks were filled with immigrants of virtually every nation and variety, while its officers were the best and brightest of New York society and had been through the famous Plattsburgh officer training program, which in the years immediately preceding America's entry into the war had trained some 17,000 men as reserve officers. As the first draft division in France, the 77th had a serious mission. All eyes were on it both at home and in France and it could not fail, for if it did it would indicate that the draft army experiment was not going to work. Almost immediately, however, there were problems, as the 77th Division's relief of the 4th did not come off well. Part of the problem was the strong rivalry between the regiments of the division, spurred in part by the nationalistic pride of the immigrant groupings within each regiment. The other problem was the inexperience that more generally plagued the AEF.

When General Haan again registered displeasure with his 63rd Brigade commander, Pershing saw an opportunity to solve two problems. Knowing

Alexander to be a strong and organized commander whose intense ego was unlikely to allow him to entertain any thought of failure, General Pershing issued orders detaching Alexander from the 32nd Division and sending him to assume command of the 77th Division from temporary commander Brigadier General Evan Johnson. On the day Alexander arrived to assume command, 27 August, the 77th had launched an attack on the ruined town of Bazoches. Exactly how successful the action was, is still up for debate. Alexander thought it a failure, stating in his memoirs: "The attempted occupation of Bazoches [as conducted] was, in my opinion, especially unfortunate." He described the attack as "tactically unsound and… directed against an objective which the enemy could make valueless at will."[1]

Alexander called a halt to the attack and started making the rounds along the front line, personally visiting his officers and men when and where he could, impressing upon them the need for interdivisional coordination and especially the doctrine of open warfare. Owing in large part to his stern and domineering personal leadership, the 77th was achieving results. He was gassed slightly at the beginning of September, which put him in bed for several days and was something of a blessing. His tendency to wander the battlefield exhausted his staff and he was not very well thought of by many of his subordinates from the beginning.

On 14 September, the 77th Division began its move from the Vesle sector to the Meuse–Argonne, in preparation for the coming major American offensive. The division was positioned on the American left flank, at the base of the western half of the Argonne Forest. To the right was the 28th Division with the mission to clear the eastern half of the Argonne and to drive up the Aire River Valley east of the forest. To Alexander's left was the French Fourth Army, which had the mission to drive up the Aisne River Valley west of the forest. The 77th's job was to keep steady and even pressure against the forest itself, squeezing out what was assumed would be a retreating enemy. If the Germans in the forest did not retreat, they risked being enveloped and cut off by the Americans on one side, and the French on the other. The time allotted for this phase of the battle was 72 hours, but it actually took two weeks to clear the forest.

From the beginning of the battle on 26 September, the Argonne proved to be a nightmare of steep hills and narrow ravines, swamp-filled draws, and vegetation so thick it was almost impenetrable. The Germans had been there for four years and established a veritable fortress, as the soldiers of the 77th quickly and painfully learned. Adding to this challenge was that the division had received replacements at the start of the battle, but many of them were untrained, with results that should have been predictable. Despite this, Alexander issued orders each morning demanding that his regiments meet their objectives. It was slow-going, tough work. Few on the staff were aware of the true nature of the terrain they were fighting through, Alexander included.

The 72-hour objective quickly collapsed, as the units on both sides of the Argonne failed to advance as far and as fast as anticipated. Alexander received orders from Lieutenant General Hunter Liggett, commander of I Corps, that the 77th would have to take the forest by direct attack. The French had lost 120,000 men there in the first two years of the war, and the line hadn't moved since. Alexander, however, took it as a challenge and now put the whip to his division.

With pressure mounting to achieve results, and knowing that Pershing would relieve any commander not performing to expectation, Alexander issued orders to advance at all costs, regardless of casualties. The 77th, however, only advanced at a crawl, with all four regiments in line and in places gaining only yards per day. Alexander again started wandering the battlefield to cajole his leaders to make progress. The commander of the 153rd Infantry Brigade, Brigadier General Edmund Wittenmyer, was an old friend who understood how Alexander operated. However, the commander of the 154th Infantry Brigade, Brigadier General Evan Johnson, whom Alexander had replaced as commander of the division, was far less accepting.

With Alexander bullying both of his brigade commanders, the 154th Brigade started to outpace the 153rd, but just barely. Alexander used that fact as leverage against Wittenmyer, and then he lied to Johnson, telling him that the 153rd was outpacing him. It was a tactic that Alexander would use often as his division tried to plow its way through the forest. Meanwhile, casualties mounted in the relentless grinder of the Argonne.

The battle came down to small-unit actions, as the troops inched their way forward. All the while, Alexander issued commands parroting Pershing's orders to attack, without regard to the flanks or losses. Results were what mattered, results were what Pershing wanted, but results from the 77th were lacking. Day after day, with no indication anywhere that the German line in the Argonne might break, Alexander grew increasingly irascible.

The tenacious defense of the Argonne by the Germans posed a direct threat to Pershing's entire campaign. Control of the high ground in the Argonne enabled the Germans to fire into the left flank of the American main advance up the Meuse Valley east of the Argonne. Any movements up the valley in this area were subject to German artillery, sniper, and machine-gun fires. From Pershing's perspective, the Argonne simply had to be cleared, and quickly.

In early October, Alexander began getting push-back from his brigade commanders, particularly Johnson, with whom he argued regularly on the phone. Despite his battlefield wanderings, Alexander never got up far enough to the action to see firsthand the difficulties the men at the platoon and squad levels were facing. Initially, Johnson had not spent adequate time forward either. When he finally did see what the conditions were like on the front lines, he tried to tell Alexander, but the division commander would not listen. He instead issued orders that he would replace anyone not achieving the required results. He grew ever more demanding, cajoling and threatening as the battle ground relentlessly on. Members of Alexander's staff later remarked how his hot and quick temper often led to regular outbursts of screaming and uncontrollable rage. At such times, the staff officers closed the door to his office and tried to find other places to be, but the situation was to take a serious turn.

Early on 2 October, the French Fourth Army, together with the AEF's I Corps, launched an attack. Several French Fourth Army units managed to break through the German lines west of the Argonne. This caused the Germans to shift several of their regiments out of the Argonne to encircle and eliminate the French units trapped behind the lines, resulting in a small gap in the German defenses in the forest in front of the American 77th Division. In the late evening of 2 October, Alexander took a call from Johnson; there had been a breakthrough achieved in 154th's area of operation by a mixed unit, barely battalion-sized. It included elements of the 1st and 2nd Battalions, 308th Infantry, and elements from two companies of the 306th Machine Gun Battalion, totaling around 600 men. The Americans had driven over a heavily defended hill that afternoon via the gap in the German defenses. Crossing the narrow Charlevaux Ravine, they reached the objective they had been battling toward for two days. Led by Major Charles Whittlesey and Captain George McMurtry, the mixed unit dug in on the northern slope of the ravine, about a mile ahead of the main American line. Elated at the first good news in days, Alexander began working with Johnson to support the breakthrough by bringing a battalion of the 307th Infantry up on Whittlesey's right, and reinforcing Whittlesey's left with the 3rd Battalion, 308th Infantry, and the remaining elements of the 2nd Battalion.

The attempt to execute the relief plan that night fell apart when only one company of 97 men from the 3rd Battalion, 307th Infantry, managed to get through to the Charlevaux Ravine. Meanwhile, the Germans found the break in the line through which Whittlesey and his men had made their way, closed it, and brought up additional troops to encircle and reduce the "*Amerikaner Nest*." By early morning on 3 October, the force in the Charlevaux Ravine, now totaling some 700 men, was completely surrounded by the German troops of a slightly larger force. Alexander was facing a situation that was spiraling rapidly out of control.

Throughout that morning, Alexander badgered Johnson about the situation, as pigeon messages started coming in from Whittlesey's isolated command. Although the situation did not look good, Alexander was loath to admit that the problem was a major crisis. Several heated conversations between Alexander and Johnson occurred that morning and only resulted in more pressure on the commander of the 308th Infantry Regiment, Colonel Cromwell Stacey. Alexander and Stacey knew each other from their time in the Philippines, where Stacey was decorated for heroism.

With the situation deteriorating in the Charlevaux Ravine, Alexander was called to First Army headquarters for a division commanders' meeting on the afternoon of 3 October. The main topic of the meeting was how to re-energize the faltering Meuse–Argonne offensive. During the meeting, however, the I Corps commander Hunter Liggett publicly questioned Alexander about the situation in the Charlevaux Ravine. Liggett had learned about it through regimental reports that had been coming in that morning. Realizing that his position was precarious, Alexander deflected the blame, first to the 308th's commander Stacey, and then to the brigade commander Johnson. To his corps commander, he tried to downplay the whole thing as a temporary setback. Officers who were present later commented on Alexander's performance with disgust.

As the situation in the Charlevaux Ravine deteriorated, Alexander was handicapped by his lack of information upon which to act, communications limited to those via messenger pigeon. On 4 October, Johnson attempted to launch a heavy assault against the forces in Whittlesey's rear, while coordinating artillery fire to the front of the position to keep the Germans at bay. But the artillery fire fell short. Alexander was largely unaware of the effort until a final carrier pigeon named Cher Ami arrived during the attack that afternoon from the ravine, with a message informing the regimental commander that Whittlesey's force was being hit by American artillery. When Alexander heard about the situation, he was livid and contacted the commander of the 152nd Field Artillery Brigade, Brigadier General Manus McCloskey, for answers. He was told that the Americans were receiving French fire, which Alexander knew to be untrue. Nonetheless, he issued orders that no such attempts were to be made again without his approval. But the damage was done, with 89 of the trapped Americans being either killed or wounded by American artillery.

The situation continued to deteriorate on 5 October, when Colonel Stacey suffered a mental breakdown and had to be taken off the line. Still not understanding the absolutely horrible conditions he was forcing his division to fight through, and with no one else available, Alexander ordered brigade commander Johnson to lead the 308th Infantry in a relieving attack. That afternoon, Liggett himself appeared at Alexander's headquarters with a further personal directive from General Pershing, stating, "Direct that a vigorous attack be made this afternoon to relieve the companies of the 77th Division that are cut off…"[2]

Feeling increasingly under pressure, Alexander paid a personal visit to the commander of the 307th Infantry Regiment, Lieutenant Colonel Eugene Houghton. Alexander was wearing both hats as division commander and effective commander of the 154th Brigade, since Johnson was now fighting at the head of the 308th Infantry. Pressing Houghton for a solution to the problem of relieving the Americans trapped in the Charlevaux Ravine, Alexander lied to Houghton by telling him that his 307th Infantry's failure to advance was holding back the 308th Infantry's attack to relieve Whittlesey. Houghton, however, refused to be bullied by Alexander. Standing up to his division commander, Houghton continued to make his own plans to break through to Whittlesey.

On the morning of 6 October, Alexander finally made it up to the sector of the 308th, where he was met by an exhausted and wounded Brigadier General Johnson. Now having seen the area of operations of the 154th Brigade up close for the first time, Alexander began to understand the situation. This didn't stop him from riding Johnson hard to get through to Whittlesey, however, loudly threatening to relieve him if he was not through to Whittlesey by that evening. At that point the two officers walked off into the woods together, Johnson taking Alexander by the arm. No one knows what passed between them, but one may be assured it wasn't pretty. Coming out of the trees, Alexander stalked off without a word.

That afternoon, Alexander, Johnson, and Houghton were summoned to the 77th Division's headquarters on the orders of General Hunter Liggett. At 1500 hours, they met with Captain Albert Rich, special investigator for I Corps, who had been sent to gather statements about the Charlevaux Ravine situation for General Pershing. Stories of the "Lost Battalion" were starting to appear in the American press; General Pershing was not pleased. With the spotlight shining directly on Alexander, he knew that his career was on the line. Brigadier General Johnson and Colonel Houghton explained their understanding of the situation and its causes, while not shying away from Alexander's role in the matter. Alexander started out by repeating the deflecting act that he had performed earlier at I Corps, trying to downplay the situation and laying the majority of blame at the feet of Colonel Stacey and Brigadier General Johnson. Captain Rich later wrote in his private memoirs that he found Alexander to be "quite disagreeable" and "very arrogant" in manner and attitude.

Nevertheless, by the afternoon of 7 October, the situation was finally being resolved. After four days of frontal attacks, I Corps brought up the 82nd Division to advance up the Aire Valley and then swing west behind the German lines in the Argonne. This threatened the Germans with encirclement and triggered orders for them to pull back several miles late on 7 October. This opened the way for Houghton's 307th Infantry to advance up to Whittlesey's position where they found a mere 194 survivors of the nearly 700. Alexander appeared in the Charlevaux Ravine in person on 8 October, meeting with Whittlesey, whom he promoted to lieutenant colonel on the spot. Later that day, Alexander briefed Hunter Liggett and recommended Whittlesey for the Medal of Honor. Privately, however, his attitude was one of dismissive condescension. To the press he alternated between booming praise for Whittlesey and disdain for the whole affair. Pershing, while holding Whittlesey up for praise, never made his personal feelings about Alexander known.

The 77th Division continued pressing forward until 15 October, when it was relieved from the line for rest and reconstitution. By that time Alexander had replaced General Johnson – despite all the hard fighting he had done for him – as well as several other officers. But those actions further alienated Alexander from many in his command. The 77th reentered the line on 31 October and participated in the breakout/pursuit of the Germans until the Armistice of 11 November. He accompanied the division home in May 1919 and led them during their victory parade in New York.

While the Lost Battalion episode became legend in the years following the war, Alexander's hand in it changed in time as well. As early as 1919 he began publicly accepting responsibility for the whole affair in the Charlevaux Ravine, but those in the division associated with the story were not fooled. One officer who had been in the Charlevaux went so far as to state, "He would have stood all his officers up against a wall and had them shot if he thought it would gain him promotion."[3]

Having fallen out of Pershing's favor, and largely disliked by his fellow division commanders in I Corps, Alexander faded into obscurity after the war. In 1919, the Army reverted him to his prewar permanent rank of colonel and he commanded the 3rd Field Artillery Brigade. Upon his retirement in 1927, the Army restored his wartime rank of major general. After leaving the Army, he was rarely sought out for public appearances and never invited to the Lost Battalion Survivors Association meetings. His *Memories of the World War 1917–1918* was published to little acclaim in 1931. His caustic personality comes through clearly in the tone and phrasing of the book's opening pages. Alexander died on 25 August 1941 in Manhattan and was buried in Arlington National Cemetery.

PART SIX

THE SPECIALIST OFFICERS

CHAPTER 18

BRIGADIER GENERAL WILLIAM "BILLY" MITCHELL

James S. Corum

General Billy Mitchell is arguably Pershing's most famous lieutenant. He was both a charismatic and effective commander as well as a constantly troublesome subordinate incapable of repressing his opinions. During, and especially after the war, he styled himself an airpower prophet and, like most prophets, had little use for criticism or contrary views. During the war Pershing found good use for Mitchell's talents, but his postwar advocacy of airpower and his political maneuvering finally got him dismissed from the Army. Even today Mitchell is revered by many in almost hagiographical terms. But a more objective assessment would rate him as a good commander but flawed prophet.

William Mitchell was born in Nice, France, on 29 December 1879 to a wealthy and politically prominent Wisconsin family. His father was elected a U.S. senator in 1893 and served as chair of the Senate Banking Committee. Mitchell enjoyed an excellent education and, at age 18, was ready to go to university and move into the family career of business and politics. However, the Spanish–American War changed Mitchell's destiny. At the outbreak of war, Mitchell signed up as a private in the 1st Wisconsin Volunteer Infantry. Mitchell did not remain a private for long as his senator father intervened and within a week Mitchell had a commission as a second lieutenant. Mitchell trained with his regiment, but when it was clear that the unit was not going to be sent to Cuba or Puerto Rico, he arranged a transfer to the Signal Corps so he could see some action. In late 1898, he was sent to Cuba.[1]

In Cuba, the young lieutenant proved himself to be an exceptionally energetic and capable officer. He was given his first command, of a signal detachment, and had to organize the laying of telegraph lines from the Santiago Province to Havana, directing Cuban laborers as well as U.S. soldiers in a countryside infested with disorder and banditry. His ability to lead, innovate, and get the job done came to the attention of the chief signals officer in Cuba. The Army was in a period of massive expansion in order to garrison the vast new empire acquired in the Spanish–American War and was looking for good material for the regular officer corps. Mitchell was a good candidate for the regulars. Seeing that there was not likely to be any further combat action in Cuba, Mitchell arranged a transfer to the Philippines, where a major insurrection had broken out against the Americans and he was sure to see combat.

In the Philippines, Mitchell was given command of a signals company, and as in Cuba, he proved himself to be an excellent field officer, working with the infantry and laying telegraph wire throughout the Philippines. He fought in several firefights with the Filipino rebels and again came to the favorable attention of his superiors, including the army commander in the Philippines, General Arthur MacArthur. When Mitchell became eligible for a Regular Army commission in 1900 (the requirement was to be age 21) the Army retained him and promised him an assignment to the Army Signal School at Fort Myer, Virginia.

In 1901, the Army's chief signal officer, Major General Adolphus Greeley, detailed Mitchell to Alaska to lay the military telegraph lines there. As in Cuba and the Philippines, Mitchell efficiently carried out the mission under difficult conditions and returned to Washington in 1903 to be married. Greeley was so impressed with Mitchell's performance that, at age 24, Mitchell was promoted to captain – the youngest captain in the Regular Army. In 1904 Mitchell was sent to Fort Leavenworth to attend the Infantry and Cavalry School, where he graduated as the distinguished honor graduate. For the next eight years Mitchell held a series of fairly routine Army assignments, yet he retained the support of some senior officers who saw in him great potential.

In 1912 Mitchell was given a position on the Army General Staff, then a relatively new organization. Mitchell served in both the Signal Corps office and as an intelligence officer, collecting and evaluating intelligence reports from attachés. As World War I broke out, pressure built for the U.S. Army to expand the Aviation Branch of the Signal Corps. Meanwhile, Colonel George Owen Squier of the Signal Corps, who was then the U.S. military attaché in London, closely followed the progress of the war and realized that aviation was playing a major role, and thus the U.S. needed to expand its minuscule aviation force into a genuine Aviation Corps.

During Mitchell's work on the General Staff, he had shown another character trait by his readiness to get involved in politics, even being prepared to disregard military regulations and traditions to advance a cause he felt important. Mitchell wrote press stories and openly lobbied senators and congressmen to support a multimillion dollar aviation bill, which would provide a foundation for American military aviation. Playing politics won Mitchell some friends, but also earned him the animosity of other officers. In 1916 Mitchell became the temporary chief of the Aviation Branch of the Signal Corps while awaiting Colonel Squier's return from Europe to take the position.[2]

Mitchell believed that aviation was an important new way of warfare, and in fall 1916 learned to fly on his own time. The Army would not release Mitchell to attend a military flight school, so Mitchell paid $1,470 out of his own pocket to learn to fly on weekends with civilian instructors. When Squier, now a brigadier general, took up his duties as chief of the Aviation Branch he believed that it was essential to have a specialist observer of aviation in Europe to monitor the European war. Mitchell – an excellent linguist who spoke French fluently and could now fly an airplane – was the ideal candidate. With his political activities promoting the Aviation Appropriations Bills, Mitchell had also created something of an uproar in Washington. Squier sought to protect Mitchell, seeing that a European assignment would be the best thing for him. Accordingly, in March 1917, Mitchell arrived in Paris and began collecting information on the European war. Three weeks after his arrival, America declared war, and Major Mitchell found himself the man on the spot in Europe.

With Mitchell already in France as the U.S. entered World War I, he quickly employed his excellent contacts with the French government to develop good relations with key French and British politicians and military leaders who could help form the American Air Service. Mitchell cultivated the friendship of Pierre Flandin, the French Under-Secretary for Aviation. Flandin ensured that the French Air Service would cooperate to the full to help establish the American Expeditionary Forces (AEF). On 20 April, less than two weeks after America entered the war, Mitchell began an extensive tour of the Western Front. With the French Aviation Force, he first visited fighter and bomber units, balloon units, air parks, and observation units. He studied subjects such as the use of aerial photographs. On 24 April, he flew in a French observation aircraft over the front, the first from the AEF to do so. He met with General Philippe Pétain to discuss his requirements. Of course, Pétain wanted manpower and airplanes in large numbers from the Americans. Experienced French aviation officers were appointed to Mitchell's small staff and Mitchell, with his excellent fluency in French, maintained a close relationship with the French Army.

One of the key people that Mitchell met in April and May was General Hugh Trenchard, commander of the British Royal Flying Corps in France. Mitchell made several visits to Trenchard's headquarters and developed a very cordial relationship with him. Mitchell was already on his way to believing that strategic bombing would be a very important part of warfare. With his firm belief in independent airpower and strategic bombing, Trenchard had a considerable influence upon Mitchell.[3]

In May 1917 Mitchell was promoted to lieutenant colonel. When Pershing arrived with his staff on 30 June, Mitchell was made chief aviation officer of the AEF. Mitchell briefed Pershing on aviation requirements and Pershing set in motion a vast program for a U.S. training center for aviators at Issoudun and coordinated with the French and British for the training of air personnel. Mitchell was appointed to the AEF's Aviation Board, which was charged to lay out a complete aviation program. Mitchell thus had considerable influence over the creation of the U.S. aviation force in France.

In the summer of 1917 General Squier dispatched a mission under Major Reynal Bolling to report back to the General Staff in Washington on the aviation requirements for the AEF. Bolling so impressed Pershing that he was retained in France, kept on the AEF staff, and promoted, like Mitchell, to lieutenant colonel. Bolling was assigned to command the air activities in the zone of the interior, while Mitchell was to command the air activities in the zone of the advance. The problem with this arrangement, with two well-qualified men holding these positions, was that nobody was actually in charge of the American Air Service, so that any disputes between Bolling and Mitchell went to General James Harbord, Pershing's chief of staff. To remedy the confused situation, Pershing in September appointed Colonel William Kenly, commander of the 7th Field Artillery Regiment, to be chief aviation officer of the AEF. Kenly was not an aviator, but he was trusted by Pershing as a manager, a team player (very important to Pershing), and a capable staff officer. In recognition of Mitchell's contributions to the AEF, he was promoted to full colonel in consolation for not being made aviation chief. Yet, Mitchell resented Kenly's appointment and failed to understand Pershing's viewpoint on playing "on the team."

Mitchell did not work well with Kenly, which was the beginning of Mitchell's often difficult relationship with the AEF commander and his staff. The 1st Aero Squadron arrived in September 1917, the first actual U.S. air unit in France. As America had gone to war with only 131 air officers and 56 rated pilots, expertise in airpower was sadly lacking. As the U.S. began planning for a large field army, Mitchell continued to push his idea that the British approach of an all-out offense using massed airpower was the best way to fight. He also promoted the British position of employing airpower as an independent arm. Mitchell was already moving toward the view that air could be the decisive arm in combat – certainly not a view that would have been accepted by Pershing's more conservative Army staff.

In the fall of 1917, Colonel Benjamin Foulois arrived in France with a large aviation staff comprised of mostly non-aviators commissioned directly into the Army from business and engineering careers. Like Mitchell, Foulois had come into the Army during the Spanish–American War, and his excellent performance had won him a Regular Army commission. Foulois was one of the first aviators in the American military and had learned to fly from the Wright Brothers six years before Mitchell had undergone flight training. Upon his arrival, Foulois was named by Pershing to replace Kenly as chief of aviation for the AEF. Foulois had served as commander of the 1st Aero Squadron under Pershing during the Mexican intervention and had impressed Pershing. Under the new command structure, both Mitchell and Bolling reported to Foulois, and Foulois was promoted to brigadier general. Mitchell deeply resented it, and he derided Foulois' large staff of non-aviators; but such supporting expertise was needed for the vast task of procuring aircraft and managing the resources of the American air arm.[4]

Mitchell also clashed with Colonel Hugh Drum, the chief of the AEF's Training and Operations Section. Drum was marked as another of Pershing's men, who saw him as capable of greater things. Drum, a brilliant staff officer, was the same age as Mitchell and held different views on the role of aviation in modern war. Drum emphasized aviation as a supporting arm rather than an independent arm, and he doubted Mitchell's claims that aviation could determine the outcome of the war.[5]

Mitchell was aviation chief for the zone of advance, but with no American units ready for combat in the fall of 1917, Mitchell had no one to command at the time. Indeed, the United States was very slow in sending squadrons – even partially trained ones – to France. However, some of the squadrons that had arrived and undergone initial training at Issoudun began advanced training near the front. Under pressure from the French and British in early 1918, the U.S. was pushed to start forming corps and larger forces that could serve on the Western Front. When U.S. I Corps was formed, Mitchell was put in command of I Corps Aviation.

In early 1918 Mitchell wrote doctrinal manuals for pursuit, observation, and bomber units. Essentially, he copied the French and British practices, which were highly developed and effective. Mitchell also worked out complete tables of organization for the U.S. squadrons and groups. Mitchell formed an air brigade staff following the model borrowed from Trenchard and the Royal Flying Corps. In developing his tables of organization, Mitchell insisted that the commanders and operations officers for groups and wings all had to be rated pilots. Mitchell asserted that only airmen could understand the problems of airmen.

By the end of March, just as the Germans began their great Spring Offensives, the 94th and 95th Pursuit Squadrons and 1st Observation Squadron were ready to begin operations under French command. Mitchell also began working with Major General Hunter Liggett, who took command of I Corps in January 1918. Foulois, meanwhile, was not coping well with managing the zone of the interior without the assistance of Bolling, who in December had been appointed as the American representative on air matters to the Allied Supreme Air Council. Foulois and Mitchell were constantly battling, and both men developed an intense dislike of each other. Pershing noted from several quarters that the airmen, while good soldiers and competent in their specialties, were working at cross purposes. Accordingly, on 29 May 1918 Pershing solved his command and control problem by appointing his West Point classmate, Brigadier General Mason Patrick, to command the Air Service of the AEF.[6]

Immediately upon taking over, Patrick assessed the messy situation of the AEF Air Service headquarters. He quickly rationalized and reorganized the Air Service, eliminated several offices, and established clear lines of authority. Although not an aviator, Patrick was experienced and senior enough as a commander that he could handle the personality disputes among the Air Service senior leaders. Patrick recognized that despite the personality clashes, both Foulois and Mitchell both brought great talent and ability to the Air Service and that both men were needed. Patrick sent Foulois to command the aviation of the U.S. First Army, which was being formed but not yet officially active. But that made Foulois Mitchell's superior.

Foulois clashed with Mitchell when he took over Mitchell's headquarters to make it his own. Mitchell took it badly, and the confrontation between the two became so unpleasant that Foulois unsuccessfully demanded Mitchell's relief. Mitchell also came into conflict with Colonel Malin Craig, soon to be promoted to brigadier general, who was chief of staff of I Corps. Craig insisted that all observation aircraft should come under direction of the corps' G-3 Operations, while Mitchell insisted that all orders and directions for air units should be issued by the corps air commander. Since there was no clear American air doctrine defining roles and responsibilities, such clashes continually bedeviled Mitchell, his commanders, and indeed the entire AEF.[7]

Having lost most of the good will and favorable reputation he had won in setting the foundations for the AEF's Air Service, Mitchell redeemed himself by his performance as a field commander. By early June Mitchell's aviation brigade contained the 1st Pursuit Group (four squadrons), the 1st Observation Group (four squadrons), three balloon companies, and a bomber squadron. The first major American corps-level operations came in response to the German BLÜCHER offensive that began on 26 May and carried the German Army to the Marne by the first week of June. The manpower-strapped French called for American support to stop and counterattack the Germans. Mitchell's brigade was thrown into the battle to support the American troops during June and early July. In the latter half of July, U.S. I Corps, supported by Mitchell's brigade, played a key role in the successful French counterattack at Soissons. The Germans were forced to retreat in the first of the great Allied attacks that would break the German Army. Mitchell's airmen had helped establish air superiority and had carried out relentless ground attacks against the Germans. The main problem had been numerous instances of a lack of effective communications and coordination between the infantry divisions and their supporting observation squadrons. This was a problem that would bedevil the U.S. Army to the end of the war, because the American divisions and their air squadrons had been thrown into battle before they had had a chance to train together. Then, as now, air–ground coordination was an art that took a lot of practice. The British and French had perfected the techniques that made air support so effective, but the U.S. had neither the time nor opportunity in 1918.

Pershing and the Allied commanders were impressed by Mitchell and the performance of his air brigade. In early August Mitchell was named commander of the air service for the U.S. First Army, which was activated that month. That made Mitchell the air commander in the zone of advance, with Foulois as air commander in the rear area. It was a command arrangement that worked well and leveraged the strengths of both men.

Mitchell's next mission was to prepare for the AEF's first offensive as an army at the Saint-Mihiel salient on 12–14 September. Mitchell threw himself into the planning, and the French provided extensive support, including their elite 1st Air Division (600 aircraft). More than 1,400 aircraft, including 700 American, supported the First Army's attack.[8] Many of the American air units were barely trained. The 1st Day Bombardment Group had only been formed two days before the offensive. Despite bad weather that kept many American aircraft on the ground, the Saint-Mihiel operation was a solid victory. American and Allied aircraft dominated the sky.[9] Mitchell flew over the front every day of the offensive, personally conducting reconnaissance for the ground troops. Pershing was so impressed by Mitchell's performance that he recommended Mitchell for the Distinguished Service Medal and approved his promotion to brigadier general in October.

The next major American operation was not so easy. The Meuse–Argonne offensive, from 26 September to 11 November, was a long and bloody campaign. When the French pulled their 1st Air Division away to support their own offensives, Mitchell was left with 700 American aircraft and 200 French aircraft to support an operation much larger than Saint-Mihiel. The Meuse–Argonne offensive quickly bogged down. The sector was key terrain for the Germans, who threw in some of their best army and air units to stop the Americans. Americans in the Meuse–Argonne sector outnumbered the Germans in the air, but the Germans committed some of their best air units, including the elite 1st Jagdgeschwader (1st Fighter Wing). American air losses were heavy, but the U.S. air units were generally able to maintain air superiority. As at Saint-Mihiel, the early stages of the Meuse–Argonne battle saw poor coordination between the American divisions and the observation squadrons assigned to support them. The main problem, as before, was the lack of combined training of the ground and air units before the battle.

The French and American soldiers on the ground in the Meuse–Argonne had adequate air cover during the first few days of the campaign. However, this changed in the following weeks as the French withdrew a large portion of their aircraft to support the French Fourth Army attack west of the Argonne. Additionally, Mitchell directed his aviators to focus on interdiction of German targets farther behind the lines. This surrendered the skies over the troops in contact to the Germans, who took advantage of this vulnerability with considerable effect. By mid-October, the situation was serious, as it appeared to the soldiers on the front line that the AEF had ceded air superiority to the Germans. The Doughboys complained of the daily German strafing of their positions, and the subsequent artillery that it brought on them, with little to no AEF aircraft contesting the air above.[10] When Hunter Liggett took command of the First Army in mid-October, he directed Mitchell to shift his focus from interdiction to close air support and to provide air superiority over the troops in contact. This had an immediate positive effect on the situation. These different visions of the utility of airpower, namely whether to use it to support the ground troops in contact, or to focus on deeper "strategic targets," would come to a head during the Allied strategic bombing campaign in World War II.

Overall, Mitchell had proved to be a capable combat commander who pushed his units hard. He had a charismatic style that was appreciated by the airmen under his command, even if it hugely irritated his peers and superiors. As the battle progressed and the Americans learned to fight, the air support by the observation squadrons improved. Mitchell also directed bombing raids of up to 100 American bombers to attack German logistics in the rear. In the latter stages of the battle American fighter planes roamed the battlefield attacking German columns and rear areas. Despite the early problems and frictions that Mitchell faced, especially in his ongoing dispute with First Army chief of staff Hugh Drum about command of reconnaissance missions, by 11 November it was acknowledged that the Air Service had performed well and had contributed to the American victory.

Mitchell returned to America in 1919 expecting to be named chief of the U.S. Army Air Service. Instead he was appointed chief of training and in 1921 made assistant chief of the Air Service under his old commander

Mason Patrick. Mitchell now saw himself as America's visionary for airpower and in a series of popular magazine articles, and also in congressional testimony, he advocated for a single department of national defense with an air force as an independent service equal to the Army and Navy. Mitchell played directly to the public and won some prominent politicians to his cause; but he earned the ire of the Navy by ridiculing the Navy's aviation program.

Mitchell made front-page news and won national acclaim when his bombers sank the captured German battleship *Ostfriesland* during bombing tests in the Chesapeake Bay in 1921. Mitchell proclaimed that his bombing tests proved battleships were obsolete and that American shores could be best protected by aircraft – a doubtful proposition considering that Mitchell had sunk a stationary ship without antiaircraft defenses, and with aircraft flying at low level from airfields only 20 miles away.[11] Mitchell's popular writing, often openly critical of the military establishment, sometimes made a good deal of sense – such as his advocacy of a strong civil aviation system. In some cases, Mitchell's vision for airpower eventually became true, such as his prediction of the importance of strategic bombing. In other cases, Mitchell's prophecies proved incredibly wrong, such as his discounting naval torpedo planes or asserting that ground-based air defense could ever be effective.

Mitchell was such a controversial and public figure, and had so thoroughly irritated his superiors, including the Secretary of War and the President, that his four-year appointment as assistant chief of the Air Service was not renewed. In early 1925 he was sent to be air officer for VIII Corps in Texas and reverted to the rank of colonel. But no one expected Mitchell to be quiet for long. Used to being in the limelight and the center of attention, in September 1925 Mitchell called six reporters to his office and issued a 6,000-word statement about the loss of the Navy dirigible *Shenandoah* in an accident. Mitchell blamed the senior military leadership for the disaster and described the "almost treasonable negligence of our national defense by the Navy and War Departments."[12] Mitchell subsequently was charged with "conduct to the prejudice of good order and military discipline and in a way to bring discredit upon the military service."[13]

His court-martial in Washington, D.C. was one of the spectacular news stories of the decade.

Mitchell had a U.S. Congressman as his defense attorney and hoped to make the trial a case against the American military leadership for ignoring airpower. In fact, Mitchell put up a very poor defense, and many of his claims were shown up as exaggerations. Mitchell bored the court by reading long excepts from his recent book *Winged Defense*, a work long on opinion and short on solid fact. Mitchell was found guilty and suspended from his rank and pay for five years – a light sentence considering that Mitchell was clearly guilty. Mitchell, instead, resigned his commission and retired to his estate in Virginia, where he continued to write popular articles about airpower.

The Air Corps Bill, which reorganized the Air Service and provided the Air Corps with an assistant secretary of war and a degree of autonomy, was passed in 1926. It was a huge step forward for American military airpower and the person behind it was not Mitchell, but General Patrick.[14] Mitchell was still visited and revered by younger Air Corps officers, but his writing did not attract the attention it once had, and U.S. military aviation progressed steadily without any guidance from Mitchell. After the 1932 election Mitchell hoped to get a call from President Roosevelt to serve as national aviation advisor – but the call never came. Mitchell died suddenly in New York City on 19 February 1936 from influenza.

CHAPTER 19

COLONEL GEORGE S. PATTON, JR.

Carlo D'Este

General George S. Patton's fame rests primarily on his deeds on the battlefields of World War II: the TORCH landings in November 1942; resurrecting American prestige and fighting ability at El Guettar in Tunisia in March 1943; his heroics in Sicily, which landed him on the covers of both *Time* and *Newsweek* in August 1943; for his exploitation with Third Army during the breakout from the Normandy bridgehead at the end of July and beginning of August 1944; and perhaps – most of all – his dramatic and prophetic actions in December 1944, when he was the only Allied senior commander to anticipate the great German counteroffensive in the Ardennes, where he overnight turned Third Army 90 degrees from Lorraine into the Ardennes and orchestrated the relief of Bastogne during the worst winter weather in Europe in 50 years.

These actions, along with his unfortunate propensity to garner bad publicity through his flamboyance and self-destructive acts, such as the two slapping incidents in Sicily in August 1943, are all part of the Patton legend. Since his death in December 1945, his fame and legacy have endured: from the 1970 film starring George C. Scott that won seven Academy Awards, to the tribute that appeared on a large sign placed outside a corps headquarters in Saudi Arabia during the 1991 Gulf War, upon which was emblazoned one of his principles: "Hold 'em by the nose and kick 'em in the ass."

All of this would certainly suggest that Patton's true legacy stems from his World War II achievements. However, one of the finest examples of his military genius occurred not in World War II but during World War I, when Patton was a very junior officer assigned to General John J. Pershing's American Expeditionary Forces (AEF) in France.

George Smith Patton, Jr., was born 11 November 1885 in San Marino, California into a wealthy family with Confederate roots – his grandfather, Confederate States of America (CSA) Colonel George Smith Patton, Sr., Virginia Military Institute (VMI) Class of 1852, was killed at the 1864 Third Battle of Winchester while his great-uncle, CSA Lieutenant Colonel Waller T. Patton, VMI Class of 1855, died during Pickett's Charge at the Battle of Gettysburg. Home-tutored until age 11, young Patton, an enthusiastic and accomplished horseman who avidly read classical military history, attended Stephen Clark's School for Boys in Pasadena for six years of formal education. Visitors to the Patton home during his youth included family friend CSA Colonel John Singleton Mosby, the South's legendary "Gray Ghost."

Determined to pursue a military career, Patton unsuccessfully sought an appointment to West Point at age 17, but was accepted to VMI, his father's and grandfather's alma mater, in 1903. After a year at VMI, in 1904 Patton received a Congressional appointment to the U.S. Military Academy, Class of 1908. Although excelling in military studies, he flunked plebe mathematics and was "turned back" a year to the Class of 1909, eventually graduating that year 46th of 103 graduates (his classmates notably included future World War II generals John H. C. Lee, Robert L. Eichelberger, and William Hood Simpson). Commissioned in the Cavalry branch, Lieutenant Patton was a modern pentathlon event competitor on the U.S. team at the 1912 Olympic Games in Stockholm. Subsequently, he designed the U.S. Model 1913 Cavalry Saber, now commonly known as the "Patton Sword," the primary "*arme blanche*" of American Army mounted units. In 1915, Lieutenant Patton's 8th Cavalry Regiment was assigned to border patrol duty and based in Sierra Blanca, Texas, along the Rio Grande River.

Patton and Pershing first met in 1916 at Fort Bliss, Texas, in the wake of Pancho Villa's raid on Columbus, New Mexico that led to the Punitive Expedition in Mexico during what proved to be a futile attempt to find and capture or kill Villa. Patton was a young, recently promoted cavalry captain, newly assigned to Fort Bliss, Texas, after duty at Fort Riley, Kansas. When he learned that the Punitive Expedition was being formed, Patton persuasively talked Pershing into taking him on to his staff as an aide-de-camp. During the Punitive Expedition, Patton led a patrol in search of Villa and got into a deadly shoot-out at a hacienda with one of Villa's henchmen, whom he killed with his revolver. The incident was reported in newspapers throughout America and for the first time Patton's name became nationally known.

As the trouble on the Mexican border played out, Patton nearly became Black Jack's brother-in-law, a then very likely event that Patton did not particularly welcome – fearing that, if it happened, any rise he later made in the Army would be chalked up to "nepotism" and not any advancement that he had earned on his own merits. In 1916–17 Pershing became enamored with Patton's younger sister Anne Wilson Patton – known as "Nita" – and although he was 27 years older than the 29-year-old Nita, Pershing and Patton's sister became engaged when Black Jack gave her a diamond ring in 1917. Yet, eventually, the demands of World War I and his postwar international fame cooled Pershing's ardor for Nita and he broke off their engagement in 1919. Nita never married; Pershing remained a widower, and although he had several post-World War I paramours, he confided in Patton years after the war that he regretted his breakup with Nina.

When America entered World War I in 1917 and President Woodrow Wilson appointed Pershing to command the American Expeditionary Forces, Patton accompanied him to France. Initially, Patton served in Paris, and later, when Pershing moved his headquarters to Chaumont, in the capacity of a combination of headquarters commandant, adjutant, provost marshal, and jack of all administrative trades: an assignment that bored him and, with combat looming, from which he sought every means of escape. "I am a sort of 'Pooh-Bah' and do everything no one else does. I can't see for the life of me where I am going to do much in this war," he lamented in a letter to his wife, Beatrice.[1]

Unknown to Patton, there were events occurring that would soon alter his life and career. In 1916, the British employed the first tanks in combat during the Battle of the Somme. They were the first operational tracked armored vehicles produced by the British, who in 1915 were spurred to create them by their aggressive and innovative First Lord of the Admiralty, Winston Spencer Churchill. When Churchill learned that such a vehicle might be created that would help to end the awful carnage of the stalemate and trench warfare on the Western Front, he applied his boot to a large number of backsides and demanded – and got – action.

At Cambrai, in November 1917, the British launched an offensive with five infantry divisions and 324 tanks that penetrated 10,000 yards into the fourth level of the Hindenburg Line and caught the Germans flatfooted, capturing 8,000 prisoners. In six hours they took more ground than 100,000 troops had in the massive and deadly Third Battle of Ypres in July 1917. Unfortunately, British success came mostly to naught when 180 of the tanks broke down and there was no plan in place for the infantry to seize the initiative.

At about the same time, the French were also developing their own version of the tank, which was designed as an infantry personnel carrier by the Renault works. The French version, first employed in the spring of 1917, was both lighter and more mobile than the British tanks, known as "Big Willies."

A joint Anglo–French tank board was also created but each side failed to agree on a common doctrine – with the British favoring the use of their heavy tanks independently, while the French preferred close cooperation between the light Renault tanks and the infantry. What the British and French were doing did not go unnoticed by observers from the American Military Mission, whose reports began to interest Washington in the tank as a future weapon of war. Eventually, a copy of one of these reports landed on Pershing's desk. He quickly endorsed the potential of the tank and appointed both an AEF tank board and a lieutenant colonel to head it.

The officer, LeRoy Eltinge, who would soon become his mentor, summoned Patton and asked if he would consider becoming a tank officer. Patton thought about it and found the idea appealing, in no small part because he could read and speak passable French. Pershing approved of Patton's selection. At the end of 1917 Patton was 113th on the list of eligible cavalry captains for promotion. Nevertheless, despite his lack of seniority he was tasked by Pershing to create the first ever American tank force.

What Patton managed to accomplish was astonishing: in 1918 he was promoted from captain to full colonel, organized and trained the first U.S. tank brigade, led his troops in the battle of Saint-Mihiel, won the Distinguished Service Cross, and was badly wounded and nearly died on the first day of the Meuse–Argonne campaign. Because the AEF arrived in France almost completely ill-trained, Pershing created a series of training schools to prepare his troops for their first combat. With Pershing's blessing, Captain Patton became the first U.S. Army soldier to be assigned to the newly created Tank Corps. On New Year's Day 1918 Patton and a young lieutenant, who was appointed his assistant, became its only two members.

Patton was directed to report to the city of Langres in eastern France to establish the U.S. First Army Tank School. At its inception, the Tank Corps had no tanks, no equipment, no uniforms, no standing operating procedures, no real precedents except for the limited and divergent experience of the British and French, no doctrine, no training school and – except in Patton's mind – no clue about how it would be created and function.

For Patton to succeed he had to take a crash course in tanks, tank warfare, and tank maintenance. He spent two weeks with the French, where he familiarized himself with the Renault tank; he drove it, fired its gun, and pronounced himself thrilled by the experience. He also visited British Colonel J. F. C. Fuller to learn firsthand about the Battle of Cambrai. The lessons Patton learned from the British and the French soon led to the writing of his first paper on the subject. It outlined specific recommendations, both historical and technical, and presented a clear rationale for the new tank force. Patton later correctly called it "the best technical paper I ever wrote."[2]

It noted that tanks and infantry were mutually supporting but it also foreordained the future role of the tank in modern warfare. Patton wrote: "If resistance is broken and the line pierced, the tank must and will assume the role of pursuit cavalry and ride the enemy to death."[3] He also observed that tanks failed whenever they got ahead of the infantry, thus losing the benefit of their natural and mutual support. For someone whose knowledge of the tank was barely a month old, it was an astonishing reflection of the visionary aspect of Patton's mind. In an upbeat mood, he wrote to his wife: "I am fitted for it as I have imagination and daring and exceptional mechanical knowledge."[4]

He established his tank school in the town of Bourges, where the first order of business was the removal of heaps of manure that littered his new training area. As officers and men began arriving in Bourges, Patton spent his days in a whirlwind of organization, drawing up plans and lectures, designing training, conducting close order drill, and continuing to visit the French and British to discuss the employment of tanks. The first American tanks were still on the drawing board and months away from becoming a reality and Patton's first real challenge was acquiring tanks in which to train. When a number of French Renault tanks arrived by train Patton was the only one who knew how to drive them off the flatcars.

A hallmark of his tank school was its rigid discipline. Patton demanded and received unquestioned obedience. He conducted foot drills and arm and hand signals for what they would later do aboard their tanks, and taught them how tanks would be employed on a battlefield and how to troubleshoot gasoline engines. Patton also gave lectures on a variety of subjects such as camouflage, reconnaissance, map reading, and reading of aerial photographs. All were things he would teach and focus on in World War II.

His emphasis on discipline and on spit and polish was designed to instill *esprit de corps*, and just as he would proclaim in World War II that they should not die for their country but make the other poor dumb bastard die for his country, Patton cautioned his officers that the Germans were disciplined but he and his men would be even more disciplined. "It is by discipline alone that all your efforts, all your patriotism, shall not have been in vain. Without it, heroism is futile. You will die for nothing.

With discipline you are irresistible," he proclaimed.[5] Saluting became so smartly executed that the byword became "Give 'em a George Patton."

Throughout his long military career Patton never once lowered his high standards or his microscopic attention to the smallest detail. Usually in colorful language he demanded toughness and insisted it would save lives. Many did not like it, and more epithets were directed at Patton than perhaps any soldier in modern military history, but most of the men in his charge flourished, and it was the secret to his success as a commander and trainer of troops. Through two world wars, Patton was never seduced by the lure of weapons of war as cure-alls that would defeat a resilient enemy such as the German Army. For Patton, the fighting man was the key to winning. Then came his famous dictum: "Wars may be fought with weapons, but they are won by men. It is the spirit of the men who follow and the man who leads that gains the victory."[6] These words are as true today as when Patton uttered them nearly a century ago. By April 1918 he was a lieutenant colonel but it was not until mid-September 1918 that were there enough tanks for the two battalions Patton had organized and trained to go to war.

The Renault FT tank of 1918 was exceptionally crude and consisted of a two-man crew: a commander and a driver. The commander could only signal the driver by a series of kicks: a kick in the back meant go forward. A kick on either shoulder told the driver where to turn. A kick in the head meant stop and repeated kicks to the head meant go in reverse. Thus, striking an enlisted man, normally a court-martial offense in the U.S. Army, became an accepted means of operating a tank in World War I. Keeping them running, however, was an absolute nightmare and most of the time Patton counted himself lucky to have a handful of his tanks actually operational. Nevertheless, what Patton accomplished in the spring and summer of 1918 was nothing less than dazzling. In addition to attending a 12-week course at Pershing's Army General Staff College at Langres, Patton had to train his own school, all the while pouring out lectures, directives, and notes. The pressures were endless and the results impressive.

By the time Patton and his men were ready for battle in September 1918 he commanded 50 officers and 900 enlisted men in what was now called the 1st Brigade, Tank Corps, which consisted of the 344th and 345th Tank Battalions. It was decided that the AEF would fight in the Saint-Mihiel sector of the front. Pershing's objective was to seize both the sector and a strategic railroad. To prepare himself for the forthcoming offensive, Patton went forward into no-man's land to reconnoiter personally, crawling for well over a mile until he came to the German outer wires.

In the rain on 12 September 1918 Patton personally led his brigade into combat at Saint-Mihiel through fog and mud. It was messy: his tanks routinely outran the infantry when they were not breaking down. He had been directed to remain in telephone contact with his boss at the AEF, Colonel Samuel Rockenbach, who had replaced Colonel Eltinge. Telephone contact was by means of wire but by 0700 hours Patton could no longer resist the lure of the battlefield, and leaving his adjutant to man the phone, strolled into the battle zone on foot. Before long, on a hillside outside the village of Essey he encountered the most highly decorated officer serving in the AEF, Brigadier General Douglas MacArthur, who commanded a brigade of the famous 42nd Rainbow Division.

Much has been made of this chance encounter but it was actually brief and inconsequential. A few words were exchanged before Patton moved on. What was significant about it was that one well-placed German shell that morning would have wiped out two of the most significant and controversial figures of World War II at a single stroke.

From there, Patton led his tanks forward riding atop a tank, in total disregard for the bullets flying everywhere around him. Later, he caught hell from Rockenbach for leaving his command post but it was typical of Patton's aggressive leadership that he was determined to lead from the front. And he vowed (privately, of course) that he would do it again.

Given that this was the first ever day of combat for the new Tank Corps, it was ultimately far more important for Patton to set the example by being seen, than remaining in the rear. His presence that day was incalculable and sent the strong message that he practiced what he preached.

Saint-Mihiel was brief but decisive for the future of armored operations. As a result, what Patton began to envision and refine during the interwar years leading up to World War II was that tanks were far more than a support arm of the infantry. He grasped the enormous potential of the tank as a decisive factor on the modern battlefield: the concept of mobile warfare.

By 1928, Patton would state that with the advent of the tank and the airplane there was now a solution to the problem of delivering a *coup de grâce* to an enemy force. Hold them until the decisive moment, then employ them ruthlessly, and en masse.

The AEF had a mere ten days to shift its forces from the Saint-Mihiel sector to the Meuse–Argonne, which was a major logistical feat under the crude conditions of the rainy season. The mission given Patton and his tanks was to support two divisions of I Corps. As was his custom, he made a personal reconnaissance of the battlefields and learned that his tanks would encounter major problems in the form of inhospitable terrain and a river between the two divisions that would disrupt mutual support.

On 26 September 1918 Patton's career and life nearly ended on the first day of the Meuse–Argonne offensive. In dense fog and under murderous machine-gun and artillery fire, American infantry and tanks became stalled. Near the village of Cheppy, Patton encountered a bottleneck and a very dangerous situation that called for leadership to rally a besieged force.

Tanks were milling around and piling up, infantry were confused, and no one knew what to do except Patton. Exposing himself, he rallied the troops, gave orders on how the tanks and infantry should attack a German strongpoint, and restored a semblance of order before being hit in the upper thigh by a machine-gun bullet that nearly killed him. Patton had been utterly terrified that morning, yet he reacted with perhaps the finest leadership of his career at a decisive moment. Five of the six men around him were killed that deadly morning. It took some hours before Patton could be rescued and moved to an aid station. He spent weeks in the hospital recuperating, was promoted to full colonel, and was later awarded the Distinguished Service Cross for his bravery on the battlefield on 26 September.

On 11 November 1918, World War I ended. In the months and years that followed Patton was haunted by his experience in the Meuse–Argonne. Although he emerged from the war with honors and acclaim, the year 1918 took its toll and the price was indeed high. Contrary to his image as a tough guy, Patton was deeply affected by the horror of war and suffered from post-traumatic stress. What had been a high on the battlefield turned into the giant letdown that is so common to soldiers who have been in combat.

In the years that followed he suffered bouts of depression and wrote dark and gruesome poetry about death. Again and again, a bleak consequence of his combat experience was reflected in letters to his wife and in his poetry, which became an important means of expression. A vivid example was a poem he called "The Moon and the Dead" that reads in part:

The roar of the battle languished
The hate from the guns grew still,
While the moon rose up from a smoke cloud, and
looked at the dead on the hill.
Pale was her face with anguish
Wet were her eyes with tears
As she gazed at the twisted corpses
Cut off in their earliest years.
Some were bit by the bullet,
Some were kissed by the steel,
Some were crushed by the cannon
But all were still, how still![7]

What Patton accomplished in France, and indeed throughout his life, was all the more challenging because of his dyslexia. To understand Patton, it is vital to appreciate the role dyslexia played in dominating his life. At an early age his parents realized their son possessed a learning disability that prevented him not only from reading but from attending school until he was 11. Although unable to identify the source, young Patton unquestionably suffered from dyslexia, a disorder afflicting one person in every seven. Some famous dyslexics include such prominent names as Leonardo da Vinci, Albert Einstein, Thomas A. Edison, Richard Branson, Henry Ford, Tom Cruise, and Woodrow Wilson.

Dyslexia was virtually unknown in the United States until the 1920s and in Patton's case he never learned what afflicted him; he simply knew that he was different. In addition to difficulty reading and writing, dyslexia also includes a tendency to boast, use of profanity, sharp mood swings, hyper-activity, obsessions, impulsiveness, and feelings of inferiority and stupidity – all Patton traits.

Like Patton, many dyslexics are able to overcome their disorder and lead very productive lives. It has been said that it is easy for dyslexics to think outside the box because they have never been inside the box. In Patton's case dyslexia was the most compelling reason for his success.

In World War I, this was reflected in Patton's leadership and initiative in forming, training, and leading the first American tanks into combat. After arriving in France in 1917 as a junior captain, he returned home as the leading battlefield commander and expert of the Tank Corps. He wore the eagles of a full colonel and on his breast were the Distinguished Service Cross, four battle stars, the French Croix de Guerre, and a Distinguished Service Medal.

It was an extraordinary triumph. Although he would earn undreamt of fame in World War II, what Patton accomplished almost singlehandedly in 1918 will endure as one of his greatest achievements and an acknowledgment of Pershing's foresight in selecting him to create and lead America's first tank force.

In the wake of his astounding World War II accomplishments, George S. Patton, Jr., the U.S. Army's most famous "warrior-general," suffered a most un-warrior-like demise. On 8 December 1945, Patton's chief of staff, Major General Hobart Gay, organized a surprise farewell pheasant hunt on the eve of Patton's scheduled return to the States. But during the long drive to the hunt in bad weather, Patton took pity on his poor hunting dog riding behind his Cadillac staff car in an open Jeep in the cold, nasty conditions. Patton gave up his warm, comfortable position in the staff car's front passenger seat near the car's heater to the wet, shivering animal, and moved to a seat in the right rear of the sedan beside Gay. Shortly after Patton surrendered his comfortable seat to the dog, his car struck a deuce-and-a-half U.S. Army truck that suddenly and unexpectedly turned in front of his staff car. Although the collision was at a low speed, the impact thrust Patton forward and upward, resulting in his head striking the car's dome light (or, possibly, the metal frame of the sliding glass window separating the sedan's front from its rear seats) and he suffered a paralyzing injury. Twelve days later, on 21 December, Patton died of pulmonary edema and congestive heart failure in the U.S. hospital in Heidelberg, Germany. He was 60 years old. Patton was buried amongst his soldiers in Luxembourg American Military Cemetery.

PART SEVEN

THE REGIMENTAL OFFICERS

CHAPTER 20

COLONEL WILLIAM J. DONOVAN

Kevin McCall

William J. Donovan was combat leader, envoy, unconventional warrior, spymaster, and ambassador. His leadership in the 165th Infantry Regiment of Pershing's American Expeditionary Forces (AEF) during the Great War demonstrated his courage, ability, and potential to become one of the most influential (and famous) Americans of his time. He received some of the nation's highest decorations for heroism and public service. In doing so, he became the future patron of two elite U.S. organizations – the Central Intelligence Agency and the U.S. Army's Special Forces – both of which claim descent from the Office of Strategic Services he would later found to conduct the deadly, secret, unconventional combat missions of World War II.

The sobriquet most identified with William J. Donovan is "Wild Bill." It is a complete misnomer. He was not "wild" either in the sense of being undisciplined or uncontrolled. Donovan was, in fact, quite the opposite. He was a man of extraordinary focus and discipline who deliberately developed and nurtured what biographer Anthony Cave Brown termed *character militaris* – the character of combat leadership in war necessary to survive and prevail. Donovan studied, practiced, developed, and imparted into his men an indomitable belief in his leadership and their own abilities. That belief was reflected in the wartime record of his battalion in multiple campaigns of World War I. The apocryphal background of the nickname "Wild Bill" purportedly came from an overheard conversation between several of Donovan's soldiers arguing about the arduous training he had led his men through in the run up to combat. Regimental Chaplain and confidant Father Francis Duffy recorded:

> The majority of his battalion have always looked upon him as the greatest man in the world. But certain numbers were resentful and complaining on account of the hard physical drilling he has continually given them to keep them in condition for just the sort of thing they had to go through last week. As a result of watching him through six days of battle – his coolness, cheerfulness, resourcefulness – there is no limit to their admiration for him. What I overheard was the partial conversation of the last dissenter. He still had a grouch about what he had been through during the past year, and three other fellows were pounding him with arguments to prove Donovan's greatness. Finally he said grudgingly: "Well, I'll say this: Wild Bill is a son of a b**** but he's a game one."[1]

Donovan always publicly decried the nickname, but his wife Ruth knew that deep down he loved it.

His grandfather emigrated from County Cork in the winter of 1846–47. Grandfather Donovan shoveled grain in the ships' docks and then he worked Buffalo's railroad yards. His fourth son, Timothy, mirrored his father's temperance, diligence, discipline, and religious devotion, and in doing so rose from greasing locomotives on the Erie and Lackawanna Railroad to yardmaster of the Blackrock terminal. By his efforts, "Young Tim" and his wife Anna moved up in Buffalo society, attaining a level of prosperity and respectability known in the parlance of the day as "lace curtain Irish."

Donovan was born into an Irish immigrant family in Buffalo, New York, on New Year's Day 1883. William (called "Will"), the firstborn, was followed in short order by a brother Timothy and a sister Mary, and later a brother Vincent. Meningitis killed the next four children until another sister, Loretta, was born when Will was a teenager. Despite an insatiable appetite for books, Will was initially a poor student. At 13 he was enrolled at Saint Joseph's Collegiate Institute and did well at oration and athletics – marginally improving his overall grades along the way. Following three years at the Catholic Niagara University and Seminary, Donovan gained admission to Columbia College in New York City. He graduated with a bachelor's degree and athletic renown as a pugnacious back-up quarterback for Columbia in 1905. Despite mediocre scholarship he went directly into Columbia's law school where he studied under future Supreme Court Justice Harlan Fiske Stone. After graduation Will returned to Buffalo to practice law and move about in the upper reaches of Buffalo society.

In 1912 he joined with other youth of means in Buffalo in forming an Army National Guard cavalry unit: Troop I, 1st New York Cavalry. For most of his colleagues, it was a social outlet of outdoor activities, nicknamed "The Business Men's Troop." (The local wags called them "The Silk Stocking Boys," in reference to their wealth and social standing.) In this egalitarian atmosphere, Donovan quickly went from trooper to sergeant, and was elected captain shortly thereafter. Donovan assumed the responsibility of command which included educating himself on strategy, tactics, and logistics.

Donovan's first exposure to active military campaigning came in 1916 after receiving a telegram while in Europe on behalf of the War Relief Commission of the Rockefeller Foundation. Troop I was mobilized to active duty in support of the Mexican Punitive Expedition under General John J. Pershing. By August 1916, Donovan and his troop were in McAllen, Texas, under Pershing's command. It was here that Donovan instituted a training process so vigorous in its intensity that fifty years later, a survivor wrote: "Probably the most vivid memory of Border Days come from those early morning hours when you put us through those damnable exercises... But you made us realize what lay ahead of us, you got us to quit playing around at being soldiers."[2] It was to become Donovan's hallmark as a commander: he trained his men mercilessly, was often unpopular for his efforts, and was as unsparing of himself as his soldiers.

As the expedition in Mexico wound down, General Pershing and his staff commenced an extensive training regimen in anticipation of deploying to Europe. Donovan took advantage of the opportunity to redouble his efforts, and in the process was first noticed by Pershing and his staff as a promising young officer of extraordinary character, temperament, and leadership. Donovan's troop returned to New York on 12 March 1917. Three days later he received orders to report to the New York National Guard Armory in Manhattan, where he joined the 69th Infantry, a New York Irish Regiment of U.S. Civil War fame. By August, the regiment was redesignated the 165th Infantry, with Major Donovan commanding its 1st Battalion, assigned to the 42nd Division destined for France. Donovan immediately took to training his battalion at Camp Mills, Long Island. His routine requirements of his new soldiers were arduous – daily 3- and 4-mile runs followed by close combat training, brutal and often barehanded – which made Donovan extremely disliked.

In late October 1917, his battalion shipped for Europe via convoy off of Nova Scotia. Even in transit, Donovan was focused on preparing for the ensuing fight in France. In a letter to his wife Ruth (whom he had married in 1914), he noted: "It is a small ship and it is difficult to drill and discipline the men. I have insisted that the officers give their entire time to the men at the sacrifice of their own."[3] The battalion landed at Liverpool, took a 12-hour train ride to Gosport, and boarded cross-Channel steamers to Le Havre. From there, "the Micks," as Donovan came to call his battalion, trudged the muddy roads to their cantonment in Champagne, France.

As he had in the Southwest desert and Camp Mills, Long Island, Donovan disciplined and trained his men strenuously and without letup. Of his relentless efforts to prepare his men for the rigors of combat, the famed unit chaplain, Father Francis Duffy, observed:

> Major William J. Donovan, who commands the first Battalion was transferred to us from Brigade Staff, but he is no stranger to us. On the Border when he was Captain of Troop I of the 1st Cavalry he was the best-known man of his rank in the New York Division... He is cool, untiring, strenuous, a man that always uses his head. He is preparing his men for the fatigues of open warfare by all kinds of wearying stunts. They too call

> him "Wild Bill" with malicious unction, after he has led them over a cross country run for four miles. But they admire him all the same, for he is the freshest man in the crowd when the run is over. He is a lawyer by profession, and a successful one, I am told. I like him for his agreeable disposition, his fine character, his alert and eager intelligence. But I certainly would not want to be in his Battalion.[4]

In addition to the preparations for the physical exertions of combat, Donovan attended to intellectual requirements as well. In his personal study he sought out insight for the actions required for infantry combat. At Christmas in 1917, he received a packet of historical treatises on military affairs, including: *An Essay on the Command of Small Detachments* (1766); *The Manual of Exercise with Explanations* (1766); *Manoeuvres for a Battalion of Infantry by a German Officer* (1766); *Manoeuvres for a Battalion of Infantry, Upon Fixed Principles* (1767); and *Wolfe's Instructions to Young Officers* (1768). He read them cover to cover, and to his wife expressed delight with the gift.[5]

His own continuous focused study of war made him consider not only the theoretical but the practical requirements of campaigning. To ensure the efficacy and understanding of his junior officers, he prepared a list of questions for them that they were required to memorize and to know upon demand:

1. Do I know my particular job here?
2. Do I know the amount of reserve ammunition I have on hand?
3. Do I know the use and purpose of each and every signal at this post?
4. Have I instructed my men in and do they know the place of each in time of attack?
5. Am I doing my utmost in looking out for the men in my platoon?
6. Can I conscientiously say that I am giving the best attention to the feet of my men?[6]

In February 1918, Donovan's "Micks" moved into the line as part of the French Sixth Army. The following month, he came to the notice of the AEF high command when the French government determined to award him the Croix de Guerre for rescuing a score of soldiers buried alive by a German artillery barrage in the regimental dugout at Rouge Bouquet. Donovan refused the medal when made aware that the Jewish sergeant who assisted him in saving the men was denied the same award. The French relented, both received the medal, and the "Micks" took note.

His efforts on behalf of the men in his own battalion were similarly noteworthy. Donovan wrote of an event later that spring, when an infantry patrol returned with two men missing:

> I went to the Colonel and told him that these men had last been seen outside the wire in No Man's Land. That they might be wounded, and that it was our duty to make a real search for them, that the entire regiment should turn out to find them, so each man would know however mean and despicable he was if lost in the performance of his duty we would go after him. I insisted that it was vitally important to the morale of the men; also that I should be permitted to conduct the patrol.[7]

Donovan went out with two lieutenants and 36 men. They spent the night combing the sector in no-man's land and returned at dawn without the missing "Micks." The two men were found alive six days later, wandering in the wire of a neighboring regiment. His personal example made the men determined to obey his orders, follow his leadership, and persevere regardless of circumstance.

On 27 July, Donovan's battalion was given objectives as part of a much greater effort of the Aisne–Marne campaign northeast of Paris. The campaign was designed to roll back well-established enemy defenses along a tributary of the Seine River. His orders were to conduct an assault following a brief artillery preparation while restricting his troops to the use of bayonets in the intended surprise attack. To approach his battalion's objectives, Donovan would have to lead his men down an exposed valley to the Ourcq River, cross the shallow water, and climb the equally exposed approach to Meurcy Farm near the hamlet of Sergy. In and around that small town, unbeknownst to the approaching "Micks," lay not the expected second-rate Landwehr Division, but at least three German divisions of infantry supported by an elite Guards Division.

The night before the assault, two of Donovan's company commanders were wounded while conducting a leaders' reconnaissance as they came upon "a very hot and bloody fight" between U.S. and German units along the route. In the ensuing shelling, Donovan got "a beautiful mouthful of gas." After a brief treatment of boracic acid for his eyes and a head-clearing dose of ammonia, Donovan led the "Micks" 6 miles to relieve the French unit in the sector. With the relief completed, his unit advanced through the day until reaching the rise overlooking the Ourcq Valley. As night fell, Donovan pulled the battalion back to the reverse slope of the hill, dug in for the night, and prepared for the attack.

The advance began at 0430 hours and the "Micks" crossed the Ourcq with few casualties. However, as the regiment advanced up the approach to Meurcy Farm, intense interlocking fires from dug-in German machine guns forced the battalions back on Donovan's flanks, leaving his men exposed to fire from three sides. The "Micks" remained in place and fought for possession of the farm and town by continually attacking the Germans who were determined to maintain it. As the casualties mounted, every officer of Donovan's staff (save one) were killed or wounded. In the last two days of July, the division finally moved up to Donovan's relief. In Major Donovan's battalion of approximately 1,000 men, 600 were killed, wounded or missing along with three-quarters of the officers; and yet they prevailed. Donovan's assessment of his men's performance is illustrative of his determination to guarantee their military efficiency:

> One thing I am glad of, and that is the system which I used in the training of these men justified itself. Their discipline and their training, and above all their spirit, held them full of fight in a position that had been given up by two other outfits. These men who had all along thought me too strict and felt that I had made them work when others did not work, and I held them to too high a standard, are now convinced that I was right, and that I would ask them to do nothing that I myself would not do. This one tribute is greater than any honor that my superior officers can give me...[8]

Nevertheless, Donovan's superior officers approved the Distinguished Service Cross for his performance at Meurcy Farm and General Pershing awarded it personally.

By October 1918, Donovan had been promoted to lieutenant colonel and commanded the 165th Regiment. The task was more daunting than it appeared. In addition to the losses sustained by Donovan's battalion the previous July, the regiment as a whole had lost 1,750 of its original 3,000 men as well as 66 of its officers at the Ourcq River fight. The replacements for men and officers lost were, for the most part, green troops, lacking the discipline, training, and experience of their predecessors. An unofficial regimental history bluntly stated: "The men obtained were for the greater part crude and raw, some not knowing how to load their rifles and don their gas masks when they reached us."[9]

On 14 October, the 42nd Division relieved the 1st Division in the Meuse–Argonne sector and took up the assault on the Kriemhilde Stellung on the Hindenburg Line south of Sedan. Lieutenant Colonel Donovan had spent the previous weeks organizing them and immediately understood that the green 165th leadership replacements were not likely to be up to the task and that he would have to personally lead the attack. To do so, Donovan revealed the depth and breadth of the military character he had so assiduously developed. Eschewing the practice of removing identifying insignia, instead he "went out as if I were going to a party, insignia, ribbons, Sam Brown[sic] belt," and all. Father Duffy's narrative described the scene: "As soon as the advance began to slow up under the heavy losses, he passed to the front line of the leading elements… It was more like a Civil War picture than anything we have seen in this fighting to watch the line of troops rushing forward led by their Commander."[10]

The night of 14 October found the regiment within 500 yards of the German lines with orders to resume the attack supported by tanks at 0730 hours the following day. When his field telephone failed after midnight, Donovan was incommunicado with the units on his flanks. "Zero hour came but no tanks, so we started anyway."[11] He emerged from his hole, still in dress uniform, and led the men forward in what would be described as the modern equivalent of the Irish Brigade's experience at the 1862 Battle of Fredericksburg. But, Donovan's "Fighting Irish" pressed ahead until the attack withered in the face of overwhelming German machine-gun fire. Undaunted, Donovan led his men forward, offering words of encouragement along the way until he was knocked down by a machine-gun round which penetrated his leg just below the knee. A lieutenant tore his trousers open and bandaged the wound. Donovan refused evacuation – for five hours. During that time, he and his men were continually shelled and gassed and then subjected to a German counterattack. In affidavits after the war, it came out that Donovan had deliberately remained to blunt the counterattack with his mortar platoon and to await the arrival of a fresh battalion.

For his actions in the October assault on the Kriemhilde Stellung, Donovan was awarded an Oak Leaf Cluster to his Distinguished Service Cross. Unbeknownst to Donovan, Father Duffy, ever the soul of the regiment, lobbied to have him awarded the Medal of Honor. Duffy submitted to AEF headquarters more than a dozen testimonies of officers and sergeants regarding Donovan's actions of 14 and 15 October. The following year in April, Donovan, having been promoted to colonel, led the Irish Regiment in a parade up Fifth Avenue in New York and received the key to the city.

As a result of Duffy's persuasion, General Pershing, then chief of staff of the Army, approved the upgrade in 1923. The Medal of Honor was awarded in the New York City Armory in a ceremony attended by the survivors of the regiment. Colonel Donovan declined to keep the medal, placing it in the armory and saying that it was not his to keep but belonged "to the boys who are not here, the boys who are resting under white crosses in France or the cemeteries of New York, also to the boys lucky enough to come through."[12]

After the war, Donovan resumed his legal profession, serving as the U.S. Attorney for the Western District of New York. When Donovan's former law professor Judge Harlan Fiske Stone was appointed Attorney General in 1925, he in turn appointed Donovan as the head of the Anti-Trust Division where he served until 1929. He ran on the Republican ticket to succeed Franklin D. Roosevelt in the New York governor's mansion, losing in the Democratic sweep of 1932. Despite differing political points of view, Roosevelt and Donovan were cut in many ways of the same cloth. Roosevelt personally respected Donovan's political skills and was once known to opine that had Donovan been a Democrat, he could have been President.

By 1939, Donovan assessed that another European conflict was looming. As "part of an informal network of American businessmen and lawyers who closely tracked and collected intelligence on foreign affairs," he travelled, collecting information on foreign leaders (including Mussolini and Hitler) while developing networks of well-placed informants in what would become the Axis Powers. In 1940 and 1941, Donovan traveled to Britain as an informal emissary for President Roosevelt to discern British prospects against Germany in the face of the defeatist assessments of U.S. Ambassador Joseph P. Kennedy. During his fact-finding mission, Prime Minister Churchill (desperate for U.S. aid) gave Donovan almost unfettered access to British plans, strategy, and intelligence analysis including trips to the British posts in the Balkans and Middle East. The resulting report strongly supported the U.S. aid, and when judiciously leaked to the press, columnist Walter Lippmann opined that Donovan's insight on British determination and capabilities "almost singlehandedly overcame the unmitigated defeatism which was paralyzing Washington."[13]

In June 1941, Donovan responded to a request from the President with an outline for a centralized intelligence service for the upcoming war. His proposal was to create an organization to gather information and analyze it in conjunction with that collected by existing US organizations. The following July, Roosevelt appointed Donovan "Coordinator of Information" (COI). Donovan, who hoped for command of a division in the upcoming conflict, reluctantly accepted the appointment. He set about developing an intelligence organization with alacrity. By June 1942, working with British intelligence cooperation and mentoring, the COI established worldwide espionage, analysis, sabotage organizations, training sites, international front companies, and networks while hiring across a spectrum of employees from artists to forgers and intellectuals to criminals. On 13 June 1942, Donovan returned to active duty as a colonel. The COI moved under the Joint Chiefs of Staff, was given responsibility to conduct "special operations not assigned to other agencies," and was renamed the Office of Strategic Services (OSS).

The OSS contributions to the war effort included clandestine intelligence collection, analysis, propaganda, sabotage, and unconventional warfare with varying degrees of involvement and success, performed in nearly every theater throughout World War II. Donovan was promoted to brigadier general in March 1943 and to major general in November 1944. During that period, he not only oversaw the development, training, and deployment of OSS officers, but also demonstrated his familiar leadership style of *character militaris* by personally going ashore at the landings of the Salerno, Anzio, and Normandy invasions and flying "over the hump" to observe operations behind Japanese lines in Burma.

At the conclusion of the war, the OSS was dissolved by President Harry Truman. The following year, Truman created the Central Intelligence Group which became the Central Intelligence Agency (CIA) in 1947. The CIA claims its direct legacy from Donovan's OSS, and at his death in 1959, after he had also served as U.S. Ambassador to Thailand, CIA station chiefs worldwide received a cable stating: "The man more responsible than any other for the existence of the Central Intelligence Agency has passed away."[14]

U.S. Special Operations Forces similarly reflect Donovan's legacy of *character militaris*. U.S. Army Special Forces claim lineage from Donovan's Burma OSS Detachment 101, while U.S. Special Operations Command, founded in 1987, similarly pays homage to Donovan's discipline, leadership, and standard of strenuous training by using an identical gold spearhead on a black oval background – the OSS design – on its insignia. Deep down, Wild Bill would have loved it.

CHAPTER 21

LIEUTENANT COLONEL THEODORE ROOSEVELT, JR.

Douglas V. Mastriano

Theodore Roosevelt, Jr., or "Ted," as his friends called him, lived up to the legacy of his father and namesake, President Theodore Roosevelt. The younger Roosevelt was a proven combat leader in both world wars, an aspiring politician, a successful businessman, an accomplished hunter and explorer, as well as governor of Puerto Rico and the Philippines. Theodore Roosevelt, Jr., like his father, received the Medal of Honor, one of only two father–son duos to be awarded America's highest honor (the other being Arthur MacArthur and Douglas MacArthur). Roosevelt rose through the ranks during the Great War, ending it as a lieutenant colonel commanding the 26th Infantry Regiment in the 1st Division. He participated in numerous engagements in 1918, which included Cantigny, Soissons, and the Meuse–Argonne campaign. He was cited for bravery, wounded in action, the first reserve officer to command a regiment in combat, and was the spearhead of the American attempt to liberate the French city of Sedan in the waning hours of the war.

Theodore Roosevelt, Jr. was born on 13 September 1887 at Oyster Bay, New York. Although a great admirer of his dad's legendary action with the Rough Riders at San Juan Hill, the burden of living up to such expectations as the eldest son caused considerable anxiety for the young man. Journalist Jacob Riis wrote a profile of the family in the White House in 1902 and said that Ted was "like his father… in his absolute fearlessness and occasional disregard for conventionalities." "Absolute fearlessness and occasional disregard for conventionalities" captured the essence of Ted's leadership style in both World War I and II.[1]

He graduated from Harvard and then entered upon a series of successful business ventures that brought him wealth before America entered World War I. Ted married Eleanor Butler Alexander in 1910 and they had four children. Eleanor would play an important role in Ted's combat experience in France. After the sinking of the RMS *Lusitania* in 1915, most Americans believed that the nation would eventually enter the war. This was a view not shared by the passive Wilson Administration, which did nothing to prepare for war. Out of frustration by the lack of proactive measures by President Wilson, "preparedness groups" popped up, as well as a military training camp at Plattsburgh, New York, which in effect created a cadre of future leaders for the war. The National Defense Act of 1916 supported this endeavor and established the Reserve Officers' Training Corps (ROTC). Roosevelt volunteered to be a part of this training, as so many young men likewise did before America entered the war. Ted captured the frustration of his generation, writing, "The administration never takes a step in advance until literally flailed into it; and the entire cuckoo population of the 'don't criticize the President' type play into the hands of the pro-Germans, pacifists, and Hearst people, so that a premium is put on our delay and inefficiency."[2]

When the United States finally entered the war in April 1917, Ted wasted no time to be among the first Americans in uniform deployed to France. For the first time in his life, he asked his dad (T. R.) for help to make this happen – something that T. R. was delighted to do. T. R. knew Pershing personally from the Spanish–American War and crafted a letter asking that his sons Ted and Archie be selected to join him immediately in France. The letter to General Pershing from T. R. in part said:

> I write you now to request that my two sons, Theodore Roosevelt, Jr… and Archibald B. Roosevelt… both of Harvard, be allowed to enlist as privates with you to go over with the first troops. The former is a Major and the latter a Captain in the Officer's Reserve Corps. They are at Plattsburg for their third summer.[3]

The letter, with a bit of help from Ted's wife Eleanor, resulted in the Roosevelt brothers boarding the S.S. *Chicago* on 20 June 1917 for France.

Eleanor was determined to be close to her husband during the war and hurriedly volunteered to serve in the Young Men's Christian Association (YMCA), before rules went into effect preventing wives of soldiers from working in volunteer organizations serving frontline troops. Many Christian and Jewish organizations sprang into action to help ameliorate the soldiers' sacrifices in this time of war. Among the most active were the Knights of Columbus, the Jewish Welfare Board, YMCA, the Red Cross, and the Salvation Army. These organizations deployed volunteers across the United States at military bases as well as in Europe to provide the soldiers with food, comfort, music, entertainment, and Bibles. Eleanor skyrocketed into the YMCA's leadership, designed their field uniforms, and became one of the leading advocates in France of taking care of the soldiers.

The Salvation Army became one of the favorites of the Doughboys in France. The volunteers were often Bible-toting evangelical Christian young ladies, who baked thousands of donuts daily to hand out to the men coming into or going out of the battle lines. The women were given the moniker of "Donut Lassies" by the men. Ted Roosevelt was so impressed that he wrote, "Before the war I felt that the Salvation Army was composed of a well-meaning lot of cranks. Now what help I can give them is theirs."[4]

Once in France Ted and Archie reported to General Pershing in Paris and asked to serve in combat with frontline troops. Pershing wrote, "Two of the Roosevelt boys, Theodore, Jr., and Archie, reported yesterday. Unable himself to participate, their father's fine spirit is represented by his sons."[5] Archie was assigned to the 6th Regiment, but Ted was sent to a training unit. He confided in a letter to his wife the anguish: "Well, it's dreadful to have those we love go to the front; but it is even worse when they are not allowed to go to the front."[6]

Ted's wait to get an assignment to a frontline combat unit would not take long. Colonel George B. Duncan, who would later be promoted to major general and command the 77th and 82nd Divisions, needed an officer to command 1st Battalion in the 26th Infantry Regiment, in the 1st Division. Ted eagerly agreed to leave the training unit for this opportunity to serve in what would be America's most celebrated division in World War I. As the first American division in France, the unit trained hard to prepare for combat. Ted bemoaned that much of the training was inadequate. In his view, the maneuver training that focused on the bayonet and rifle was not realistic, and this put him at odds with General Pershing's assumption that the Americans once in battle would break the stalemate and quickly enter open warfare. In one case, during an exercise observed by General Pershing himself, the result was potentially catastrophic. Ted wrote of this:

> Once we had a maneuver of this kind before General Pershing. The company officers were lined up and afterward were asked their opinion as to how the men had conducted themselves. The first one to answer was a game little fellow named Wortley… He said that he thought everything went off very well and he didn't think he had anything to criticize. The next lieutenant said that he thought that a few men of his company had got a little mixed up. This was a cheerful point of view for him to have, for, as a matter of fact, two thirds of his company had gone astray. His company had been selected to deliver a flank attack over the top, but when this took place it consisted of one lieutenant and two privates.[7]

Fortunately, General Pershing did not notice this glaring error. Also present during this episode was the 1st Division's assistant chief of staff for training, Major George C. Marshall, who had a good relationship with Ted. This friendship would serve Ted well in the dark days of World War II in 1943, in the months following the Allied operations in North Africa.

Ted and the 1st Division spent the latter part of 1917 and early 1918 gaining experience in the trenches along the quieter sectors of the Western Front. By May 1918, it was the Americans' turn to finally play an active role in the fighting. The 1st Division was rushed north by train to the Somme and given the mission of liberating the destroyed French village of Cantigny. A brigade of the division that included Ted's unit was given the mission of what would be America's biggest yet engagement of the war. Supported by French tanks, aircraft, and artillery, the Americans launched an impressive attack that drove the Germans both out of Cantigny and the surrounding areas. For the next three days, the German Army launched a series of failed counterattacks to drive the Americans back. Ted played a key role leading his battalion in the defense of Cantigny. Although suffering from gas poisoning, Ted stayed in the line and continued to valiantly lead his men in the thick of the action. According to his official citation for the Silver Star:

> During the operations connected with the capture and defense of Cantigny, France, 27 to 31 May 1918. Major Roosevelt during an enemy raid, displayed high qualities of courage and leadership in going forward to supervise in person the action of one of the companies of his battalion which had been attacked; on the day of our attack upon Cantigny, although gassed in the lungs and gassed in the eyes to blindness, Major Roosevelt refused to be evacuated and retained command of his battalion, under heavy bombardment, throughout the engagement.[8]

In addition to the Silver Star, Ted also was awarded the French Croix de Guerre for this action.

As the guns fell silent at Cantigny, Ted heard rumors that Paris was about to be overrun by the Germans. Fearing for the safety of his wife Eleanor, Ted awoke Lieutenant Colonel George C. Marshall for permission to find his wife. Marshall rebuked him, saying, "For heaven's sake Roosevelt, go and get some rest! You've been gassed and look like the dickens. Your wife will be alright." To this, Ted answered, "That's may as be, but I've got to be sure. You see, she's the only wife I've got."[9] The appeal worked and Ted was given permission to rush to Paris only to find Eleanor doing quite well.

After a short period of rest, the 1st Division made its way northeast of Paris to participate in the offensive to liberate Soissons. As the men prepared for the attack, Ted heard the news of his brother Quentin being killed in action after being shot down by a German fighter plane. His brother Archie was likewise seriously wounded. The war was taking a heavy toll on the Roosevelt family.[10]

Sensing that the German offensives had culminated,[11] Allied Supreme Commander Foch directed that the Allies retake the ground lost earlier in the year around Soissons. Lasting from 18 to 22 July, the attack included the American 1st and 2nd Divisions, two British divisions, and 24 French divisions. The attack, although costly, was superbly executed, forcing the Germans to lose nearly all the ground that they had captured two months earlier. As expected, Ted led his men from the front on the first and second days of the battle. As they advanced on 19 July, a German machine gun opened fire, resulting in Ted and the men around him dashing forward in a sprint to eliminate this threat. As Ted charged, a bullet crashed into his knee, causing him to crash into the ground. The enemy machine gun was taken, but Ted suffered a wound that would follow him throughout his life.

Ted refused adequate treatment and hopped in a motorcycle sidecar to visit his wife Eleanor, who was still in Paris helping to lead the YMCA effort. Eleanor was surprised to see him and helpless to convince him to have the wound taken care of properly. Providentially, a mutual friend, Lieutenant Colonel Richard Derby, dropped in for a visit. Derby was the chief surgeon with the 2nd Division and evaluated the wound; seeing that it was severe, he advised that if it was not treated right away, Ted could lose his leg. This was enough for Ted, who agreed to be taken to a nearby hospital. Ted was awarded the Distinguished Service Cross for his leadership and bravery during the Battle of Soissons.

After nearly two months of convalescing, Ted reported to a training unit in France in mid-September 1918 and was soon thereafter promoted to lieutenant colonel. Although not healed of his wounds, Ted was looking for a chance to return to the 1st Division. This came in late October, when Brigadier General Frank Parker called to inquire about his health. Parker was looking to give command of the 26th Regiment to Ted if he was well enough to take it. Roosevelt jumped at the chance and left his training unit without orders to join the 1st Division preparing for the final push of the Meuse–Argonne offensive. Ted arrived in time for the division's advance during the final week of the war.

The AEF had finally broken through the German lines on 1 November 1918 and was now in pursuit of the enemy to the Meuse River. The 1st Division joined the push on 6 November and within hours was redirected from advancing north toward the Meuse River, and instead ordered to swing west across the U.S. I Corps sector to seize the occupied French city of Sedan. A confusing set of circumstances triggered this dangerous maneuver. General Pershing expressed his desire that Sedan should be taken by the Americans and that his favorite division, the 1st, should have the honor of liberating it. As a result, U.S. First Army issued a muddled memorandum late on 5 November (see Introduction, pp. 51–53) that resulted in the chaos of the 1st Division cutting across the front of the sector of U.S. I Corps, and pushing other American troops into the sector of the French Fourth Army. Ted Roosevelt and his regiment led the 1st Division. The results were catastrophic. The advance of an entire American corps was halted; there were incidents of fratricide, and outrage from the French. Roosevelt was literally about to order his men the few remaining miles forward into Sedan when he was ordered back.

With this, the Armistice went into effect, thus ending the war. As the 1st Division limped back, Ted was surprised to find his wife Eleanor looking for him. She was in the area with the YMCA leadership to set up additional forward sites at the front. Upon hearing that the war was ending, she set off to reunite with Ted. After this brief reunion with his wife, Ted and the rest of the 1st Division were ordered to serve as part of the Allied occupational forces in the Rhineland, Germany, where his stay was brief. In early 1919, he returned to France, helped to establish the American Legion, and thereafter went back to the United States.

After World War I, Ted launched a political career; he was elected to the New York State Assembly, and then, like his father many years before, appointed as the Assistant Secretary of the Navy. His political future seemed endless until he ran for governor of New York in 1924. Widespread Democrat Party voter fraud and a smear campaign led by Ted's cousin

Franklin Delano Roosevelt (FDR) were blamed for his defeat. Ted was outraged by FDR's betrayal and the breach between the two would never be healed. Yet, the son of Theodore, Sr. had a reputation similar to his father's, was a genuine war hero, adventurer, hunter and explorer, and thereby remained ever present in the public's imagination. As a result, he was appointed to serve as the governor of Puerto Rice from 1929 to 1932 and the governor general of the Philippines.

As the clouds of another world war gathered, Ted returned to the United States Army in 1940, at 53 years of age, was promoted to colonel and given command of his 26th Infantry Regiment in the 1st Infantry Division. He went in with the assault wave to hit the beaches in Oran, Algeria during Operation TORCH in North Africa. During the initial attack, Ted continually pushed to the front and was awarded the Bronze Star Medal for fighting off a French patrol while riding shotgun in his jeep. The legacy of Pershing's orders in 1918 for officers to always be out front was still with Ted two decades later. Major General Omar Bradley captured the essence of Roosevelt's leadership style in North Africa, recollecting that he was "a brave… undersized man who trudged about the front with a walking stick… His cheery bullfrog voice had echoed reassuringly among the troops in every Tunisian wadi in which riflemen fought the Germans."[12]

Yet, the performance of the Americans in North Africa in early 1943 was far from splendid. The flaws of an inexperienced army, facing a determined adversary, were evident in battle, especially in the disastrous Battle of Kasserine Pass. Eisenhower assigned George S. Patton in March of 1943 to take command of II Corps in North Africa to get the Americans in shape. The spit and polish Patton was the polar opposite of the 1st Infantry Division commander, Major General Terry Allen and Ted Roosevelt (now a brigadier general and the division's assistant division commander). This notwithstanding, The Big Red One, as the 1st Infantry Division was called, helped redeem the reputation of the Americans at the Battle of El Guettar, which, together with the advance of Field Marshall Bernard Montgomery's British Eighth Army push from the east resulted in the defeat of Axis forces in North Africa.

The victory in North Africa was followed by the Allied landings at Sicily in July 1943, an operation in which the 1st Infantry Division and

Ted Roosevelt played a key role. The performance of the division and its leaders notwithstanding, Patton, now the U.S. Seventh Army Commander, conferred with Eisenhower to have Allen and Roosevelt reassigned under the guise of "rotation of command." Eisenhower agreed, with Patton making a statement that the reassignment of Ted would cause a bit of a furor, saying, "There will be a kick over Teddy, but he has to go, brave but otherwise, no soldier."[13]

After several months serving as a liaison officer with the French Army fighting in Italy, Ted was reassigned to the United Kingdom to serve as the 4th Infantry Division's assistant division commander to prepare for what would be Allied landings at Normandy on 6 June 1944. This lateral assignment did not reflect any punishment by Eisenhower of Roosevelt for his unique leadership style. When the time for the landings arrived, Ted appealed to the division commander, Major General Raymond "Tubby" Barton, for permission to land on Utah Beach with the first wave. Barton was initially opposed to this, but relented to Roosevelt's insistence that it was where he needed to be to ensure success. At 56 years of age, Ted indeed hit the beach of Normandy, France, in the first wave. Upon landing, he took stock of the situation and realized that the landing craft had drifted more than a mile southeast of the planned landing beaches. After a few moments of thought, Ted gave his famous order: "We'll start the war from right here!"

With that, Brigadier General Roosevelt greeted each successive wave of landing craft, giving them specific orders on where to advance. His grasp of the situation was superb, and his clarity of orders indeed was what was needed to secure the beachhead and beyond. For the next month, Ted continued to perform brilliantly in France and was recommended by Lieutenant General Omar Bradley for promotion to major general and command of the 90th Infantry Division. However, before this was approved, Ted died of a heart attack on 12 July 1944. Roosevelt was posthumously awarded the Medal of Honor for his actions on Utah Beach. His award citation states:

> For gallantry and intrepidity at the risk of his life above and beyond the call of duty on 6 June 1944, in France. After two verbal requests to accompany the leading assault elements in the Normandy invasion had

> been denied, Brig. Gen. Roosevelt's written request for this mission was approved and he landed with the first wave of the forces assaulting the enemy-held beaches. He repeatedly led groups from the beach, over the seawall and established them inland. His valor, courage, and presence in the very front of the attack and his complete unconcern at being under heavy fire inspired the troops to heights of enthusiasm and self-sacrifice. Although the enemy had the beach under constant direct fire, Brig. Gen. Roosevelt moved from one locality to another, rallying men around him, directed and personally led them against the enemy. Under his seasoned, precise, calm, and unfaltering leadership, assault troops reduced beach strong points and rapidly moved inland with minimum casualties. He thus contributed substantially to the successful establishment of the beachhead in France.[14]

The legacy and influence of General Pershing cast a long shadow over the life of Ted Roosevelt. The relentless drive to lead from the front, in harm's way, was the type of leadership that Pershing demanded in 1918 and that Ted maintained throughout his service in both world wars. His selfless service personified many of the virtues of both his family and Pershing's ideals for leaders. Foremost of these was his bravery in leading his men from the front. His awards for heroism and leadership not only included the Medal of Honor, but the Distinguished Service Cross, Distinguished Service Medal, four Silver Stars, and the Legion of Merit. Although differing in his view of what a leader should look like, Patton conceded that Roosevelt was "one of the bravest men I've ever known." Ted, however, had a distinct style that did not necessarily embrace Pershing's (and later Patton's) rigid spit-and-polish outward image. His personable style and his tireless endeavors to be at the front with his men motivated and inspired those who served with him. Ted Roosevelt lived up to his namesake and left a legacy worthy of emulation.

CHAPTER 22

MAJOR HARRY S. TRUMAN

Dave Theis

Harry S. Truman was born on 8 May 1884 to John and Martha Truman in Lamar, Missouri. Truman was, from an early age, an avid reader. He showed a special interest in military figures, having closely read about, among others, Alexander the Great, Hannibal, Julius Caesar, Napoleon Bonaparte, and Robert E. Lee. Truman's poor eyesight did not deter him from his reading program. At the same time, he learned to play the piano.

Both he and his playmates liked playing soldier. When he was 14, the Spanish–American War erupted. The young men formed a "Junior Brigade" composed of friends from the area. They spent much time conducting military-style drills, camping out, and shooting .22-caliber rifles. With the close of the war, Truman expressed the idea of attending the U.S. Military Academy at West Point but with his poor eyesight, he was not good enough for the academy. His only alternative was to join an artillery unit of the Missouri National Guard in 1905. His initial service in the National Guard was six years, which included monthly drills and a training encampment each summer, which covered fundamental military skills, marksmanship, and basic artillery procedures. During these years, Truman also spent time helping on the family farm. As the farm workload grew, he left the National Guard in 1911, at the end of his initial term of service.

When America entered the war in the spring of 1917, Truman, at 33 years of age, was too old for the newly instituted draft, but wanted to serve. In a letter to his sweetheart, Bess Wallace, he wrote, "I felt that I was a Galahad after the Grail."[1] He re-enlisted in the Missouri National Guard on 22 June 1917 and was assigned to the 129th Field Artillery, 35th Division. As opposed to the units of the Regular Army, whose soldiers come from all regions of the country, soldiers in National Guard units typically come from the same area. The advantage this provides is quick cohesiveness, but it also increases the possibility for many of a single region to become casualties together. It also was standard practice at the time for National Guard units to elect their own officers from those in the unit believed to be the best leaders. The members of Battery F, 129th Field Artillery, elected Truman as their first lieutenant. His date of commission was retroactive to 22 June 1917, the date he re-enlisted.

Battery F mobilized for federal service on 5 September 1917 and was one of six batteries in the 129th. Each battery was commanded by a captain, and had 200 men and four French 75mm guns. The unit deployed for training to Camp Doniphan, which was a sub-post of Fort Sill, Oklahoma. Camp Doniphan was a hastily constructed tent camp, offering very few frills. Sanitary conditions were rudimentary. The 129th Field Artillery trained there for eight months. As a new officer, Truman learned to compute firing barrages and conducted live-firing practice with the 75mm guns.

Truman took action to improve the soldiers' living conditions. He worked with the mess hall to improve the food service and with Sergeant Eddie Jacobson he opened a canteen for the troops. They offered candy, cakes, apples, soft drinks, and a barbershop. They used Truman's 1911 Stafford car to get the necessary supplies for the canteen, insuring a steady stream of soldier-oriented items. By the time the 129th finished training at Camp Doniphan, the canteen showed a profit of $15,000 – a sizable sum, especially when considering gasoline in those days was only pennies per gallon. While he was at Camp Doniphan, Truman also met Jim Pendergast of Battery B, who was related to Tom Pendergast, the leader of the Pendergast political machine in Kansas City. This contact would bear fruit a few years after World War I.

Truman was one of 14 officers selected to deploy to France with the 129th Field Artillery's advanced party. Landing in Brest, France on 13 April 1918, he attended the U.S. II Corps Artillery School at Montigny-sur-Aube. The school was an extremely intensive six-week course. The focus was on mathematics and gunnery techniques. In a letter to Bess, he noted that the school was very difficult. Two days after he returned to his unit in June, he was informed by Colonel Karl Klemm, the commander of the 129th Field Artillery, that he had been promoted to captain and given command of Battery D, 129th Field Artillery.

Battery D had a fearsome reputation. Its men were undisciplined, but loyal, cohesive, and athletic. One of Battery D's members, Private Vere Leigh, said the unit members were wild kids, but not dummies. Another, Eugene Donnelly, said, "We were a pretty rough bunch of boys. We'd already got rid of four commanding officers."[2] Almost all were high school graduates, and many had been to college. When he assumed command on 11 July 1918, the new battery commander faced 200 bad-tempered young men. Private Leigh said: "We'd had all kinds of officers, and this was just another one, you, know."[3] As Truman later recalled, "I've been very badly frightened several times in my life and the morning of July 11, 1918, when I took over that battery was one of those times."[4] Sergeant Edward McKim also remembered that Truman's "Knees were knocking together."[5]

After receiving their new commander's comments and upon being dismissed, almost all of the battery gave a very loud "Bronx Cheer." Later that same day, the men of Battery D staged a horse stampede, and then had a drunken brawl. The following day, 12 July 1918, Truman posted a notice on the battery bulletin board announcing that half of the non-commissioned officers and most of the privates first class were demoted. Later that day at a meeting with the few remaining NCOs, Truman said, "I didn't come over here to get along with you. You've got to get along with me. And if there are any of you who can't, speak up right now and I'll bust you right back."[6]

The new battery commander insisted upon uncompromising discipline, and his efforts to energize his chain of command proved largely successful. Punishments increased, but so did rewards. The food got better. The soldiers were required to write regularly to their mothers and sweethearts, in accordance with General Pershing's orders that soldiers write home. Truman wrote his sweetheart Bess Wallace often.

On 31 July 1918, Truman wrote to Bess and was proud that his Battery D had out-fired all the other batteries in the battalion on the training range. He wrote similar letters to Bess on 4 August, saying he was going to the range again the next day. On 5 August, in a letter to his first cousin Mary Ethel Noland, he wrote that his battery had fired 611 rounds at the range, and all were on target. In late August, the batteries of the 129th Field Artillery, along with the rest of the 35th Division, deployed to an active but relatively stable sector of the front in the Vosges Mountains, near Gérardmer. On 29 August, the 129th was scheduled to fire a barrage of about 3,000 gas rounds against the Germans. The other batteries were in old French positions, but Battery D was in an ancillary position several miles from the others.

At 1900 hours, the barrage started all along the line. The Battery D first sergeant was told to have the horses back at the firing position at 2030 hours, to displace the battery before the expected German counter-battery fire. According to Private Leigh, "We were firing away and having a hell of a good time doing it until [the Germans] began to fire back."[7] It was the first time under fire for all the troops. But the first sergeant and the horses did not get back to the battery's position until 2100 hours. By that time, most of Battery D's guns were mired in mud, with incoming German fire. As the first sergeant arrived at the position, he yelled for the troops to run. A number of them did. Truman and six or seven privates did not run, and Truman began yelling at the fleeing soldiers. As he later recalled, "I got up and called them everything I knew."[8] He focused on their bravery and their mothers, two subjects the troops were sensitive about. It worked. The troops returned and began march-ordering the guns. It took all of the battery's horses together to haul out the two mired guns. The battery went back and recovered the other two the following day. Leigh later commented on his battery commander, "I don't think he'd ever been under fire before either, and it didn't bother him a damned bit."[9]

Truman confided in a letter to Bess that his legs were very anxious to carry him away. The battalion commander wanted the first sergeant court-martialed, but Truman chose to demote him and transfer him to Battery B. The incident became known throughout Battery D as the "Battle of Who Run." Many years after the war, Truman commented, "I never did give anybody Hell. I just told the truth and they thought it was Hell."[10]

When Battery D left the Vosges sector it moved to Bayon. After getting off the train, it began a long road march to Toul Hill, near Nancy. The march lasted several days through rain and mud. It was an exhausting march, and many of the men steadied themselves on the limbers and caissons, which was a forbidden practice because it added strain on the horses. As they approached Toul Hill, a colonel saw this and became agitated. He ordered Battery D to double time up the hill. Truman instead decided to get his men off the road and let men and horses get a good night's sleep.

Battery D was in reserve for, but did not participate in, the Saint-Mihiel offensive. On 15 September, it started marching again to redeploy for the Meuse–Argonne offensive, where it was to fire in support of the 35th Division, which was in the first echelon of the attack. The march covered more than 100 miles over bad roads, and lasted until 22 September. The battalion deployed near Hill 290, southwest of the village of Boureuilles and south of the town of Varennes. Both towns were in German hands.

The 129th and 128th Field Artillery Regiments were part of the 60th Field Artillery Brigade, commanded by Colonel Lucian Berry. On the morning of 26 September, Battery D's mission was to saturate Boureuilles with fire and the adjacent area to its east. After the initial preparation fire, the guns would then shift their fires to deliver a creeping barrage to the north, toward the village of Cheppy. The fires would support the advance of the 35th Division's infantry through and past Boureuilles, and support the advance of the 344th Tank Battalion, part of Colonel George S. Patton's 1st Tank Brigade.

As part of the kickoff of the Meuse–Argonne offensive, the preparatory artillery fire began at 0330 hours. When the creeping barrage reached the Cheppy-to-Varennes east–west line, both the 128th and 129th Field Artillery were to displace their guns and follow the infantry closely. The

Germans, however, had blown a large crater in the Boureuilles–Varennes road, slowing any movement. The 129th pulled back, and the battalion commander, Major Marvin Gates, and Truman conducted a forward reconnaissance. After fording the Aire River, they found an opening east of Varennes and then started to bring the guns forward. Battery D was forced to double-team the horses at 12 to a gun to move across the muddy fields. By 1000 hours it was about halfway between the German front-line, around Boureuilles, and the road to the north from Cheppy to Varennes.

Truman went northeast of Varennes to observe and direct fire in support of the American tank attack toward Charpentry. About this time, Truman found himself 200 yards ahead of the infantry regiment he was to support. Looking around, he took up a position where he could observe the most likely German advance, and from where he could observe the Aire River (west of Varennes) and the Argonne Forrest, which was to the west. That area was the operations area of the 28th Division, operating on the west flank of the 35th Division. Truman did not know that the 28th Division's artillery was caught in a traffic jam and could not move forward to provide fire support. And with the 28th Division hanging back, the 35th Division had an exposed left flank. The Germans were pouring artillery fire into the 35th, but no return fire was coming from the 28th. The U.S. II Corps operations prohibited artillery fire in areas closer than 4 miles from infantry frontline positions. Also, no firing was permitted across divisional boundaries without prior coordination. The consequence, for the 28th Division, was that it was not able to use its 155mm general support artillery until 29 September.

From Truman's observation post on 27 September, he saw a U.S. plane drop a flare to the west of his position in the 28th Division's sector. He also observed a German artillery battery going into firing position in about the same spot. He waited until the German battery was in place and its horses withdrawn. He then ordered Battery D to fire without prior coordination across the divisional boundary, destroying the German guns. Next, he ordered the battery to displace forward 300 yards immediately, avoiding the German counterfire that fell on its old firing position. On the morning of 28 September, Truman observed the Germans setting up an observation post in an abandoned mill, again in the 28th Division's sector. Calling in fire from Battery D, he destroyed that position. Later that day, another German artillery battery began moving in the 28th Division's sector. Battery D again fired across the divisional boundary, forcing the German guns to withdraw.

Tactical expediency aside, Truman was worried that Colonel Klemm might court-martial him for directing uncoordinated fire across the divisional boundary. That same day, Pershing visited the 35th Division commander, Major General Peter E. Traub. Pershing was concerned about the slowness of advance. Traub said part of the problem was that, because of the standing order, he could not fire out of his own sector. Pershing responded, "But surely you do not obey that order?"[11]

On 29 September, the 35th Division attacked to liberate the town of Exermont, but it was thrown back by the 30th. On 1 October, the 1st Division relieved the 35th Division in the line. Battery D fired in support of the 1st Division that day and the next. Truman's battery then moved back south to the vicinity of Bar-le-Duc, and remained there from 5 to 12 October. Then it moved to the northeast on the opposite side of the Meuse River, north of Verdun and close to Fort Douaumont, over which the Germans and French had fought so hard in 1916. Battery D fired in support of the 35th Division, and then the 81st Division.

By the time the war ended on 11 November, Battery D had fired more than 10,000 rounds against the Germans since 29 August. It moved back to Bar-le-Duc, and then to Brest. On 9 April 1919, it boarded the USS *Zeppelin*, arriving in New York on 20 April. On 3 May Battery D returned to Kansas City, Missouri, to a triumphal welcome. Truman received his discharge on 6 May, and his war was over. Battery D had not lost a single man.

In June 1919, Truman married Bess Wallace, a marriage that would last their entire lives. Truman contacted Eddie Jacobson, with whom he had run the highly successful canteen in Camp Doniphan. Together they opened a haberdashery in Kansas City, which initially was successful. Truman wished to continue as a citizen soldier, and in 1920, he joined the Officer's Reserve Corps at the rank of major. Throughout the 1920s, and 1930s, he continued to attend summer encampment training. However, 1921 brought bad luck and a business turndown, and the haberdashery business folded in 1922.

During the summer of 1921, Jim Pendergast, of Battery B, 129th Field Artillery, and his father Jim, visited with Truman. Both were part of the Pendergast political machine in Missouri. They wanted to know if Truman had any interest in politics. Because of his business troubles, he was very interested. Pendergast needed someone to run for one of three local judge positions. Pendergast reasoned that since many veterans of the 129th Field Artillery lived in the county, Truman would have a solid base of support. Pendergast was correct; Truman won.

Never neglecting his Army Reserve duties, Truman continued to do summer training. He also became a founding member of the Reserve Officers Association in Kansas City, and was active in the American Legion. An open U.S. Senate seat beckoned in 1934. Truman ran, and won. Even during his initial term in the Senate, he continued as a citizen-soldier. He attended summer encampments in 1934 and 1935, and those in 1936 and 1937 at his own expense. He ultimately rose to the rank of colonel of field artillery. During Truman's first term in the Senate, he adopted the American Legion's position on national defense as his own. One of the key elements of that position was the case for military readiness. Speaking to the American Legion in Washington, D.C. on 7 March 1938, he said:

> The Congress is considering a plan for industrial mobilization which, I think has merit. It is proposed to draft industry and labor in time of emergency. I believe in an adequate defense program. Andrew Jackson, the fighting old President, said, "We shall more certainly preserve peace when it is understood that we are prepared for war." I hope we shall never have to fight again, and the best way to keep from it is to be adequately prepared for all contingencies.[12]

War came to America again on 7 December 1941. The 57-year-old Truman visited Army chief of staff General George C. Marshall and told him that he was ready to serve again. Marshall declined, advising Truman his support for the U.S. Army was needed in the Senate. On 1 March 1941, Truman had introduced Resolution 71, which resulted in the establishment of the Senate Special Committee to Investigate the National Defense Program. The committee, soon called the Truman Committee, helped oversee military policy and appropriation, seeking to ensure the government was not overcharged for goods and services. It was very successful, eventually saving an estimated $15 billion dollars throughout the course of World War II. Partly in recognition of the committee's success, President Franklin D. Roosevelt selected Truman as his running mate for vice president in the 1944 election.

After Roosevelt's untimely death on 12 April 1945, Harry Truman succeeded him as President. The war in Europe was almost over, but the war in the Pacific continued. Europe was devastated, and at home, a new weapon of war, the atomic bomb, was close to the end of its development. Overtures were made to Japan without success, and Truman then made the decision to bring the war to as rapid a conclusion as possible by using the atomic bomb. On 6 August 1945, the "Little Boy" atomic bomb exploded nearly 2,000 feet above Hiroshima. The city was devastated. On 9 August 1945, the "Fat Man" bomb was dropped on Nagasaki. Again, devastation resulted. But by 10 August 1945, Japan had not yet surrendered, which resulted in a bombing attack on Japan by U.S. air forces in the Pacific on 14 August. Of the 1,000 attacking bombers, 828 were the B-29 Super Fortress. Before the last B-29 landed after the mission, Truman was able to announce the Japanese surrender. Historians arguing from hindsight debate the "morality" of using atomic weapons against Japan. Many of those historians on one side of the argument today maintain that the decision to end the war as quickly as possible, although brutally, saved more lives in the long run, both Japanese and American. Unlike so many who pontificate on this topic, the commander-in-chief in the White House who made the final decision knew war firsthand.

Truman also understood the mistakes made by the United States after World War I. Among the missteps after World War I, those Truman understood and acted on were:

1. The peace treaty at Versailles was punitive, and helped the rise of German nationalism – and Hitler.
2. Postwar economic policies helped bring on a depression.
3. After World War I, the United States returned to isolationism.

President Truman supported the Marshall Plan ensuring that Germany made a quick economic recovery. The United States provided leadership around the world, and supported the United Nations. Truman also integrated the armed forces racially, expanded the National Guard and Reserve, supported universal military training, and supported a reorganization of the American military, which resulted in the establishment of the U.S. Air Force as a separate service. In response to the greatest military challenge to civilian authority in American history, the former World War I artillery captain in the White House fired General of the Army Douglas MacArthur during the Korean War for trying to dictate national strategy to the President.

Truman always remembered those citizen soldiers with whom he had served. At his presidential inauguration in January 1948, he saw to it that many members of his World War I Battery D walked on both sides of his car in the inaugural parade. On 31 January 1953, only a few weeks after Truman left the White House, he retired from the United States Army Reserve as a colonel of field artillery. Harry Truman died in Kansas City, Missouri on 26 December 1972.

APPENDIX

U.S. Army Professional Military Education in the Early 20th Century

Douglas V. Mastriano and David T. Ząbecki

The United States established its first school for the training of future military officers at West Point, New York, in 1802. Unlike many of its foreign counterparts, then and even now, the U.S. Military Academy was from the start a four-year, bachelor's degree-granting institution. In its earliest years, West Point focused on training officers in the highly technical branches of Engineers and Artillery. Over time, the program of instruction at West Point evolved into one that educated and trained officers to serve in all branches. The Navy followed with the establishment of the U.S. Naval Academy in 1845; and the U.S. Air Force Academy was established in 1954, after the Air Force became an independent branch of the military in 1947.

Although the U.S. Army expanded and shrank drastically several times over the course of the 19th century, West Point was never its sole source of officers. Officers in the militias of the various states often managed to secure regular commissions, and the U.S. Army has a long tradition of selective commissioning of soldiers directly from the ranks. During the course of the 19th century, a number of state-sponsored and civilian higher educational institutions came into being that also provided concentrated military education. Many of the graduates of those institutions secured commissions in the Regular Army, while others were commissioned into their respective state militias. Many of those militia officers went on to serve with considerable distinction in America's 19th- and 20th-century wars. George Marshall received his Regular Army commission upon his graduation from Virginia Military Institute. By the dawn of the 20th century, the most important of what are today called the Senior Military Colleges (SMCs) included:

- Norwich University: 1819
- Pennsylvania Military College: 1821
- Virginia Military Institute: 1839
- The Citadel, The Military College of South Carolina: 1842
- Virginia Polytechnic Institute and State University (Virginia Tech): 1872
- University of North Georgia (The Military College of Georgia): 1873
- Texas Agricultural and Mechanical University: 1873

In 1862 America expanded its base of officer pre-commissioning training with the passage of the Morrill Act, which established the land-grant colleges. One of the U.S. federal government's key requirements for these schools was the inclusion in their curriculum of a formal course of military training and tactics, for which the Army provided the instructors and the professors of military science. As a first lieutenant, John J. Pershing served in one of those positions at the University of Nebraska. The program established under the Morrill Act was the foundation of what in 1916 became the Reserve Officers' Training Corps (ROTC).

Many American colleges and universities today have ROTC programs. The successful graduates receive commissions in the U.S. Army Reserve, while those among the top tier of graduates are offered commissions in the Regular Army. The graduates of the SMCs also earn their commissions through ROTC, but the programs in the SMCs are fundamentally different than the standard civilian colleges and universities that offer ROTC on an elective basis, and they fall under different provision of U.S.

federal law. In addition to ROTC, the SMCs must maintain a corps of cadets in which all students wear military uniforms. The schools must maintain military standards and discipline similar to those of the federal service academies. The members of the corps of cadets live in a constant military environment, not just during normal school hours. With one exception, all of the SMCs listed above remain in operation to this day. In 1972, Pennsylvania Military College, the second oldest of the group, fell victim to the virulent anti-military atmosphere of the Vietnam War era, and transformed itself into a civilian institution now called Widener University.

When America entered the war in April 1917, the U.S. Army rapidly expanded from a force of only a couple of hundred thousand to almost 4 million at the end of 1918. The existing officer training programs could not come close to producing the 200,000 officers that such a force required. Following the sinking of the *Lusitania* in May 1915, General Leonard Wood, the former chief of staff of the U.S. Army, and Theodore Roosevelt, the former President of the United States, launched the Preparedness Movement in anticipation of American entry into the war. A key element of the program was the Citizens' Military Training Camps, otherwise known as the Plattsburgh Program. In May 1917, some 5,000 men, largely from the upper social classes, reported to a training camp at Plattsburgh, New York, prepared to undergo a strenuous training course that would qualify them for commissions as reserve line officers. By the end of 1917, more than 17,000 had completed the program, including Theodore Roosevelt, Jr.

When America formally entered the war, the Plattsburgh Program became the model for the 90-day officer training camps established at military posts throughout the country. The training programs were rudimentary at best, weighted heavily on dismounted drill. Some of the training camps were oriented toward a specific branch, such as the Field Artillery Central Officers Training School (FACOTS) at Camp Zachary Taylor, Kentucky. By the end of 1918, the various officer training camps had trained almost half of all commissioned Army officers. As American military historian Timothy Nenninger has noted, the most astonishing aspect of the American 19-month rapid build-up was the training and commissioning of some 200,000 officers, "most of them competent."[1]

Professional military training is a never-ending process throughout a soldier's career. Once an officer is sufficiently trained for commissioning, he then has to be trained in the technical and tactical specifics of his branch of service. Throughout most of the 19th century, that took place on an on-the-job-training basis, once the officer was assigned to his new unit. The regimental or unit commander, working through his senior officers, had the primary responsibility for making sure his new officers learned how to do their jobs. But that system showed serious shortcomings as military technologies grew increasingly complex. Assigned to small, isolated posts throughout the country, Army officers in the years immediately following the Civil War became experts in small-unit administration and the daily operations of such posts, but they developed little grasp of larger unit tactics and operations, and virtually none of strategy. There was a clear need for post-commissioning training.

One of the U.S. Army's first specialist schools was the Artillery School of Practice, established in 1824 at Fort Monroe, Virginia. Renamed the Artillery School of the U.S. Army in 1867, the program of instruction was always heavily weighted toward coastal artillery, rather than field artillery. In 1866, just after the end of the Civil War, the Army Signal Corps School was established at Fort Whipple, Virginia.

In 1881, General William, T. Sherman, who was then the commanding general of the U.S. Army, established the School of Application for Infantry and Cavalry at Fort Leavenworth, Kansas. It was the foundation of the Army's modern-day schools system. In 1886 the school was renamed the U.S. Infantry and Cavalry School. In the following years, the Army established other branch-specific schools. Established at Fort Riley, Kansas, in 1893, the training at the Cavalry and Light Artillery School focused almost exclusively on the horse, the central element of those two mounted branches. In 1907 it was renamed the Mounted Service School, where Lieutenant George Patton later served as an instructor of mounted swordsmanship. In 1911 the School of Fire was established at Fort Sill, Oklahoma, for the training of Field Artillery officers. In 1917 it was renamed the Field Artillery School. Meanwhile, the Artillery School at Fort Monroe had been re-designated in 1907 as the Coast Artillery School. In 1918, the Infantry School opened at Fort Benning, Georgia. All of these new branch schools conducted focused training programs for both officers and enlisted soldiers.

The Germans established their General Staff in 1806, and their General Staff training school, the Kriegsakademie, in 1810. The U.S. Army did not establish a general staff until 1903. Four years later, the Army Staff School was established at Fort Leavenworth. That same year, the Infantry and Cavalry School was renamed the School of the Line. The Signal School and Field Engineer School also were established at Leavenworth in 1907. The four Leavenworth schools were grouped together under the Army Service Schools. By 1916, however, only about 700 officers had graduated from the various Leavenworth Army Service Schools.

The School of the Line, which was now opened to Field Artillery officers as well, was a one-year course. The highest-ranking graduates were selected to attend the Army Staff School, which was another year. The Army now had the formal system in place to train General Staff officers. By 1916, however, only about 200 had completed the Staff School. The problem was that the graduates had little opportunity to apply their new skills, because until 1916 the Army had no field level headquarters higher than the regiment. Nonetheless, the Leavenworth graduates came to have an overwhelming influence on the American Expeditionary Forces in France. Of the AEF's 26 divisions, 23 had Leavenworth-trained chiefs of staff. On the other hand, only five of the 26 divisions had Leavenworth-trained commanders.

In the face of massive mobilization, the Leavenworth schools closed in 1916, and all the schools' officers (students, faculty, and administration) were ordered to rejoin their parent regiments. But once the AEF started to establish itself in France, the critical need became readily apparent for trained General Staff officers capable of planning and coordinating the operations and movements of the huge American divisions. Under Pershing's direction, a large number of American schools and training centers were established in France. The most important was the U.S. Army General Staff College at Langres, France. Between November 1917 and December 1918, the Langres Staff College conducted four three-month-long crash course cycles. A total of 777 officers attended Langres; but only 537 of those completed the course rated as qualified to perform General Staff officer duties. The faculty of the

Langres Staff College consisted of what few former Leavenworth instructors the AEF could scrape together, augmented by a small handful of British and French qualified General Staff officers. Oddly enough, while the Langres school was officially named a General Staff *college*, the one at Leavenworth was called a General Staff *school*, and would continue to be called such when it re-opened after the war. Presumably, the AEF officers called their institution a college to suggest a sort of equivalency with the British Army Staff College at Camberley, England.

The capstone of American professional military education was, and still is, the U.S. Army War College. It was established in Washington, D.C. in 1901 as an initiative of Secretary of War Elihu Root, specifically to address the military failings of senior leaders to mobilize and deploy forces during the Spanish–American War. The War College was established at Washington Barracks (now known as Fort Lesley J. McNair), with its first class graduating in 1904. The intent of the War College was loosely based upon the German model and had a focus on the conduct of strategy and leadership at higher levels of command. Yet, lack of adequate funding and an obsession with fighting small wars, such as in the Philippines, shifted its focus away from its founding principles. Additionally, the far-left peace ideals of the Wilson Administration severely restricted the ability of the War College even to contemplate a basic strategic focus. Even with a nascent group of War College graduates in the Army, any thinking outside the norms of the Wilson Administration was severely restricted, and the Army's senior leaders were kept from thinking and acting strategically.

Established six years before the Army Staff School at Leavenworth, the Army War College initially had a role in the training of General Staff officers; but the focus was on service on the Army General Staff in Washington. Thus, for the years preceding World War I, there was something of an overlap between the War Collage and the Leavenworth Staff School, although the latter was clearly oriented on the higher field levels of command. The role of the War College in General Staff officer training ended in 1916, and that same year the school was closed for the duration of the war.

World War I was the first time that the U.S. Army and the U.S. Marine Corps operated in combat as an integrated force. The much smaller

Marine Corps contributed not only a brigade-sized unit to the AEF, but also several important general officers. As a branch of the Navy, most Marine officers of the time either had received direct commissions, or were commissioned from the U.S. Naval Academy at Annapolis, Maryland. Most of the Marine officers who served in the AEF also had been trained at the Marine Corps School of Application, established in 1891 at Quantico, Virginia. The Marines had no equivalent school to train General Staff officers, but Marine generals such as John A. Lejeune and Wendell C. Neville had devoted much of their careers to intensive self-study of the profession of arms.

Both the Leavenworth Army Staff School and the Army War College re-opened in 1919. That same year the Mounted Service School at Fort Riley was renamed the Cavalry School. In 1922 the Army Staff School was renamed the Army Command and General Staff School, with its focus on training future battalion and brigade commanders, as well as training officers in the use of combined arms and the staff functions for division and corps as they related to tactics and logistics. The mission of the War College was now more clearly focused on command at the divisional level and above; the strategic level of war; and the effects of political, social, and economic factors on national defense. Successful completion of the Command and General Staff School became a minimum requirement for attendance at the War College.

Immediately following World War II, the Cavalry School at Fort Riley and the Coast Artillery School at Fort Monroe closed, as those branches were phased out of the Army. The Command and General Staff School at Leavenworth was renamed the Command and General Staff College, which remains its current name. In 1951, the Army War College moved to Carlisle Barracks, Pennsylvania, its current home. In the U.S. Army of the 21st century, all officers after commissioning complete an officer branch basic course as new lieutenants, and an officer branch advanced course as captains. Completion of the Command and General Staff College is required for promotion to lieutenant colonel; and completion of the War College is required for promotion to the general officer ranks.

ENDNOTES

Foreword

1 Robert Alexander, *Memories of the World War* (New York: Macmillan, 1931), p. 1.

Introduction

1 Dr. Lennox frequently uses this quote during his live discussions. He credits the famed English journalist Malcolm Muggeridge for his version of the quote. Muggeridge's original quote is "All new news is old news happening to new people."

2 Richard Striner, *Woodrow Wilson and World War I: A Burden too Great to Bear* (New York: Rowman and Littlefield, 2014), p. 1.

3 Carl von Clausewitz, *On War*, Michael Howard and Peter Paret, trans and eds (Princeton, NJ: Princeton University Press, 1976), Book 2, chapter 1, pp. 131–32.

4 For the Warren and Baker quotations, see Donald Smythe, *Pershing: General of the Armies* (Bloomington, IN: University of Indiana Press, 1986), p. 4.

5 Quoted in Smythe, p. 6.

6 John J. Pershing, *My Experiences in the World War* (New York: Frederick A. Stokes Company, 1931), Vol. 1, p. 259.

7 Ibid., Vol. 1, p. 259.

8 Smythe, pp. 70–71.

9 Ibid., pp. 23–24.

10 Pershing, Vol. 1, p. 114. In his memoirs, Pershing rarely passes up an opportunity to criticize both the French and the British for their unwillingness to accept what he considered to be his far superior tactical theories of infantry-centric combat. The Allies, however, had learned through three years of bitter experience that those concepts no longer worked in modern warfare.

11 Ibid., Vol. 1, p. 153.

12 Ibid., Vol. 2, p. 28.

13 Ibid.

14 Smythe, p. 115.

15 Gary Sheffield and John Bourne, eds, *Douglas Haig: War Diaries and Letters* (London: Weidenfeld and Nicholson, 2005), p. 409.

16 Pershing, Vol. 2, pp. 244–47.

17 Ibid., Vol. 2, pp. 248–50.

18 "Foch to Pershing," No. 3480 (1 September 1918). United Kingdom National Archives, Kew, Great Britain. Record Group WO 158/05 358215.

19 Pershing, Vol. 2, pp. 293.

20 Diary of Lieutenant Colonel P. L. Stackpole, A.D.C. to General Liggett: January 25, 1918 to August 2, 1919 (Washington, D.C.: U.S. Library of Congress), 29 September 1918 [hereafter referred to as Stackpole Diary].

21 Stackpole Diary, 16 October 1918.

22 George C. Marshall, *Memories of my Services in the World War, 1917–1918* (Boston, MA: Houghton Mifflin Company, 1976), p. 189.

23 James G. Harbord, *The American Army in France, 1917–1918* (Boston, MA: Little Brown and Company, 1936), pp. 455–56.

24 Hunter Liggett, *A.E.F.: Ten Years Ago in France* (New York: Dodd, Mead and Company, 1928), pp. 229–30.

25 Pershing, Vol. 2, p. 381.

26 Cited in Smythe, p. 292.

27 "Preliminary Report of the Commander-in-Chief," G-3, GHQ, AEF: 1123 (19 November 1918). United States Department of the Army. United States Army in the World War 1917–1919: Military Operations of the American Expeditionary Forces, Vol. 12, Center of Military History (reprint), Washington, D.C.: 1989.44.

28 Pershing, Vol. 1, p. 153.

29 Mark E. Grotelueschen, *The AEF Way of War: The American Army and Combat in World War I* (Cambridge and New York: Cambridge University Press, 2007), pp. 353–54.

Chapter 1

1 Promotions for Hines are detailed in the "Statement of the Military Service of John Leonard Hines," by the Department of the Army, dated 20 April 1996 and found in Box 2 of the John L. Hines Collection [hereafter referred to as *Papers*] in the USAMHI Archives at Carlisle Barracks [hereafter referred to as *Hines Service*]. The easiest reference for Eisenhower's promotions is provided by the National Archives located at https://www.eisenhower.archives.gov/all_about_ike/chronologies.html#dde. Ambrose and D'Este also detail Eisenhower's promotions. Stephen E. Ambrose, *Eisenhower: Soldier, General of the Army, President-Elect, 1890–1952* (New York: Simon and Schuster, 1983); Carlo D'Este, *Eisenhower: A Soldier's Life* (New York: Henry Holt and Company, 2002).

2 "Oldest Academy Graduate, Gen. Hines Honored by Point Cadets on Labor Day," *Service Stripe*, 8 September 1967 (Washington, D.C.: Walter Reed Army Medical Center), Vol. XXIII, No. 36; *Papers*.

3 *Hines Service*, p. 1.

4 Robert W. Fraser, *Forts of the West* (Norman, OK: University of Oklahoma Press, 1977), pp. 81–82; *United States Military Reservations, National Cemeteries and Military Parks, "Montana"*(War Department: GPO, 1937), pp. 3–4.

5 Steven T. Messenger, "The Trains Stop at Tampa: Port Mobilization During the Spanish–American War and the Evolution of Army Deployment Operations," *Army History*, No. 104 (Summer 2017), U.S. Army Center of Military History, p. 43. Also of value in understanding the logistical challenges of mobilization and Tampa is *The Sinews of War: Army Logistics 1775–1953* (Office of the Chief of Military History: United States Army, 1966), pp. 280–86; Frederick B. Shur, *One Hundred and Forty Years of Service in Peace and War: History of the Second Infantry United States Army* (Detroit, MI: Strathmore Press, 1930).

6 Charles L. Bolte, Unpublished Manuscript on Hines (Carlisle, PA: USMHI). Provides great detail on Hines during the Spanish–American War, pp. 22–27; John L. Hines Papers, Letter Box 1 [hereafter referred to as *Manuscript*].

7 Theodore Roosevelt, *The Rough Riders, An Autobiography* (Library of America Edition, 2004), pp. 50, 488.

8 *Manuscript*, p. 27.

9 *Hines Service*, p. 6.

10 Major Thomas Marshall Spaulding, "The Lessons of the World War as Applied to Our Detailed Staff System; and the Effect of Modifications of this System as Contained in Act of June 4, 1920," *Infantry Journal* (Washington, D.C.: The United States Infantry Association), Vol. XIX, July 1921 to December 1921, p. 57

11 *Hines Service*, p. 4.

12 Spaulding, p. 57.

13 Martin A. Kreidberg and Merton G. Henry, *History of the Mobilization of the United States Army 1775–1945*. (Washington, D.C.: Department of the Army, DA Pam 20-212, 1955), pp. 221, 246.

14 Phase lines are military operational command and control tools that show some positional dependency or relation to the passage of time, most often the changing phases of a military operation. Shown as notional lines drawn on operational maps, phase lines are used to coordinate the maneuver and fires of various units during specific phases of an operation. Phase lines are usually distinguished with different code names, varying by the particulars of the mission, such as the location and nature of a specific required action.

15 *Manuscript*, pp. 39–40.

16 Timothy K. Nenninger, "John J. Pershing and Relief for Cause in the American Expeditionary Forces, 1917–1918," *Army History*, No. 61 (Spring 2005), p. 29.

17 Louis A. Peake, *Major General John L. Hines: Chief of Staff and the Army, 1924–1926* (Marshall University: Unpublished Thesis, 1976), p. 21 [hereafter referred to as *Peake*].

18 *Peake*, p. 38.

19 *Peake*, p. 36.

20 "General Hines, at Fort Harrison in 1898, to Inspect Guard Here." *Helena Daily Independent*, 11 May 1929, p. 1. *Papers*.

21 Letter from Hines to Bach, 6 July 1927. AWC 3996, *Papers*.

22 Ibid.

23 Letter from Bach to Hines, 12 August 1927, *Papers*.

24 "Statement on Critics of the Army," 7 February 1925 (War Department: John L. Hines Papers), Scrapbook No. 7, *Papers*.

25 *Manuscript*, p. 59.

26 Charles S. Kilburn, "Service with General John L. Hines, United States Army," *Papers*.

Chapter 2

1 Charles P. Summerall, *The Way of Duty, Honor, Country: The Memoir of General Charles Pelot Summerall*, Timothy K. Nenninger, ed. (Lexington, KY: University of Kentucky Press, 2010), p. 47.

2 W. Gary Nichols, *American Leader in War and Peace: The Life and Times of WWI Soldier, Army Chief of Staff and Citadel President General Charles P. Summerall* (Shippensburg, PA: Whitemane Books, 2011), p. 302.

3 Ibid.

4 Summerall, p. 6.

5 Nichols, pp. 177, 209.

6 Ibid., p. 177.

7 Ibid., p. 197.

8 Douglas MacArthur, *Reminiscences* (New York: McGraw-Hill, 1964), p. 47.

9 Theodore Roosevelt, Jr., *T. Roosevelt Papers* (Washington, D.C.: Library of Congress, 1959).

10 Nichols, p. 302.

11 Summerall, p. 4.

12 Nichols, p. 12.

13 Summerall, pp. 20–21.

14 Nichols, p. 26.

15 Summerall, pp. 232–33.

16 Ibid., p. 233.

17 Ibid.

18 Ibid., p. 107.

19 John J. Pershing, *My Experiences in the First World War* (New York: Da Capo Press, 1931, 1995), Vol. 2, pp. 100–01.

20 Summerall, p. 103.

21 MacArthur, p. 53.

22 Summerall, p. 233.

23 Pershing, Vol. 2, p. 60.

24 Summerall, p. 233.

25 Nichols, p. 173.

26 Pershing, Vol. 2, pp. 323–24.

27 Forrest C. Pogue, *George C. Marshall: Education of a General, 1880–1939* (New York: Viking Press, 1963), p. 183.

28 Pershing, Vol. 2, pp. 336–37.

29 MacArthur, pp. 66–67.

30 Thomas Johnson, *Without Censor* (Indianapolis, IN: Bobbs-Merrill Company, 1927), p. 257.

31 Pershing, Vol. 2, p. 340.

32 Ibid., p. 375.

33 Pogue, pp. 187–88.

34 Quoted in Pogue, pp. 187–88.

35 Pershing, Vol. 2, p. 381,

36 Summerall, p. 158.

37 Ibid., p. 155.
38 Johnson, p. 370.
39 Summerall, p. 155.
40 United States Army Center of Military History, *American Armies and Battlefields in Europe* (Washington, D.C.: U.S. Government Printing Office, 1992; first published 1938), p. 511. "This decoration was originally a small [3/16-inch] silver star worn on the ribbon of a service medal [typically the World War I Victory Medal] but in 1932 it was replaced by a separate medal."
41 Nichols, p. 302.
42 Ibid., p. 181.
43 Ibid., pp. 323, 335.
44 Ibid., p. 335.
45 Summerall, p. 205.
46 Quoted in Carlo D'Este, *Eisenhower: A Soldier's Life* (New York: Henry Holt and Company, 2002), p. 206.
47 Summerall, pp. 194–95, 215.
48 Quoted in Carlo D'Este, *Patton: A Genius for War* (New York: HarperCollins, 1995), p. 107.
49 Quoted in Carlo D'Este, *Patton: A Genius for War* (New York: HarperCollins, 1995), p. 294.
50 D'Este, *Eisenhower*, p. 206.

Chapter 3

1 U.S. Army Center of Military History, *Medal of Honor Recipients: Civil War (M-R)*. https.//history.army.mil/moh/civilwar_mr.html#MacARTHUR. Arthur MacArthur received his Medal of Honor 30 June 1890.
2 Frazier Hunt, *The Untold Story of Douglas MacArthur* (New York: Signet, 1954), p. 60.
3 Geoffrey Perret, *Old Soldiers Never Die: The Life of Douglas MacArthur* (New York: Random House, 1996), p. 72.
4 William Manchester, *American Caesar: Douglas MacArthur, 1880–1964* (Boston: Little, Brown and Company, 1978), p. 76.
5 Douglas MacArthur, *Reminiscences* (New York: McGraw-Hill, 1964), p. 47.
6 Ibid.
7 Ibid., p. 45.
8 Ibid., p. 46.
9 Ibid., p. 53.

10 "Approximate average strength… of [Western Front] combat divisions… during 1918: American 25,500; British 11,800; French 11,400; German 12,300." United States Army Center of Military History, *American Armies and Battlefields in Europe* (Washington, D.C.: U.S. Government Printing Office, 1992; first published 1938), p. 501.

11 MacArthur, p. 53.

12 Ibid.

13 Ibid.

14 Ibid.

15 Arthur Herman, *Douglas MacArthur: American Warrior* (New York: Random House, 2016), p. 104.

16 MacArthur, p. 53.

17 Herman, p. 104.

18 MacArthur, p. 53.

19 Herman, p. 104.

20 MacArthur, p. 53.

21 Herman, p. 105.

22 Ibid.

23 Ibid., p. 110.

24 MacArthur, p. 54.

25 Perret, p. 87.

26 Herman, p. 113.

27 Quoted in MacArthur, p. 70.

28 Quoted in MacArthur, p. 70.

29 Herman, p. 112.

30 MacArthur, p. 70.

31 Herman, p. 116.

32 Ibid., p. 117.

33 Ibid., p. 118.

34 Perret, p. 94.

35 *American Armies and Battlefields in Europe*, p. 511. "This decoration was originally a small [3/16-inch] silver star worn on the ribbon of a service medal [typically the World War I Victory Medal] but in 1932 it was replaced by a separate medal." MacArthur, as Army Chief of Staff in 1932, instituted this medal and revived the Purple Heart medal to replace World War I wound chevrons.

36 *Medal of Honor Recipients*. https.//history.army.mil/moh. MacArthur was nominated three times for the Medal of Honor (1914, 1918, and 1942), receiving it on 1 April 1942: "For conspicuous leadership in preparing the

Philippine Islands to resist conquest, for gallantry and intrepidity above and beyond the call of duty in action against invading Japanese forces, and for the heroic conduct of defensive and offensive operations on the Bataan peninsula."

37 Herman, p. 143.

38 Perret, p. 112.

39 *American Armies and Battlefields in Europe*, pp. 515–17.

40 Herman, p. 149.

41 Ibid., p. 151.

42 Perret, p. 128; Herman, p. 151.

43 Herman, p. 151.

44 A mass demonstration of World War I veterans, many of whom were impoverished by the Great Depression and demanding early payments of their promised war service bonuses.

Chapter 4

1 Hunter Liggett, *A.E.F.: Ten Years Ago in France* (New York: Dodd, Mead and Company, 1928), p. 30.

2 Ibid., p. 307.

3 Ibid., p. 28.

4 Diary of Lieutenant Colonel P. L. Stackpole, A.D.C. to General Liggett: January 25, 1918 to August 2, 1919 (Washington, D.C.: U.S. Library of Congress), 27 January 1918.

5 Liggett, p. 140.

6 Ibid., p. 188.

7 Liggett, p. 230.

8 Martin Blumenson, ed., *The Patton Papers: 1885–1940* (Boston, MA: Houghton Mifflin Company, 1972), p. 872.

9 Mark S. Watson, *Chief of Staff: Prewar Plans and Preparations, United States Army in World War II* (Washington, D.C.: Center of Military History, 1950), p. 85.

Chapter 5

1 Bland, Larry I. et al., eds, *The Papers of George C. Marshall*, Vol. 1, *The Soldierly Spirit*, December 1880–June 1939 (Baltimore, MD: Johns Hopkins University Press, 1981), pp. 189–90.

2 Quoted in Forrest Pogue, *George C. Marshall: Ordeal and Hope, 1939–1942* (New York: Viking, 1963), p. ix.

3 Bland et al., pp. 121–22.
4 George C. Marshall, *Memoirs of My Services in the World War, 1917–1918* (Boston, MA: Houghton Mifflin, 1976), p. 18.
5 Ibid., pp. 78–79.
6 Ibid., p. 99.
7 Ibid., p. 124.
8 Ibid., p. 124.
9 Ibid., p. 125.
10 Ibid., p. 129.
11 Ibid., p. 126.
12 Ibid., p. 137.
13 Ibid., pp. 137–38.
14 Ibid., p. 139.
15 Ibid., p. 138.
16 Ibid., p. 139.
17 Ibid., p. 205.
18 "Foggy Bottom" is the standard nickname for the U.S. State Department.
19 "Marshall is dead in capital at 78; World war chief," *New York Times*, 17 October 1959, p. 1.

Chapter 6

1 As reported in Merrill Bartlett, "The Genesis of the U.S. Marine Corps' Amphibious Assault Mission, 1890–1934," in Tristan T. A. Lovering, ed., *Amphibious Assault: Maneuver from the Sea* (Portsmouth: Royal Navy, 2005), p. 63.
2 Pronounced "Lejern," with an R-sound, not the incontrovertibly wrong "Lejoon." P. T. Brent, "Lejeune, Lejern and How to Say It," *Leatherneck Magazine*, 91, no. 4, April 2008, pp. 16–19.
3 John W. Thomason, *Fix Bayonets!* (Annapolis, MD: U.S. Naval Institute Press, 1923; reprinted 1994), p. 23.
4 John A. Lejeune, *Reminiscences of a Marine* (Philadelphia, PA: Dorrance and Company, 1930), p. 335.
5 *Marine Corps Manual* (Washington, D.C.: Department of the Navy, 1980), Par. 1100, "Military Leadership", 1-21–1-23.
6 Ibid., Par. 1400, "Marine Corps Birthday," 1-33–1-34.

Chapter 7

1 "MG John A. Lejeune Fitness Report on BG Wendell C. Neville, 28 July–30 September 1918," in Alan Millett and Jack Shulimson,

Commandants of the Marine Corps (Annapolis, MD: U.S. Naval Institute Press, 2004), p. 218.

2 Ibid.

3 John A. Lejeune, *Reminiscences of a Marine* (New York: Dorrance and Company, 1930), p. 300.

4 Ibid., p. 290.

5 Mark E. Grotelueschen, *The AEF Way of War: The American Army and Combat in World War I* (Cambridge and New York: Cambridge University Press, 2007), p. 248.

6 Ibid.

7 Ibid., p. 110.

8 Lejeune, p. 308.

Chapter 8

1 John J. Pershing, *My Experiences in the World War* (New York: Frederick A. Stokes Company, 1931), Vol. 2, p.180.

2 Ibid., Vol. 2, p. 38.

3 Richard Holmes, *The Western Front* (London: BBC Books, 1999), p. 203.

Chapter 9

1 Quoted in Edward Cox, *Grey Eminence: Fox Conner and the Art of Mentorship* (Stillwater, OK: New Forums, 2011), p. 102.

2 George S. Patton, *The Patton Papers: 1885–1940*, Martin Blumenson, ed. (Boston, MA: Houghton Mifflin Company, 1972), pp. 527–28.

3 Harbord, James G., *The American Army in France, 1917–1918* (Boston, MA: Little Brown and Company, 1936), p. 459.

4 Charles P. Summerall, *The Way of Duty, Honor, Country: The Memoir of General Charles Pelot Summerall*, Timothy K. Nenninger, ed. (Lexington, KY: University Press of Kentucky, 2010), p. 153.

5 Douglas MacArthur, *Reminiscences* (New York: McGraw-Hill, 1964), p. 68.

6 Quoted in Cox, p. 94.

7 Ibid., p. 79.

Chapter 10

1 Speech by General James Harbord at the Annual Meeting of the New York Society of Military and Naval Officers of the World War, 16 April, 1941, *James G. Harbord Papers*, New York Historical Society, Box 39, Folder 8.

2 Hugh Drum's World War I diary, 31 March, 1918, *Drum Papers* (Carlisle, PA: USAHEC).

3 John J. Pershing, *My Experiences in the World War* (New York: Frederick A. Stokes Company, 1931), Vol. 2, p. 212.

4 George C. Marshall, *Memoirs of My Services in the World War 1917–1918* (Boston, MA: Houghton Mifflin Company, 1976), p. 139.

5 Edward M. Coffman, *The Regulars: The American Army, 1898–1941* (Cambridge, MA: Belknap Press, 2007), p. 213.

6 James G. Harbord, *The American Army in France, 1917–1918* (Boston, MA: Little Brown and Company, 1936), pp. 455–56.

7 Edward M. Coffman, *The War to End All Wars: The American Military Experience in World War I* (Lexington, KY: University Press of Kentucky, 1998), p. 349.

8 Diary of Lieutenant Colonel P. L. Stackpole, A.D.C. to General Liggett: January 25, 1918 to August 2, 1919 (Washington, D.C.: U.S. Library of Congress), 8 November 1918.

9 Quoted in Elliott L. Johnson, *The Military Experiences of General Hugh A. Drum from 1898–1918*, p. 367, from Drum Lecture "Lecture on School of the Line," Vol. 5, Training, Part I – Lectures (1919–20) (Carlisle Barracks, PA: Army War College).

10 Quoted in Coffman, *The War to End All Wars*, p. 300. Also quoted in Mark E. Grotelueschen, *The AEF Way of War: The American Army and Combat in World War I* (Cambridge and New York: Cambridge University Press, 2007), p. 99.

11 Quoted in Coffman, *The War to End All Wars*, p. 338. Also quoted in *United States Army in the World War 1917–1919: Organization of the American Expeditionary Forces*, Vol. 1, Center of Military History, p. xxii.

12 Pershing, *My Experiences in the World War*, Vol. 2, p. 255.

13 Quoted in Johnson, p. 361, from efficiency reports in *Papers of General John J. Pershing*, Box 23, Record Group 316, National Archives, College Park, MD.

14 Marshall, p. 206.

Chapter 11

1 Charles G. Dawes, *A Journal of the Great War*, Vol. 1 (Boston and New York: Houghton Mifflin Company, 1921), p. 21.

2 "War Department General Order 12, 1919," listed in *American Decorations: Awarded Under the Authority of the Congress of the United States, 1862–1926* (Washington, D.C.: Government Printing Office, 1927), p. 695.

3 Annette B. Dunlap, *Charles Gates Dawes: A Life* (Evanston, IL: Northwestern University Press, 2016), p. 144.

4 Budget and Accounting Act of 1921, sec. 312 (a).

5 Dunlap, p. 179.

Chapter 12

1 John J. Pershing, *My Experiences in the World War*, Vol. 1 (New York: Frederick A. Stokes Company, 1931), pp. 193–94.

2 Hunter Liggett, *A.E.F.: Ten Years Ago in France* (New York: Dodd, Mead and Company, 1928), p. 31.

3 David F. Trask, *The AEF and Coalition War Making 1917–1918* (Kansas, KS: University of Kansas Press, 1993), pp. 30, 43.

4 Hunter Liggett, *Commanding an American Army: Recollections of the World War* (Boston, MA: Houghton Mifflin, 1925), pp. 49–50.

5 B. H. Liddell Hart, *Reputations: Ten Years After* (New York: Little, Brown and Company, 1928), pp. 274–75.

6 John J. Pershing, *Final Report of John J. Pershing* (Washington, D.C.: Government Printing Office, 1919), pp. 38–43; Pershing, *My Experiences in the World War*, Vol. 2, pp. 269–73.

7 Liggett, p. 207.

8 Ibid., p. 204.

9 Ibid., pp. 229–30.

10 Ibid., p. 159.

Chapter 13

1 *Who Was Who in American History: The Military* (Chicago, IL: Marquis Who's Who, 1975), p. 73.

2 John J. Pershing, *My Experiences in the World War* (New York: Frederick A. Stokes Company, 1931), Vol. 1, p. 88.

3 Donald Smythe, *Pershing: General of the Armies* (Bloomington, IN: University of Indiana Press, 1986), p. 68.

4 George C. Marshall, *Memories of My Service in the World War 1917–1918* (Boston, MA: Houghton Mifflin Company, 1976), pp. 97–98.

5 Diary of Lieutenant Colonel P. L. Stackpole, A.D.C. to General Liggett: January 25, 1918 to August 2, 1919 (Washington, D.C.: U.S. Library of Congress), 6 August 1918.

6 Douglas V. Mastriano, *Thunder in the Argonne: A New History of America's Greatest Battle* (Lexington, KY: University Press of Kentucky, 2018), p. 79.

7 Frank L. Roberts, *The American Foreign Legion: Black Soldiers of the 93rd in World War I* (Annapolis, MD: U.S. Naval Institute Press, 2004), p. 48.

8 Allan R. Millett, *The General: Robert L. Bullard and Officership in the United States Army, 1881–1926* (Westport, CT: Greenwood Press, 1976)

9 Edward G. Lengel, *To Conquer Hell: The Meuse–Argonne, 1918* (New York: Henry Holt and Company, 2008), p. 90.

Chapter 14

1 Joseph T. Dickman, *The Great Crusade: A Narrative of the World War* (New York: D. Appleton and Company, 1927), pp. 2–4.

2 Ibid., pp. 32–34.

3 Ibid., p. 49.

4 Ibid., p. 54.

5 Letter from Joseph Dickman to Clement Stueve, 5 August 1918, University of Notre Dame Library.

6 Letter from Joseph Dickman to Clement Stueve, 11 September 1918, University of Notre Dame Library.

7 Letter from Joseph Dickman to Mary Dickman, 24 October 1918, University of Notre Dame Library.

8 Letter from Joseph Dickman to Mary Dickman, 29 October 1918, University of Notre Dame Library.

9 Letter from Joseph Dickman to Clement Stueve, 18 October 1918, University of Notre Dame Library.

10 Ibid.

11 Dickman, p. 208.

12 Letter from Joseph Dickman to Mary Dickman, 12 December 1918, University of Notre Dame Library.

Chapter 15

1 Mark E. Grotelueschen, *The AEF Way of War: The American Army and Combat in World War I* (Cambridge and New York: Cambridge University Press, 2007), p. 181.

2 Ibid., pp. 185–86.

3 Liggett, Hunter, *A.E.F.: Ten Years Ago in France* (New York: Dodd, Mead and Company, 1928), p. 199.

4 Robert H. Ferrell, *America's Deadliest Battle: Meuse–Argonne, 1918* (Lawrence, KS: University Press of Kansas, 2007), p. 172, n. 3.

5 Edward G. Lengel, *To Conquer Hell: The Meuse–Argonne, 1918* (New York: Henry Holt and Company, 2008), p. 308.

6 Charles P. Summerall, *The Way of Duty, Honor, Country: The Memoir of General Charles Pelot Summerall*, Timothy K. Nenninger, ed. (Lexington,

KY: University Press of Kentucky, 2010), p. 142. Summerall was in error about Cameron and Pershing being classmates. Cameron was actually three years ahead of Pershing, who graduated in 1886.

7 Diary of Lieutenant Colonel P. L. Stackpole, A.D.C. to General Liggett: January 25, 1918 to August 2, 1919 (Washington, D.C.: U.S. Library of Congress), 22 October 1918.

Chapter 16

1 Michael E. Shay, *Revered Commander Maligned General: The Life of Clarence Ransom Edwards 1859–1931* (Columbia, MO: University of Missouri Press, 2011), p. 157.

2 Ibid., p. 162.

3 Diary of Lieutenant Colonel P. L. Stackpole, A.D.C. to General Liggett: January 25, 1918 to August 2, 1919 (Washington, D.C.: U.S. Library of Congress), 24 July 1918.

4 Shay, p. 187.

Chapter 17

1 Robert Alexander, *Memories of the World War 1917–1918* (New York: MacMillan Company, 1931), p. 111.

2 Records Group 120; Records of the Headquarters Section/308th Infantry/77th Division, NARA II, College Park, MD.

3 Personal observation of Lieutenant Sherman M. Eager, Company G/308th Infantry, Private memoir, copy in the author's collection.

Chapter 18

1 *Who Was Who in American History: The Military* (Chicago, IL: Marquis Who's Who, 1975), p. 387.

2 James J. Cooke, *Billy Mitchell* (Boulder, CO: Lynne Rienner Publishers, 2002), pp. 49–52.

3 Ibid., pp. 53–54, 64.

4 Donald Smythe, *Pershing: General of the Armies* (Bloomington, IN: University of Indiana Press, 1986), pp. 143–44.

5 Cooke, pp. 66–67, 97–99.

6 John J. Pershing, *My Experiences in the World War* (New York: Frederick A. Stokes Company, 1931), Vol. 2, p. 50.

7 Cooke, pp. 72–74.

8 Pershing, p. 260.

9 Cooke, pp. 87–89, 91–93, 98–99.
10 Edward G. Lengel, *To Conquer Hell: The Meuse–Argonne, 1918* (New York: Henry Holt and Company, 2008), pp. 6, 145–46, 198, 206.
11 Cooke, pp. 125, 129.
12 Ibid, p. 178.
13 Ibid, p. 180.
14 Ibid, p. 163.

Chapter 19

1 Letter from Patton to his wife, 19 July 1917, *The Patton Papers, 1885–1940*, Martin Blumenson, ed. (Boston, MA: Houghton Mifflin Company, 1972), p. 409.
2 Carlo D'Este, *Patton, A Genius for War* (New York: HarperCollins, 1995), p. 208.
3 Ibid.
4 Letter from Patton to his wife, 23 December 1917, *The Patton Papers, 1885–1940*, p. 502.
5 D'Este, p. 219.
6 George S. Patton, "Mechanized Forces: A Lecture," *Cavalry Journal* 42 (September–October 1933), pp. 5–8.
7 Quoted in D'Este, pp. 237–38.

Chapter 20

1 Francis P. Duffy, *Father Duffy's Story* (New York: Doran, 1919), p. 220.
2 Letter from Hill Jones to WJD, in file marked "Major General William J. Donovan, 1883–1959," Vol. 1, WJD Family Collection, quoted in Anthony Cave Brown, *The Last Hero: Wild Bill Donovan* (New York: Time, 1982), p. 36.
3 Letter from WJD to Ruth Donovan, 28 October 1917, quoted in Brown, p. 38.
4 Duffy, p. 25.
5 Letter from WJD to Ruth Donovan, 7 January 1918, quoted in Brown, p. 41.
6 Letter from WJD to Ruth Donovan, 1918, B: 132A, WJDP, MHI, Carlisle, PA, quoted in Douglas Waller, *Wild Bill Donovan: The Spymaster Who Created the OSS and Modern Espionage* (New York: Free Press, 2011), p. 22.
7 Letter from WJD to Ruth Donovan, 3 May 1918, quoted in Brown, p. 44.

8 Letter from WJD to Ruth Donovan, 7 August 1918, quoted in Brown, p. 55.

9 "Story of the Fighting 69th, 165th Infantry," unsigned, undated leaflet published on the regiment's return to New York, William J. Donovan Miscellaneous Collection, quoted in Brown, p. 57.

10 Duffy, p. 271.

11 Letter from WJD to Ruth Donovan, 23 October 1918, quoted in Brown, p. 62.

12 Douglas C. Waller, *Wild Bill Donovan: The Spymaster who Created the OSS and Modern American Espionage* (New York: Free Press, 2011), p. 35.

13 Ibid., p. 61.

14 Quoted in Brown, p. 834.

Chapter 21

1 Quoted in Tim Brady, *His Father's Son: the Life of General Ted Roosevelt, Jr.* (New York, New American; 2017), p. 32.

2 Theodore Roosevelt, *Average Americans* (New York: Putnam, 1919), p. xiv.

3 Eleanor Butler Roosevelt, *The Day Before Yesterday* (Garden City, NY: Doubleday, 1959), pp. 70–72.

4 T. Roosevelt, *Average Americans*, p. 93.

5 John J. Pershing, *My Experiences in the World War* (New York: Frederick A. Stokes Company, 1931), Vol. 1, p. 91.

6 T. Roosevelt, *Average Americans*, p. viii.

7 Ibid., p. 103.

8 *Valor, Military Times*, https://valor.militarytimes.com/hero/2922.

9 E. Roosevelt, *The Day Before Yesterday*, p. 98.

10 All three of his brothers, Quentin, Archie, and Kermit, served in World War I. Along with Ted, Archie and Kermit also served in World War II.

11 One of the most important military operational concepts, introduced in the mid-19th century by the German military theorist General Carl von Clausewitz. He defined culmination as the point in time and space when the attacker's combat power no longer exceeds that of the defender, or when the defender no longer has the capability to resist the attacker successfully.

12 Quoted in Brady, p. 242.

13 Quoted in Brady, pp. 266–70.

14 Theodore Roosevelt, Jr., Medal of Honor Citation, http://www.cmohs.org/recipient-detail/2972/roosevelt-theodore-jr.php.

Chapter 22

1 National Park Service (NPS), "Harry S Truman and the Influences of His Service in World War I," Harry S Truman National Historic Site, 1.

2 Quoted in Merle Miller, *Plain Speaking: An Oral Biography of Harry S. Truman* (New York: Berkeley Publishing Group, 1974), p. 95.

3 Quoted in NPS, 1.

4 Quoted in NPS, 1.

5 Quoted in NPS, 1.

6 Dennis M. Giangreco, *The Soldier from Independence: A Military Biography of Harry Truman, Vol 1: 1906–1919* (Minneapolis, MN: Zenith Press, 2009), p. 96

7 J. R. Fuchs, "Oral History Interview with Vere C. Leigh" (Kansas City, MO: Truman Library and Museum: 1970), p. 21.

8 Giangreco, p. 139.

9 Quoted in Fuchs, p. 20.

10 Michael Waldman, *My Fellow Americans: The Most Important Speeches of America's Presidents* (Naperville, IL: Sourcebooks Incorporated, 2010), p. 137.

11 Dennis M. Giangreco, "Capt. Harry Truman and Battery D, 129th Field Artillery in Action in the Argonne," *Journal of the Royal Artillery* (Autumn 2003), p. 59.

12 Seavey, Mark, comp, Harry Truman "Speech to American Legion Post 1, March 7, 1938," *The American Legion Magazine* (1939), p. 36.

Appendix

1 Timothy K. Nenninger, "American Military Effectiveness in the First World War," Alan Millet and Williamson Murray, eds, *Military Effectiveness*, Vol. 1, *The First World War* (Boston, MA: Unwin Hayman, 1988), p. 134.

SELECT BIBLIOGRAPHY

Introduction

Ferrell, Robert H., *America's Deadliest Battle: Meuse Argonne, 1918* (Lawrence, KS: University Press of Kansas, 2007)

Grotelueschen, Mark E., *The AEF Way of War: The American Army and Combat in World War I* (Cambridge and New York: Cambridge University Press, 2007)

Harbord, James G., *The American Army in France, 1917–1918* (Boston, MA: Little Brown and Company, 1936)

Lengel, Edward G., *To Conquer Hell: The Meuse–Argonne, 1918* (New York: Henry Holt and Company, 2008)

Liggett, Hunter, *A.E.F.: Ten Years Ago in France* (New York: Dodd, Mead and Company, 1928)

Marshall, George C., *Memoirs of My Services in the World War, 1917–1918* (Boston, MA: Houghton Mifflin Company, 1976)

Mastriano, Douglas V., *Thunder in the Argonne: A New History of America's Greatest Battle* (Lexington, KY: University Press of Kentucky, 2018)

Nenninger, Timothy K., ed., *The Way of Duty, Honor, Country: The Memoir of General Charles Pelot Summerall* (Lexington, KY: University Press of Kentucky, 2010)

Pershing, John J., *My Experiences in the World War* (New York: Frederick A. Stokes Company, 1931)

Sheffield, Gary and John Bourne, eds, *Douglas Haig: War Diaries and Letters* (London: Weidenfeld and Nicholson, 2005)

Smythe, Donald, *Pershing: General of the Armies* (Bloomington, IN: University of Indiana Press, 1986)

Trask, David F., *The AEF and Coalition Warmaking, 1917–1918* (Lawrence, KS: University Press of Kansas, 1993)

Ząbecki, David T., *The Generals' War: Operational Level Command on the Western Front in 1918* (Bloomington, IN: Indiana University Press, 2018)

Chapter 1

American Battlefield and Monuments Commission, *1st Division Summary of Operations in the World War* (Washington, D.C.: Government Printing Office, 1944)

American Battlefield and Monuments Commission, *4th Division Summary of Operations in the World War* (Washington, D.C.: Government Printing Office, 1944)

Bullard, Robert Lee, *Personalities and Reminiscences of the War* (New York: Doubleday, Page and Company, 1925)

Johnson, Douglas V., II and Hillman, Rolfe I., Jr., *Soissons 1918* (College Station, TX: A&M University Press, 1999)

Messinger, Steven T., "The Trains Stop at Tampa: Port Mobilization During the Spanish–American War and the Evolution of Army Deployment Operations," *Army History*, No. 104 (Summer 2017), US Center of Military History

Nenninger, Timothy K., "John J. Pershing and Relief for Cause in the American Expeditionary Forces, 1917–1918," *Army History*, No. 61 (Spring 2005)

Peake, Louis A., *Major General John L. Hines: Chief of Staff and the Army, 1924–1926*, Unpublished Thesis (Marshall University, 1976)

Chapter 2

D'Este, Carlo, *Patton: A Genius for War* (New York: HarperCollins, 1995)

D'Este, Carlo, *Eisenhower: A Soldier's Life* (New York: Henry Holt and Company, 2002)

Johnson, Thomas, *Without Censor* (Indianapolis, IN: Bobbs-Merrill Company, 1927)

MacArthur, Douglas, *Reminiscences* (New York: McGraw-Hill, 1964)

Nenninger, Timothy K., ed., *The Way of Duty, Honor, Country: The Memoir of General Charles Pelot Summerall* (Lexington, KY: University of Kentucky Press, 2010)

Nichols, W. Gary, *American Leader in War and Peace: The Life and Times of WWI Soldier, Army Chief of Staff and Citadel President General Charles P. Summerall* (Shippensburg, PA: Whitemane Books, 2011)

Pershing, John J., *My Experiences in the First World War* (New York: Da Capo Press, 1995; first published 1931)

Pogue, Forrest C., *George C. Marshall: Education of a General, 1880–1939* (New York: Viking Press, 1963)

Roosevelt, Theodore, Jr., *T. Roosevelt Papers* (Washington, D.C.: Library of Congress, 1959)

United States Army Center of Military History, *American Armies and Battlefields in Europe*. (Washington, D.C.: U.S. Government Printing Office, 1992; first published 1938)

Chapter 3

Herman, Arthur, *Douglas MacArthur: American Warrior* (New York: Random House, 2016)

Hunt, Frazier, *The Untold Story of Douglas MacArthur* (New York: New American Library, 1964)

MacArthur, Douglas, *Reminiscences* (New York: McGraw-Hill, 1964)

Manchester, William, *American Caesar: Douglas MacArthur, 1880–1964* (Boston, MA: Little, Brown and Company, 1978)

Perret, Geoffrey, *Old Soldiers Never Die: The Life of Douglas MacArthur* (New York: Random House, 1996)

United States Army Center of Military History, *American Armies and Battlefields in Europe* (Washington, D.C.: U.S. Government Printing Office, 1992; first published 1938)

United States Army Center of Military History, *Medal of Honor Recipients: Civil War (M–R)*, https.//history.army.mil/moh/civilwar_mr.html#MacARTHUR

Chapter 4

Bell, William Gardner, *Commanding Generals and Chiefs of Staff, 1775–2013: Portraits and Biographical Sketches of the United States Army's Senior Officers* (Washington D.C.: Center of Military History, 2013)

Grotelueschen, Mark E., *The AEF Way of War: The American Army and Combat in World War I* (Cambridge and New York: Cambridge University Press, 2007)

Liggett, Hunter, *A.E.F.: Ten Years Ago in France* (New York: Dodd, Mead and Company, 1928)

Pogue, Forrest C., *George C. Marshall: Education of a General, 1880–1939* (New York: Viking Press, 1963)

Stackpole, Pierpont L., Diary of Lieutenant Colonel P. L. Stackpole, A.D.C. to General Liggett: January 25, 1918 to August 2, 1919 (Washington D.C.: U.S. Library of Congress)

Watson, Mark S., *Chief of Staff: Prewar Plans and Preparations, United States Army in World War II* (Washington D.C.: Center of Military History, 1950)

Chapter 5

Bland, Larry I. et al., eds, *The Papers of George C. Marshall* (Baltimore, MD: Johns Hopkins University Press, 1981–2016)

Marshall, George C., *Memoirs of My Services in the World War, 1917–1918* (Boston, MA: Houghton Mifflin, 1976)

Pogue, Forrest C., *George C. Marshall: Education of a General, 1880–1939* (New York: Viking Press, 1963)

Chapter 6

Amerman, Annette D., *Reducing the Saint Mihiel Salient, September 1918* (Quantico, VA: History Division, U.S. Marine Corps, 2018)

Bartlett, Merrill L., *Lejeune: A Marine's Life, 1867–1942* (Columbia, SC: University of South Carolina Press, 1991)

Gilbert, Oscar E. and Canseir, Romain, *First to Fight: The U.S. Marines in World War I* (Havertown, PA: Casemate Publishers, 2017)

Grotelueschen, Mark E., *The AEF Way of War: The American Army and Combat in World War I* (Cambridge and New York: Cambridge University Press, 2007)

Lejeune, John A., *Reminiscences of a Marine* (New York: Dorrance and Company, 1930)

Mastriano, Douglas V., *Thunder in the Argonne: A New History of America's Greatest Battle* (Lexington, KY: University Press of Kentucky, 2018)

McClellan, Edwin N., *The United States Marine Corps in World War I* (London: Forgotten Books and Dalton Ltd., 2017)

Millett, Alan and Shulimson, Jack, *Commandants of the Marine Corps* (Annapolis, MD: U.S. Naval Institute Press, 2004)

Thomason, John W., *Fix Bayonets!* (Annapolis, MD: U.S. Naval Institute Press, 1994; first published 1923)

Ząbecki, David, T., *The Generals' War: Operational Level of Command on the Western Front in 1918* (Bloomington: Indiana University Press, 2018)

Chapter 7

Bettez, David J., *A Kentucky Marine; Major General Morgan Freland and the Making of the Modern USMC* (Lexington, KY: University of Kentucky Press, 2014)

Catlin, Albertus W., *With the Help of God and a Few Marines: The Battles of Chateau Thierry and Belleau Wood* (New York: Doubleday, 1919)

Gilbert, Oscar E. and Canseir, Romain, *First to Fight: The U.S. Marines in World War I* (Havertown, PA: Casemate Publishers, 2017)

Grotelueschen, Mark E., *The AEF Way of War: The American Army and Combat in World War I* (Cambridge and New York: Cambridge University Press, 2007)

Lejeune, John A., *Reminiscences of a Marine* (New York, Dorrance and Company, 1930)

McClellan, Edwin N., *The United States Marine Corps in World War I* (London: Forgotten Books and Dalton Ltd., 2017)

Millett, Alan and Shulimson, Jack, *Commandants of the Marine Corps* (Annapolis, MD: U.S. Naval Institute Press, 2004)

Ząbecki, David, T., *The Generals' War: Operational Level of Command on the Western Front in 1918* (Bloomington, IN: Indiana University Press, 2018)

Chapter 8

Cooke, James J., "James Guthrie Harbord," in David T. Ząbecki, ed., *Chief of Staff: The Principal Officers Behind History's Great Commanders*, Vol. 1, *Napoleonic Wars to World War I* (Annapolis, MD: U.S. Naval Institute Press, 2008), pp. 208–19.

Ferrell, Robert H., *America's Deadliest Battle: Meuse Argonne, 1918* (Lawrence, KS: University Press of Kansas, 2007)

Grotelueschen, Mark E., *The AEF Way of War: The American Army and Combat in World War I* (Cambridge and New York: Cambridge University Press, 2007)

Harbord, James G., *The American Army in France, 1917–1918* (Boston, MA: Little Brown and Company, 1936)

Holmes, Richard, *The Western Front* (London: BBC Books, 1999)

Lengel, Edward G., *To Conquer Hell: The Meuse–Argonne, 1918* (New York: Henry Holt and Company, 2008)

Marshall, George C., *Memoirs of My Services in the World War, 1917–1918* (Boston, MA: Houghton Mifflin Company, 1976)

Mastriano, Douglas V., *Thunder in the Argonne: A New History of America's Greatest Battle* (Lexington, KY: University Press of Kentucky, 2018)

Nenninger, Timothy K., ed., *The Way of Duty, Honor, Country: The Memoir of General Charles Pelot Summerall* (Lexington, KY: University Press of Kentucky, 2010)

Pershing, John J., *My Experiences in the World War* (New York: Frederick A. Stokes Company, 1931)

Rabalais, Steven, *General Fox Conner: Pershing's Chief of Operations and Eisenhower's Mentor* (Havertown, PA: Casemate, 2016)

Smythe, Donald, *Pershing: General of the Armies* (Bloomington, IN: University of Indiana Press, 1986)

Trask, David F., *The AEF and Coalition Warmaking, 1917–1918* (Lawrence, KS: University Press of Kansas, 1993)

Ząbecki, David T., "The U.S. Marines' Mythic Fight at Belleau Wood: Piercing the Fog of History to Separate Legend from Fact," *Military History* (March 2012), pp. 40–49

Chapter 9

Blumenson, Martin, ed., *The Patton Papers: 1885–1940* (Boston, MA: Houghton Mifflin Company, 1972)

Cox, Edward, *Grey Eminence: Fox Conner and the Art of Mentorship* (Stillwater, OK: New Forums, 2011)

Eisenhower, Dwight D., *At Ease: Stories I Tell My Friends* (New York: Doubleday, 1967)

Harbord, James G., *The American Army in France, 1917–1919* (Boston, MA: Little Brown and Company, 1936)

Liggett, Hunter, *A.E.F.: Ten Years Ago in France* (New York: Dodd, Mead and Company, 1928)

MacArthur, Douglas, *Reminiscences* (New York: McGraw-Hill, 1964)

Marshall, George C., *Memories of my Service in the World War, 1917–1918* (Boston, MA: Houghton Mifflin Company, 1976)

Nenninger, Timothy K., ed., *The Way of Duty, Honor, Country: The Memoir of General Charles Pelot Summerall* (Lexington, KY: University Press of Kentucky, 2010)

Pershing, John J., *My Experiences in the World War* (New York: Frederick A. Stokes Company, 1931)

Rabalais, Steven, *General Fox Conner: Pershing's Chief of Operations and Eisenhower's Mentor* (Havertown, PA: Casemate Publishers, 2016)

Chapter 10

Cooke, James J., *Pershing and His Generals: Command and Staff in the AEF* (Westport, CT: Praeger, 1997)

Drum, Hugh, *World War I Diary & Drum Papers* (Carlisle, PA: USAHEC)

Grotelueschen, Mark E., *The AEF Way of War: The American Army and Combat in World War I* (Cambridge and New York: Cambridge University Press, 2007)

Harbord, James G., *The American Army in France, 1917–1918* (Boston, MA: Little Brown and Company, 1936)

Lengel, Edward G., *To Conquer Hell: The Meuse–Argonne, 1918* (New York: Henry Holt and Company, 2008)

Marshall, George C., *Memoirs of My Services in the World War, 1917–1918* (Boston, MA: Houghton Mifflin Company, 1976)

Mastriano, Douglas V., *Thunder in the Argonne: A New History of America's Greatest Battle* (Lexington, KY: University Press of Kentucky, 2018)

Pershing, John J., *My Experiences in the World War* (New York: Frederick A. Stokes Company, 1931)

Rabalais, Steven, *General Fox Conner: Pershing's Chief of Operations and Eisenhower's Mentor* (Havertown, PA: Casemate Publishers, 2016)

Stackpole, Pierpont L., Diary of Lieutenant Colonel P. L. Stackpole, A.D.C. to General Liggett: January 25, 1918 to August 2, 1919 (Washington D.C.: U.S. Library of Congress)

Chapter 11

Dawes, Charles G., *A Journal of the Great War*, Vol. 1 (Boston and New York: Houghton Mifflin Company, 1921)

Dunlap, Annette B., *Charles Gates Dawes: A Life* (Evanston, IL: Northwestern University Press, 2016)

Goedecken, Edward A., "A Banker at War: The World War I Experiences of Charles Gates Dawes," *Illinois Historical Journal*, 78 (3), 1985, pp. 195–206

Schuker, Stephen A., *The End of French Predominance in Europe: The Financial Crisis of 1924 and the Adoption of the Dawes Plan* (Chapel Hill, NC: University of North Carolina Press, 1976)

Chapter 12

Grotelueschen, Mark E., *The AEF Way of War: The American Army and Combat in World War I* (Cambridge and New York: Cambridge University Press, 2007)

Hart, Liddell B. H., *Reputations Ten Years After* (Boston, MA: Little, Brown and Company, 1928)

Liggett, Hunter, *A.E.F.: Ten Years Ago in France* (New York: Dodd, Mead and Company, 1928)

Liggett, Hunter, *Commanding an American Army: Recollections of the World War* (Boston, MA: Houghton Mifflin, 1925)

Marshall, George, *Memoires of My Services in the World War 1917–1918* (Boston, MA: Houghton Mifflin Company, 1976)

Mastriano, Douglas V., *Thunder in the Argonne* (Lexington, KY: University of Kentucky Press, 2018)

Pershing, John J., *My Experiences in the World War* (New York: Frederick A. Stokes Company, 1931)

Pershing, John J. and Liggett, Hunter, Major General, *Report of the First Army, American Expeditionary Forces, 10 August 1918 – 20 April 1920* (Fort Leavenworth, KS: General Service Schools Press, 1923)

Shay, Michael E., *Hunter Liggett: A Soldier's General* (College Station, TX: A&M University Press, 2019)

Shipley, Thomas, *The History of the A.E.F.* (New York: George H. Doran Company, 1920)

Trask, David F., *The AEF and Coalition War Making 1917–1918* (Lawrence, KS: University Press of Kansas, 1993)

United States Army Center of Military History, *American Armies and Battlefields in Europe* (Washington, D.C.: U.S. Government Printing Office, 1992; first published 1938)

Ząbecki, David, ed., *Chief of Staff: The Principal Officers Behind History's Great Commanders, Vol. 1, Napoleonic Wars to World War I* (Annapolis, MD: U.S. Naval Institute Press, 2008)

Chapter 13

Bullard, Robert Lee, *Personalities and Reminiscences of the War* (New York: Doubleday, 1925)

Fax, Gene, *With Their Bare Hands: General Pershing, the 79th Division, and the Battle for Montfaucon* (Oxford: Osprey Publishing, 2017)

Ferrell, Robert H., *Unjustly Dishonored: An African American Division in World War I* (Columbia, MO: University of Missouri Press, 2011)

Grotelueschen, Mark E., *The AEF Way of War: The American Army in Combat in World War I* (Cambridge and New York: Cambridge University Press, 2007)

Lengel, Edward, *Thunder and Flames: Americans in the Crucible of Combat, 1917–1918* Lawrence, KS: University Press of Kansas, 2017)

Millett, Allan R., *The General: Robert L. Bullard and Officership in the United States Army, 1881–1926* (Westport, CT: Greenwood Press, 1976)

Roberts, Frank L., *The American Foreign Legion: Black Soldiers of the 93rd in World War I* (Annapolis, MD: U.S. Naval Institute Press, 2004)

Chapter 14

Dickman, Joseph T., *The Great Crusade: A Narrative of the World War* (New York: D. Appleton and Company, 1927)

Joseph T. Dickman Papers, Archives of the University of Notre Dame, South Bend, Indiana.

Grotelueschen, Mark E., *The AEF Way of War: The American Army and Combat in World War I* (Cambridge and New York: Cambridge University Press, 2007)

Lengel, Edward G., *To Conquer Hell: The Meuse–Argonne, 1918* (New York: Henry Holt and Company, 2008)

Mastriano, Douglas V., *Thunder in the Argonne: A New History of America's Greatest Battle* (Lexington, KY: The University Press of Kentucky, 2018)

Stueve, Mary Clement, "An Ohio Army Officer of World War I: Major General Joseph T. Dickman," *Ohio History Journal*, Vol. 63 (January 1954), pp. 34–63

Chapter 15

Bach, Christian Albert, and Hall, Henry Noble, *The Fourth Division: Its Services and Achievements in the World War* (Published by the Fourth Division, 1920)

Ferrell, Robert H., *America's Deadliest Battle: Meuse–Argonne, 1918* (Lawrence, KS: University Press of Kansas, 2007)

Grotelueschen, Mark E., *The AEF Way of War: The American Army and Combat in World War I* (Cambridge and New York: Cambridge University Press, 2007)

Lengel, Edward G., *To Conquer Hell: The Meuse–Argonne, 1918* (New York: Henry Holt and Company, 2008)

Liggett, Hunter, *A.E.F.: Ten Years Ago in France* (New York: Dodd, Mead and Company, 1928)

Mastriano, Douglas V., *Thunder in the Argonne* (Lexington, NY: University Press of Kentucky, 2018)

Nenninger, Timothy K., ed., *The Way of Duty, Honor, Country: The Memoir of General Charles Pelot Summerall* (Lexington, NY: University Press of Kentucky, 2010)

Stackpole, Pierpont L., Diary of Lieutenant Colonel P. L. Stackpole, A.D.C. to General Liggett: January 25, 1918 to August 2, 1919 (Washington D.C.: U.S. Library of Congress)

Wright, William M., *Meuse–Argonne Diary: A Division Commander in World War I* (Columbia, MO: University of Missouri Press, 2004)

Chapter 16

Byerly, Carol R., *Fever of War: The Influenza Epidemic in the U.S. Army During World War I* (New York: New York University Press, 2005)

Finnegan, Terrance J., *A Delicate Affair on the Western Front: America Learns How to Fight a Modern War in the Woëvre Trenches* (Cheltenham: The History Press, 2015)

Pershing, John J., *My Experiences in the World War* (New York: Frederick A. Stokes Company, 1931)

Shay, Michael E., *Revered Commander, Maligned General: The Life of Clarence Ransom Edwards, 1859–1931* (Columbia, MO: University of Missouri Press, 2014)

Shay, Michael E., *The Yankee Division in the First World War: In the Highest Tradition* (College Station, TX: A&M University Press, 2008)

Stackpole, Pierpont L., Diary of Lieutenant Colonel P. L. Stackpole, A.D.C. to General Liggett: January 25, 1918 to August 2, 1919 (Washington D.C.: U.S. Library of Congress)

Chapter 17

Alexander, Robert, *Memories of the World War* (New York: The MacMillan Company, 1931)

Grotelueschen, Mark E., *The AEF Way of War: The American Army and Combat in World War I* (Cambridge and New York: Cambridge University Press, 2007)

Laplander, Robert, *Finding the Lost Battalion* (Waterford, WI: Lulu Press, 2018)

Liggett, Hunter, *A.E.F.: Ten Years Ago in France* (New York: Dodd, Mead and Company, 1928)

McKeogh, Arthur, *The Victorious 77th Division in the Argonne Fight* (New York: John H. Eggers Co., 1918)

Miles, Louis W., *History of the 308th Infantry* (New York; G.P. Putnam's Sons, 1927)

Chapter 18

Cooke, James, *Billy Mitchell* (Boulder, CO: Lynne Rienner Publishers, 2002)

Cooke, James, *Pershing and His Generals: Command and Staff in the A.E.F.* (Westport, CT: Praeger, 1997)

Hurley, Alfred, *Billy Mitchell: Crusader for Air Power* (Bloomington, IN: Indiana University Press, 1975)

Maurer, *The U.S. Air Service in World War I* (Washington, D.C.: Office of Air Force History, 1978)

Mitchell, William, *Memoirs of World War I* (New York: Random House, 1960; originally published in *Liberty Magazine* in 1926)

Mitchell, William, *Winged Defense* (New York: Putnam's Sons, 1925)

Tate, James, *The Army and its Air Corps, 1919–1941* (Maxwell AFB, AL: Air University Press, 1998)

Chapter 19

Blumenson, Martin, ed., *The Patton Papers: 1885–1940* (Boston, MA: Houghton Mifflin Company, 1972)

Coffman, Edward M., *The War to End All Wars: The American Military Experience in World War I* (Lexington, KY: University Press of Kentucky, 1998)

D'Este, Carlo, *Patton: A Genius for War* (New York: HarperCollins, 1995)

Fuller, J. F. C., *Tanks in the Great War, 1914–1918* (London: John Murray, 1920)

Priori, Carmine A., ed., *Lines of Fire: The Poems of General George S. Patton, Jr.* (Lewiston, NY: Edwin Mellin Press, 1991)

Wilson, Dale E., *Treat 'Em Rough: The Birth of American Armor, 1917–1918* (Novato, CA: Presidio Press, 1990)

Chapter 20

Brown, Anthony C., *The Last Hero: Wild Bill Donovan* (New York: Time, 1982)

Donovan Papers (355 boxes), U.S. Army Military History Institute Carlisle Barracks, Carlisle, PA 17013-5008

Duffy, Francis Patrick Fr., *Father Duffy's Story* (New York: George H. Doran Company, 1919)

Dunlop, Richard, *Donovan, America's Master Spy* (Chicago, IL: Rand McNally, 1982)

Harris, Stephen L., *Duffy's War: Fr. Francis Duffy, Wild Bill Donovan and the Irish Fighting 69th in World War I* (Washington, D.C.: Potomac, 2008)

Reilly, Henry J. and Heer, F. J., *Americans All, the Rainbow at War: The Official History of the 42nd Rainbow Division in the World War* (Columbus, OH: F.J. Heer Printing Co., 1936)

Waller, Douglas C., *Wild Bill Donovan: The Spymaster who Created the OSS and Modern American Espionage* (New York: Free Press, 2011)

Chapter 21

Brady, Tim, *His Father's Son: the Life of General Ted Roosevelt, Jr.* (New York, New American; 2017)

Hess, Stephen, *America's Political Dynasties* (Garden City, NY: Doubleday, 1966)

Marshall, George C., *Memories of My Service in the World War 1917–1918* (Boston, MA: Houghton Mifflin Company, 1976)

Nenninger, Timothy K., ed., *The Way of Duty, Honor, Country: The Memoir of General Charles Pelot Summerall* (Lexington, KY: University of Kentucky Press, 2010)

Pershing, John J., *My Experiences in the World War* (New York: Frederick A. Stokes Company, 1931)

Roosevelt, Eleanor Butler, *The Day Before Yesterday* (Garden City, NY: Doubleday, 1959)

Roosevelt, Theodore, Jr., *Average Americans* (New York: Putnam, 1919)

Terraine, John, *To Win a War* (London: Papermac, 1978)

Trask, David F., *The AEF and Coalition War Making 1917–1918* (Lawrence, KS: University Press of Kansas, 1993)

Chapter 22

Fuchs, J. R., "Oral History Interview with Vere C. Leigh" (Kansas City, MO: Truman Library and Museum, 1970)

Giangreco, Dennis M., "Capt. Harry Truman and Battery D, 129th Field Artillery in Action in the Argonne," *Journal of the Royal Artillery* (Autumn 2003), pp. 56–59.

Giangreco, Dennis M., *The Soldier from Independence: A Military Biography of Harry Truman, Vol. 1: 1906–1919* (Minneapolis, MN: Zenith Press, 2009)

"Heroes or Corpses: Captain Truman in World War I," Truman Library and Museum, Kansas City (2018)

McCullough, David, *Truman* (New York: Simon and Schuster, 1992)

Miller, Merle, *Plain Speaking: An Oral Biography of Harry S. Truman* (New York: Berkeley Publishing Group, 1974)

National Park Service, "Harry S Truman and the Influences of His Service in World War I," Harry S. Truman National Historic Site, www.nps.gov (2018)

Seavey, Mark (compiler), Harry Truman "Speech to American Legion Post 1, March 7, 1938," *The American Legion Magazine* (1939), pp. 34–40

"Special Committee to Investigate the National Defense Program," United States Senate, www.senate.gov (n.d.)

Waldman, Michael, *My Fellow Americans: The Most Important Speeches of America's Presidents* (Naperville, IL: Sourcebooks Incorporated, 2010)

Ząbecki, David T., "Captain Harry," *Field Artillery Journal* (Fort Sill, OK, 1981), pp. 58–61

INDEX

References to lieutenants' main entries are in **bold**; references to maps are in *italics*.